retu

# China and the EU in Context

# China and the EU in Context

## Insights for Business and Investors

Edited by

**Kerry Brown**

*Professor and Director, China Studies, University of Sydney; Team Leader, Europe China Research and Advice Network; Associate Fellow, Asia Programme, Chatham House*

palgrave
macmillan

First published 2014 by
PALGRAVE MACMILLAN

Palgrave Macmillan in the UK is an imprint of Macmillan Publishers Limited, registered in England, company number 785998, of Houndmills, Basingstoke, Hampshire RG21 6XS.

Palgrave Macmillan in the US is a division of St Martin's Press LLC, 175 Fifth Avenue, New York, NY 10010.

Palgrave Macmillan is the global academic imprint of the above companies and has companies and representatives throughout the world.

Palgrave® and Macmillan® are registered trademarks in the United States, the United Kingdom, Europe and other countries.

ISBN 978–1–137–35238–5

This book is printed on paper suitable for recycling and made from fully managed and sustained forest sources. Logging, pulping and manufacturing processes are expected to conform to the environmental regulations of the country of origin.

A catalogue record for this book is available from the British Library.

A catalog record for this book is available from the Library of Congress.

Typeset by MPS Limited, Chennai, India.

# Contents

# List of Figures and Tables

## Figures

## Tables

# Notes on Contributors

**Thierry Apoteker** is the founding partner and Chief Executive Officer of TAC. He is a lecturer at HEC Paris and the University of Rennes 1.

**Robert Ash** is Professor of Economics with reference to China and Taiwan at the School of Oriental and African Studies (SOAS), University of London.

**Kerry Brown** is Executive Director of the China Studies Centre, and Professor of Chinese Politics at the University of Sydney. He leads the Europe China Research and Advice Network (ECRAN), funded by the European Commission, and is Associate Fellow on the Asia Programme at Chatham House. He is the author of eight books on China, the most recent of which is *The New Emperors: China's Fifth Generation Leadership* (2014).

**Jeremy Clegg** is Director of the Centre for International Business, and Jean Monnet Professor of European Integration and International Business Management at the Leeds University Business School.

**Michael Dillon's** books include *Contemporary China: An Introduction; China: A Modern History* (long-listed for the ICAS 2013 humanities prize) and *Xinjiang: China's Muslim Far Northwest. Deng Xiaoping: A Political Biography* and *Xinjiang and the Expansion of Chinese Communist Power: Kashghar in the Early Twentieth Century* will be published in 2014.

**Bates Gill** is Professor of Politics and Chief Executive Officer of the United States Studies Centre at the University of Sydney. He was previously Director of the Stockholm International Peace Research Institute (SIPRI) from 2007 to 2012 and led major Asia-related programmes at the Center for Strategic and International Studies (CSIS) and the Brookings Institution in

Washington, DC. In 2013 he received the Royal Order of the Commander of the Polar Star, the highest award bestowed upon foreigners by the Swedish monarch, for his services to Sweden.

**Christian Göbel** is Professor of Modern China Studies at Vienna University. Previous to this, he held positions at Lund University and Heidelberg University. He is the author of *The Politics of Rural Reform in China* (Routledge 2010) and *The Politics of Community Building in Urban China* (Routledge 2011, with Thomas Heberer) and has published widely on topics related to state-society relations and political reform in China and Taiwan.

**Jikun Huang** is Founder and Director of the Center for Chinese Agricultural Policy of Chinese Academy of Sciences, and Professor at the Institute of Geographical Sciences and Natural Resources Research. His research focuses on agricultural policy and rural development. He has published about 400 journal papers with 200 papers published in international journals.

**Kevin Latham** is Senior Lecturer at the School of Oriental and African Studies, University of London. Having worked for more than 20 years on Chinese media in Chinese contexts, ranging from Cantonese opera in Hong Kong, to journalism in Southern China and the use of mobile phones and the Internet in Beijing and Guangdong, he has recently started out in a new research direction looking at experiences of networks, place, mobility and media use among Chinese immigrants in Italy and Europe more broadly. His previous research has also covered consumption and popular culture in China.

**Yuelai Lu** is Head of the Secretariat of UK-China Sustainable Agriculture Innovation Network (SAIN) and a Research Fellow at University of East Anglia. He is specialised in sustainable agriculture and rural development with experience in China and Africa. He has been a consultant to ADB, FAO, World Bank, EU, Dfid, BIS and FCO on various projects.

**David Norse** CBE is Emeritus Professor of Environmental Management, at UCL Environment Institute, and has worked on agricultural development problems in Africa and the Caribbean and then worked with Defra, the OECD and the UNFAO. He contributed to Agenda 21, the IPCC's first report, and the Stern Review. He is an active researcher on policy solutions to food security and agro-environmental problems in China and globally.

**Lynette H. Ong** is Associate Professor of Political Science at the University of Toronto. She is the author of *Prosper or Perish: Credit and Fiscal Systems in Rural China* (2012). Her publications have appeared in *Comparative Politics, China Quarterly, International Political Science Review, Foreign Affairs, Journal of East Asian Studies*, among others.

**Robin Porter** holds a PhD from SOAS, University of London, and since 1968 has taught at universities in Canada, Australia and the UK. He has also served as Counsellor for Science and Innovation at the British Embassy in Beijing. He is currently a Visiting Professor at the University of Bristol, and his latest book is *From Mao to Market: China Reconfigured* (2011).

**Andrew Small** is Transatlantic Fellow with the Asia programme at the German Marshall Fund of the United States, which he has helped lead since 2006. His research focuses on US-China relations, EU-China relations, Chinese policy in South and South-West Asia, and China's role in 'problem' and fragile states.

**Tim Summers** writes on the politics, economy and international relations of contemporary China. He is Senior Consulting Fellow with Chatham House, teaches at the Chinese University of Hong Kong, and advises corporations and investors on China. He began his career as a British diplomat, culminating in a posting as Consul-General in Chongqing, southwest China, from 2004 to 2007. He holds a PhD in Chinese Studies.

**Hinrich Voss** is Lecturer in International Business at the Centre for International Business University of Leeds (CIBUL). Before joining CIBUL, Hinrich was Postdoctoral Research Fellow at the White Rose East Asia Centre/National Institute for Chinese Studies.

**Bin Wu** is Senior Research Fellow and Convenor of the Centre for Chinese Migration Studies (CCMS), in the School of Contemporary Chinese Studies, University of Nottingham. His research interests include Chinese international migration and diasporic Chinese in the UK and Europe; Chinese student migration and integration; globalisation, social justice and higher education reform in China and beyond.

# List of Abbreviations

| | |
|---|---|
| ARF | ASEAN Regional Forum |
| ASEAN | Association of Southeast Asian Nations |
| ATT | Arms Trade Treaty |
| BIT | Bilateral Investment Treaty |
| BRICS | Group of five emerging national economies: Brazil, Russia, India, China, and South Africa |
| CAPSiM | China's Agricultural Policy Simulation Model |
| CAS | Chinese Academy of Sciences |
| CCAP | Centre for Chinese Agricultural Policy |
| CCP | Chinese Communist Party |
| CCPCC | Chinese Communist Party Central Committee |
| CCS | EU-China Cooperation on Carbon Capture and Storage |
| CDM | Clean Development Mechanism |
| CIA | Central Intelligence Agency (United States) |
| CIC | China Investment Corporation |
| CIS | Commonwealth of Independent States |
| CNOOC | China National Offshore Oil Corp |
| CNPC | China National Petroleum Corporation |
| COFM | ChinaObs/FDImonitor |
| CPPCC | Chinese People's Political Consultative Conference |
| CSI | Container Security Initiative |
| CTBT | Comprehensive Test Ban Treaty |
| CYL | Communist Youth League |
| EC | European Commission |
| ECRAN | Europe China Research and Advice Network |
| EEAS | European External Action Service |
| EEC | European Economic Community |
| EEP | EU-China Energy and Environment Programme |
| EFSF | European Financial Stability Facility |
| ERA | European Research Area |

| | |
|---|---|
| ERIA | Economic Research Institute for ASEAN and East Asia |
| FAO | Food and Agriculture Organization of the United Nations |
| FMCT | Fissile Material Cut-off Treaty |
| FUE | Fertilizer Use Efficiency |
| FYP | Five Year Programme |
| GDP | Gross domestic product |
| GOC | Government of China |
| GEZ | Greater Europe Zone |
| GHG | Greenhouse gas |
| G8 | Group of 8 |
| G20 | Group of 20 |
| GM | Genetically modified |
| ICSID | International Centre for the Settlement of Investment Disputes |
| ICT | Information and Communication Technology |
| IFPRI | International Food Policy Research Institute |
| IIAs | International Investment Agreements |
| IMF | International Monetary Fund |
| IPR | Intellectual Property Right |
| ITER | International Thermonuclear Experimental Reactor |
| MAC | Middle Class and Affluent Consumer |
| MEP | Ministry of Environmental Protection |
| Mha | Million hectares |
| MHRUD | Ministry of Housing and Urban–Rural Development |
| MLR | Ministry of Land and Resources |
| MOA | Ministry of Agriculture People's Republic of China |
| MOST | Ministry of Science and Technology |
| MOF | Ministry of Finance |
| MOFCOM | Ministry of Commerce People's Republic of China |
| Mt | Megatonne: a million tonnes |
| MWR | Ministry of Water Resources |
| NATO | North Atlantic Treaty Organization |
| NBS | National Bureau of Statistics |
| NBSC | National Bureau of Statistics of China |

| | |
|---|---|
| NDRC | National Development Reform Commission |
| NEA | National Energy Administration |
| NEC | National Energy Commission |
| NFS | National Food Survey |
| NSFC | Natural Science Foundation of China |
| NPC | National People's Congress |
| NPT | Nuclear Non-proliferation Treaty |
| NSG | Nuclear Suppliers Group |
| ODI | Overseas Direct Investment |
| OECD | Organisation for Economic Cooperation and Development |
| OFDI | Outward Foreign Direct Investment |
| OFIC | Outbound Foreign Investment Catalogue |
| PLA | People's Liberation Army |
| PRC | People's Republic of China |
| R&D | Research and Development |
| RMB | Renminbi (official currency of the People's Republic of China) |
| SAFE | State Administration of Foreign Exchange People's Republic of China |
| SAG | State Administration of Grain |
| SAR | Hong Kong Special Administrative Region |
| SCO | Shanghai Cooperation Organisation |
| SFIC | Strategic Forum for International S&T Cooperation |
| SME | Small and medium enterprises |
| SOE | State-Owned Enterprise |
| S&T | Science and technology |
| STI | Science, technology and innovation |
| SWF | Sovereign Wealth Funds |
| UNCTAD | United Nations Conference on Trade and Development |
| UNCOM | United Nations Commodity Trade |
| UNSC | United Nations Security Council |
| USDA | United States Department of Agriculture |
| WTO | World Trade Organization |
| WUE | Water Use Efficiency |

# Acknowledgements

I am extremely grateful to Chloe Sageman and Angelika Meier, my colleagues on the ECRAN project, and to Professor Shaun Breslin, Professor Lina Song and Professor Shujie Yao for their help as key experts in assessing and providing feedback for some of the papers here. I am also extremely grateful to Franz Jesson, and his successor Rebecca Fabrizi at the EEAS for their support for the ECRAN project, and to their colleagues in the China section, in particular Dr Jolita Pons and Liliana Strugariu. I would also like to thank Gigi Hancock and Georgia Regan for editorial help. Finally, of course, I am extremely grateful to the authors of each of the papers here, who worked so hard, and have produced such excellent and valuable research. I would also like to convey my thanks to Tamsine O'Riordan of Palgrave Macmillan for steering this book through to publication.

# Introduction: The EU and China, a Relationship in Context

*Kerry Brown*

The articles collected in this book are the first long research pieces produced as part of the Europe China Research and Advice Network (ECRAN), a four-year project funded by the European Union (EU) to provide policy advice and analysis, and support research to the European External Action Service (EEAS). The EEAS was established as the formal diplomatic service of the EU under the Lisbon Treaty implemented in 2009.

ECRAN was a unique endeavour to build deeper communication links between the EU policy making apparatus and expert communities on China across the 28 Member States of the Union. Its main work has been to supply short and long policy papers, and briefing and public events, in order to inform decision making and the public discussion of relations between the EU and China. The chapters assembled here are the first selection of the longer research pieces, commissioned after competitive tender from some of the world's leading experts on China and issues relating to China. They embrace social, economic and political issues, and give some flavour of the different approaches and frameworks within which China and its relations with the EU can be viewed. They also give insights into the evolution of these issues within China.

## Context of the Relationship

The EU and China have formal relations dating back to 1975, when they first extended diplomatic recognition to each other. This was a very particular moment in their individual development.

For the People's Republic of China (PRC), it marked the twilight of the Cultural Revolution which had been ongoing since 1966, and which had seen major political campaigns in the country which had, at one point, reduced its representation at ambassadorial level abroad down to one country (Egypt). China's internal politics during this era had been convulsed, its decision making processes preoccupied by elite power struggles and factional battles which had resulted in the removal of two of Mao Zedong's potential successors (Liu Shaoqi in 1967 and Lin Biao in 1971), and the conduct of hugely disruptive campaigns. One of the great paradoxes of this period, however, was the startling rapprochement with the United States in 1972, and the gradual diversification of the country's international links after a period of intense, albeit brief, introspection from the 1950s onwards.

By the year that China and the European Economic Community (EEC), as it then was, accorded recognition to each other, they were both seeking a larger global role. For the EEC, this took the form of the transition from an alliance between nation states in Europe based purely on economic joint interests to something that would, within two decades, become a much deeper political union. The highly economic nature of the EEC is recognised by the EU-China Trade and Cooperation Agreement signed in 1985. This remains the legal basis of the relationship to this day, and yet it reads largely as an agreement on tariffs and market access. It was only with the ratification of the Maastricht Treaty in February 1992 that the EU came into existence a year later, replacing the EEC, expanding the ambitions of an enlarged Union to formally embrace joint social and political values. A process of enlargement over the next two decades meant that by 2013, the Union had acquired 28 members, and had become the world's largest single trading bloc and the single largest economy, accounting for almost a third of global gross domestic product (GDP).

In these four decades of radical change since 1975, the EEC/EU and the PRC underwent parallel journeys of existential change. The EU now is a very different entity from that which existed in 1975. But in some ways, the PRC despite its continuation as a unified sovereign state is even more radically different. In 1975, a year before the death of Mao Zedong, who had been the undisputed supreme leader for most of the last three decades since 1949 and the foundation of the country, the Chinese economy was a centrally planned one controlled by the state. It was primarily an agrarian system where almost 90 per cent of people lived in rural areas, a place where there was hardly any foreign capital, and where the market existed at the very edges of society, and with no legal protection.

Over the next decade, and particularly with the immense impetus given to the country at the third plenum of the Eleventh Party Congress held in Beijing in December 1978, all of this was to change. By 1985, when the Trade and Cooperation agreement was signed with the EEC, China had laws allowing for foreign capital to enter the country through joint ventures, had embraced the market by allowing farmers to sell surplus crops back to the state for a profit and set up town and village enterprises engaged in profit making activities, had started to open its internal market up to the outside world and was experimenting with private sector reform. Despite some hiccoughs, over the ensuing three decades all these trends have not only continued, but deepened. China joined the World Trade Organization (WTO) in 2001, and quadrupled the size of its economy by 2013, to become the world's second largest in terms of purchasing power parity (PPP) by 2010. According to the Organisation for Economic Cooperation and Development (OECD), over half of economic productivity was through the non-state sector by 2005.[1] It had started to become a significant outward investor, and the world's second largest importer. Over this period, unsurprisingly, its trade relations with the EU burgeoned, so that by 2011 EU and China bilateral trade had risen to €423 billion, with the EU being the largest destination for Chinese exports, and the second largest supplier of goods to China. Even during the harsh years of trade from 2007 to 2011, trade rose almost 9 per cent per annum, almost double China's trade with the rest of the world. China accounted for 17 per cent of EU imports, and nearly 9 per cent of exports.[2]

This is a relationship of transformed partners, who, in the second decade of the twenty-first century have a series of dialogues at almost every possible conceivable level around them. There were 56 of these as of 2013, covering areas ranging from human rights (one of the most controversial areas) to intellectual property and scientific cooperation. One informal calculation estimated that in the Brussels central bureaucracy there were 100 officials dealing solely with issues relating to China. In fact, across the EU governance system, and into the separate bureaucracies of the Member States there were probably many thousands who were involved, at different levels and to different degrees of intensity, with China, or China-related issues. The EU-China bilateral relationship has become almost as labour intensive as the construction of the Great Wall, with armies of officials, analysts, diplomats and other facilitators on both sides putting intellectual, administrative and economic effort into understanding each other.

One thing that is striking, and which these chapters all, in their different ways, testify to is that this is a complex relationship. That complexity is asymmetrical and existential. The EU is not like the PRC, because it is a collection of sovereign states, an alliance where these states have radically different identities, cultures, languages and internal politics. They work to a common purpose within the framework of an agreement which had been articulated over many years and after immense effort. Their alliance is not, as Benedict Anderson said, some kind of imagined community but something built on hard-nosed, pragmatic negotiations and tight definitions amongst each of the nation states, of self-interest.[3] For the PRC, its notion of identity is different, something born of a long history of state development, and predicated, at least by the current political elite within the ruling Communist Party of China in Beijing, on unified and centralised rule. In an odd way, the experience of disunity and its terrible outcomes is something that links these two polities. China's fragmentation in the Republican Period from 1911 led to the darkest period of colonial suffering, when it experienced the Sino Japanese war from 1937 and its own Civil War from 1946 to 1949. During this period, central governance structures effectively ceased. Warlords famously administered large swathes of the country, or, during the war period, were co-opted either by Nationalist, Communist or Japanese forces. For the EU, the horrifying results of the political divisions from the 1930s leading to all consuming total war from 1939 was the foundation of the project to ensure that this never reoccurred. And so, while the founding purpose of the Union from the European Steel and Coal Community formally established by the Treaty of Paris with six member states in 1951 may have been economic, at its heart there was always a project of deeper

European integration, something which had become more explicit as the decades wore on. The Treaty of Rome established the EEC itself in 1956, which remained in existence till 1993. We can see a journey towards a highly contended greater political unity, and one which remains controversial even to this day. Even so, the aspiration to forge unity where there is so much potential disunity is one that, in very different ways (and certainly ways that neither likes to explicitly refer to) both have in common to this day.

Since the global financial crisis of 2007–8, the EU has undergone a series of profound economic shocks, which have undermined what was seen as a sometime imperious and often self-regarding attitude that it had towards China. China itself had, through the very act of joining the WTO in 2001, signed up to an acceptance of global norms and standards, at least in the economic realm. It had, in many ways, conceded to a system forged and directed by developed, and mostly democratic, countries. And yet, rather than creating a more profound sense of common purpose, there were ways in which EU-China relations from this period grew progressively tougher. The start of the decade was good. China produced one of its first bold statements on the meaning of the relationship in 2003. In a White Paper produced by the State Council, it declared:

> The common ground between China and the EU far outweighs their disagreements. Both China and the EU stand for democracy in international relations and an enhanced role of the UN. Both are committed to combating international terrorism and promoting sustainable development through poverty elimination and environmental protection endeavours. China and the EU are highly complementary economically thanks to their respective advantages. The EU has a developed economy, advanced technologies and strong financial resources while China boasts steady economic growth, a huge market and abundant labour force. There is a broad prospect for bilateral trade and economic and technological cooperation. Both China and the EU member states have a long history and splendid culture each and stand for more cultural exchanges and mutual emulation. The political, economic and cultural common understanding and interaction between China and the EU offer a solid foundation for the continued growth of China-EU relations.[4]

To a degree, the EU reciprocated, producing a document entitled 'EU-China: Closer Partners, Growing Responsibilities' in 2006. This declared:

> Europe needs to respond effectively to China's renewed strength. To tackle the key challenges facing Europe today – including climate change, employment, migration, security – we need to leverage the potential of a dynamic relationship with China based on our values. We also have an interest in supporting China's reform process. This means factoring the China dimension into the full range of EU policies, external and internal. It also means close coordination inside the EU to ensure an overall and coherent approach.[5]

By 2013, however, a number of entrenched issues meant the heady days of this earlier idealism were over. The EU had failed, as a result of US pressure, to lift the arms embargo imposed on China after the Tiananmen Square uprising in June 1989; it had failed, despite intense lobbying on China's part, to accord the PRC market economy status, and it had been embroiled in a number of difficult trade disputes, the most recent of which was the growing spat from 2012 onwards over solar panels and claims on the EU side that China was subsidising manufacturers who were then flooding the European market. On top of this, the two had clashed on Tibet, the awarding of the Nobel Peace Prize to the Chinese dissident Liu Xiaobo and the execution, in late 2009, of British national Akmal Shaikh for drug smuggling, the first EU citizen to have been sentenced to death since the late 1950s.

## Knowing Each Other Better

The chapters in this collection cover key aspects of the economic relationship between the EU and China, but also the major issues of China's internal governance and its own leadership, and the geopolitical context in which this critical relationship is located. They also look at the practical and highly concrete question of migration by Chinese into the EU Member States.

Investment is a big issue, simply because flows of capital over the decade from 2001 have risen steeply. A book about

EU-China relations in 1995 that contained two major essays on this subject would have been regarded as puzzling. At that time, Chinese overseas investment was hardly noticeable, and mostly in developing countries and the resources sector. But by the turn of the second decade of the twenty-first century, this issue had become one of the most important ones. The contribution by Jeremy Clegg and Hinrich Voss looks at the highly topical issue of what kinds of Chinese investment there has been in the EU up to 2011, what the sectorial and regional distribution of this has been, where it is deployed most heavily, and, perhaps most critically, where it has come from. Their treatment captures the immediate problem of getting good data. But in Europe and China, there are issues about how investment is defined, how to track investment that comes via other sources (in the case of China, in particular, the Hong Kong Special Administrative Region, where almost two-thirds of Chinese outward investment now initially goes) and how to quantify it. Their chapter shows that different sources give different figures, but that the underlying story they tell is the same: that Chinese investment, while still modest, is increasing, and that all the key drivers for its growth are likely to remain in place over the coming years. For policy makers and business people too, their detailed research shows that countries in the EU with the infrastructure to attract Chinese investment proactively have gained – Germany, the UK and France are significant here. Those who take a passive 'wait and it will come' approach are less successful. The European market, with its superficial unity but its deep differences legally, culturally and administratively, is still a daunting one to Chinese potential investors, no matter how much capital they may have to deploy. If the EU wants more investment, therefore, it needs to think about giving more practical help. And it also needs to reflect hard on the narrative that it presents to Chinese state and non-state companies coming here, who often get welcomed with a message that on the one hand tells them they are needed, and on the other tells them they are regarded as a threat and a problem.

Thierry Apoteker's contribution looks at the countries in the Greater Europe Zone – and in particular, the dominating economies in this area of Russia and Turkey. Chinese investments here are large, but concentrated in one key area, that of resources.

There is still the same problem of finding credible data as Clegg and Voss highlight, perhaps because the methods by which statistics are collected vary profoundly from country to country. Russia absorbs the bulk of Chinese investment – perhaps unsurprising in view of its rich resources and the almost limitless need by the Chinese economy for energy. But even with this strong connection of complementing needs – China's for resources, Russia's for capital – Chinese investment is lower than might be expected. And there are ways in which the EU can figure this emerging Chinese interest in the resource market in Russia particularly as competition, largely because so much of its current and projected future energy needs are due to come from this area. In this chapter, therefore, we see Chinese investment not as a largely positive phenomenon, but more as a new and growing dynamic in an increasingly competitive global market place, and one where the EU needs to formulate responses.

One of the arguments behind the EU's insistence that China not be accorded market economy status is because the state still plays a significant part in the structuring and operation of the Chinese economy. The most overt sign of this is the continuing existence of central state macro-economic planning, the most visible element being the Five Year Programmes (called 'Plans' up to the late 1990s). The most recent of these, published in 2011, is the twelfth since they began in 1953. In the twenty-first century, they are more like grand budget statements, which set out the key objectives for growth over the coming five years. But as Robert Ash, Robin Porter and Timothy Summers make clear in their analysis of the Twelfth Programme, they are the most detailed indication that the outside world gets of the priorities that the Chinese government through its various national ministries and provincial decision making bodies has set itself. Their chapter concentrates in particular on the aspirations set out from 2011 to make China a greener economy, and one which is more innovative and produces higher value goods. Greening the Chinese economy is critical now, since the effects of three decades of intense industrialisation on the environment are both visible and quantifiable. Pan Yue, the previous outspoken Vice-Minister in the national environment ministry stated in the mid-2000s that the cost of cleaning up China's environment after this era of deep modernisation and activity might be equivalent to all the wealth created over the same period. This is a sobering reminder of the seriousness of China's challenges here, and something that the Twelfth Programme explicitly sets targets for. For Ash, Porter and Summers, however, the real issue is how the government continues to deliver what it calls 'fast, sustainable growth'. Is this possible? Can 7 per cent annual GDP growth be sustained, doubling the size of the economy in the next decade, and can resources, environment, water and food be preserved? There are clearly ways in which China's massive challenges here are also opportunities for collaboration and engagement with outside partners. As with investment, therefore, the terms of an EU-China engagement in this area, within the framework articulated in the Programme, are promising ones, and they should expand. The main thing is to look closely at the ways in which the Programme document spells out the government's own understanding of its internal priorities and then see in what ways partners across the EU can speak to these in ways they can benefit.

During the period 2011 to 2013, the issue of elite leadership loomed over all these issues. From the Seventeenth Party Congress in 2007, it was clear that two figures in particular, who were promoted that year to the all-important Standing Committee of the Politburo, the summit of power in contemporary China, were in pole position to replace the serving Party Secretary Hu Jintao, and the Premier and Head of the State Council and Executive Wen Jiabao. Xi Jinping and Li Keqiang came to their Politburo positions with rich provincial experience, and with deep links to various networks in the Party. But they were also operating in a context in which the laws of leadership succession for the Communist Party were undergoing profound change, and where there were no clear explicit rules. Previous successions had been complex, and often failed. The main issue in 2012, when the Eighteenth Party Congress which would see this changeover take place was due, was to achieve this with minimal fuss and with maximum legitimacy.

Michael Dillon is a long term observer of Chinese politics, and his contribution uses Chinese and English language sources both to track the startling fall of one of the main contenders for promotion in 2012, Bo Xilai, through a series of scandals involving his wife, but also through the complex interplay of alliances and struggles between different elite leaders and the networks around them. For all its institutionalisation, therefore, the Communist Party in the twenty-first century still runs on the basis of powerful individuals and their accrual of political capital and influence. Dillon maps these out, with detailed descriptions of the backgrounds of Li and Xi, and some analysis of where their policy interests might lie. His account supports the notion that trying to understand modern China without some historic background is impossible. The historic parallels and context he offers is invaluable, because it is these individuals, the ones who came out as victors of the whole process in 2012 and into 2013, that will guide the vast project of nation building and economic strengthening in China in the coming critical decade as it works towards being a middle-income country by 2020.

The country that they rule is one of the most challenging, if not the most challenging, on the planet. It is geographically vast, divided into 31 different provinces, autonomous regions and municipalities under the central government, each of them with different internal political, economic and cultural dynamics. Gansu in the North-west is a wholly different sort of polity from Shanghai, on the coast, with vastly different GDP levels, consumption patterns and industrial patterns. This is a country where governance is a huge and time consuming task, and one which Lynette Ong and Christian Göbel show is beset by internal struggles. Different interest groups clash with each other, some contending for land rights, some for pension payments, many for access to justice which they feel the legal system has failed to give them. Ong and Göbel's field research, undertaken specially for this chapter, shows that Chinese rural areas and provinces are run by leaders who have, as their main criterion, production of growth, and who are mandated to deal with social management and outbreaks of unrest in any way they can that at least alleviates the problems. The outcomes of this are not pleasant, but they have, at least until 2013, maintained stability in a society undergoing profound development and transformation. One issue that Ong and Göbel address is what in fact constitutes unrest in China. It might be demonstrations involving a few people, or vast uprisings as occurred most famously in Wukan, Guangdong province in 2010–11. There are no standard templates by which leaders respond to these incidents, or a manual that they use to show them how to face these issues.

In some, negotiation is used, in others brute violence. The conclusion that this chapter guides one towards is an appreciation of just how much conflict there is in China in the era of 'harmony' and 'scientific development', and now outsiders cannot be too complacent about the overall stability of the system that the elite leaders in Dillon's chapter seem to dominate.

Outside, of course, China presents a different image – a wealthy, powerful and unified one. Bates Gill and Andrew Small are two of the most astute and experienced observers of China's international behaviour, and their chapter wrestles with the issue of how the relationship between the EU, China and the US might be balanced, in a period in which they seem to be pulled in different, and more competitive directions. With the establishment of G8, G7 and then G20 in the last few decades, and with some even talking since the late 2000s of the G2 consisting of just the US and China, the question guiding this chapter is in what ways we might sensibly talk of a G3, adding the EU. In terms of economic importance, the concept has some traction. It is odd that the world's three largest unified trading blocks are not ever in a room together, working out common strategies. They constitute, after all, over half of global GDP. Even so, the EU, China and the US have widely different identities, and are often bemused by each other, sometimes to the extent that China and the EU have common cause against the US, or the US and China against the EU. Nothing illustrates the flexibility and fluidity of international relations in the modern era more than the shifting allegiances and definitions of common interest as the relationship between these three partners. And while Gill and Small's conclusion is that definition of common ground, while it exists between the three, is modest, there are ways in which they can, and should, work better with each other.

The final chapters deal separately with two of the most practically important, but contentious issues, China's internal development and the bilateral issues between the EU and China. Food security was an issue on which China tragically failed in the Maoist period. The memory of the vast famines from the late 1950s to 1962 lie heavy on the country to this day, with passionate debate inside and out about how many might actually have died at this time (even the lowest estimates are tens of millions). China solved its food needs by greater efficiency in the agricultural sector and a steep rise in productivity in the 1980s. But in the twenty-first century, the country is faced with a whole new set of challenges: reduction in farming land through intense urbanisation, changes in diet as people eat more Western style meat based diets, issues of environmental degradation and its impact on farming. David Norse, Yuelai Lu and Jikun Huang in their important contribution show the new dependencies that are being created in China as it seeks to feed its population through efficiencies and reform of the agricultural sector, still a quarter of China's economy. Migration is more a bilateral issue. Once more, the issue of statistics is a controversial one here, with Kevin Latham and Bin Wu undertaking audits across the EU Member States of exactly where Chinese migrant communities have historically existed, and where new patterns have emerged. There are, perhaps unsurprisingly, widely different trends as progress takes place across the EU terrain. For some, like the UK, there has been a steady flow through the contact with Hong Kong over the last century, and a large influx of students in the decade after 2000. But for others, like countries in Eastern Europe, the arrivals have been more modest, and mostly consisted of business people. Chinese migration into Italy illustrates the contentiousness, with large influxes through links with the textile industry, in long-established cities in the north of the country like Prato, leading to political and social outcomes that have been challenging. In some communities, arrivals of new migrants from China have been welcomed, and integrated. In others, there have been tensions. The need for a coherent migration policy has been obvious in many EU states. Latham and Wu show the economic benefits that Chinese migrants have brought, and offer some evidence of the very real bridges that they then offer back to communities in China. It is clear that in the future these links will be increasingly important. However, the relatively low levels of political representation from the ethnic Chinese communities in EU countries is worrying – the UK, with one of the oldest and best established Chinese diasporas has never yet had an ethnically Chinese Member of Parliament. Policy makers at national and subnational level are therefore confronted in Latham and Wu's chapter with a group in society that has huge importance and value who are, at the moment, too marginalised and often stereotyped.

These chapters, taken together, give an overview, often in great detail, of a crucial relationship, and one that is developing and evolving almost constantly. They are written by experts with considerable experience in their area, with strong analytic tools from across the disciplines, but who are also dealing with fresh data. The common element between these contributions is of a field of engagement and study in which, almost daily, we are presented with new facts, new data collections and information, and new demands by which to structure and make sense of these. This book therefore is a contribution to that larger debate, a debate in which two of the world's key geopolitical and economic players in the twenty-first century deepen their understanding and engagement with each other. The most powerful message from this collection in the end is an optimistic one. China and the EU have much more in common than they think, and many more possible ways of working together. Their differences are real, and often deep – but the scope by which they can enhance their collaboration and draw their polities and economies closer together is also huge. These contributions show how thorough and up-to-date research and sound analysis can offer policy makers, whether in government, the non-state sector, or in the wider community, real value. We hope that they are useful, and that they contribute to the flourishing of EU and China relations in the coming years.

## Notes

1. See 'Economic Survey of China 2005' by the OECD, http://www.oecd.org/eco/surveys/economicsurveyofchina2005executivesummary.htm, available at: accessed 22 July 2013.
2. See EU-China summit September 2012, Factsheet, available at: http://eeas.europa.eu/china/summit/summit_docs/20120920_factsheet_en.pdf, accessed 8 January 2014.
3. Benedict Anderson, 'Imagined Communities: Reflections on the Origin and Spread of Nationalism', Verso London, 1983.
4. China's EU Policy Paper', State Council Information Office, October 2003, available at: http://www.china.org.cn/e-white/20050817/, accessed 8 January 2014.
5. http://eur-lex.europa.eu/LexUriServ/site/en/com/2006/com2006_0631en01.pdf, accessed 8 January 2014.

# 1 Chinese Overseas Direct Investment into the European Union

*Jeremy Clegg and Hinrich Voss*

## Introduction

The purpose of this chapter is to review the factors that have driven and constrained mainland Chinese investments in the EU from 2000 to 2013, and to outline the policy recommendations that arise for the EU and its Member States wishing to increase their share of Chinese foreign direct investment (FDI). The geographical focus of investment for this chapter is the EU of 27 Member States (EU-27). The narrower boundaries of the EU of 15 Member States (EU-15) will be used when we refer to time periods before 2004 (i.e. the pre-Fifth-Enlargement members).

We focus on FDI by mainland Chinese firms, that is, where the ultimate parent company is Chinese. This can be determined by using mergers and acquisitions (M&A) data, but not with conventional FDI statistics. Thus portfolio investments, government bond purchases and direct investments from the Hong Kong Special Administrative Region (SAR), from the Macao SAR, from Taiwan or from any offshore tax haven are not considered here. Direct investments from Japan, South Korea and the US are included only for comparative reasons, to put Chinese investments in the EU into international perspective. A Chinese foreign direct investment in the EU is taken to mean investment owned by a Chinese-resident enterprise in an EU-resident enterprise, with the intention of establishing a lasting interest while exercising a significant degree of management influence. Such influence is inferred if the investor has 10 per cent or more of equity-based voting power (see UNCTAD 2009, p. 38; OECD 2008, para. 117). Chinese firms that invest overseas (including in Hong Kong, which is still regarded as autonomous from the People's Republic of China (PRC) except in foreign policy and defence), thus owning productive assets in at least two countries, are classified as multinational enterprises (MNEs). This is regardless of their size or form of ownership. Forms of ownership addressed in this chapter cover state-owned and privately owned firms. Chinese listed firms can also fall into either of these categories. Sovereign wealth funds (SWFs), such as the China Investment Corporation (CIC) and the State Administration of Foreign Exchange (SAFE) Investment Fund, are government-owned investment vehicles, not state-owned enterprises. They are not solely, nor even predominantly, FDI-focused organisations. They are therefore treated as a separate form of investor. Monetary values are presented in Euros and US dollar.

Our analysis comprises a Chinese and a European perspective. The Chinese perspective is applied when we consider the investment pattern and motivation of Chinese state-owned and privately owned investors. Firms invest internationally in order to expand or to defend their overseas market (so-called market-seeking investment); to secure better access to raw materials such as oil and minerals (resource-seeking); to secure better access to technologies, brands, distribution channels (strategic asset-seeking); and/or to reduce overall production costs by utilising cheaper inputs, generally labour, or to achieve greater productivity (efficiency-seeking). Depending on the investment motive (and often several motives are present at a time), potential investors consider and evaluate host-country characteristics comparatively. Such characteristics encompass Chinese government attitudes and the Chinese institutional framework towards investing abroad. Indeed, one aspect that must not be overlooked in the Chinese context is the role of the government, which has been central in guiding the domestic economy to today's economic success. The stance of central government policy has changed towards outward investment in recent years. Although cross-border investments were first permitted in the late 1970s, they were heavily restricted by the government. This slowly changed during the 1980s and 1990s as a regulatory framework was developed and state-owned enterprises incrementally gathered experience in operating in foreign markets. The most prominent initiative to signal that the government deemed Chinese companies sufficiently prepared was the 'Go Global' policy, formally decreed in 2000. We note in outline the relaxation of official Chinese policy, but we do not go into detail or predict the future. We give priority to what lies within the policy domain of the EU to win its share (and influence the quality) of China's outward FDI rather than the aggregate quantity of its outward foreign direct investment (OFDI).

To complement the Chinese perspective, a European perspective is employed in order to analyse the attractiveness of Chinese investors and to evaluate the success of EU Member States in bringing them to Europe. Market, institutional and policy conditions are assessed for the way in which they support Chinese investments (through, for example, investment promotion agencies, specialised investment and trading hubs) but also hinder them (through restrictive work permits, visa regulations and so on).

## Chinese Outward FDI Globally and the Role of the EU

The importance and magnitude of Chinese direct investments to, and within, the EU cannot be assessed properly without first being contextualised. We therefore begin by presenting an analysis of Chinese direct investment globally. This is done in two parts: (1) its distribution in terms of absolute values and growth figures, from which we infer the importance of the EU to Chinese investors, and (2) the industrial distribution of Chinese investments globally.

## Structure of Chinese Global Outward FDI Distribution

In 2011, Chinese firms made investments of €53 billion (US$70 billion) overseas (NBS, MOFCOM and SAFE, 2012). Early investments from China were directed towards the industrialised countries Australia, Canada and the USA. But this has changed since the mid-1990s, and today the majority of Chinese investments are directed to emerging and developing countries. A major pull factor for Chinese investments globally is the level of natural resource endowment of host countries, in particular oil (Kolstad and Wiig, 2012; Duanmu, 2012).

The EU saw an increase in Chinese inward investment from €0.3 billion (US$0.4 billion) to €5.8 billion (US$7.6 billion) between 2003 and 2011 (NBS, MOFCOM and SAFE, 2012). This was an annual growth rate of Chinese outward FDI stock to the EU-27 of 59.4 per cent, much above the 42.7 per cent growth rate of the global Chinese FDI stock. In 2006–9, the progress of Chinese investment in the EU became decoupled from the global trend. Chinese investments there were rising faster than the global average until the Anglo-American financial and economic crisis. Then the downward pressure on investment worldwide translated into a far steeper decline of Chinese FDI in the EU (and North America). In particular, a majority of Chinese SMEs expressed the intention to reduce their overseas investments, and a desire to seek more advantageous host economies (CCPIT, 2009). The crisis also heralded changes in the motivation for investment by Chinese firms. The strategic intent of Chinese investors in the EU market shifted almost entirely away from the resource-rich regions, as Chinese enterprises became opportunistic acquirers of firms, and parts of firms, in response to the shrinkage of EU corporations' equity value during the crisis. Overall, however, movements of Chinese FDI into the EU over the period average out; and the share of Chinese investment secured by the EU has returned to around 2.5 per cent in 2009 (the same level prior to the crisis). Since then, the share has then increased to 5 per cent of China's outward FDI stock.

## Distribution of OFDI by Sector

In 2003 China reported, for the first time, OFDI statistics that were in line with OECD and IMF definitions (Cheung and Qian, 2009; NBS, MOFCOM and SAFE, 2010). This resulted in a revaluation downwards of mining and manufacturing investments while investments in business services and finance were revealed as more substantial than previously appreciated. These two service sectors are important in supporting the internationalisation of home-country enterprise: firms from these service sectors either follow their major domestic clients or prepare the path on to which their domestic clients step. The underlying increase in share of these sectors can be regarded as part of the continuous intensification in the internationalisation process of Chinese firms.

Bilateral trade, in the form of exports and imports to and from the host country, are important determinants of the geographical pattern of Chinese OFDI (Buckley, Clegg, Cross et al., 2007; Kolstad and Wiig, 2012). The published Chinese statistics do not enable us to see the simultaneous industry-by-country distribution of Chinese OFDI. Cuervo-Cazurra (2007) observed that emerging-market firms tend to locate sales, marketing and R&D-related activities in host countries where they can exploit their home-country advantages and that they locate manufacturing activities in hosts when the cross-border transfer of end products is difficult or when host country advantages of location can be exploited. It follows from this that Chinese investments in the more advanced economies of the EU-15 should be characterised by smaller-scale, knowledge-exploring, high-value manufacturing and goods-trading investments. The Fifth-Enlargement Member States, which joined the EU in 2004 and 2007, are more likely to receive predominantly standardised manufacturing or assembly-related FDI. The small share of Chinese FDI destined for the European Union raises a number of questions that we intend to address in the following sections. In particular, are Europeans making a sufficient effort to attract Chinese investments or are the wrong Chinese investors being courted? Are there artificial or natural barriers to Chinese investments? Before we can answer these questions, it is important to understand better what is happening in the EU.

## Chinese Outward FDI in the EU

The distribution of Chinese investment across the EU is an important indication of the ability of Chinese firms to invest and of their motivation for investment. However, there are limits to the extent to which we can determine competitiveness by using aggregate data. Chinese affiliates may simply be handling goods produced in China, in which case these firms' competitiveness must inevitably owe more to the locational (comparative) advantage of China as a production base than to abilities specific to them. Chinese direct investments in the economically developed countries indicate a motivation to acquire technologies and brands as well as a degree of capability and competitiveness intrinsic to the firms concerned. On the other hand, investments in the Fifth-Enlargement countries of the EU point towards low-cost production strategies that target only the European market without upgrading the abilities of the investing Chinese firms.

The distribution of investments is also instructive for assessing the potential impact of Chinese FDI. For those of the Fifth-Enlargement countries that otherwise receive little FDI, Chinese investment can offer a valuable contribution to industrialising their economy.

## Structure of Intra-EU Distribution

Chinese investment in the EU has always been concentrated in a small number of countries. France, Germany and the United Kingdom have together attracted on average 51 per cent of annual Chinese investment from 2003 to 2011 (NBS, MOFCOM and SAFE, 2012). We shall look at the distribution of Chinese outward investment in the European Union countries using three alternative measures, in order to build a picture of the true commitment of Chinese firms to the European market.

Figure 1.1, using data from Eurostat (Eurostat, 2011a) and from the NBS, MOFCOM and SAFE statistical bulletin (2011), shows clearly that the distribution of Chinese OFDI is highly concentrated within the European Union. The top four investment locations account for 39.2 per cent of all Chinese investment there, according to Eurostat data. The ranking of the major host countries differs between the Eurostat data and the MOFCOM data, but we can see that the dominance by major host countries remains. And although there are significant conflicts between the two data sources, they do agree that the UK and Germany are major host countries to inward Chinese FDI.

The major disagreement between the two data sources concerns Denmark and France. They complete the leading four host countries, according to the Eurostat data; but Luxembourg and the Netherlands replace them in the top four, according to the MOFCOM data. This can be explained by known deficiencies in the data. Eurostat data are not reported for Luxembourg, and that immediately distorts the basis for comparison. This underlines the value of using MOFCOM data to identify where Chinese investments are directed. At the same time, Luxembourg is known to be an investment gateway into the EU, and so the recording of Chinese FDI entering Luxembourg is not necessarily that of where the investment remains. Data collected by the United Nations Conference on Trade and Development (UNCTAD) also supports this interpretation that Luxembourg is, in many cases, not the ultimate destination of investment (UNCTAD, 2011). We should also note that investment into Luxembourg is characteristically 'lumpy': it tends to be built up by the accumulation of a relatively few large-value investments.

Greater confidence in the data is yielded by a comparison of the two sources, as the absolute difference in the valuations for individual countries (for which both data sources are reported) is not excessive; and there is no evidence of significant systematic under- or overvaluation. Generally, the Eurostat data estimate Chinese FDI in the EU to be a little higher than the Chinese data (for example in 2009, €5.7 billion (in dollar terms, US$8 billion) as compared with €4.5 billion (US$6.3 billion)). Such differences in valuation are not unusual. It is deficiencies in reporting at Member State level that are the most problematic; in particular, the absence of Eurostat data for Luxembourg distorts the picture. For certain states, we see that FDI positions may be negative, or might diminish rapidly. Although this might seem to suggest that FDI is zero, it actually signifies that affiliates are in credit with parent enterprises, and it may have much to do with financial repositioning internal to MNEs after the financial and economic crisis.

A combined analysis of both data sources suggests a clustering in the distribution of investments. First, there are the top two hosts, the UK and Germany, then the 'super-cluster' of Denmark, France and the Netherlands. After these countries, China invests in Austria, Italy, Poland and the like. A large number of Member States have received very little Chinese investment or record negative FDI positions, according to Eurostat. The

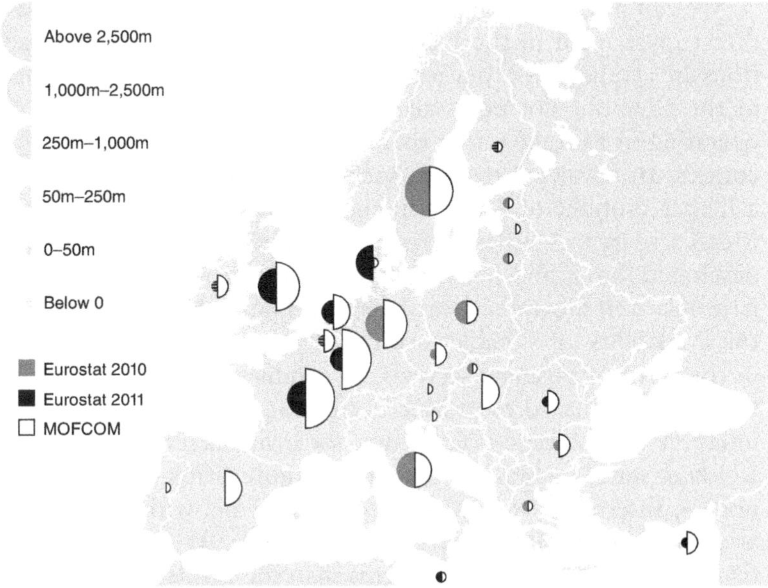


Figure 1.1 **Distribution of Chinese OFDI in the EU-27 by 2009 (€ million)**

*Note*: Black/grey denotes Eurostat data and white denotes NBS, MOFCOM and SAFE data.

*Source*: Eurostat (2011a) and NBS, MOFCOM and SAFE (2010).

remarkable concentration shown in Figure 1.1 suggests that the large-market countries of the Union received Chinese investment precisely because of the size of their domestic market. It suggests too that Chinese investors do not at present perceive the EU as a single integrated market. If this were the case, there would probably be a more even distribution in Chinese investment across the EU. Of course, the availability of acquisition targets is also skewed towards the large advanced markets of the Union. Moreover, a skewed distribution might reflect concentrated manufacturing facilities serving the entire European market, as is evident for investments from South Korea (in central and east European states) and Japan (in Germany and the UK). Besides the attraction of economic size, the concentration of Chinese investments in these states is arguably the outcome of sound bilateral international economic relations and the effective promotion of inward investment.

We can also employ M&A data to build a picture of Chinese direct investment in the EU. In practice, most of these transactions are acquisitions: they represent the takeover of a firm located in the EU (but not necessarily owned by European owners or operating in Europe) rather than the merger of two separate legal entities. In advanced markets such as the EU, we would expect a higher number of M&As in the inflow of FDI. The bulk of M&A activity by Chinese investors is, again, located in those most developed, large and favoured economies for investment, which have relatively liberalised markets (see Figure 1.2). This reflects the availability of suitable investment targets and the expertise, in the form of business services, to conduct merger and acquisition transactions. As most M&As are straight acquisitions, we can interpret the Chinese predilection for investment in the leading EU host states to indicate that they acquire firms for their technology, international brands, international networks of subsidiaries and international distribution channels. At present, Indian firms acquire more European firms than the Chinese do (Ernst & Young, 2011; Sun et al., 2012), but the rate and spread of Chinese acquisitions is on a rising trend.

Companies in the United Kingdom, Germany, France, Italy and the Netherlands are the main subjects of Chinese takeovers. Acquisition activity is found predominately in the same countries in which the aggregate FDI data indicate the greatest inflow of Chinese investment. We cannot expect the FDI data, which are reported on an OECD FDI definition basis, to agree with the M&A data, as these are recorded on a transaction basis. However, these transaction data do support our overall finding that the international EU-China relationship is primarily a result of the decision by Chinese investors to invest in the Member State concerned.

An advantage of acquisition data is that, unlike the aggregate FDI position data collected by Eurostat and by NBS, MOFCOM and SAFE, they allow us to gain insight into the nature of the Chinese investor's form of ownership. This is a controversial matter. The advances by Huawei, the telecommunications equipment manufacturer, to acquire Marconi (UK) stumbled over its suggested close links with the Chinese government and armed forces. China National Offshore Oil Corporation (CNOOC) (oil) and Lenovo (IT) encountered similar problems in the US. The

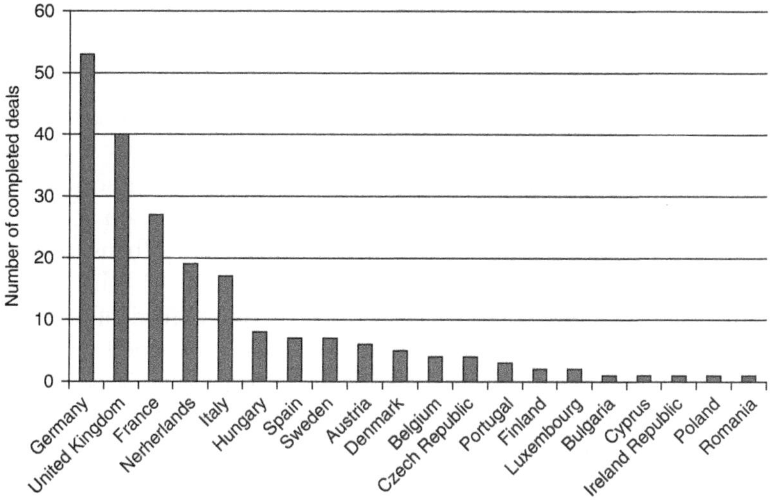


Figure 1.2 **M&As by Chinese firms in the EU-27, 2000–13 (April)**

*Note*: EU Member States not listed above did not record deals in 2000–10.

*Source*: Thomson Reuters (2013).

underlying host-country concern is about the perceived influence that the Chinese government may exert on the operations and activities in the host country through the Chinese investor.

There are four ownership categories of Chinese investor. The 'investor' category refers either to a consortium of several investors or to equity investors who do not fall into the other categories. Government investors are those who form part of the Chinese state, such as SOEs. Public investors are corporations with shares that are publicly traded. But this does not mean that a significant proportion of their equity cannot lie in Chinese government hands, either directly or indirectly. Therefore, it is not possible to say that these publicly listed firms are strictly comparable to the majority of publicly listed firms in the EU. Finally, private investors are those firms that are non-state-owned joint-stock companies; they remain in private hands and are not listed. There is a growing cohort of Chinese SMEs that invests abroad. These firms are becoming increasingly important to the growth of Chinese OFDI, and therefore for the crafting of policy initiatives in both the EU and China (CCPIT, 2009, 2010, 2011).

Since 2001, we can infer from the development of private investors that the private sector is revealing a clear strategic intention to build up its equity commitment in EU Member States. Around 50 per cent of the total number of Chinese acquisitions is accounted for by their investment. Putting this together with the aggregate data discussed above, we can surmise that these acquisitions are likely to be conducted with the ambition to gain access to strategic resources owned by European firms or by firms located in Europe but ultimately owned by foreign (non-EU) investors. State-owned Chinese investors reveal a strong record of acquisition that has varied somewhat over the years. It declined dramatically in 2008 but recovered in 2009 and 2010, probably as a result of the increased availability of acquisition targets in the EU after the financial and economic crisis. Least stable is the category of public investor, whose instability may be in part a result of variable access to finance with which to leverage M&A deals. The data show that a majority of acquisitions are not made by SOEs. With respect to the value of acquisitions, data are reported for 30 deals. Public enterprises acquired European firms of a value in excess of €9.8 billion, SOEs in excess of €5.4 billion and private firms in excess of €1.7 billion. Because of their smaller number of deals, public Chinese firms also lead in terms of average deal value while government and private firms report similar average deal values.

## Sectoral Distribution of Investments

The data originating from China's MOFCOM do not detail the industry distribution of Chinese investments in the European Union. We therefore rely here on Eurostat data for the general investment pattern and on Thomson Reuters data for information on acquisition-related patterns.

Although there is much year-on-year variation, European firms in the 'industrials' and 'materials' sectors have been the main targets for acquisition in the first decade of the twenty-first century. The 'consumer staples' industry sector is a constant feature in the acquisition pattern, but 'high technology' firms have only recently become targets.

Government, or state-owned enterprises are often associated with investment in the natural resources sector, particularly in developing countries. In the EU, the sectors in which Chinese state-owned acquirers are most active are industrials, materials, and energy and power. However, the profile shifts a good deal from one year to the next owing to the nature of acquisitions and the 'lumpiness' of investments.

Foreign acquirers' business motives and Member States' locational advantages together explain the industry patterns we observe in Table 1.1. The United Kingdom has a wide range of targeted industries, including a good representation in the service sector. Germany is more focused on industrial and physical goods. This would seem to match with the strategic targeting by Chinese firms of enterprises with intangible assets, such as technology, capabilities and brands.

There is a further dimension to Chinese acquisition. The evidence which shows Chinese acquirers to be buying the operations of firms in the EU, but in the telecommunications and infrastructure sectors, also suggests that they are doing so to acquire the networks of operations of firms that have become multinationalised in Europe, particularly since the mid-1980s. Since the year 2000, the range of industries in which Chinese firms have acquired EU firms has broadened appreciably, both at the Member State level and at the European level. From an early focus on high technology, infrastructure and heavy industry, Chinese firms have now moved into the services sector, including healthcare, finance, media and entertainment, and into liberalised infrastructure sectors such as telecommunications equipment. This points to the growing strength of Chinese firms outside the manufacturing sector. Finally, in order to more precisely identify the motive for Chinese acquisitions in the EU, we now look at the breakdown of ownership of the Chinese acquiring firm and the main location of operations of the target firm. Table 1.2 presents the distribution of the location of the target enterprise and of the ownership of the target.

There has been an upward trend in the number of EU-located and -parented companies acquired by Chinese firms between 2000 and 2010, with annual acquisitions averaging in the mid-teens and amounting to a cumulative total of 83 by 2010. This testifies to those firms' growing appetite and capacity to acquire European enterprises with a view to competing head-to-head with established firms in the Union if, as yet, on a modest scale.

**Table 1.1** Industry distribution of EU acquisition target firms, 2000–13 (April)

| | 2000–3 | | 2004–7 | | 2008–10 | | 2011–13 | |
|---|---|---|---|---|---|---|---|---|
| Austria | | | | | Industrials | 1 | Industrials | 4 |
| | | | | | | | Energy and power | 1 |
| Belgium | | | Consumer products and services | 1 | | | Consumer staples | 1 |
| Bulgaria | | | | | Financials | 1 | | |
| Cyprus | | | | | | | Materials | 1 |
| Czech Republic | | | | | | | Industrials | 2 |
| | | | | | | | Consumer products and services | 1 |
| | | | | | | | materials | 1 |
| Denmark | | | Industrials | 1 | | | | |
| | | | | | Energy and power | 1 | Energy and power | 1 |
| | | | | | High technology | 1 | High technology | 1 |
| Finland | | | | | Healthcare | 1 | | |
| | | | | | High technology | 1 | | |
| France | Materials | 1 | Materials | 1 | | | Materials | 3 |
| | Industrials | 1 | Industrials | 1 | Industrials | 2 | Industrials | 2 |
| | High technology | 1 | | | High technology | 1 | | |
| | | | Consumer staples | 1 | Consumer staples | 3 | Consumer staples | 5 |
| | | | Telecommunications | 1 | | | Telecommunications | 1 |
| | | | | | | | Consumer products and services | 1 |
| | | | | | | | Energy and power | 1 |

| | | | | | | | | |
|---|---|---|---|---|---|---|---|---|
| | | | | | | | Healthcare | 1 |
| | | | | | | | Media and entertainment | 1 |
| Germany | Materials | 1 | Materials | 2 | | | Materials | 2 |
| | High technology | 1 | | | | | High technology | 7 |
| | | | Industrials | 7 | Industrials | 2 | Industrials | 22 |
| | | | Consumer products and services | 1 | Consumer products and services | 1 | Consumer products and services | 2 |
| | | | Energy and power | 1 | | | | |
| | | | | | | | Financials | 1 |
| | | | | | | | Telecommunications | 2 |
| Hungary | | | | | Materials | 3 | Materials | 1 |
| | | | | | Real estate | 2 | | |
| Ireland | | | | | High technology | 1 | | |
| Italy | Consumer staples | 1 | Consumer staples | 1 | Consumer staples | 1 | Consumer staples | 1 |
| | | | Industrials | 2 | Industrials | 2 | Industrials | 1 |
| | | | | | High technology | 2 | High technology | 1 |
| | | | | | Materials | 1 | | |
| | | | | | | | Telecommunications | 1 |
| Luxembourg | | | | | Financials | 1 | High technology | 1 |
| The Netherlands | Telecommunications | 1 | Telecommunications | 2 | | | | |
| | Consumer products and services | 1 | Consumer staples | 1 | | | Consumer staples | 1 |
| | | | Industrials | 1 | Industrials | 1 | Industrials | 2 |
| | | | | | High technology | 1 | High technology | 2 |
| | | | | | Materials | 1 | Materials | 1 |
| | | | | | Healthcare | 1 | Healthcare | 1 |
| | | | | | | | Financials | 1 |

*(continued)*

**Table 1.1** Continued

| | 2000–3 | | 2004–7 | | 2008–10 | | 2011–13 | |
|---|---|---|---|---|---|---|---|---|
| Poland | | | | | | | Industrials | 1 |
| Portugal | | | | | Consumer staples | 1 | Energy and power | 2 |
| Romania | | | | | | | High technology | 1 |
| Spain | Energy and power | 2 | Materials | 1 | Industrials | 1 | Industrials | 2 |
| | | | | | | | High technology | 1 |
| | | | | | | | Media and entertainment | 1 |
| Sweden | | | | | Industrials | 2 | Industrials | 1 |
| | | | | | | | Energy and power | 1 |
| | | | | | | | High technology | 1 |
| | | | | | | | Telecommunications | 1 |
| | | | | | | | Consumer products and services | 1 |
| United Kingdom | | | Industrials | 5 | | | Industrial | 4 |
| | | | Materials | 4 | Materials | 1 | Material | 5 |
| | | | Energy and power | 3 | Energy and power | 1 | Energy and power | 3 |
| | | | High technology | 1 | | | High technology | 1 |
| | | | Consumer products and services | 1 | Consumer products and services | 1 | | |
| | | | | | Consumer staples | 1 | Consumer staples | 1 |
| | | | | | Retail | 1 | Retail | 1 |
| | | | | | Media and entertainment | 1 | | |
| | | | | | | | Real estate | 1 |

*Note:* No M&As in other EU countries have been recorded. Industry classification follows Thomson Reuter's Macro Industries.
*Source:* Thomson Reuters (2013).

**Table 1.2** Mergers and acquisitions in the EU by ownership and location of operation, 2000–10

| **Number of completed M&A deals, 2000–10** | **2000** | **2001** | **2002** | **2003** | **2004** | **2005** | **2006** | **2007** | **2008** | **2009** | **2010** | **2000–10** |
|---|---|---|---|---|---|---|---|---|---|---|---|---|
| EU-located target owned by an EU parent | 0 | 4 | 3 | 1 | 7 | 11 | 5 | 13 | 8 | 15 | 16 | 83 |
| EU-located target owned by an non-EU parent | 0 | 1 | 0 | 0 | 0 | 1 | 2 | 0 | 4 | 1 | 1 | 10 |
| Non-EU target owned by an EU parent | 3 | 6 | 5 | 9 | 7 | 6 | 9 | 5 | 8 | 8 | 12 | 78 |

*Note:* Of the 10 EU firms belonging to a non-EU parent that were acquired by a Chinese firm, four already belonged to a Chinese parent company.

*Source:* Thomson Reuters (2013).

Although classified as business transactions, acquisitions may appear from the host country's perspective to be simply the swapping of existing third-country ownership for Chinese ownership. There were ten cases in this category between 2000 and 2010, including four that involved the replacement of one Chinese parent enterprise by another.

To complete the picture of Chinese acquisitions in relation to the EU, of the 78 non-EU target firms belonging to EU parents that were acquired by Chinese companies, 49 were located in China and eight in Hong Kong. This shows how the strategy of many Chinese acquirers is very much focused on the home, or regional, economy. Given official and public concern about the Chinese acquisition of European-owned assets, and the fear of job losses, it is important to bear in mind that a number of these takeovers pertain to operations outside the EU.

Indeed, acquisitions in the EU may well be motivated by factors extraneous to the EU economy. The important general point is that Chinese firms are acquiring international networks of affiliates and that by acquiring these international networks of affiliates of EU multinationals, they may rapidly become highly multinational and diversified. The implication is that the European economy inevitably becomes subject to international linkages of more extensive complexity. As a consequence, the need for EU policies that encourage internationally linked multinational groups (whether EU or Chinese-owned) to retain and grow their productive activity within the Union, is becoming ever more pressing.

How far any of these changes in ownership through Chinese acquisition will impact on the Member States' economies and the EU economy, and what kind of impact that might be, are not fathomable from these data. However, current understanding would suggest that the performance of Chinese-owned affiliates, following a decline immediately after the change in ownership, and after a lag, should likely improve in most cases. Detailed research, probably involving both case study and econometric research methods, would be necessary in order to understand the outcomes of Chinese acquisitions in depth.

## Chinese Policies for Outward FDI and for FDI in the EU

The Chinese government today generally supports cross-border investments by Chinese firms and, in some instances, actively supports them. Since the mid-1980s, it has issued policy regulations designed to structure and co-ordinate cross-border direct investments. In order to decentralise, streamline and improve investment approval, it has enabled the responsible institutions of government to enhance their competence to assess, monitor and evaluate such investments. The Go Global policy has accelerated this decentralisation process and encouraged a more 'hands-off' approach to outward FDI. Notwithstanding this evolution in the Chinese outward investment policy regime, national government organisations and their provincial equivalents are still much involved in the setting of policy and the approval of investments. At the national level, these bodies are the State Council, the National Development and Reform Commission (NDRC), MOFCOM and SAFE. Other ministries and organisations may be involved depending on the investment and the industry concerned.

The increasing 'hands-off' approach, indicating the development of an industrialised-country approach to outward investment, is illustrated by actions undertaken by the relevant government bodies. SAFE lifted restrictions on the amount of foreign exchange available annually to domestic investors' outbound investments and announced in 2009 that Chinese firms can seek financing from multiple sources. MOFCOM simplified and shortened the approval procedures in 2009, and the NDRC reiterated in 2011 its desire to decentralise the outward investment approval decision process (Luo, Xue and Han, 2009; Voss, Buckley and Cross, 2009; Buckley et al., 2012).

## Chinese Policies for Outward Investment

The Go Global policy has led to the establishment of new organisations and regulations specifically to encourage outward investment. Supportive measures include workshops and conferences on outward FDI, for example the annual conferences of the Zhejiang Investment and Trade Symposium (www.zjits.com) or the China Council for the Promotion of International Trade (www.goglobal.org.cn) and, under certain conditions, the provision of finance in the form of equity and debt financing. Conditions for support are fulfilled if outward investment promotes domestic development by securing natural resources, stimulates Chinese exports or focuses on R&D. Some measures of support are industry-specific. The NDRC stated in 2005 that its objective is to promote the establishment of conditional production bases and marketing networks in sectors such as light industry, textiles, home appliances and other manufacturing and to actively encourage key service sector industries (that is, trade, distribution, banking, insurance, and telecommunications) to 'go out'. Recently, financial services have received special attention from MOFCOM, which intends to promote the globalisation of China's commercial banking. MOFCOM supports firms that invest in world-renowned brands, advanced technology, marketing networks and research institutions. The Ministry of Finance (MOF) and MOFCOM issued financing guidelines in 2010 to clarify when direct subsidies to outward investment are available. These subsidies would be for the upfront costs of professional services, investigation costs, fees for project feasibility, study reports and the preparation of safety assessments and also transportation fees for the import of resources and fees for the registration of foreign patents.

In 2011, MOFCOM announced that, *inter alia*, banks should increase Go Global credit support for enterprises in certain sectors, such as mineral resource companies; that the Export-Import Bank should improve its offers; that local governments should guide funding better; and that the granting of support for equity investment and bond financing should be accelerated. Other instruments of support also came under the spotlight for improvement, such as the provision of credit insurance and the strengthening of co-operation between international organisations and foreign insurance institutions. Controversy exists over the extent to which these government measures constitute unfair competition.

The Chinese government owns the sovereign wealth fund CIC (established in 2007); and through SAFE, it owns the Hong Kong-based subsidiary SAFE Investment Company (SIC, established in 1997), which invests much like a SWF. The objective of both funds is to secure good returns on investments. Jointly, the two funds hold assets in excess of US$1 trillion. The CIC is heavily involved in domestic Chinese investments but was also employed to acquire 9.9 per cent of the American private equity firm Blackstone Group in 2007, along with other American financial institutions that have interests in natural resource-related investments abroad (Sekine, 2011; Thomas and Chen, 2011). The SIC has holdings of portfolio investments (without management control) in the European oil companies BP and Total (Thomas and Chen, 2011); and since 2005, it has increased its cross-border direct investments from €0.52 billion (US$0.65 billion) to €2.35 billion (US$3.11 billion) in 2010 (SWF Institute, 2011). Given their current focus on portfolio and other types of investment, these funds are not considered in depth in this chapter. However, we should note that as they seek to diversify their growing portfolios of wealth holdings, they are inexorably led towards the ownership of real assets, as opposed to paper (financial) assets, and towards direct investment as their holdings pass the 10 per cent threshold for FDI. Indeed, many EU states are keen to secure SWF capital for large infrastructure projects.

Finally, the Chinese government is supporting the global establishment of 50 'economic co-operation and trade zones'. These zones are open to any investor but tend to be, as in the African case, used predominantly by Chinese firms (Bräutigam, 2011). With the China-Africa Development Fund and the China-ASEAN Co-operation Fund, the Chinese government has established bodies to increase Chinese business activities in specific regions. No such fund exists for investments in the EU.

## Chinese Policies for Outward Investment to the EU

China's policies towards Chinese direct investments in the EU will be analysed through an assessment of China's Outbound Investment Catalogue, China's Global Economic and Trade Co-operation Zones in relation to the observable investment pattern in the EU.

## China's Outbound Investment Catalogue

The Chinese government departments MOFCOM and the Ministry of Foreign Affairs published the first Outbound Foreign Investment Catalogue (OFIC) in 2004. Mirroring the structure of the Foreign Investment Catalogue (for inward FDI), the OFIC indicates in which sectors and countries Chinese firms should invest. The country coverage of the catalogue was expanded in the 2005 and 2007 updates to include 128 countries. No further updates or amendments have been released since then.

For the EU-27, the catalogue generally emphasises investments in industrial sectors, followed by services. Encouragement to invest in natural resources, such as forestry, fishing or mining, is focused on the Czech Republic, Finland, Poland and Spain, where the relevant resources can be found in abundance.

Of the leading European economies, only Germany and the United Kingdom are identified as attractive host countries (see Table 1.3). The respective comparative advantages of these states explain their attraction for Chinese firms. The UK scores well in services (trade, distribution, R&D, warehousing, logistics and transportation, finance and legal services) and Germany in manufacturing (television sets, communications equipment, computers and other electronic equipment, electrical machinery and equipment, pharmaceuticals and chemicals and chemical products).

Romania, Poland, the Czech Republic, Hungary and Portugal are the other most attractive European countries. All these Fifth-Enlargement states are identified as being of greater importance for Chinese firms that seek to manufacture in the EU than the EU-15 countries. They are identified as locations for the manufacturing of textiles, leather goods and luggage (with the exception of Portugal), television sets, communications equipment, computers and other electronic equipment (Poland, Portugal, Romania) as well as electrical machinery and equipment (Czech Republic, Hungary, Poland). These are all industries in which China has export strength but in which it has faced increasing pressure in recent years from importing nations to reduce its balance of trade surplus. Although generated by Chinese firms' export competitiveness, this trade imbalance is nevertheless politically contentious. It is voiced against the Chinese government, and reflected in the 55 anti-dumping measures and one anti-subsidy measure in force in the EU against Chinese imports as of 30 June 2011.

The highlighting of these sectors for FDI can therefore be explained as encouraging trade-substituting and import barrier-avoiding investment in low-cost EU countries in order to defend existing market share. The Czech Republic (forestry) and Poland (mining) also feature as hosts for activities focused on natural resources. The split in official encouragement along the lines of comparative advantage – whether it arises for natural reasons (resource endowments) or man-made reasons (firms' created assets) – supports the view that Chinese firms invest for strategic asset-seeking purposes in the advanced European economies. And it also suggests market-seeking and efficiency-seeking motives. Of course, we have to infer the motives of Chinese firms by dissection of the Chinese government's policy intentions, not by analysis of firm-level data.

There is a lack of sector guidance (encouragement) for the Member States Italy, Latvia, Luxembourg and Malta. The reasons for this apparent oversight are not immediately clear, but they could be inadequacy of domestic market size (Latvia and Malta), clear comparative advantage in line with Chinese economic priorities or barriers to doing business. Yet Italy has thriving manufacturing, textile and leather industries. The Chinese government has encouraged investments in those industries in other states, such as the Czech Republic, France, Lithuania, Poland and Spain, which offer either large domestic markets or

**Table 1.3** Attractiveness of EU Member States

| | Number of attractive sectors identified per Member State | | | |
|---|---|---|---|---|
| | **Total** | **Natural resources** | **Industry** | **Services** |
| Germany | 8 | 0 | 4 | 4 |
| Romania | 8 | 0 | 5 | 3 |
| Poland | 7 | 1 | 4 | 2 |
| Czech Republic | 6 | 1 | 4 | 1 |
| Hungary | 6 | 0 | 4 | 2 |
| Portugal | 6 | 0 | 4 | 2 |
| United Kingdom | 6 | 0 | 2 | 4 |
| Austria | 5 | 0 | 3 | 2 |
| Denmark | 5 | 0 | 3 | 2 |
| Estonia | 5 | 0 | 3 | 2 |
| France | 5 | 0 | 3 | 2 |
| Sweden | 5 | 0 | 3 | 2 |
| Bulgaria | 4 | 0 | 3 | 1 |
| Belgium | 4 | 0 | 1 | 3 |
| Greece | 4 | 0 | 2 | 2 |
| Ireland | 4 | 0 | 2 | 2 |
| The Netherlands | 4 | 0 | 2 | 2 |
| Spain | 4 | 1 | 2 | 1 |
| Cyprus | 3 | 0 | 2 | 1 |
| Finland | 3 | 1 | 1 | 1 |
| Slovenia | 3 | 0 | 2 | 1 |
| Slovakia | 2 | 0 | 2 | 0 |
| Lithuania | 1 | 0 | 1 | 0 |
| Italy | 0 | 0 | 0 | 0 |
| Latvia | 0 | 0 | 0 | 0 |
| Luxembourg | 0 | 0 | 0 | 0 |
| Malta | 0 | 0 | 0 | 0 |

*Note:* The table lists the number of sectors mentioned per country out of 35 possible sectors.

*Source:* MOFCOM and Ministry of Foreign Affairs (2004–7).

low-labour cost production (by EU standards) and from which goods can be exported to the rest of the EU. This points to official guidance away from high-labour-cost locations when Chinese import-substituting FDI is undertaken in order to defend export market shares and when the motive is to secure increased market share, or strategic assets, in larger markets.

The catalogue highlights manufacturing sectors in which China has a comparative advantage at home coupled with significant exports to the EU (see Figure 1.3). Investments in those areas can therefore be regarded as advantage-exploiting strategies. Industries and functional activities in which Chinese firms are disadvantaged vis-à-vis competitors in the EU are regarded as priority areas for investment. Such exploration and learning activities are common among Chinese investors globally and follow in the footsteps of strategies pursued by firms such as Haier and Huawei, leading to increasing overseas activities for a new cohort of firms. By contrast, Chinese outward investors have lagged behind in activities such as R&D and financial and legal services, although improvements in those activities are now afoot in order to support the internationalisation of Chinese investors in other industries.

Neither the sectoral nor the country emphasis of the Outward Foreign Investment Catalogue square well with the observed investment pattern. As analysed in this chapter, Germany and the UK receive the largest share of Chinese investment, and the peripheral countries receive considerably less than their industry structures would suggest is appropriate. The prominence of international trade-related FDI is evident in the data, as in the catalogue. Sectors that have not been picked up by investors include textiles, leather and luggage manufacturing and tourism. The apparent mismatch between the government-devised catalogue and firms' investment decisions indicates a certain independence of mind regarding commercial investment decisions, at least by some Chinese outward investors.

The financial and economic crisis should leave its mark on the country and sector focus of Chinese OFDI. The economic situations of Portugal, Ireland, Greece and Spain pose severe risks for international investors, especially those with little international experience. In different macro-economic circumstances, however, Chinese firms have shown their skill in identifying

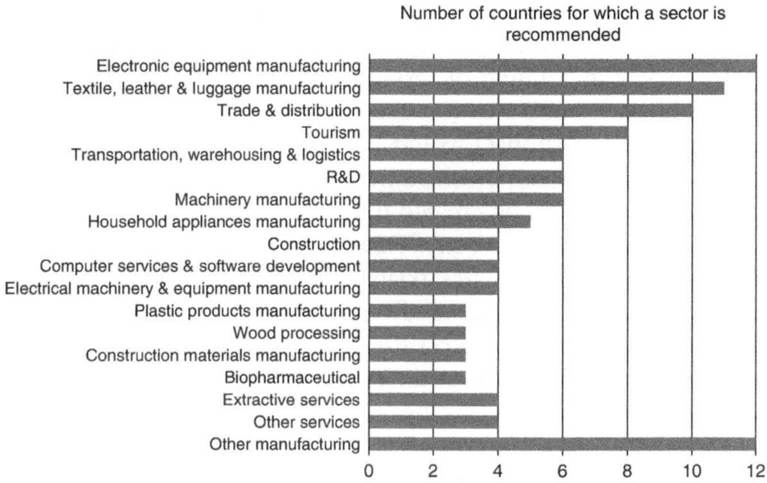


Figure 1.3 **Sector distribution in the Outbound Investment Catalogue, in force in 2013**

*Note*: Electronic equipment manufacturing includes: TV, communications equipment, computers and other electronic equipment manufacturing. Other services and extractive services each comprise three sectors, other manufacturing comprises nine sectors.

*Source*: MOFCOM and Ministry of Foreign Affairs (2004–7).

promising business opportunities, as when acquiring ailing German Mittelstand (medium-sized) firms.

## Conclusion

Chinese direct investment outflows today are equal to or greater than those of large industrialised economies and are set to rise still further. The Chinese economy, and its FDI, has shown resilience in the financial and economic crisis that the advanced economies can only envy. It is therefore a challenge that the European Union as a whole is only a minor recipient of Chinese direct investment abroad. This would be more worrying had the EU striven hard to secure Chinese FDI. But it has not presented a unified face to China, and has to date not been in a position to conclude an investment agreement. With the Treaty of Lisbon and the passing of ultimate competence for FDI policy to the EU-level, the EU and China are working towards an

International Investment Agreement (European Commission, 2006, 2010a, b and c, 2011). The interests of European firms (particularly in a range of services) that would like to invest in China but are unable to (on account of limits to China's WTO obligations to liberalise) would be well served by such an agreement. And at the same time a new EU-level investment-friendly environment would be created for Chinese investors.

The current, post-Lisbon, FDI regime is still largely the product of individual Member States' bilateral investment treaties with third countries on market access and on investment protection. As with China, the focus has been on EU investment in these third countries, rather than on Chinese investment into the EU. We can surmise that the transitional arrangements preserve most of the benefits of the status quo of International Investment Agreement (IIA) in general, but do not address the question of how best to promote the right kind of Chinese inward FDI to the EU. The analysis of data shows that the EU cannot afford to take a back seat in the global competition to attract and provide for investment from, and to, all parts of the world. The work of the Member States in encouraging inward FDI is largely the preserve of their individual investment promotion authorities and sub-national, even city-level, bodies.

Besides encouraging inward Chinese FDI in quantity, the EU and Member States must design policy to encourage investment high in quality. The range of benefits to EU hosts flow from the competitive effect of inward FDI, directly and indirectly raising, or preserving, income and employment. Private sector investors bring entrepreneurship, and sovereign wealth funds offer the potential for large-scale investment, for example in infrastructure. Unlike Japanese FDI in the EU or US FDI before it, Chinese FDI is not so likely to transfer management skills and new technology. If anything, Chinese firms may be seeking to learn, at least in some respects. And this may be the key to making the EU truly distinctive, and attractive, as a host. Inward investment promotion is best when it recognises the specific needs of investors. Inward investors could be mentored on their business models and on encouraging larger-scale Chinese investments, and those with greater R&D intensity naturally offer greater linkage and spillover potential for the EU and local economies. Investment promotion agencies throughout the Member States should be encouraged to attract exactly this kind of investment, to bring about a better and targeted fit with local economies. Helping to arrange mentoring, linkages and joint ventures for Chinese firms would embed them in the local economy and potentially lead to opportunities in China for EU firms.

To date, the impact of Chinese FDI at the EU level has been minor. But in certain sectors, e.g. telecommunications equipment, there are already signs of a positive competitive effect. And although the operating profile of Chinese FDI is quantitatively small, at its best it clearly indicates productive activity with substantial income and employment generation for the host country. In some states, the profile suggests that affiliates primarily handle imports from China and distribute them EU-wide. We need to know more about these profiles, to help develop a coherent policy to encourage FDI in sectors that will benefit the EU and as a counterpart to China's Outbound Foreign Investment Catalogue. Further dynamic benefits to the EU are possible. We need to find out more about how opportunities for European businesses, especially small and medium-sized firms, to enter new markets can be stimulated by Chinese investment in the EU.

Commentators in China have perceived a hostile stance in the EU towards Chinese investments. This perception might be informed by the media's penchant for alarmist reports of an influx of Chinese investors buying up Europe. In fact, the vast majority of cross-border investments are based on mergers and acquisitions, and the number of European acquisitions by Chinese firms is actually very small. This point underlines that any policymaking (and reporting) on FDI across the EU needs to be better informed and to be supported by appropriate data, which is the responsibility of Eurostat. EU-level action and Member State co-operation, underpinned by the EU's new FDI competence, will be necessary for the Union to have as clear a picture of inward FDI as China does of inward FDI from the EU. Anything less places the EU at a distinct disadvantage.

Chinese firms have only recently started to internationalise. There is still a long way to go until they have the same status in the EU that firms from the US, Japan and South Korea enjoy. But it is no unrealistic prediction to say that with a concerted European policy and a positive attitude towards Chinese inward investment, Chinese (consumer) brands will become household names in the EU. And Chinese investment will provide a much-needed competitive stimulus to EU growth and entrepreneurial and technological dynamism in the Internal Market.

## Appendix: Methodology

We drew on multiple data sources and analytical methods in order to gain a holistic and deep understanding of Chinese direct investments in the European Union.

### Secondary numerical data sources

In order to gain insight into the distribution and impact of Chinese cross-border direct investments, we collected data from publicly and non-publicly available data sources. The public sources are Eurostat and the Chinese Ministry of Commerce. From Eurostat we collected data on the distribution of Chinese direct investments across the Member States and data on the operations of Chinese affiliates in Europe. The Chinese Ministry of Commerce annually publishes the influential but quite aggregate Statistical Bulletin on Chinese Outward Direct Investment. This aggregate data, although not necessarily entirely reliable or comprehensive, was used to cross-check the Eurostat data. Our chosen non-publicly available data source is Thomson ONE from Thomson Reuters, from which we collected information on cross-border mergers and acquisitions. All monetary values were converted from the currency of reporting into euros based on the annual average foreign exchange rate as published by Eurostat (Eurostat, 2011b).

### Secondary written data sources

The policy dimension in Europe and China on Chinese cross-border investments in the EU has been addressed through an analysis of published secondary data sources. This includes European and Chinese laws and regulations and comments and interpretations thereupon, academic articles and trade and business press material on the overseas expansion of Chinese firms.

## Note

This is an abridged version of 'Chinese Overseas Direct Investment into the European Union' briefing paper for the EU-funded Europe China Research and Advice Network (ECRAN), 2012, by Jeremy Clegg and Hinrich Voss.

## References

Bräutigam, D. (2011), 'Chinese aid to Africa: what, where, why, and how much?', in J. Golley and L. Song (eds), *China Update 2011*, Canberra: Australian National University.

Buckley, P.J., Clegg, L.J., Cross, A.R., Liu, X., Voss, H. and Zheng, P. (2007), 'The determinants of Chinese outward foreign direct investment', *Journal of International Business Studies*, 38(4): 499–518.

Buckley, P.J., Voss, H., Cross, A.R. and Clegg, L.J. (2012), 'The emergence of Chinese firms as multinationals: the influence of the home institutional environment', in R. Pearce (ed.), *China and the Multinationals: International Business and the Entry of China into the Global Economy*, Cheltenham: Edward Elgar.

Cheung, Y.-W. and Qian, X. (2009), 'Empirics of China's Outward Direct Investment', *Pacific Economic Review*, 14(3): 312–41.

China Council for the Promotion of International Trade (2009), *2009 Survey on Current Conditions and Intention of Outbound Investment by Chinese Enterprises*, Beijing: CCPIT.

China Council for the Promotion of International Trade (2010), *2010 Survey on Current Conditions and Intention of Outbound Investment by Chinese Enterprises*, Beijing: CCPIT.

China Council for the Promotion of International Trade (2011), *2011 Survey on Current Conditions and Intention of Outbound Investment by Chinese Enterprises*, Beijing: CCPIT.

Cuervo-Cazurra, A. (2007), 'Sequence of value-added activities in the multinationalization of developing country firms', *Journal of International Management*, 13, 258–77.

Duanmu, J.-L. (2012), 'Firm heterogeneity and location choice of Chinese Multinational Enterprise (MNEs)', *Journal of World Business*, 47(1): 64–72.

Ernst & Young (2011), *Destination UK: Sustaining Success in the New Economy – Ernst & Young's 2011 UK Attractiveness Survey*, London: Ernst & Young.

European Commission (2006), Upgrading the EU Investment Policy, Note for the Attention of the 133 Committee, European Commission, Issues paper. European Commission Directorate-General for Trade, Brussels, 30 May.

European Commission (2010a), Establishing Transitional Arrangements for Bilateral Investment Agreements between Member States and Third Countries, Regulation of the European

Parliament and of the Council. European Commission, Brussels, 7 July, COM (2010)344 final.

European Commission (2010b), Towards a Comprehensive European International Investment Policy, Communication from the Commission to the Council, the European Parliament, the European Economic and Social Committee and the Committee of the Regions Brussels, 7 July, COM (2010)343 final.

European Commission (2010c), Q&A: Commission Launches Comprehensive European International Investment Policy, Memorandum, Directorate-General for Trade, Brussels, 7 July, http://trade.ec.europa.eu/doclib/press/index.cfm?id=590.

European Commission (2011), Public Consultation on the Future Investment Relationship between the EU and China, Directorate-General for Trade, Brussels, 2 May.

Eurostat (2011a), EU Direct Investment Flows, Breakdown by Partner Country and Economic Activity [bop_fdi_flows], European Commission, Luxembourg, 6 April.

Eurostat (2011b), Euro/ECU exchange rates – Annual data [ert_bil_eur_a], European Commission, Luxembourg, 30 August.

Kolstad, I. and Wiig, A. (2012), 'What determines Chinese outward FDI?', *Journal of World Business*, 47(1): 26–34.

Luo, Y., Xue, Q. and Han, B. (2009), 'How emerging-market governments promote outward FDI: experience from China', *Journal of World Business*, 45(1): 68–79.

Ministry of Commerce (MOFCOM) and Ministry of Foreign Affairs (MFA) (2004–2007), *Outward Investment Catalogue*, Beijing: MOFCOM and MFA.

NBS, MOFCOM and SAFE (2010), *2009 Statistical Bulletin of China's Outward Foreign Direct Investment* (data of the National Bureau of Statistics of China (NBS), Chinese Ministry of Commerce of China (MOFCOM) and State Administration of Foreign Exchange (SAFE)), September. MOFCOM website: http://hzs.mofcom.gov.cn/accessory/201009/1284339524515.pdf.

NBS, MOFCOM, and SAFE (2012), *2011 Statistical Bulletin of China's Outward Foreign Direct Investment, English version* (data of the National Bureau of Statistics of China (NBS), Chinese Ministry of Commerce of China (MOFCOM) and State Administration of Foreign Exchange (SAFE)), September.

Organisation for Economic Co-operation and Development (OECD) (2008), *OECD Benchmark Definition of Foreign Direct Investment*, 4th edn, Paris: OECD.

Sekine, E. (2011), 'The governance of China Investment Corporation on its way to becoming a sophisticated institutional investor', *Nomura Journal of Capital Markets*, 2(3), http://www.nicmr.com/nicmr/english/report/backno/2011win.html.

Sun, S.L., Peng, M.W., Ren, B. and Yan, D. (2012), 'A comparative ownership advantage framework for cross-border M&As: the rise of Chinese and Indian MNEs', *Journal of World Business*, 47(1): 4–16.

SWF Institute (2011), *SAFE Investment Company*, http://www.swfinstitute.org/swfs/safe-investment-company/.

Thomas, S. and Chen, J. (2011), 'China's Sovereign Wealth Funds: origins, development, and future roles', *Journal of Contemporary China*, 20(70): 467–78.

Thomson Reuters (2013), Thomson ONE,http://banker.thomsonib.com/.

UNCTAD (2009) World Investment Report 2009. UN: Geneva and New York.

United Nations Conference on Trade and Development (UNCTAD) (2011), *UNCTADstat* (UNCTAD online database), New York and Geneva: United Nations. UNCTADstat, http://unctadstat.unctad.org/.

Voss, H., Buckley, P.J. and Cross, A.R. (2009), 'An assessment of the effects of institutional change on Chinese outward direct investment activity', In I. Alon, J. Chang, M. Fetscherin, C. Lattemann and J.R. McIntyre (eds), *China Rules: Globalization and Political Transformation*, London: Palgrave Macmillan, pp. 135–65.

# 2 Chinese Investment in the Greater Europe Zone

*Thierry Apoteker*

## Introduction

### Concepts and definitions

Investments are financial flows that purchase financial and productive assets. Foreign investments are investments in enterprises that operate outside the domestic territory of the investor. These can be classified in two ways: (1) foreign portfolio investments are financial flows that enter equity or bond markets, possibly for a short time, and market prices are usually a fundamental driver for the foreign investor; (2) foreign direct investments (FDIs) involve significant foreign ownership (at least 10 per cent of voting stock) of productive assets. Inward FDI is defined as capital entering an economy attracted by favourable economic factors; outward FDI (sometimes noted as outward direct investment or ODI/OFDI) is a flow of capital moving abroad.

The economic literature that looks at the determinants of FDI is vast,[1] and consistently points towards (1) the strengthening of an existing market structure or the expansion of a business to new markets (market-seeking FDI), (2) gaining access to resources in host countries (resource-seeking FDI) and (3) the optimisation of competitiveness or economies of scale (efficiency-seeking FDI).

As part of the economic reform movement initiated in the late 1970s, the Chinese government has continued the process of institutional transformation, seeking to attract foreign capital and technology as a critical element of its strategy to catch up with the West. The impressive increase in Chinese FDI inflows throughout the 2000s has contributed to the acceleration of China's GDP growth and made it the top destination for global FDI in developing economies.

Outward FDI from China also emerged during this time with the Go Global policy, initiated by the Chinese authorities in 1999. It encourages the globalisation of domestic enterprises and therefore overseas investment by Chinese enterprises.[2] According to the United Nations Conference on Trade and Development (UNCTAD), China accounted for 3.6 per cent of total outward investment from developing countries in 1995, 10.0 per cent in 2005 and a massive 20.8 per cent in 2010 (€51.4 billion) in the midst of the global economic crisis. This made it the second-largest developing country in terms of outward FDI, beaten only by Hong Kong (ranked fourth globally in 2010), which acts as a key 'transit' point for operations in and out of China – from trade to capital flows, including investments.

In the academic literature, econometric studies emphasise the different features of Chinese outward FDI and show that large markets, cultural proximity with the host country and countries with abundant natural resources and poor institutions are the main drivers of Chinese FDI.[3] Studies also suggest that Chinese investors have different overseas investment strategies compared with other investors. Those studies argue that good institutions in target countries will reduce the risk and costs of doing business and help to improve productivity, thus increasing Chinese outward FDI flows.[4]

## Data and statistical difficulties

In reviewing and analysing investment flows, one of the main difficulties is determining how these capital flows are measured. This is certainly true at the global level, but it is even more difficult in the case of China. For example, how should one classify investments below the threshold of 10 per cent of the equity of targeted companies? How does one deal with offshore centres that act as critical intermediaries for FDI in order to avoid taxes and transparency?

The official Chinese source of data for foreign direct investments into and out of China comes from the Ministry of

Commerce (MOFCOM). MOFCOM provides free information detailing the breakdown of Chinese FDI outflows abroad by country and by industry. However, they do not provide any details for a country or industry analysis. The second official and recognised data source for FDI, at the international level, is UNCTAD. Unfortunately, UNCTAD reports only global historical figures and do not give information about bilateral FDIs or a detailed industry breakdown.

In order to improve the analysis of inward as well as outward FDI related to China, the ChinaObs/FDImonitor (COFM) database was established by the research group TAC[5] through a project funded by the European Commission.[6] COFM aggregates industry- and country-level information on all operations and deals related to foreign investment into and out of China (mergers and acquisitions (M&A) and Greenfield investments) since 2005. It allows detailed analysis country by country of investment and industries, as well as the type of investment made (equity participation, full acquisition, Greenfield, etc.).

COFM is constructed using a comprehensive investigation and review of all public information related to such investment flows, from press reports to information published by Investment Promotion Agencies and including data and details provided by banks and other financial institutions. The data collected is screened and verified systematically, and is confronted to results and information provided by two major private databases, the Thomson One database from the Thomson Reuters group, for mergers and acquisitions, and the fDi Markets database (a subsidiary of the Financial Times group) for Greenfield investments. The way information at the level of individual operations and deals is collected, analysed and screened allows the distinction between what is called the 'immediate parent' company and the 'ultimate parent' company for both the acquirer and the target company involved in FDI. The immediate parent is the company which is immediately or directly involved in the deal either as a target or as an acquirer/investor; the ultimate parent looks at the company which has a control on the immediate parent.

This distinction is critical when monitoring FDI flows as multinational companies usually operate from local or intermediate subsidiaries for acquisitions, leading to very large errors in 'attributing' the operation to a given country of origin (or destination).

For the monitoring of China's OFDI, COFM measures incorporate all operations in which the *ultimate parent* acquirer is *China* and the *parent* target *is different from China*. They specifically exclude Chinese M&A abroad by the intermediary of its subsidiaries in Hong Kong when the ultimate parent target is China.

Looking at the aggregate data for total outward FDI from China in MOFCOM, UNCTAD and COFM sources in Figure 2.1, we see that increasing Chinese FDI flows are clearly represented in all three sources (apart from differences in 2008, but still broadly comparable). However, COFM figures are frequently higher than those reported by MOFCOM while UNCTAD's figures are the lowest among the three sources (except in 2009).

A detailed analysis of these discrepancies identifies the following differences and/or uncertainties:

Likely under-reporting of FDI outflows in MOFCOM figures: in principle, investments abroad need to be pre-approved by MOFCOM, but in practice, small-scale investments do not necessarily go through this process. The recent administrative

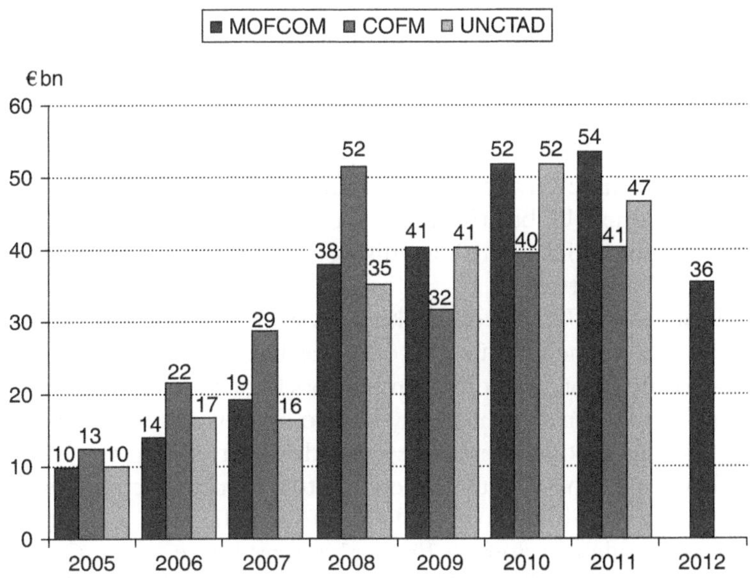


Figure 2.1 **China's outward FDI flows, 2005–2012 (€ billion)**

*Source*: COFM, MOFCOM, UNCTAD.

reforms that allow such authorisation processes to be decentralised for smaller outward investment operations are likely to increase the degree of under-reporting.

Chinese investment abroad by intermediaries or their subsidiaries or affiliates operating outside China (Hong Kong, Macao and offshore destinations such as the Cayman Islands) appears not to be properly included in MOFCOM data.

MOFCOM normally registers reinvested earnings of Chinese affiliates abroad as new outward FDI. COFM is limited only to new operations and investments.

Complex financial structures designed for large infrastructure- or commodity-related investments appear not to be included in MOFCOM data, probably because they could be classed as 'project finance' investments rather than as direct investment. COFM includes these operations when the provider of funding for any special-purpose vehicle is ultimately a Chinese entity. A similar observation is valid for outward FDI related to official bilateral aid flows from China (the 'Angola Mode',[7] whereby it is virtually impossible to disentangle genuine FDI from bilateral aid and suppliers/construction contracts).

The absence of detailed information and data discrepancies has become more of an issue as the amount of Chinese outward FDI has increased. The issue of how to become an attractive destination for Chinese ODI has taken on new importance everywhere, including the EU, but the absence of detailed information feeds into worries about China's acquisition of sensitive or large assets in foreign countries.

From the EU perspective, the analysis of China's presence and investment in neighbouring countries has a specific relevance: those countries can become competitors for attracting investment from Chinese firms, which may lead to certain countries becoming easy entry points for Chinese goods exported into the EU.

The aim of this chapter is therefore to conduct a focused review and analysis of Chinese outward FDI in a specific geographical area that is considered 'close to Europe', referred here as the Greater Europe Zone (GEZ, see Figure 2.2). In this study, the Greater Europe Zone includes the Commonwealth of Independent States (CIS) plus Turkey,[8] a mixed group of 13 countries.

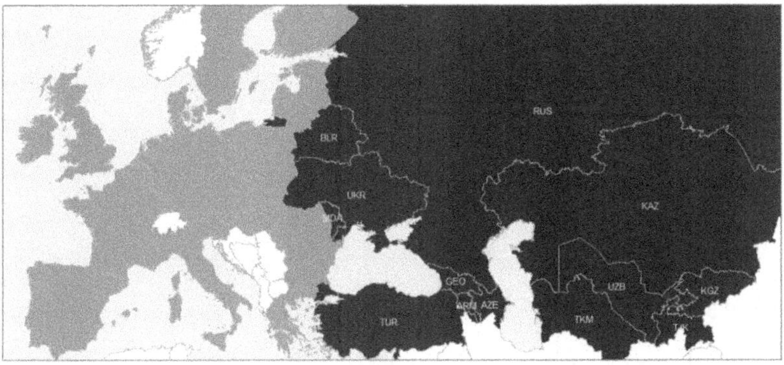


Figure 2.2 **Map of the European Union and the Greater Europe Zone**
*Note*: EU-27: grey; GEZ countries: black.
*Source*: ECRAN, 2012.

The analysis is structured in three sections. First, there is a quantitative review and analysis of trends and time patterns of China's overseas investment in the GEZ. That is followed by an analysis of the strategies and of challenges to Chinese multinational companies in the GEZ. The final section addresses China's specific policy for the GEZ and the GEZ states' response, particularly in terms of regulatory environment. We conclude with a couple of recommendations.

## Quantitative Review and Analysis

### General characteristics of China's investment in the GEZ

The irregularity of China's outward investments in the GEZ shown by COFM data reveals an opportunistic strategy that seeks to make large acquisitions when possible. However, as shown in Figure 2.3 this irregularity is not confirmed by MOFCOM figures, which show a clear and regular positive trend of outflows to the GEZ, but at around 30 per cent of the total estimated by COFM (average figures for 2005–2009).

It is obvious too that the discrepancies between these two sources are much larger for the GEZ than are demonstrated globally. It appears that important deals in the energy sector

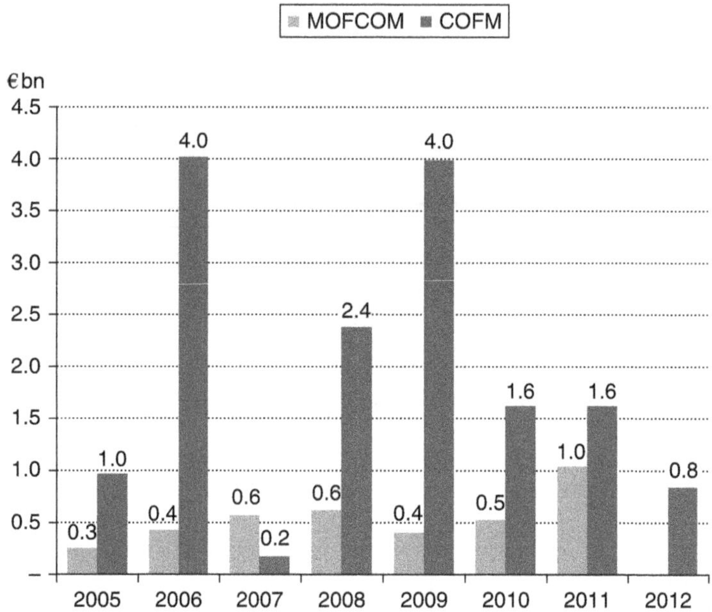


Figure 2.3 **China's outward FDI flows to the GEZ, 2005–2011 (€ billion)**

*Sources*: COFM, MOFCOM.

(particularly in oil and gas exploration and production and in constructing gas pipelines) are excluded in MOFCOM reporting. Indeed, the huge discrepancies depicted in Figure 2.3 coincide with the following important deals:

In 2006, the €2.8 billion M&A by Sinopec in Russia (OAO Udmurtneft);

In 2008, the €1.5 billion Greenfield investment by PetroChina in Turkmenistan (to build a gas pipeline between China and Turkmenistan); and

In 2009, the €1.9 billion M&A by an investment group in Kazakhstan (OAO MangistanMunaiGaz) and the €0.7 billion M&A by Fullbloom Investment Corporation (a special-purpose acquisition vehicle formed by the China Investment Corporation) in Kazakhstan (GazMunaiGas).

It is also important to mention that only 40 per cent of operations and deals extracted from COFM for Chinese outward FDI flows into the GEZ have their amount reported in the MOFCOM data. Indeed, if we include amounts for the smallest operations, which are not usually reported, we should expect the COFM total (and therefore the discrepancies between the two sources) to be even higher than that indicated in Figure 2.3.

Over the period 2005–2012, the COFM database indicates that the cumulated Chinese OFDI into the GEZ amounted to €15.6 bn for 155 different investments and acquisition.

In 2012, outward direct investment from China into the GEZ was estimated at €0.8 billion (according to COFM figures), representing 2.2 per cent of China's total outward FDI. It suggests a sharp decrease compared with 2009. However, the number of deals has trebled from the pre-financial crisis period (11 deals in 2007) to 28 operations in 2009, and it decreased only slightly in 2010, 2011 and 2012 (see Figure 2.4).

Over the whole period 2005–2012, the GEZ attracted about 10 per cent of total Chinese investment overseas, the main regions for direct investment from China being South-East Asia and East Asia (22 per cent of the cumulated OFDI), Western Europe and North America (31 per cent), and Latin America (16 per cent) and Africa and the Middle East (13 per cent).

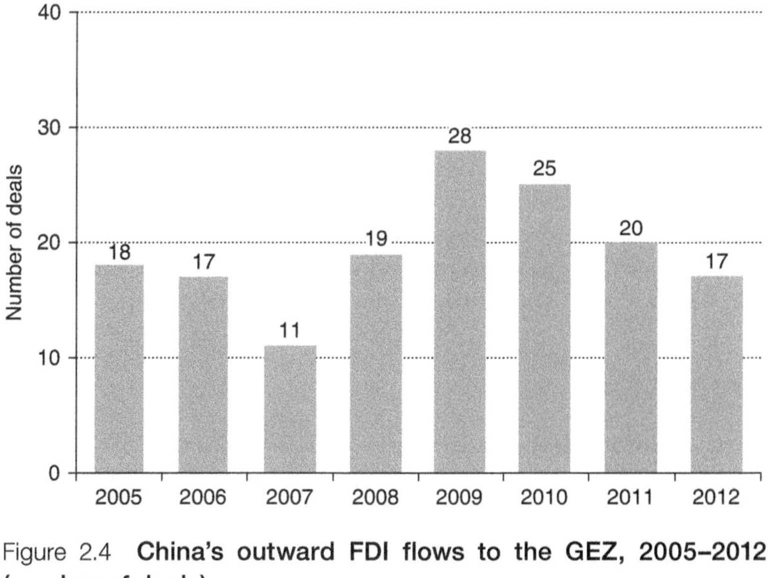


Figure 2.4 **China's outward FDI flows to the GEZ, 2005–2012 (number of deals)**

*Source*: COFM.

Chinese multinationals operate in the GEZ mainly in the form of Greenfield investments. These have accounted for 60 per cent of total investments since 2005 and 86 per cent of the total number of operations, compared with 40 per cent and 14 per cent respectively for M&As. This clearly reflects a small number of very large M&A operations; in particular, there were four 'mega-deals' during the period that substantially lifted the total value of China's OFDI in the GEZ in the form of acquisition of existing companies and assets: Sinopec in Russia in 2006, Investor Group and the Chinese government in Kazakhstan in 2009, CIC in France in 2011 and Sinopec in Portugal in 2012. If we exclude these four operations, most OFDI in the GEZ consists of Greenfield investments.

The average size of individual investments in the GEZ is also very heavily influenced by a limited number of large operations, and indeed, this average size is higher when China's annual outward FDI flows are the largest. On average during 2005–2012, the size of all OFDI from China into the GEZ was €100 mn, with €62 mn for Greenfield operations and €291 mn for M&A.

### Industry breakdown

Globally, China and its multinational companies have a very active outward foreign direct investment strategy. The main objectives include increasing access to commodity resources and achieving 'shortcuts' in order to help increase technological and commercial know-how from companies operating in more mature economies. For investments into the GEZ, the focus is very clearly on natural resources, and notably energy. Indeed, during 2005–2012, 49 per cent of total Chinese outward FDI flows to the GEZ were concentrated in the energy sector, followed by automotive and transport (21 per cent) and commodities and materials (10 per cent).

### Energy sector

Chinese investors in the GEZ's energy sector are exclusively state-owned enterprises. They operate very large M&A or Greenfield investments and have clear political and economic motivations. The economic strategic factors behind their FDIs are a combination of seeking new markets and, more importantly, securing access to commodity resources, principally fuels, ores and metals. Political motivations relate to the institutional framework in resource rich countries; academic research has shown that the quality of public institutions is a major determinant of inward FDI, although Chinese companies can gain greater competitive advantage when weaker institutions are present (for example, when there is less transparency).[9] The GEZ countries registered fast economic growth rates in the mid-2000s, often supported by significant returns on productive levels of natural resources. This created large opportunities for energy-related infrastructure development funded by Chinese investors, who expanded their presence particularly in the Central Asian countries of the GEZ.

Specifically, the two largest oil companies in China, the China National Petroleum Corporation (CNPC)/PetroChina and the China Petroleum and Chemical Corporation (Sinopec Group), have invested in oil and gas production/exploration and in transnational oil and gas pipelines. China is almost entirely dependent on the international oil market for its oil supply, as its oil fields are ageing and their reserves to production ratios are low. As a result, it became a net oil importer in 1993. The national oil companies' objectives in investing in Central Asia are to support energy production capacities in some countries of the GEZ, as well as to diversify and expand China's access to oil and gas reserves. These goals are the top priority of China's Go Global policy.

### Other sectors

The distribution of outward FDI by sector has been influenced by the development of China's industrial structure, which has been increasingly orientated towards heavy industry and transportation equipment during the past several decades.

Excluding the energy sector, China invested mostly in the motor and transport (€2.9 billion during 2005–2012), commodities and materials (€1.5 billion), construction (€0.8 billion), real estate (€0.7 billion) and electronic, software and IT (€0.7 billion) sectors. Conversely, the chemicals, food and beverages, healthcare, aerospace and consumer products and services did attract a very limited amount of operations and investment during this period.

## Country breakdown

Studying the breakdown of outward FDI flows from China to individual countries between 2005 and 2012 (see Table 2.1) enables the definition of a typology of Chinese foreign investment in the GEZ. Over that period, Russia was the most attractive country for outward Chinese FDI (with cumulated flows of €7.5 billion), followed by Kazakhstan (€3.3 billion) and Turkmenistan (€1.7 billion). This correlates with China's opportunistic strategy of investing massively in the energy sector and in commodities and materials. Chinese foreign investments in Uzbekistan and Tajikistan remained small, at €342 million and €121 million respectively, and irregular.

A comparison of the total number of Chinese investment deals with the GEZ countries over the period with FDI flows to them shows that Russia had the largest number of deals (87), followed by Turkey, Kazakhstan and Belarus (with 17, 11 and 11 deals respectively). Conversely, only five deals were registered

**Table 2.1** China's outward FDI flows to the GEZ states*, 2005–2012 (€ million)

| | 2005 | 2006 | 2007 | 2008 | 2009 | 2010 | 2011 | 2012 | 2005–12 |
|---|---|---|---|---|---|---|---|---|---|
| **Russia** | 868 | 3,827 | – | 136 | 891 | 1,290 | 513 | 14 | 7,539 |
| **Kazakhstan** | – | – | – | 585 | 2,543 | – | – | 156 | 3,284 |
| **Turkmenistan** | – | – | 167 | 1,496 | – | – | – | – | 1,663 |
| **Turkey** | – | – | – | – | 538 | 38 | 18 | 661 | 1,255 |
| **Uzbekistan** | 85 | 159 | – | 61 | – | – | 36 | – | 341 |
| **Azerbaijan** | – | – | – | – | – | – | 251 | – | 251 |
| **Tajikistan** | – | – | – | 99 | 22 | – | – | – | 121 |
| **Kyrgyzstan** | – | – | 1 | – | – | – | 47 | – | 48 |
| **Moldova** | – | – | – | – | – | 45 | – | – | 45 |
| **Belarus** | – | 1 | – | – | – | – | 36 | 8 | 45 |
| **Ukraine** | – | 28 | – | – | – | – | – | – | 28 |
| **Total** | 953 | 4,015 | 168 | 2,377 | 3,994 | 1,373 | 901 | 839 | 14,620 |

**Note*: China's ODI flows into Armenia, Azerbaijan and Georgia are not reported in COFM between 2005 and 2010. A dash (-) signifies no ODI flows from China to the country for that year. For Tajikistan, the rounded total for 2005–2010 represents the addition of the non-rounded amounts for 2008 and 2009.

*Source*: COFM.

in Turkmenistan – one in 2007, two in 2008, one in 2011 and one in 2012 – but the average size of Chinese investment deals was much higher there (€333million) and in Kazakhstan (€298 million) than in Russia (€86 million). Chinese investments in Turkmenistan and Kazakhstan concentrated on substantial projects when strategic opportunities emerged. The more significant presence of Chinese companies in the Russian market was consolidated through several direct investment deals, which have remained roughly constant over recent years.

### Country/industry breakdown

Within China's OFDI into the GEZ in the energy sector, Russia accounts for the largest share (51 per cent of amounts invested in the sector in the GEZ, 30 per cent of the number of deals, here again clearly indicating larger operations in Russia than elsewhere in this energy sector). Among those deals, the 96.86 per cent share acquisition in OAO Udmurtneft, a Russian oil producer, by Sinopec Group in 2006 for €2.8 bn stands out and bespeaks the importance to the two countries of significantly strengthening their partnership in the commercial and technical development of energy projects. This acquisition has allowed, for the first time, a Chinese company to produce crude oil in Russia, the world's second-largest oil supplier at the time; but its importance lies more in China's efforts to increase and secure its energy supplies. In 2009 and 2010, China concluded four further deals with Russia in the energy sector. Among them was a 45 per cent share acquisition of the Nobel Oil Group, a company active in oil exploration and production, by the Chinese sovereign wealth fund, the China Investment Corporation (CIC), for €216 million. This investment confirms China's resource-seeking strategy, especially as the CIC has a long-term investment perspective in supporting Chinese companies' overseas development.

In the dominant energy sector, Chinese enterprises also made substantial investments in Kazakhstan and Turkmenistan in 2008 and 2009, seizing nascent opportunities to expand and secure long-term energy supplies with new partners. Indeed, investments in the energy sector constituted all Chinese FDI outflows to Kazakhstan and 90 per cent of flows to Turkmenistan between 2005 and 2010. China's interest in these two countries lies in their geographical location: they form the eastern and northern shores of the Caspian Sea, an area rich in hydrocarbon resources.

Direct investment in the energy sector in Kazakhstan cumulatively reached some €3.3 billion between 2005 and 2012. The two deals registered in 2009, amounting to a massive €2.6 billion, concerned the acquisition of Kazakh companies engaged in oil and gas production. The first acquisition (approximately €0.7 billion) was a minority stake purchase (11 per cent of the capital) of JSC KazMunaiGas Exploration Production by Fullbloom Investment Corporation, a wholly owned subsidiary of the CIC. The second transaction (€1.9 billion) was the joint purchase of MangistauMunaiGaz, one of Kazakhstan's largest oil producers, by the state-owned China National Petroleum Company and Kazakhstan's KazMunaiGaz. Interestingly, the deal was concluded thanks to a €1.3 billion loan from the CNPC to KazMunaiGaz. At the same time, an additional €3.6 billion loan was agreed between the Export-Import Bank of China (China Exim Bank) and the Kazakhstan Development Bank for other oil and gas projects in the country.

China's presence in Turkmenistan is related to the CNPC's investment (€1.5 billion) in the Amu Darya Natural Gas Project, completed in 2008. The CNPC has a production-sharing agreement to explore and develop gas fields, as well as a natural gas sale-and-purchase agreement with its Turkmen partners for the export of 30 billion cubic meters of natural gas to China annually for 30 years. Construction on the Amu Darya river of a natural gas processing plant, the most technologically advanced and the largest-capacity plant in Central Asia, started in 2008. The plant became operational in 2009.

When excluding energy, there is again a pre-eminence of Russia, which accounts for about 58 per cent of operations and 53 per cent of total invested amounts. Chinese (non-energy) investments in Russia are orientated mostly towards the commodities and materials sector (50 per cent of invested amounts in Russia excluding energy); the other noteworthy sectors for Chinese investment into Russia include construction and real estate, chemicals, and motor and transport.

Turkey and Belarus are also prominent recipients of Chinese investment in terms of number of deals (16 and 11 respectively). But while total flows from China into Turkey reached €1,255 million, Belarus received only €44 million between 2005 and 2012.

Two Chinese Greenfield investments in Turkey were realised in 2009. First, the state-owned car manufacturer Chery completed construction of a €360 million plant in the European part of Turkey. It has a capacity of 20,000 units per year and is expected to serve the EU car market. Second, Dongfeng Motor, the third-largest Chinese car-maker, finished a €180 million production facility in Turkey – its estimated annual production is 52,000 units per year – to support Dongfeng's expansion in Europe, the Middle East and Africa.

China's strategic expansion of domestic industries, largely state-owned companies, is intended to align foreign investments with the country's long-term development strategies. National industry champions thus have access to overseas natural resources in selected countries. The government's involvement ensures that improved resource allocation is achieved, in particular in energy security, combined with positive spillovers for international competitiveness. The country destination choice for outward investment also has strong links to the Chinese authorities' main geopolitical goal of developing and securing good relations with neighbouring countries, including Russia, Kazakhstan, Kyrgyzstan and Tajikistan in Central Asia.

## Strategies and Challenges

As evidenced in the previous section, China's motives for outward investment in the GEZ are primarily resource-seeking. But as well as with direct investments, Chinese enterprises are accessing GEZ markets in other ways.

### The different forms of resource-seeking strategy

China engages in strategic partnerships at the sovereign and corporate levels. The main arm of China's overseas activity is the China Exim Bank, whose mission is to assist Chinese companies in their offshore contract projects and outbound investment. Unfortunately, its English-language website does not provide detailed lists of financial transactions, but two major projects in the GEZ are listed in its annual reports:

The Tajikistan–Uzbekistan Highway Restoration and Reconstruction Project was completed in 2010 with the support of a concessional loan.[10] The China Road and Bridge Corporation undertook the general design, full reconstruction and expansion of the 355 km Tajikistan–Uzbekistan Highway under an engineering, procurement and construction contract.

The 500 kV North–South Transmission Line Project in Tajikistan: in 2008, the China Exim Bank provided a preferential export buyer's credit (for an estimated €192 million) to address the power supply imbalance and transmission bottleneck in the country.[11]

Projects financed by the China Exim Bank are related mainly to energy and infrastructure development in the GEZ. China has successfully completed several projects on cross-border communications (highways and railways), transforming the cities of Kashgar and Urumqi, in the westernmost provinces of China, into major trade hubs in Central Asia. It has also constructed oil and gas pipelines in the neighbouring GEZ, most notably a 2,200-kilometre oil pipeline from the Caspian shore of Kazakhstan to the Xinjiang autonomous region in China. This was completed in 2009 and provides about 5 per cent of China's annual oil consumption. Gas pipelines are under construction in Turkmenistan, Uzbekistan and Kazakhstan up to the Chinese border. In 2012, the Export-Import Bank of China also financed a crude oil refinery processing project in Kazakhstan (US$1.7 bn), which is contracted by the Sinopec Group.

Local Chinese governments in the western provinces have sought the central government's support for a new strategy to advance their underdeveloped markets through better integration with neighbouring countries. The central government's major Go West policy, which aims to develop the Chinese hinterland, helped local governments to address their specific economic development agendas. Moreover, international organisations, such as the Asian Development Bank (ADB) and the United Nations Development Programme (UNDP), are working closely with the Chinese central government on pan-Asian connectivity initiatives.

Over the years, China has devoted huge funds to implement new projects, with the aim of taking full advantage of regional programmes. In 2009, the China Exim Bank and the ADB concluded a co-financing agreement worth €2.2 billion, of which the disposable part was allocated mainly to the Asian Infrastructure Financing Initiative. China also promised a €7.2 billion loan for infrastructure development within the Shanghai Cooperation Organisation framework – bilateral cooperation within a regional multilateral structure but without international institutions such as the ADB.

China has an important role in regional project management too. It often acts as a catalyst and a coordinator, and becomes an essential part of the design and implementation of projects. China has built a strong competitive advantage through the active participation of its officials in exploratory studies and in planning and technical committees for regional infrastructure projects. It has therefore been able to create a strong position for itself in terms of know-how and research, giving Chinese companies a comparative advantage during international competition for construction and/or exploitation tenders.

Complementary to the favourable investment financing provided in the form of credit lines by the China Exim Bank to Chinese companies, the Chinese government has taken another important step to support outward FDI by domestic enterprises in the framework of the Go Global strategy. At the end of 2001, it set up an export credit insurance corporation, Sinosure, whose mandate is to support investment. Sinosure provides investment insurance schemes for both Chinese enterprises investing overseas and foreign enterprises investing in China. Unfortunately, Sinosure does not publish detailed lists of the projects (with country of destination and value of investment covered) that benefit from their services. Nevertheless, it shows the Chinese state's strong interest in promoting domestic enterprises' overseas investment as part of enhancing its power and influence abroad.

Another type of government support for the foreign expansion of Chinese enterprises is referred to as 'tied aid': this is when Chinese foreign aid programmes are linked to preferential commercial contracts (for example, for the awarding of construction contracts), even though this practice is generally discouraged by international aid organisations. As a case in point, the white paper on China's foreign aid (2011) mentions, among several economic infrastructure construction projects, the 2.3 kilometre Shar-Shar tunnel in Tajikistan, which much improves traffic conditions between Tajikistan and China. In fact, the Chinese government provided Tajikistan with a €32 million grant for the project, which began in October 2006, under the proviso that the China Railway Engineering Corporation would be the general contractor for the tunnel's construction.

China has indeed used its aid-giving power as an indirect way to provide new market opportunities for domestic enterprises, taking advantage of the relatively low cost of local workforces. This also respects one of the basic features of China's foreign aid policy: China promotes mutual benefit and common development through economic and technical cooperation with other developing countries.

Finally, the Chinese presence in the GEZ can be observed in the form of large engineering and construction contracts. These are not outward direct investments, but their mention is necessary in order to provide a complete view of China's strategy. The following list of large engineering and construction contracts is incomplete, as the transactions often involve a Chinese or a local firm that does not provide financial disclosure, but it is nevertheless indicative of their scale.

Sinohydro Corporation, China's major hydropower developer, signed a deal in August 2008 to carry out the design and construction of a hydroelectric power station in eastern Tajikistan worth up to €204 million.

China Minmetals Development, a subsidiary of the state-owned international metals and mining China Minmetals Corporation, signed an agreement worth around €290 million in October 2008 with the Russian mining and metal company Mechel. In this contract the parties agreed to the joint development of several projects, among them the construction of a rail and structural steel mill at Chelyabinsk Metallurgical Plant and the building of a new coal-mining complex at the Elga deposit in the far east of Russia.

China National Materials Corporation (Sinoma), one of the leading Chinese cement equipment and engineering service providers, has signed a €167 million contract with Lafarge SA to design and construct a cement production line in Mykolaiv, western Ukraine.

China's Sinopec Engineering, a subsidiary of the state-run Sinopec (Asia's largest refiner and a major producer of chemicals) and the Kazakhstan government have signed a €1 billion contract to build a polypropylene production plant in the western Atyrau region, part of a €4.8 billion gas processing complex. The China Exim Bank is providing a loan to Sinopec's counterpart, and Sinopec is responsible for the export of the plant's products.

China Triumph International Engineering has signed a €251 million contract with Norm, an Azerbaijani company to establish a new cement plant in the Garadagh district of Baku, Azerbaijan. The $350m facility, called Gizildash Cement, will employ 400 people.

## Entry points into the EU or domestic market penetration?

The trade-off between domestic market penetration and the establishment of a basis for extra-border operations is dictated by strategic decisions at the corporate level; as the nature and the size of direct investments vary, so do their expected returns. Preliminary negotiations between potential business partners are often supported and entangled in bilateral political relations. Multiple visits by Chinese leaders to the GEZ have each time encouraged a greater tie-up between the visited country and China in the fields of economic and trade cooperation and in improving business contacts and developing specific initiatives. This demonstrates the extent to which China's political leaders influence and support the activities of state-owned companies in the GEZ. Academics have suggested that the strategic shift of Chinese overseas investment occurred around the middle of the 2000s, with a combination of closer cooperation between government policy and corporate entrepreneurship and the emphasis on responses to the challenges and opportunities offered by globalisation by Chinese companies.[12]

The quantitative analysis of China's overseas investment in the GEZ presented in 'Introduction' above has shown that the predominant motivation for Chinese companies engaging in investment is to secure access to commodity resources (chiefly sources of energy). At the same time, some large direct investments in Russia and Turkey are aimed at developing the presence of Chinese companies in those markets. The sectors of particular interest, mainly commodities and materials, construction and real estate, are targeted through a specific market penetration strategy for the GEZ.

The investments of Chinese car manufacturers (Chery and Dongfeng Motor) in Turkey are clearly motivated by a desire to tap into not only the domestic market but also enlarged neighbourhood markets. Chery's production facility in Istanbul is strategically located to target the European market. Its vehicles have unencumbered access to the EU because of an EU-Turkey Customs Union agreement, and safety standards at the plant have also been put in line with EU regulations.

## China's Policy for the GEZ and the GEZ States' Response

In order to assess China's OFDI policy for the GEZ, a comprehensive review of the literature on that policy and its evolution since the launch of the Go Global policy in 1999 has been completed, as has research on bilateral investment treaties' (BITs) effects on FDI. An analysis of specific GEZ countries' proactive and/or restrictive policies towards Chinese investments highlights the nature of the relative openness of GEZ countries. Indeed, Figure 2.5 shows the strong relationship between China's trade with the GEZ and investment flows from China to the GEZ in 2005–2012. The correlation coefficients between trade and ODI are very high: above 98 per cent for imports and close to 92 per cent for exports. This suggests that the strategy of Chinese investment in the target GEZ countries has been developed thanks to trusted and significant commercial ties.

Knowledge of the local business environment in the GEZ and confidence-building with partners who export to the Chinese market provide sound support for China's investment decisions for the GEZ. In order to assess China's OFDI policy for the GEZ and to highlight the nature of the relative openness of the GEZ countries, an analysis of specific GEZ countries' policies towards Chinese investments has been made. A provisional list of bilateral agreements, from China's Ministry of Foreign Affairs

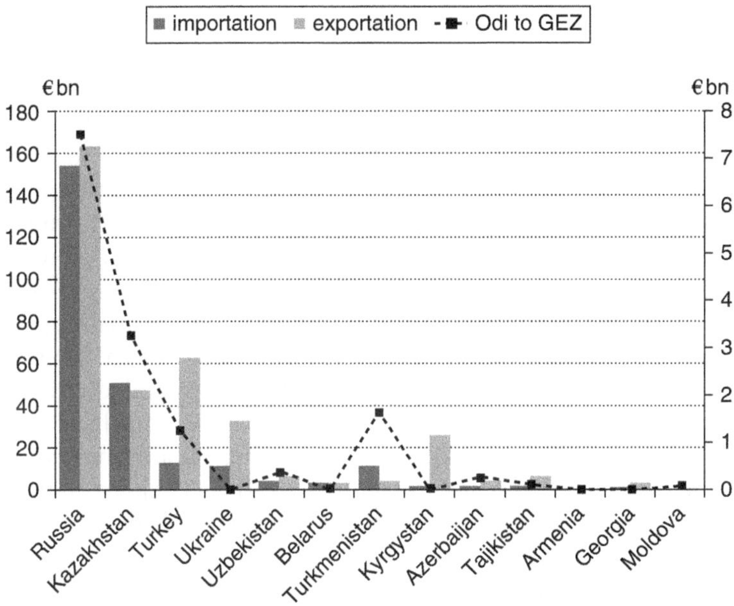


Figure 2.5 **China's trade with and outward FDI flows to the GEZ states, 2005–2012 (€ billion)**

*Source*: UN Comtrade database, COFM.

demonstrates the importance given by Chinese authorities to formalising bilateral relationships and prioritising areas of further cooperation.

## Go Global and China's ODI policy for the GEZ

This section reviews the recent evolution of China's policy regarding ODI, including the specific role of state-owned enterprises in resource-seeking strategies.

Go Global is the banner name of a national policy encouraging outward investment by Chinese firms. It was introduced in 1999 but has evolved to represent a cluster of individual policies. Previously companies had been heavily restricted from investing overseas. The policy to promote outward investment and to establish an adequate support system was officially included in the Tenth Five-Year Plan, 2001–2005. A major tool of the Go

Global policy has been the loosening of controls on outward investment by Chinese firms.[13]

Outward investment requires approval from the Ministry of Commerce, with concomitant foreign currency approval from the State Administration of Foreign Exchange (SAFE). In 2002, SAFE authorisation was decentralised from the central agency to selected local authorities for projects of about €1 million or less, with an overall investment cap of about €210 million. Decentralisation continued in 2005, when foreign exchange authorisation was extended to all provinces, municipalities and autonomous regions. The local limit was increased to about €8 million and the overall investment quota was expanded to about €4 billion. The power of authorisation was decentralised from the Ministry of Commerce to local commercial administrations in October 2004, except for large state-owned enterprises. In June 2006, the overall investment quota was abolished.

Outward investment has been encouraged further through support from the Ministry of Commerce. Some of this support has been information and bureaucratic expertise in navigating foreign investment rules. In July 2004, the Ministry of Commerce along with the Ministry of Foreign Affairs provided a 'guidance list' of industries preferred for outward investment. Additional support has come in the form of preferential treatment of outward-investing Chinese firms in terms of direct grants, tax benefits, low- or no-interest loans, access to foreign exchange, etc. This culminated in November 2004 in the creation of a formal loan support system under the authority of the National Development and Reform Commission and the China Exim Bank.

New measures in April 2009 covering the administration of outbound investments promise faster and simpler reviews of many small to medium-sized Chinese direct investments abroad and more careful reviews of others. Chinese companies proposing routine outward direct investments in foreign non-financial sectors, and also foreign sellers and joint-venture participants, can benefit from the availability of simpler and faster verification procedures of the Ministry of Commerce. However, non-routine investments will not benefit from simpler or faster verification. These include investments into the energy and mining sectors and into companies intended to be red-chips (offshore companies that hold Chinese companies' subsidiaries and are controlled by

Chinese investors but are listed on a stock exchange in Hong Kong or on a foreign market). MOFCOM's verification procedures were updated with effect on 1 May 2009 in accordance with its recently issued Measures for Administration of External Investment. The main effects of these measures, compared to the previous rules, are the availability of a three-day turnaround of an online application, without supporting documentation, for approval of a routine small to medium-size investment from MOFCOM or from a provincial-level department with authority delegated by MOFCOM.

The prominence of energy investments relates, as has been pointed out above, to China's growing dependence on imported fuels for its energy needs. The associated 'energy diplomacy' is implemented by China's central government and Chinese energy companies. This growing dependence has created a visible 'energy worry' among the Chinese leadership: there is a clear relationship between the social need for development, political stability (and the strength of the Communist Party) and the economic growth rate and access to the required energy to feed this growth. Shortages of fuel have already triggered social protests in different provinces. And the Chinese authorities' belief that the US is exerting de facto control of major supply sources in the Middle East and is in a position to control the key maritime routes, at the straits of Hormuz and Malacca, taken by oil bound for China has only added to their feelings of insecurity. Finally, the Chinese authorities see as an element in this security issue the dominance of oil markets by large (mostly US and European) multinationals and state-owned companies in 'West-friendly' producers, which creates the potential for price manipulation and volatility.

Both China's international strategic objectives (its relations with Taiwan, its role in Asia and its role as a dominant world power) and domestic ones (political stability and avoidance of economic and social disruptions) have converged to make the question of reducing this dependence a central objective for the authorities.[14] This perception is pushing the government to develop a multi-faceted strategy regarding access to oil and gas resources:

There has been a multiplication of diplomatic initiatives to secure access to resources through cooperation/long-term supply agreements with oil-producing countries. However, the Chinese authorities have clearly stated that there is little room left for such bilateral agreements: the existing contractual/marketing relations of the largest producers mean that China is pushed to establish links where other nations or companies have been reluctant to do so. Thus it has relations with Angola, Sudan, Iran and a significant number of other countries about which an objective country risk analysis would suggest being very cautious. In such countries, China has a pragmatic approach of not interfering with their domestic/governance issues and accompanying any agreement with substantial development aid and economic cooperation.

China has supported the acquisition of oil/gas fields abroad by the large state-owned oil companies. The CNPC (and its subsidiary Petrochina), Sinopec and the China National Offshore Oil Corp (CNOOC) are the key vehicles for this acquisition drive.

It has supported and funded the improvement of ground transport of energy supplies, implying the great importance of long-term relations with Central Asian countries (Kazakhstan, Azerbaijan), the need for a strategic relation with Russia and the funding of large pipeline projects from those three countries into China. There is a clear conflict of interest between China, Japan and Europe in securing supplies of oil and gas from Russia. Russia is undoubtedly determined to play this rivalry to its own advantage.

This strategy will have major implications for China's general international position as well as for energy price developments (considered less critical than access to resources). The race for energy resources is likely to increase regional tensions in Asia (e.g. with Japan and with India, which shares the Chinese interest in Kazakhstan and Myanmar). It is also likely to increase tensions over the control of international waters, as some of the most promising deep-sea oil fields are in areas (of the South China Sea) contested by China, Vietnam, Malaysia and the Philippines. The consequences will also be felt in the defence and security fields, with naval control, the ability to secure the maritime routes of energy supplies, becoming more important. This will place a large premium on the ability to gain land access to resources in Central Asia.

An important fact that helps us to understand Chinese investment strategy in the GEZ and in the rest of the world is that the

Chinese companies investing abroad are predominantly state-owned enterprises. 84 per cent of all Chinese investment in the GEZ comes from state-owned enterprises. In fact, between 2005 and 2010, only three of the main Chinese investors there were not state-owned: Huawei Technologies (four deals in the telecommunications sector), Great Wall Motors (three deals in the motor sector) and the Midea Group (three deals in the household products manufacturing sector). As most investments are made by state-owned enterprises – such as Sinopec Group, CNPC/PetroChina, Datang International Power Generation, SAIC Chery Automobile, the State Grid Corporation (power transmission and distribution), the China Huadian Corporation (power generation) and China North Industries Group – investment decisions in the GEZ often reflect political objectives, not just profit-maximisation as in the case of privately owned companies.

## Bilateral investment treaties with the GEZ countries

This section summarises the current state of BITs between China and the GEZ countries and offers a qualitative evaluation of their potential and causal effects.

BITs are agreements between two sovereign countries fixing terms and conditions for private investment by nationals and companies of one country in the other country. Under a BIT, contracting countries grant a number of guarantees to foreign investors, such as fair treatment, protection from expropriation, and repatriation of investment and returns. Developing and emerging countries sign BITs to attract and promote FDI but these agreements can also include dispute-settlement mechanisms between a national or a company and the host country. In many cases, they allow international arbitration, often under the auspices of the International Centre for the Settlement of Investment Disputes (ICSID).

According to the UNCTAD country list of BITs, China has conducted active investment diplomacy in the GEZ since the early 1990s. It has signed bilateral investment agreements with all the GEZ countries. All 13 Chinese BITs with the GEZ countries have entered into force, after an average interval from signature of two years (see Table 2.2). The ICSID database of BITs also gives the 13 signed BITs for China, based on information provided by governments (Chinese or counterparts), of which only 12 have entered into force.

For the initial BIT between China and Russia, the ICSID database reports only a signature date, 21 July 1990. The gap between this signature date and the subsequent signature date, 9 November 2006, is related to the BIT's renegotiation. This renegotiation was initiated by China and Russia in order to update the content of the agreement in response to greater bilateral economic cooperation. The entry into force of the China-Russia BIT signed in November 2006 automatically terminated the relations under the agreement signed in July 1990.

The second BIT signed between China and a member of the GEZ was with Turkey in November 1990; it entered into force more than three years later. Turkey had begun to negotiate BITs in the latter 1980s so as to provide favourable conditions for foreign investment as a means to foster economic growth. That time was when a liberal and flexible foreign investment policy had been adopted as part of a programme of economic transformation launched early in the decade. It appears that as investments by Turkish enterprises abroad increased, BITs became a main instrument for providing more predictable and transparent conditions

**Table 2.2** China-GEZ bilateral investment treaties

| Partner | Date of signature | Date of entry into force |
|---|---|---|
| Armenia | 4 July 1992 | 18 March 1995 |
| Azerbaijan | 8 March 1994 | 1 April 1995 |
| Belarus | 11 January 1993 | 14 January 1995 |
| Georgia | 3 June 1993 | 1 March 1995 |
| Kazakhstan | 10 August 1992 | 13 August 1994 |
| Kyrgyzstan | 14 May 1992 | 8 September 1995 |
| Moldova | 6 November 1992 | 1 March 1995 |
| Russia | 9 November 2006 | 1 May 2009 |
| Tajikistan | 9 March 1993 | 20 January 1994 |
| Turkey | 13 November 1990 | 20 August 1994 |
| Turkmenistan | 21 November 1992 | 4 June 1994 |
| Ukraine | 31 October 1992 | 29 May 1993 |
| Uzbekistan | 13 March 1992 | 12 April 1994 |

*Source*: UNCTAD, http://www.unctad.org/Templates/Page.asp?intItemID=2344&lang=1 (as of 30 June 2011).

for Turkish investors. Therefore, China and Turkey negotiated and concluded a BIT establishing identical rights and obligations for both parties. They agreed that disputes between the contracting parties should be submitted to an ad hoc international arbitration tribunal in accordance with the Arbitration Rules of the United Nations Commission on International Trade Law.

Soon after the dissolution of the Soviet Union and the declaration of independence of 10 republics in 1991, China initiated bilateral negotiations with the governments of the newly created CIS. The official dates of signature between the CIS countries, excluding Russia, and China were between March 1992 (with Uzbekistan) and March 1994 (with Azerbaijan).

Over the past decade, and especially since 1998, many academic studies have investigated the potential impact of BITs on FDI flows and economic growth. The potential impact of a BIT can be analysed through four channels:

A commitment effect: a binding international commitment to the satisfactory protection and treatment of foreign investors, which reduces risks and increases FDI from home partner countries.

A signalling effect: a BIT is a signal of seriousness about improved property rights in the host country applying to all investors. Thus it may stimulate FDI from all countries, not only from the BIT contracting parties.

A shortcut to improved institutional quality: foreign investors may consider BITs a substitute for improved institutional quality, and thus FDI inflows from these investors may be stimulated; and

A promotion effect: strong provisions in favour of foreign investors have a greater chance of stimulating FDI.

Applying the economic principle of efficient allocation of production factors, some studies assess the impact of the BITs on the general stock or flows of FDI with a set of control variables; these account for different economic and business environments in the partner countries. In 2009, UNCTAD conducted an analysis of 'The Role of International Investment Agreements in Attracting Foreign Direct Investment to Developing Countries', providing an overview of 15 major econometric studies that examined the impact of BITs on FDI flows into developing countries. It is particularly interesting to see that there is no consensus on the influence of BITs on FDI, mainly because of the lack of clear statistical evidence.

Some studies conclude that BITs do have an effect on FDI[15] but most conclude that BITs have only a weak effect or none at all.[16] In their 2009 report, UNCTAD concludes interestingly that 'International investment agreements (IIAs) alone can never be a sufficient policy instrument to attract FDI' but they 'can influence a company's decision where to invest, and this impact is generally stronger in the case of preferential trade and investment agreements than with regard to BITs'. Moreover, UNCTAD adds that 'although most BITs do not change the key economic determinants of FDI, they improve several policy and institutional determinants, and thereby increase the likelihood that developing countries engaged in BIT programmes will receive more FDI.'[17]

As for the influence of BITs on China's FDI outflows to the GEZ, there is little evidence about how they have contributed to the growth of FDI. After all, BITs are only one of several confidence-building measures used to improve each GEZ country's investment climate. In addition, a look at the trend of investment flows for each country of destination (see Figure 2.5 on the geographical breakdown of Chinese outward FDI flows to the GEZ between 2005 and 2010) shows clearly that BITs have had no remarkable effect on the growth of China's FDI outflows to the GEZ.

## Host countries' policies towards Chinese investments

Political relations between China and the GEZ countries, particularly its Central Asian members, have evolved considerably, due to the emergence of relative political stability in Central Asia after the collapse of the Soviet Union. State-building in Central Asian countries is complex and fragile, with varying degrees of internal and external vulnerability. Chinese interests favour their increased political and economic stability, notably to reduce security risks and ensure stability on its continental Asian border. Chinese foreign policy objectives for the region include mutual cooperation, through a permanent dialogue platform in the Shanghai Cooperation Organisation, and the diversification of China's supplies of natural resources and the options for their transportation, as endorsed by the Go Global policy.

China addresses the underlying economic challenges to stability in Central Asian GEZ countries through its provision of financial support. Its conditional lending and commercial practices are often related to purchases and hiring from China, in contrast to the conditionality traditionally attached to Bretton Woods institutions related to micro- and macroeconomic reforms. Financial relations, and in particular China's investment flows, constitute a large part of its economic diplomacy; and gaining access to natural resources in the GEZ is more important in its investment policy than sound local regulatory frameworks for direct investments. Close political relations between China and GEZ governments, and mutual interests developed by corporate leaders in the energy sector, have formed a common basis for strengthening bilateral economic relations and facilitating Chinese direct investments in the GEZ.

The Chinese investments are particularly well received in the GEZ countries as ways to improve economic conditions at the firm level and to balance Russia's influence on the region's oil and gas development. They favour inward investment, and most see it as a priority for fuelling economic growth. In comparison with many of the political attitudes shown towards Chinese investments globally (e.g. by the US, the European Union and Japan), the GEZ countries have developed welcoming policies towards Chinese companies. Global political issues, such as human rights, democracy and international intervention are not a primary concern at high-level political and economic meetings between China and GEZ states. Politically sensitive issues such as Taiwan and Tibet are often left aside by most GEZ countries, as their focus is on domestic and regional economic and social stability.

The GEZ countries have established the necessary legal conditions (liberalisation of sectors open to FDI, guarantees and protection of rights) and incentives (favourable fiscal regimes, schemes for disinvestment/privatisation of state property) to attract potential foreign investors. In addition, they have put a number of initiatives on transparency and promotion into place such as creating organisations to promote their economy and to create awareness on investment opportunities and one-stop-window agencies to inform investors of and perform all necessary legal procedures, etc.

Table 2.3 gives a provisional list of organisations in each GEZ country that aim to create a favourable investment environment

**Table 2.3** Investment promotion institutions in the GEZ

| Country | Name | Year | Type | Ownership |
|---|---|---|---|---|
| Armenia | Armenia Development Agency | 1998 | Trade promotion/ development organisation | 100% government |
| | Association for Foreign Investment and Cooperation | 1998 | Investment promotion/ development organisation | Non-profit, non-governmental business association |
| | Gegharkunik Chamber of Commerce and Industry | 2002 | Chamber of commerce | Non-governmental organisation |
| Azerbaijan | Azerbaijan Export and Investment Promotion Foundation | 2003 | Investment promotion/ development organisation | Joint public-private initiative |
| | Caspian Investment Centre | 2003 | Investment promotion/ development organisation | Private |
| Belarus | National Investment Agency | | Investment promotion/ development organisation | 100% government |
| Georgia | Georgian National Investment Agency | 2002 | Investment promotion/ development organisation, investment authority | 100% government |
| Kazakhstan | Foreign Investors' Council | 1998 | Investment promotion/ development organisation | 100% government |
| | Kazakhstan Investment Promotion Centre | 1998 | Investment promotion/ development organisation | 100% government |
| Kyrgyzstan | none | | | |
| Moldova | Moldovan Investment and Export Promotion Organisation | 1999 | Investment promotion/ development organisation | 100% government |

| | | | | |
|---|---|---|---|---|
| Russia | National Agency for Direct Investment | 2001 | Investment authority | Independent, non-commercial partnership |
| | Foreign Investment Advisory Council | 1994 | Investment promotion/ development organisation | Joint public-private initiative |
| Tajikistan | State Committee on Investments and State Property Management | 2006 | Investment promotion/ development organisation Investment authority | 100% government |
| Turkey | Investment Support and Promotion Agency | 2006 | Investment promotion/ development organisation | 100% government |
| Turkmenistan | none | | | |
| Ukraine | Centre for Foreign Investment Promotion | 2005 | Investment promotion/ development organisation | Independent non-profit investment agency |
| Uzbekistan | Chamber of Commerce and Industry of Uzbekistan | 2004 | Chamber of commerce | Joint public-private initiative |
| | Uzbek Information and Commercial Centre | 1992 | Trade promotion/development organisation | 100% government |

*Source*: UNESCAP (2009), U.S. Department of State (2011).

for foreign direct investors. The progressive implementation of new regulations for investment, particularly foreign-orientated strategies, has promoted a competitive environment for attracting FDI into the GEZ. A special coalition representing the interests of 'international capital' often helps to shape the region's FDI-friendly economic policies. This coalition consists of sections of the ministry of industry and trade and the ministry of foreign affairs, local branches of Western consulting firms and their local competitors, and companies providing services to foreign investors.

Even though Kyrgyzstan has a liberal investment regime with laws on foreign investment that guarantee protection from expropriation and nationalisation for foreign investors, its outdated regulatory framework has not yet put in place an agency that deals specifically with foreign investments. Despite the government of Turkmenistan's intention to improve investment conditions and its adoption of legal reforms on foreign investment and licensing in 2008, the lack of an established rule of law, inconsistent regulatory practices and unfamiliarity with international business norms are major disincentives for foreign investment.

National policies related to foreign investment in the GEZ generally have no specific objective regarding China's inward investment. Nevertheless, governments in the GEZ welcome and encourage Chinese OFDI in their economies. A wide range of actions both at the domestic level and on a bilateral basis enhance the GEZ's attractiveness for Chinese investment, such as business leaders' meetings, regular political dialogue and (temporary or permanent) country-focused programmes for investment promotion. For example, Moldova has prepared and implemented a strategy to develop trade and investment with a specific country-focus on China and seven other countries (OECD Investment Compact, 2006).

The BITs signed with China form the principal means of enabling a better environment for Chinese OFDI. Even though a BIT does not constitute a legal investment framework in each GEZ country, it provides an incentive for Chinese multinationals, guaranteeing their protection and security and the fair and equitable treatment of direct investments. In addition, the GEZ countries have favourably orientated their bilateral political relations towards the sectoral interests of Chinese companies.

For example, memorandums of understanding (MoUs) signed between Russia and China detail bilateral cooperation in the oil, nuclear and gas sectors.

In the case of the Russian energy sector, the government of Russia has granted strategic status to a limited number of large state-owned companies. These corporations usually enjoy a dominant position in the domestic market in their area of activity (Gazprom in the oil sector, Rosneft in the gas sector, Rosatom in nuclear energy, Sovkomflot in shipbuilding, etc.). The government, which controls inward and outward foreign investment, has adopted a development strategy in the energy sector that resulted from strategic alliances with foreign companies. The 2006 initial public offering (IPO) of Rosneft tapped several international strategic investors, and the CNPC bought a stake of about €400 million in a landmark IPO of €8.5 billion. This purchase is only one milestone in Russia-China relations, as Rosneft and the CNPC established in 2010 a new joint venture for the construction/exploitation of a refinery with an annual capacity of 13 million tonnes as a part of energy cooperation between the two companies.

## Conclusions and Recommendations

Under the Go Global policy implemented in the past decade, the Chinese government has provided support for Chinese enterprises engaging in outward direct investment.[18] Large enterprises, mainly state-owned companies, have expanded their presence in the GEZ. Their main focus has been on the energy sector, to fulfil China's quest for energy. Chinese investments in the GEZ have a clear strategic motivation. Indeed, the main strategic factor behind much FDI is to seek access to commodity resources.

China's total FDI in the GEZ reached €14.6 billion in the period between 2005 and 2012, but the pace of investment was irregular, peaking in 2006, 2009 (both at €4 billion) and 2010 (€1.4 billion), 2011 (€0.9 billion) and 2012 (€0.83 billion). Russia is the major destination for Chinese FDI in the GEZ, receiving approximately €7.5 billion over this period (52 per cent of FDI there), followed by Kazakhstan (€3.3 billion) and

Turkmenistan (€1.7 billion). The average size of an investment is larger in Turkmenistan than in other GEZ countries and five times the size of an average investment in Russia.

The sectoral distribution of Chinese direct investments in the GEZ is highly concentrated in energy, which accounts for 50 per cent of total Chinese investments (€7.2 billion between 2005 and 2012). The two next most significant sectors are motors and transport (20 per cent) and commodities and materials (10 per cent). But in terms of the number of deals, a fourth sector is also important: the electronics, software and IT sector takes 15 per cent of the 161 deals in the GEZ, against 21 per cent for motors and transport, 14 per cent for energy and 17 per cent for commodities and materials.

Globally, Chinese FDI's focus on the energy sector is motivated by the strategic imperative of securing access to natural resources at a time of rapidly growing Chinese energy (and other raw materials) demand and potential tensions in international supply. China's central government and the state-owned energy companies are actively implementing an 'energy diplomacy', with the aim of gaining access to readily available/developing oil and gas reserves. To this end, the Chinese authorities have engaged in multiple strategic initiatives. These include cooperation/long-term supply agreements with oil- and gas-producing countries in the GEZ (notably in Kazakhstan, Russia and Turkmenistan); the acquisition of foreign assets by large state-owned oil companies (the CNPC and its subsidiary Petrochina, Sinopec and the CNOOC); and the construction of ground transport of energy supplies.

The policy of the GEZ countries towards Chinese direct investments is driven by economic considerations. The GEZ countries registered fast economic growth rates in the mid-2000s, in line with the development of their energy sector. This has created big opportunities for Chinese companies in the development of energy-related infrastructure, and several Chinese companies have since expanded their presence in Central Asia. The regulatory framework for direct investment into the GEZ is at different stages of development, but the conclusion of BITs between China and individual members of the GEZ ensures full protection and security, and fair and equitable treatment, for Chinese direct investments in the region.

We can therefore draw two broad conclusions with policy implications from these findings:

1 Chinese investments in the GEZ have a clear focus on energy and commodity-related industries. The GEZ is a major supplier of energy to the EU. GEZ countries, Russia and Kazakhstan in particular, clearly intend to use the implicit strategic resource competition between the EU and China to their advantage. The very large investments made by Chinese companies and their connection with explicit policy objectives (and policy-related financial resources) mean that the EU risks being left behind in this long-term competition.
2 There is scant evidence of a Chinese EU market penetration strategy that uses the GEZ countries as a production platform for exporting into the EU. Most of the non-commodity-related investments by China in the GEZ are in Russia and to a lesser extent Turkey, and such operations target primarily those domestic markets.

## Notes

1. For example Bevan and Estrin (2000, 2004), Botric and Skuflic (2005), Campos and Kinoshita (2003), Meyer (2005) and Tondel (2001).
2. Wu and Chen (2001).
3. Kolstad and Wiig (2009), Buckley et al. (2007) and Chou, Chen and Mai (2011).
4. Blonigen (2005), Globerman and Shapiro (2002), Asiedu (2006) and Gani (2007).
5. More information on TAC at www.tac-financial.com.
6. EU-China Economic Observatory, Framework Contract FWC COM Lot 1.
7. In this mode, the Chinese government reaches a framework agreement with a country to undertake a development project in exchange for access rights to natural resources, e.g. oil. No money is usually directly transferred to the recipient government. In return, the Chinese government awards a construction contract to a Chinese company and a Chinese oil company acquires rights to begin exploration/production. Sometimes the Chinese oil company can acquire an interest for cash in a joint venture

with a local government. It is presumed that Chinese official FDI statistics cover only a part of these financial packages under the 'Angola mode'.

8. The GEZ countries are Armenia, Azerbaijan, Belarus, Georgia, Kazakhstan, Kyrgystan, Moldova, Russia, Tajikistan, Turkey, Turkmenistan, Ukraine and Uzbekistan.
9. Benassy-Quere et al. (2005).
10. Export-Import Bank of China, 2010 Annual Report.
11. Export-Import Bank of China, 2008 Annual Report.
12. Hong and Sun (2006).
13. Davies (2010).
14. Holslag (2010).
15. Neumayer and Spess (2005).
16. Hallward-Driemeier (2003) or UNCTAD (2009).
17. UNCTAD World Investment Report, 2009, pp. xi–xiii.
18. Lemoine (2011).

## References

Asiedu, E. (2006), 'Foreign direct investment in Africa: The role of natural resources, market size, government policy, institutions and political stability', *The World Economy*, vol. 29(1), pp. 63–77.

Benassy-Quere, A., Coupet, M. and Mayer, T. (2005), 'Institutional Determinants of Foreign Direct Investment', CEPII, WP No. 2005-05.

Bevan, A. and Estrin, S. (2000), 'The Determinants of Foreign Direct Investment in Transition Economies', William Davidson Institute, WP No. 342, October.

Bevan, A. and Estrin, S. (2004), 'The determinants of foreign direct investment into European transition economies', *Journal of Comparative Economics*, vol. 32(4), pp. 775–787.

Blonigen, B. (2005), 'A review of the empirical literature on FDI determinants', *Atlantic Economic Journal*, vol. 33(4), pp. 383–403.

Botric, V. and Skuflic, L. (2005), 'Main Determinants of Foreign Direct Investment in the South East European Countries', Second Europhrame Conference on Economic Policy Issues in the European Union – 'Trade, FDI and Relocation: Challenges for Employment and Growth in the European Union?', 3 June, Vienna.

Buckley, P., Clegg, J., Cross, A., Liu, X., Voss, H. and Zheng, P. (2007), 'The determinants of Chinese outward foreign direct investment', *Journal of International Business Studies*, vol. 38(4), pp. 499–518.

Campos, N. and Kinoshita, Y. (2003), 'Why Does FDI Go Where It Goes? New Evidence from the Transition Economies', International Monetary Fund, Working Paper No. 03/228.

Chou, K. H, Chen, C. H. and Mai, C. C. (2011), 'The Impact of Third-Country Effects and Economic Integration on China's Outward FDI', *Economic Modelling*, vol. 28(5), September, pp. 2154–2163.

Davies, K. (2010), 'Outward FDI from China and Its policy context', Columbia FDI Profiles, Vale Columbia Center on Sustainable International Investment.

Export-Import Bank of China, Annual Reports 2008 and 2010.

Gani, A. (2007), 'Governance and foreign direct investment links: Evidence from panel data estimations', *Applied Economic Letters*, vol. 14(14), pp. 753–756.

Globerman, S. and Shapiro, D. (2002), 'Global foreign direct investment flows: the role of governance infrastructure', *World Development*, vol. 30(11), pp. 1898–1919.

Hallward-Driemaier, M. (2003), 'Do bilateral investment treaties attract FDI? Only a bit and they could bite', World Bank Policy Research Paper WPS 3121.

Holslag, J. (2010), 'China's Roads to Influence', *Asian Survey*, vol. 50(4), pp. 641–662.

Hong, E. and Sun, L. (2006), 'Dynamics of internationalization and outward investment: Chinese corporations′ strategies', *The China Quarterly*, vol. 187, pp. 610–634.

Information Office of the State Council, The People's Republic of China (2011), *White Paper on China's Foreign Aid*.

Kolstad, I. and Wiig, A. (2009), 'What determines Chinese outward FDI?', Chr. Michelsen Institute Working Paper, WP 2009:3.

Lemoine, F. (2011), 'Les investissements internationaux de la Chine: stratégie ou pragmatisme?', *Revue d'Economie Financière*, no. 102 (2-2011), pp. 133–148.

Meyer, K. (2005), 'Foreign Direct Investment in Emerging Economies', Policy Discussion Paper, Templeton College, Oxford, December.

Ministry of Commerce, People's Republic of China (2011), 2010 Statistical Bulletin of China's Outward Foreign Direct Investment.

Ministry of Foreign Affairs of the People's Republic of China, Department of European-Central Asian Affairs, http://www.fmprc.gov.cn/eng/. Website accessed on 30 June 2011.

Mlachila, M. and Takebe, M. (2011), 'FDI from BRICs to LICs: Emerging Growth Driver?', International Monetary Fund, Working Paper No. 11/178.Neumayer, E. and Spess, L. (2005), 'Do bilateral investment treaties increase foreign direct investment to developing countries?', *World Development*, vol. 33(10), pp. 1567–1585.

OECD Investment Compact (2006), 'Moldova – Foreign Direct Investment and Export Development – Vision and Strategy: 2006–2010'.

TAC (2005–2010), 'EU-China Economic Observatory', unpublished reports for the European Commission – DG Relex (in particular Issue 6, December 2007; Issue 8, June 2008; Issue 10, June 2009 and Issue 13, December 2010).

Tondel, L. (2001), 'Foreign Direct Investment during Transition. Determinants and Patterns in Central and Eastern Europe and the former Soviet Union', Chr. Michelsen Institute Working Paper, WP 2001:9.

UNCTAD (2009), 'The Role of International Investment Agreements in Attracting Foreign Direct Investment to Developing Countries', UNCTAD Series on International Investment Policies for Development, UNCTAD/DIAE/IA/2009/5.

UNESCAP (2009), 'Directory of Trade Promotion-Development Organizations of Developing Countries and Areas in Asia and the Pacific', ST/ESCAP/2533.

U.S. Department of State (2011), 'Investment Climate Statements 2011', http://www.state.gov/e/eb/rls/othr/ics/2011/index.htm. Website accessed on 30 June 2011.

Wu, H. and Chen, C. (2001), 'An assessment of outward foreign direct investment from China's transnational economy', *Europe-Asia Studies*, vol. 53(8), pp. 1235–1254.

# 3 Rebalancing towards a Sustainable Future: China's Twelfth Five-Year Programme

*Robert Ash, Robin Porter and Tim Summers*

## Introduction

This chapter seeks to analyse and assess some of the major opportunities and challenges in China's Twelfth Five-Year Programme for Social and Economic Development (hereafter 12FYP).[1] The main economic thrust of the 12FYP is one of sustainable, balanced and innovative development; its principal social thrust is that the government should enhance its support for 'livelihoods' (*minsheng*) in order to create a 'moderately well-off' (*xiaokang*) society by 2020.[2]

We find that during the period of the Programme's implementation (2011–15), China's development trajectory will be increasingly shaped by *domestic* factors and forces, especially through a significant increase in domestic demand. This is the result firstly of the fragility of global economic conditions and Chinese leaders' sense of overexposure to global economic risk; secondly, it reflects the fact that, as its economy continues to grow, China's dependence on external drivers is likely to diminish.

This is not to suggest that China is set to re-embrace a policy of self-reliance. Moreover, the 12FYP itself highlights the continued importance of China's outward economic orientation, albeit in a context of plans to restructure its foreign trade and to give as much weight to outward as to inward flows of foreign direct investment (FDI). Chinese leaders' protestations that their country's economic fate is inextricably linked with that of the rest of the world should be interpreted as referring to its linkages with not only OECD members, but also the wider international community.

The 12FYP reveals similarities in the economic, social and welfare outcomes to which both China and the EU have committed themselves. For example, one of *EU 2020*'s priority goals – attainment of 'sustainable' and 'inclusive' growth – encompasses a range of objectives specified in China's 12FYP.[3] Such similarities highlight the potential scope for collaboration and mutual engagement, by government, commercial and academic representatives, inherent in the vision for the future set out in the two documents. However, other factors have the potential to weaken cooperation. Many of these are political. But others – for example, issues relating to the EU's bilateral trade deficit vis-à-vis China, the undervaluation of China's currency, protection of intellectual property rights (IPR) and the maintenance of non-tariff barriers to trade – are not. It is still too early to judge to what extent in the foreseeable future the strategic partnership between China and the EU will facilitate the advancement of their respective economic, social and political agendas.

This chapter focuses on issues that have potentially significant implications for the EU and its Member States. The first three sections are of a general nature. Following initial discussion (see 'The Planning Environment in China') of the planning environment in China, 'The Eleventh Five-Year Programme of Economic and Social Development' and 'The Twelfth Five-Year Programme of Economic and Social Development' review the content and outcome of the Eleventh Development Programme (11FYP) (2006–10), and analyse and assess the guidelines of the Twelfth FYP (2011–15). There follows a brief comment (see 'The 12FYP and Economic Rebalancing: The Role of Consumption') on the implications of the 12FYP for international relations, with particular reference to the EU. 'Demographic Change, the Labour Supply and Employment' examines the impact of the Programme on China's economic geography, including urbanisation. Each of the remaining six sections is organised around a major developmental theme. They address, in turn, issues relating to population change and employment; the changing role of consumption; commercial opportunities; education; technology and intellectual property rights; and sustainability (energy, climate change and environmental policies). A concluding section summarises the findings of the chapter.

## The Planning Environment in China

Since the post-1978 economic reforms, and especially China's espousal in October 1992 of a 'socialist market economy', the planning environment in China has changed dramatically. The system has evolved to embody increasingly powerful market forces, but in a context in which there is a considerable degree of residual public ownership. The government has also remained an arbiter of decision-making in some key areas of the economy.[4]

China's continued formulation of five-year plans (now called 'programmes') highlights the government's determination that it should set long-term national strategic priorities. Until the end of the 1970s, five-year plans resolved all major production and distribution issues, embodied in detailed output targets. But with subsequent reforms and non-state economic expansion in the 1980s, both the scope and the nature of planning were adjusted and the number of quantitative targets contracted markedly. In the 1990s, the main thrust of planning further shifted towards *guidance* and *supervision*.

The 11FYP was a watershed in terms of both the rhetoric and the evolution of planning under the impact of reform: for the first time a Chinese five-year plan was designated as a *guihua* ('guideline programme') rather than as a *jihua* ('plan'). This definitively signalled China's abandonment of administrative planning in favour of a more open, transparent and consultative approach towards the formulation of economic strategy.[5] The evolutionary aspect of the change was captured in the downgrading of quantitative targets (the 11FYP contained just 22 such targets) in favour of much more emphasis on qualitative principles and goals (e.g., pursuit of a 'harmonious society' or greater sustainability) and the classification of targets into two new categories, *yueshuxing* ('binding') and *yuqixing* ('predictive'). These changes, which are also embodied in the 12FYP, suggest that the Chinese government is adopting a more subtle and sophisticated approach in its efforts to guide the economy towards a more sustainable development trajectory. Further, there are in-built linkages between successive FYPs, and therefore strong policy continuity between the 11FYP and the 12FYP. Each parent FYP is also supplemented by more detailed regional, sectorial and thematic 'sub-plans', and in-built mechanisms now exist that allow adjustments to be made to both policies and targets during the implementation process itself.

The much more open and consultative nature of planning in China is reflected in the 12FYP. Halfway through the *previous* FYP period, the National Development Reform Commission (NDRC), the body that takes the lead in coordinating China's FYPs, commissioned mid-term evaluations of the 11FYP from Tsinghua University's Centre for China Studies, the State Council's Development Research Centre and the Beijing Office of the World Bank.[6] In the light of their findings, the NDRC recruited experts, scholars and business representatives over the following 12 months in order to suggest development guidelines for more than 20 priority policy areas under the 12FYP.[7] Out of this process emerged the main thrust of the new Programme, which, after discussion by senior Chinese Communist Party (henceforth Party) and government officials, was officially endorsed in February 2010. At this time, the Chinese Communist Party Central Committee (CCPCC) Politburo appointed then Vice-Premier Li Keqiang[8] to take charge of a working party for drafting an FYP 'proposal' (*jianyi*). A FYP 'Proposal' was endorsed by the Fifth Plenary Session of the Seventeenth CCPCC in October 2010, and published.[9] The final drafting of the 12FYP generated an outline document that was submitted to the National People's Congress (NPC) for discussion at its annual meeting in March. Following its formal endorsement, the Outline was published.[10] It is this document that is generally referred to when reference is made to China's 'Five-Year Programme [Plan]'.

The publication of the Outline has been followed by three further phases. In the first phase, regions (provinces and cities) and government ministries are charged with formulating sectorial and thematic special plans designed to show in greater detail how the broad goals set out in the Outline FYP are to be achieved. In the second, facilitating documents are made available, to help implement and coordinate policy. These are supplemented, in the final phase, by the release of very specific 'work programmes' and 'implementive programmes' to local officials. By the time that these have been issued, the FYP will probably have already reached its mid-point and be approaching the mid-term evaluation.

## The Eleventh Five-Year Programme of Economic and Social Development

At the heart of the 11FYP was the aim to create a 'harmonious society' (*hexie shehui*), and a more sustainable pattern of economic and social development – an ethos that also informed the 12FYP. In 2003–4 the Chinese government announced a major shift in its development strategy away from growth maximisation towards sustainability following more than two decades of rapid economic growth. This was in response to the emergence of a number of developmental fault lines, including resource pressures and shortages resulting from the pursuit of high growth; increasing economic polarisation between coastal and inland China and between urban and rural areas; and environmental costs of high growth. The 11FYP's solution was to advocate implementation of a new principle of 'scientific development' in order to create a 'harmonious socialist society'. Implicit in the new approach was a belief that growth was meaningless unless it 'put people first' (*yiren weiben*).

The 11FYP's targets relating to growth and structural change presaged an intended slowing in the rate of expansion of the GDP,[11] as the economy tilted more towards the service sector. Increasing the share of spending on R&D (research and development) in the GDP reflected the government's aspiration to move China up the value-added ladder.

As for social development indicators, maintenance of a *binding* target for population growth reflected a continuing commitment to the ethos of the one-child family policy, and increasing urbanisation underlined the government's conviction that both economic and welfare goals would thereby be served. At the same time, the looked-for major expansion in urban *employment* dictated further large-scale transfers of agricultural workers to the urban sector. Welfare and economics were simultaneously embodied in 11FYP targets in order to enhance educational standards and to expand the reach of social welfare insurance.

It is noteworthy that although most targets relating to human and social development were predictive, government concern about the environmental costs of growth was reflected in the binding status of most environmental targets.

Achievements during the 11FYP included:

- ▷ GDP grew over 11 per cent per annum on average.
- ▷ Urban disposable income growth was almost double the planned figure, while net rural income also increased well in excess of what was planned.
- ▷ Almost 58 million new jobs were created in the urban sector, most of them filled by the 45 million rural residents (overwhelmingly farm workers) who left the countryside.
- ▷ By 2010, almost all rural residents were enrolled in the rural cooperative health system, compared with less than a quarter in 2005 (albeit with enormous variation in the quality of services).
- ▷ The rate of increase in the number of urban residents with basic pension cover was considerably higher than the planned figure.
- ▷ The planned reduction in water use by industry was exceeded by a sizeable margin.
- ▷ Energy consumption per unit of GDP also fell appreciably, basically (if not literally) fulfilling the 20 per cent target.
- ▷ Compared with the 10FYP period (2001–5), during which 6.2 million hectares of arable land were lost, in 2006–10 less than 1 million hectares were lost.
- ▷ The rate of forest cover increased in the above plan (though these figures are difficult to confirm).
- ▷ Government investment in agriculture rose substantially. The agricultural tax and other farm levies were abolished; more subsidies were extended to grain farmers. Grain production rose year on year to reach a record level of 546.5 million tonnes (2010), thereby enabling China to maintain 95 per cent self-sufficiency in cereals.
- ▷ Transportation infrastructure (roads, railways, port facilities) underwent notable expansion.
- ▷ Government spending on education increased, on average, by 22.4 per cent per annum, facilitating the establishment of

a universal free urban and rural compulsory nine-year education system. Free secondary vocational education was also extended to students from low-income urban and poor rural households.

Although few quantitative targets remained unfulfilled at the end of 2010,[12] concealed within the superficially impressive official statistical 11FYP results were serious shortcomings.[13]

▷ Far from slowing, throughout the 11FYP period GDP growth was consistently well above the planned 7.5 per cent rate.
▷ The goal of *economic rebalancing* from investment and net exports as prime drivers of growth to one in which domestic demand (above all, *household* consumption) would assume a much greater role was not fulfilled, and the contribution of consumption to GDP growth *declined* (see Figure 3.1).
▷ *Insufficient progress was made in* achieving more equal regional and sectorial income distribution. For example, in nominal terms, the ratio between urban and rural per capita incomes in 2010 was virtually identical to that of 2005.

Ultimately, the outcome of a FYP overwhelmingly reflects the *internal* dynamics of policy implementation and the effectiveness of China's own implementive mechanisms. These internal dynamics embrace the reality of frequent sharp divergences

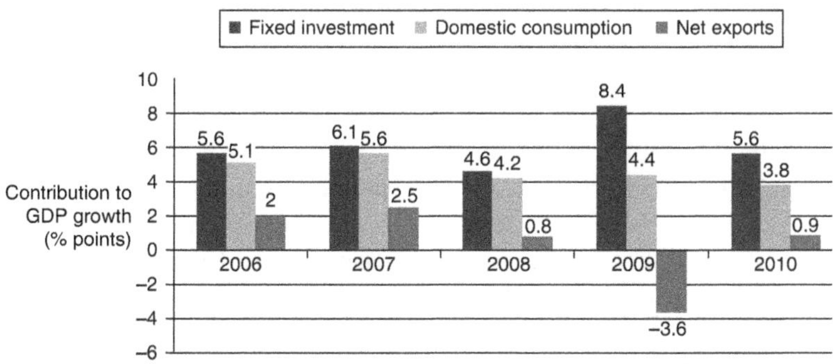


Figure 3.1 **The share of fixed investment, domestic consumption and net exports in GDP growth under the 11FYP**

*Source*: NBS, *Zhongguo tongji zhaiyao*, 2011, p. 37.

between central government's strategic, long-term priorities and the short-term vested interests of local authorities, whether at provincial, prefectural or even township level. The chain of command that worked effectively, even though to the massive detriment of incentives and efficiency, under the old central planning system has long disappeared. Binding orders from the centre can no longer be guaranteed to be carried out by local government officials, many of whom are engaged in corrupt dealings with businessmen and entrepreneurs. The lack of a robust legal framework and the existence of ill-defined property rights further complicate the situation. In short, the Chinese central government faces profound systemic institutional constraints in its efforts to implement its highly rational and potentially effective economic and social policies.

## The Twelfth Five-Year Programme of Economic and Social Development

### The 12FYP: themes, goals and targets

Both the 11FYP and the 12FYP are premised on pursuit of 'scientific development'; both aspire to achieve 'steady, fairly rapid' GDP growth; and both endorse the principle that such growth should translate into higher living standards, the benefits of which should be distributed more equally among the Chinese population. But there are also significant differences in emphasis between the two documents, reflecting the changed context in which the 12FYP has been launched:

- The post-2008 global crisis and its aftermath affected China profoundly. Although trade with the US and Japan (less with the EU) recovered quickly from the downturn in 2009,[14] the potential threat of disruption from future financial instability has underlined the urgency of economic rebalancing as a means to enhance the role of domestic consumption as a driver of growth.
- Another effect of the global crisis was to strengthen the role of fixed investment as a driver of growth as a result of the massive fiscal and monetary stimulus package launched by

China. Many regard that level of investment to have reached an unsustainable level, further strengthening the case for economic rebalancing.

▷ After 2010, China moved closer to the 'Lewis turning point',[15] as the reservoir of underemployed surplus farm workers sharply contracted. The resulting upward pressure on wages promises to stimulate an expansion of domestic demand. It also reinforces the need to shift towards higher value-added activities as China's comparative advantage begins to move towards more capital- and technology-intensive products.

▷ For many years, China benefited from a 'demographic dividend', characterised by a low dependency ratio alongside a high share of potentially productive 15- to 60-year-olds in the population. That era is now ending. China's work force will peak, perhaps as early as 2016. And as people are living longer, caring for the elderly will become a major financial burden at a time when other social insurance demands are also rising sharply.

All these factors are reflected in the new Five-Year Programme, and help to explain some of its major policy thrusts.

The 12FYP is more detailed than the 11FYP, with more chapters, more targets and more prescriptive comments in order to reach a new trajectory of sustainable development, in addition to maintaining 'steady, fairly rapid' growth, with the aim of attaining a 'comfortably well-off' (*xiaokang*) society by 2020. It lists the following core objectives:

▷ to enhance the competitiveness of the manufacturing industry in a restructured economy that gives greater weight to the service sector;

▷ to achieve more balanced urban and rural growth through accelerated urbanisation;

▷ to achieve more balanced development between regions of China;

▷ to raise educational standards and to strengthen the role of science and technology (S&T) in support of economic modernisation;

▷ through job creation, more equal income distribution and the provision of comprehensive social welfare insurance services, to translate economic growth into higher living standards and improved levels of welfare for all urban and rural residents;

- to make better use of resources and to protect the environment through implementation of measures designed to conserve energy, reduce greenhouse gas (GHG) emissions and address problems of climate change; and
- to harmonise population growth and economic development.

The quantitative targets listed in the 12FYP are reproduced in Table 3.1.

Of the 24 targets listed in the 12FYP, only four – two fewer than in the 11FYP – relate explicitly to economic growth and economic structure, although a further four address education, science and technology. By contrast, eight targets relate to resource use and environment, and nine to human and social development. There is greater weight attached to binding targets in the human, social, environmental and resource categories compared with those relating to economic growth and structural change.[16] This signals the government's determination to shift towards a more inclusive, balanced and sustainable growth model.

Important aspects of the new Programme are examined in detail in later sections of this chapter. Here we highlight a few of the key tasks to which the 12FYP addresses itself.

*Energy, environment and climate change*: Energy and environmental issues were a high priority in the 11FYP. The 12FYP reaffirms their importance, but also broadens their scope (especially in the unprecedented attention it gives to climate change).[17] Existing efforts to promote low-carbon technology will be strengthened.[18] Non-fossil fuels are expected to rise sharply in consumption and to account for 11.4 per cent of total energy use by 2015.[19]

*Development of strategic industries*: The 12FYP prioritises the development of seven 'strategic emerging industries', whose economic contribution is planned to quadruple and reach 8 per cent of GDP by 2015.[20] The choice of industries[21] reflects the priorities of the new Programme: collectively they promise to lend support to the fulfilment of China's sustainable development aspirations and to facilitate its ascent of the value chain.

**Table 3.1** Goals and targets of China's 12FYP

| Indicator | Unit | Nature of target | Plan | | |
|---|---|---|---|---|---|
| | | | **2010** | **2015** | **Growth p.a. (%)** |
| **Economic growth and structure** | | | | | |
| GDP | M yuan | Predictive | 3,980 | 5,580 | 7.0 |
| Service sector share in total value-added | % | Predictive | 43.0 | 47.0 | [4.0] |
| Spending on research and experimental development as share of GDP | % | Predictive | 1.75 | 2.20 | [0.45] |
| **Human and social development** | | | | | |
| Total population | Million | Binding | 1,341.00 | < 7.2‰ | 1,390.00 |
| Urban share of total population | % | Predictive | 47.5 | 51.5 | [4.0] |
| Number of new urban jobs | Million | Predictive | – | – | [45.0] |
| Registered urban unemployment | % | Predictive | 4.1 | <5.0 | – |
| Average per capita urban disposable income | Yuan | Predictive | 19,109 | >26,810 | >7.0 |
| Average per capita rural net income | Yuan | Predictive | 5,919 | >8,310 | >7.0 |
| Number of urban residents covered by basic pension insurance | Million | Binding | 2.57 | 3.57 | [1.00] |
| Participation rate for urban and rural | Years | Binding | 9.0 | [0.5] | 9.0 |
| residents in basic medical insurance | % | Binding | – | – | [3.0] |
| Average life expectancy | Years | Predictive | 73.5 | 74.5 | [1.0] |

(*continued*)

**Table 3.1** Continued

| Indicator | Unit | Nature of target | Plan | | |
|---|---|---|---|---|---|
| **Science and technology, education** | | | | | |
| Consolidation rate of nine-year compulsory education | % | Binding | 89.7 | 93.0 | [3.3] |
| Gross enrolment rate in senior high school education | % | Predictive | 82.5 | 87.0 | [4.5] |
| Spending on R&D as share of GDP | % | Predictive | 1.75 | 2.20 | [0.45] |
| Patents per 10,000 population | Unit | Predictive | 1.7 | 3.3 | [1.6] |
| **Resources and environment** | | | | | |
| Guaranteed arable area | M. ha. | Binding | 121.2 | 121.2 | [0] |
| Forest cover | | | | | |
| Forest coverage rate | % | Binding | 20.36 | 21.66 | [1.3] |
| Forest stock | Million $m^3$ | Binding | 13,700 | 14,300 | [6.0] |
| Increase in water efficiency coefficient in agricultural irrigation | | Predictive | 0.50 | 0.53 | [0.03] |
| Reduction in water consumption per unit of industrial value-added | % | Binding | – | – | [30.0] |
| Reduction in energy consumption per unit of GDP | % | Binding | – | – | [16.0] |
| Share of non-fossil fuels in total primary energy consumption | % | Binding | 8.3 | 11.4 | [3.1] |
| Rate of decrease in carbon dioxide emissions per unit of GDP | % | Binding | – | – | [17.0] |

| | | | | | |
|---|---|---|---|---|---|
| Reduction in emissions of major pollutants: | | | | | |
| chemical oxygen demand | % | Binding | – | – | [8.0] |
| sulphur dioxide | | | – | – | [8.0] |
| ammonia nitrogen | | | – | – | [10.0] |
| nitrogen oxides | | | – | – | [10.0] |

*Note*: GDP and per capita income estimates, including projected growth rates, are calculated in terms of 2010 prices. Figures in square brackets show the projected cumulative percentage increase between 2011 and 2015. Participation rates in basic medical insurance refer to basic insurance cover for members of the registered urban work force and non-working urban residents, as well as for rural residents enrolled in the new cooperative health system.

*Source*: CDTD, *Twelfth Five-Year Plan*, pp. 14–16 and *Gangyao*, pp. 10–11.

*Service sector expansion*: In line with efforts to create a more rational economic structure that accommodates China's strategic objectives, the 12FYP calls for the share of services in the GDP to reach 47 per cent in 2015 (in 2005, the corresponding figure was 40.5 per cent). Policy and institutional initiatives designed to facilitate this process include efforts to expand key service industries (financial, business, logistical and high-tech services) and also measures to upgrade the service sector and make it more competitive. Henceforth, the service sector will have first claim on land that is no longer needed for industrial purposes.

*Raising consumption*: At the heart of the 12FYP agenda is a renewed determination to raise the share of consumption in GDP, especially by increasing personal consumption spending by domestic households. It therefore calls for rises in disposable income, large-scale job creation, tax reform, accelerated urbanisation, the provision of more social housing and extended social welfare coverage.

*Pursuit of more inclusive growth*: Allied to efforts to rebalance the economy by raising consumption is a resolve to 'put people first' in order to halt and reverse intersectoral and interregional income and consumption gaps, which have widened since the 1980s. Tax reforms, continued subsidy payments to farmers and investment promotion are intended to help fulfil this core objective.

## China's 12FYP: substance or rhetoric?

Some initial reaction to the 12FYP was sceptical, noting its similarities to the 11FYP, and asking why it should be taken at face value, given the 11FYP's failure to attain a more sustainable development trajectory.[22] However behind the undeniable rhetoric lies serious intent. The change in mindset that has consistently informed the social and economic development strategy of the Hu Jintao-Wen Jiabao administration is a coherent and logical response to the problems arising from the first two decades of reform.[23] Shifting to a new development trajectory is a long-term process. The 12FYP further has stronger sustainability credentials, as evident in its even greater emphasis on the need for economic rebalancing, greater energy efficiency and environmental enhancement. It also owes more to consultation than any previous FYP, and it was reported that some 38 changes were made to the 12FYP[24] following its discussion by NPC delegates, whose final endorsement, as China's legislature, was required in order to translate the Programme into formal policy.

## Implementing the 12FYP: challenges

The biggest challenge is that of implementation and compliance. Implementation is difficult because of the need for reform of government structures, interministerial conflicts of interest and the complex nature of relations between central and provincial levels of government. The fragmented, even dysfunctional, nature of Chinese governance means that the central government has found it difficult to ensure that its policy scope extends to provincial and lower-level governments. For example, there are wide disparities in growth targets between the national and *provincial* levels of government; not one province has listed a planned growth rate of below 8 per cent during the 12FYP period.[25] Resolving these tensions is challenging, and requires a more effective incentive framework to ensure that officials who meet rebalancing targets are rewarded more handsomely than those who merely pursue faster growth.

These considerations are also relevant to an assessment of the role of market forces in driving economic change in China over the next five years. Under the impact of three decades of reforms, the role of market forces has increased substantially. However, one of the effects of the global financial crisis was to reassert the role of centralised and administrative mechanisms in guiding the economy. There seems no reason to suppose that the 12FYP period will see a pronounced extension of market forces. Further market liberalisation would, in fact, probably serve to intensify central-local tensions to the detriment of fulfilling centrally determined economic goals. But those who argue that the reassertion of state authority in the Chinese economy is 'squeezing out' the private sector[26] exaggerate the likely future role of central government. The private sector has been such a potent driver of China's economic growth, and will continue to be,[27] that encroachment on its activities will be limited. For the foreseeable future, therefore, the state will loom large as a shaper of strategy and a source of strategic investment, but economic change will continue to reflect the *combined* impact of market and state-led administrative policy instruments. So much seems clear from statements made by Premier Wen Jiabao in March 2011 in his government report. In this, he insisted that 'sound market forces and effective macro-control are both indispensable parts of the socialist market economy' and called on those responsible for implementing policy to 'closely integrate government control with market forces'.[28] The message implicit in Wen's remarks is that the market will be allowed to guide resource allocation but that administrative fiat and quantitative targets will continue to be used in an attempt to shape growth and the direction of structural change.

## The 12FYP and Economic Rebalancing: The Role of Consumption

At the heart of the 12FYP is an attempt to rebalance the economy by raising the share of consumption – above all, ***household*** consumption – in GDP. Many of the factors alluded to later in this chapter are designed to help fulfil this goal, including increased social insurance cover, employment expansion and higher wages, increased subsidies and raising the share of services in GDP.

### China's consumer revolution[29]

The structure of consumption has changed markedly during three decades of reform. Higher disposable incomes enable consumers to purchase more non-basic items, including consumer durables, electronics and brand-name products. Spending on services in deregulated sectors, such as housing, education, health and transport, has grown quite sharply. These changes have been most evident in cities, although the same broad patterns have begun to emerge in more prosperous parts of the countryside. The greatest potential for further expansion in consumer spending lies in newer, high-end products, for example mobile (cell) phones, computers and cars, all of which have already experienced explosive growth in recent years.

However, the benefits of the consumer revolution have not been distributed in an equal or equitable manner. Interregional, intraregional and sectorial income and consumption gaps have steadily widened, and an objective of the 12FYP is to address the reality that alongside the emergence of a sizeable Chinese middle class, there still existed a large legacy of consumption poverty in 2011.

In both aggregate and per capita terms, China's consumption spending lags well behind that of major developed countries, such as the US, Japan and Germany. This gap will persist for the foreseeable future, although the speed with which consumption behaviour is changing in China is highlighted in estimates indicating that the size of China's 'consuming middle class' has more than doubled since 2005.

## Consumption in the 12FYP

Increasing domestic consumer spending is one of the major planks of the 12FYP. Recent growth of retail spending, although rapid, has failed to keep pace with that of fixed investment. For example, in the 1990s the share of household consumption in GDP remained quite stable, but between 2000 and 2010 it fell by well over 10 percentage points, from 46.4 per cent to 33.8 per cent.[30]

The 12FYP calls for at least 7 per cent annual growth in both urban and rural per capita incomes (see Table 3.1), and the intention to increase households' consumption share of GDP is enunciated[31] thus:

> [We] will create a long-term effective mechanism for expanding consumer demand. Expanding [household] consumer demand will be the strategic focus of expanding domestic demand. We will strengthen the purchasing power of residents, raise their consumption expectations, promote upgrading of the structure of consumption, further release the consumption potential of urban and rural residents, and gradually make the overall scale of our country's domestic market one of the largest in the world by actively yet prudently carrying out urbanisation, implementing the strategy of making employment a top priority, deepening reform of the income distribution system, improving the social security system and creating a favourable consumption environment.[32]

Large-scale urban job creation, increases in per capita income and wages and the extension of social welfare insurance cover all promises, directly or indirectly, to facilitate higher household spending. The potential impact of the planned extension of health and pension coverage lies mainly in its ability to enable households to divert some of their savings towards consumption,[33] and measures to boost funding for public education[34] may have a similar effect. The emphasis on increased provision for rural education highlights the growing importance of the rural sector in stimulating future increases in consumer demand.

In addition, projected tax adjustments will help to stimulate demand. The 12FYP makes reference to the need to adjust the personal income tax threshold 'during the early part of the 12FYP period'.[35] After the publication of the 12FYP, the issue was debated by the National People's Congress Standing Committee, and from 1 September 2011 the threshold below which income tax is not payable was increased from 2,000 yuan per month to 3,500 yuan, and the minimum tax rate for low-income earners (those in receipt of between 3,500 and 4,500 yuan a month) reduced from 5 per cent to 3 per cent.[36] This change in threshold was expected to exempt an addition 60 million people (the equivalent of 19 per cent of the urban work force) from paying tax.

The changing age structure of the population is the most important factor shaping demographic change in the next five years (see 'Demographic Change, the Labour Supply and Employment'), and population ageing will have a definite impact on consumption demand. The potential importance of this is captured in the finding that in 2009, gross demand by China's elderly population was valued at around one trillion yuan, or 8.2 per cent of total household expenditure. It is estimated that this will grow in excess of 4 per cent per annum in the coming decades to reach 5 trillion yuan by 2050.[37] For the time being, the market for the elderly in China remains relatively unexplored, perhaps because in the short run the spending power of most elderly Chinese will be limited. But as economic growth continues and incomes rise, especially in cities and coastal provinces, the value of the greying market will steadily expand.

Nevertheless, demographic projections leave no room for doubt that, for the time being, the age cohort that will drive consumption is those born since 1980. This younger age group will account for more than half of China's population by the end of the 12FYP period.[38] As long as the momentum of buoyant GDP and personal income growth is maintained, their discretionary spending is expected to rise rapidly, not least fuelled by a sharp increase in the use of consumer credit spending and online shopping.[39]

## Demographic Change, the Labour Supply and Employment

Demographic change is important because of its impact not only on China's economic development but also on its social and economic stability. Under the impact of family planning, fertility rates have fallen sharply and China's population growth has fallen, according to official estimates, to a mere 0.5 per cent per annum.

### China's ageing population and the implications for healthcare and pension provision

One of the most serious consequences is the changing age profile of the population. Since 1982, while the share of the population aged 0–14 has halved (from 33.6 to 16.6 per cent), the proportion of the elderly (65 and above) has doubled, from 4.9 to 8.9 per cent.[40] The number of over-65s has risen from less than 50 million in the early 1980s to almost 120 million in 2010. The November 2010 national census showed that there were 178 million people above the age of 60 in China.[41] Projections suggest that by 2050 the number of over-65s will have reached well over 300 million, with the elderly accounting for about one-fifth of the total population. However, the text of the 12FYP only contains one short chapter, which speaks, in very general terms, of the need to 'keep the total population within bounds [the 2015 target is set at a maximum of 1.39 billion], improve the quality of the population, optimise the population structure, and promote the long-term balanced development of the population'.[42]

Within this framework, the Programme prioritises several aspects of population work, including strengthening family planning services, promoting the 'overall' development of women, enhancing the well-being of children and providing more effectively for the needs of the disabled. It also includes a section on the need to address the implications of an ageing population, although this is disappointingly short on detail.

The financial burden of meeting the government's long-term goal of providing a universally affordable healthcare system will become increasingly onerous as the demands of ageing make themselves felt.[43] Even if the social welfare insurance contributions of employers and individuals increase, the budgets of both central and local governments in China will come under severe pressure. This is explicitly acknowledged in the 12FYP through the following commitments:[44]

- ▷ to increase the number of urban and rural residents enrolled in the basic medical insurance scheme by 60 million;
- ▷ to continue to increase the level of financial subsidies in support of the basic medical insurance and new rural cooperative medical schemes and to raise the level of payment for policy holders covered by the basic medical scheme to 70 per cent;
- ▷ on a nationwide basis, to make plans for the implementation of a basic pension fund for all urban employees and to increase the number of urban residents enrolled in the basic pension scheme by 100 million;
- ▷ to increase the basic pension fund and to ensure that unemployed urban residents above the age of 60 receive basic pension remuneration; and
- ▷ to implement universal coverage under the new rural cooperative pension scheme and to increase the level of the basic pension.

Increased dialogue between relevant Chinese and EU parties promises to help facilitate anticipated major advances in the provision of healthcare services in China during the 12FYP period. There may be potential for involvement by European companies: for example, the opening up of the healthcare sector will offer opportunities for European pharmaceutical producers, hospital operators and care home providers. However, there will be competition from domestic Chinese producers, especially as increased investment, improved government support and mergers and acquisitions activities help to bring about the consolidation of domestic healthcare provision and its transformation into a more efficient sector. More widely, there is scope for deeper exchanges on related issues, such as pension provision, as China's demographic structure moves closer to that of Europe.

## Employment and wages

The challenge of accommodating accelerated population ageing is heightened by its occurrence at precisely the time when China's work force will be contracting. Between 2000 and 2010, the working-age population[45] grew by 1.2 per cent per annum, compared with 3 per cent for the elderly. Projections suggest that the working-age population could peak by the beginning of the next (13th) FYP period (2016–20). Thereafter, it will decline at an accelerating rate, and by 2050 may have fallen to around 860 million – 14 per cent less than in 2010.

Employment expansion[46] and wage increases are expected to make a key contribution towards enhancing the role of consumption as a driver of economic growth. Central to efforts to generate higher employment is the expansion of small-scale labour-intensive and service activities; tertiary sector activities create about one-third more jobs per unit of GDP than does manufacturing.[47] Raising the share of services in GDP was one of the few targets left unfulfilled under the 11FYP, and one of the predictive goals set in the 12FYP is that the tertiary sector's share in GDP should increase from 43 to 47 per cent (see Table 3.1, above).[48] Job creation will mainly be in transport and wholesale and retail trade, hotels, restaurants, leisure and healthcare. This too could create opportunities for European and other foreign investors.

The 12FYP also calls for significant growth in wages in the coming five years, contributing to the establishment of a 'harmonious' society. The Programme calls for the minimum wage to be raised by at least 13 per cent per annum during 2011–15, and stipulates that the minimum wage in any area should be at least 40 per cent of the average local wage of urban employees.[49]

Another 12FYP target is that 40 million agricultural workers should be transferred to the urban sector during the five-year period. Given the wide gap between urban and rural incomes,[50] fulfilment of this target should increase the total wage bill.

12FYP policies to raise farm incomes include enhancement of price protection measures for farm (especially grain) producers; provision of better skills training and information services for farmers; ensuring that farmers receive a 'reasonable share' of revenue from the processing and distribution of agricultural products; and even making use of 'agricultural landscape resources to develop rural service industries such as sightseeing, leisure and tourism'.[51] The Programme also commits the government to continuing direct subsidy payments for grain producers and to extending subsidies in support of farmers' purchases of seeds and agricultural machinery.

## The Regional Perspective: The 12FYP and China's Changing Economic Geography

### Regional policy: themes and guidelines

The strong coastal bias of China's recent growth trajectory has been shaped by the historical legacy of a more developed physical, economic and social infrastructure in a number of coastal regions and the relative ease with which, once China decided to open up to the outside world, coastal provinces could integrate with regional and global economies. When reforms took hold in the 1980s, this both encouraged and facilitated a high degree of concentration of investment, including FDI, in these regions, and favoured the emergence of three core regional growth hubs, centred on the Yangtze and the Pearl River deltas and the Bohai Gulf region. However this came at the expense of widening inter-regional income disparities, leading the previous Hu Jintao-Wen Jiabao administration to emphasise the attainment of a more balanced regional pattern of development.[52]

The 12FYP[53] reiterates the need to achieve more coordinated development between the various geographical regions of China, with three main themes:

- ▷ to promote development that is appropriate to the resource endowment and economic conditions of each region in order to help reduce development gaps between and within regions, as well as between urban and rural sectors;
- ▷ to make the most rational and effective use of limited land resources, especially in support of fulfilling agricultural and environmental goals; and
- ▷ to continue to promote urbanisation.

The framework in which the regional development plans are set is that of the four familiar 'mega-regions': eastern, northeastern, central and western China. Continuity of policy is evident in the priorities: to promote a new round (post-July 2010) in the policy of 'Opening Up the West' as the highest priority; to stimulate development in the northeast and the 'old industrial base areas'; to promote the rapid rise of the central regions; to support the leading development role of the eastern regions; to strengthen support for the 'old revolutionary, ethnic minority, border and poverty-stricken' areas of the country.[54]

Major policy instruments include increased investment in hard and soft infrastructure – most notably, in transport and education – implementation of more effective land-use policies, use of the tax system (for example, reducing corporate income tax[55]), and improving the investment environment. Elsewhere,[56] the Programme also highlights the need to improve 'opening up' policies in three geographical regions – coastal regions (which remain the priority), inland regions and inland border regions – but to adapt related policies to the particular characteristics of each. This includes encouraging the coastal regions to move up the value chain, attracting manufacturing investment and trade processing to central China, and opening up the western regions to China's western land neighbours.[57]

## Urbanisation

The 12FYP also calls for 'healthy' urbanisation.[58] Urbanisation in China has assumed its own indigenous characteristics, such as the simultaneous emergence of cities of enormous size – note especially the spectacular growth of cities such as Dongguan, Foshan, Zhongshan and Shenzhen in the Pearl River Delta region of Guangdong province – and of much smaller but often rapidly expanding cities. This pattern offers a distinctive and, in some ways, challenging context in which to promote continued urbanisation.

The Programme highlights, in particular, the benefits of urban *clusters* that can serve as nodes from which economic activity can develop. It is also sets out a vision of creating major vertical (north–south) and horizontal (east–west) transport arteries that will link the main urban clusters throughout the country.

The 12FYP leaves no room for doubt that as urbanisation proceeds, it is the cities in the eastern coastal belt that will be expected most strongly to strengthen their global competitiveness, and be the locations in which most of the economic upgrading anticipated under the Programme as a result of rising consumption and the expanding services trade will take place. Official reports make it clear that the urban clusters in the Yangtze and Pearl River deltas and Bohai Bay will remain the driving forces of China's future modernisation and continuing integration into the global economy (these three coastal metropolitan areas already account for almost 40 per cent of national GDP).

By contrast, ambitions on behalf of cities in central and western China, their scale depending on local conditions, are more modest, though in inland China certain growth areas stand out. These include the Chengdu–Chongqing belt, areas around Wuhan, Changsha (the Chang–Zhu–Tan 'city belt') and Xi'an, and the Beibu Gulf (Gulf of Tonkin) on the coast of Guangxi. The Programme also highlights areas that are the focus of poverty alleviation efforts and that pose serious development challenges, such as southern Xinjiang, western Yunnan and eastern stretches of the Qinghai–Tibet Plateau.

## Implications

Under the impact of faster GDP growth in central and western China,[59] we expect that a further rebalancing of the Chinese economy will take place. For the EU, this will offer new opportunities for commercial, economic and cultural engagement in regions that have previously not enjoyed significant interaction with Europe. In particular, it promises to extend quite significantly the markets for European industrial products and consumer goods, especially as more cities throughout China support a sizeable number of middle-class and affluent consumer (MAC) households.[60] Further, in contrast to coastal regional markets that are becoming saturated and experiencing increasingly strong competition from Chinese corporates, it will also create opportunities for investment – especially investment targeted at the domestic market – in areas where preferential treatment is still available. Such activities will enjoy active encouragement from China's Ministry of Commerce (MOFCOM).

The emphasis on urbanisation in the 12FYP opens up commercial opportunities generated by urban expansion and higher incomes, and scope for intensified policy dialogue on the common challenges of urban living, such as water and air quality, transport infrastructure, environmental protection and the development of cultural industries.

## The 12FYP and International Relations, with Particular Reference to the EU

The principal message with respect to international relations is encapsulated in the heading of Section 12 of the 12FYP: 'Create a Win-win Situation: Raise the Level of Opening Up'.[61] The primary mechanism for global economic governance envisaged in the 12FYP is the G20. Because this gives China a more prominent role than in the G8 framework and because in the G20 China stands *alongside* other large countries rather than in front of them, the arrangement accommodates China's policy rhetoric of 'equality' (or 'democracy') in international affairs.[62] The use of the word 'positively' to describe China's participation in economic governance points to a more active role for China at a time when its foreign policy elite is becoming more aware of growing expectations vis-à-vis China throughout the world and suggests that more proactive approaches by Chinese policymakers will gradually emerge. Chinese leaders have stressed their intention to behave responsibly and to promote global financial and economic stability.[63] Nonetheless, there is an element of gradual revisionism to the policy outlook,[64] most evident in references to promoting reform of the international economic system in order to make it more 'just and rational'.

In discussion of regional cooperation the emphasis is on the potential benefits of the further development of regional free trade arrangements. The particular priority focus here is China's relations with its immediate neighbours in East and Southeast Asia, these being the only regions mentioned by name in this part of the 12FYP. The inference appears to be that, by contrast, Europe is not such a high priority for Beijing. China remains officially supportive of the Doha Round,[65] although this is not mentioned in the 12FYP.

More widely, at the macro-level of a diplomatic and trade policy that increasingly has global reach, the 12FYP suggests that the Chinese government will seek to look at the world in terms of *regions* (Europe, Africa, the Middle East, etc.), but again with a priority focus on neighbouring areas. This, in turn, suggests that Europe will more and more be viewed from Beijing as just one of a number of regions of the world with which China deals, rather than be accorded the priority it might have enjoyed in, say, the 1990s, when a major goal of Chinese policy was to attract FDI from developed countries and to prepare for admission to the WTO.[66]As China's relative economic and political weight in the world continues to rise and it takes a gradually more proactive Chinese approach to the global economy and other global affairs, Europe's ability to set the agenda will decline, underlining the need for proactive dialogue with China on issues of global economic governance.

## The 12FYP: Commercial Opportunities, with Specific Reference to the EU

China and the EU have a close commercial relationship. China is the EU's second-largest trading partner after the US; the EU has become China's largest trading partner. In 2010, the value of bilateral merchandise trade was €395 billion (almost one-third more than in 2009). The value of Chinese exports to the EU was €281.9 billion (31 per cent above the 2009 level); that of Chinese imports was €113.1 billion (a rise of 38 per cent).[67] The EU was also the largest source of FDI in China, accounting for €5.3 billion in 2009.[68]

Opportunities for European companies, as highlighted by Chinese officials, should come from:[69]

- ▷ increased consumption spending by Chinese households;
- ▷ greater spending on social insurance programmes;
- ▷ raised share of services in GDP;
- ▷ Chinese efforts to upgrade the technological base of the Chinese economy and to expand its hi-tech sector;
- ▷ prioritisation of clean energy and 'green' growth, especially in the provision of low-carbon technologies, in which Europe is a world leader. There seems little doubt that China is set to become the largest market for environmental products in the world.

Changes are likely to be more evolutionary than radical, and the rest of this section analyses the commercial implications from structural, geographical and sectorial perspectives. *Structural* changes take as their starting point Chinese trade and investment policies and China's emergence as an increasingly powerful player in the global economy. *Geographical* changes refer to the impact of shifts in China's economic geography (outlined in 'The Regional Perspective: the 12FYP and China's Changing Economic Geography' of this chapter). The *sectorial* analysis identifies changing commercial opportunities and challenges in some of the major business sectors.[70]

## Structural shifts: policy environment

Structural changes arising from China's growing size and economic clout are changing the rules of the commercial game. China is no longer viewed primarily as an export base, but as a growing domestic market, albeit in a context in which it remains an integral part of global supply chains.[71] Separately, China's policy approach is moving from reactive responses to developments in OECD economies to a more proactive role in driving global economic policy and economic growth.

Reflecting these themes, the 12FYP[72] describes China's approach to foreign trade and investment (both inward and outward) and sets out the government's views on global economic governance and regional cooperation. It strongly advocates openness,[73] motivated by its role in helping to promote development, reform and innovation within China, and its criticism of protectionism. The 12FYP seeks to promote a 'new trend' that will enable China to shift from its previous principal status as a source of exports and FDI inflows to one in which inward FDI and outward OFDI more closely complement each other, and in which exports and imports are more closely in balance. This, in turn, implies changes in the nature and structure of exports, alongside more rapid import growth. Most significant of all is the strong encouragement given to increasing China's outward investment.[74]

Future export policy will focus on maintaining existing competitive strengths while nurturing new ('core competitive') strengths in technology, branding, quality and services. Specific goals include raising the quality and value-added of labour-intensive exports, expanding exports of electronics and high-technology products and 'strictly controlling' exports of energy and resource-intensive and polluting products. Export processing will be highly concentrated in special customs zones. Chinese enterprises are also encouraged to establish overseas sales networks and more actively to explore overseas markets.

On imports, there is specific reference to the proactive expansion of technology, parts and components (items that are key to fulfilling China's aspirations to upgrade its economy); resources that are in scarce supply in China; resource-saving and environmentally efficient products; and products that help to expand domestic consumption, rebalance the economy and/or improve the trade balance.

This menu creates opportunities for EU exporters, especially in consumer products (including, but not limited to, luxury goods) and 'green' exports. Another area of particular relevance to the EU is the 12FYP's intention to develop trade in services so as to help upgrade the economy and increase the service sector's share of GDP. Exports are to be expanded from traditional sectors – tourism and transport – to new products, such as culture, Chinese medicine, software and communications services, business services, finance and insurance. Efforts will also be made to attract service outsourcing and to 'open up' education, health and sports.

However, the plan to diversify foreign trade and to increase exports to emerging markets is likely to be less favourable to the EU, although this is understandable in the wake of the recent global crisis. In fact, the diversification of China's foreign economic relations has already been under way for some years. For example, between 2000 and 2010, Europe's share of FDI inflows to China almost halved, from 9.6 per cent to 5.3 per cent, indicating that from a Chinese perspective, the relative importance of European investment is declining.

In terms of FDI inflows, the 12FYP emphasises investment that will enable China to fulfil the goal of developing a more efficient and innovative economy, namely in high technology, cutting-edge manufacturing industries, resource-efficient and environmentally friendly sectors and also modern services, as well as to attract human resources and foreign R&D centres to China.

A reference to resisting 'protectionism' touches on politically sensitive issues not spelt out in the 12FYP, but expressed in European companies' concern about the difficulties of market access and the Chinese government's disquiet in the face of the EU's continued unwillingness to designate China a 'market economy'. It is unlikely that the 12FYP itself will markedly affect the extent to which trade tension is (or is not) reduced in the coming five years. However, the Programme's commitment to oppose protectionism could be used by the EU as a political tool in support of efforts to increase market access.

EU companies will face challenges including[75] increased competition from domestic enterprises in China, which are likely to benefit from advantages – for example, access to capital and subsidies – not available to would-be European investors; procurement policies that favour domestic Chinese firms; encroachment on profit margins associated with higher costs in China (via wage increases, higher prices for raw materials, higher value-added tax and the introduction of new environmental taxes); and difficulties in enforcing the protection of intellectual property rights (see also 'Science, Technology and Innovation').

## Geographical changes

Since 2007, GDP growth in central, western and northeastern regions of China has been faster than in the more affluent and highly developed eastern coastal provinces (see 'The Regional Perspective: The 12FYP and China's Changing Economic Geography'). This points to increasing commercial opportunities for foreign companies in inland China and in cities that previously offered fewer opportunities. At the same time, the *relative* importance of the three major coastal clusters (around Beijing, Shanghai and Guangdong/Hong Kong), which have dominated most foreign business activity in China since the 1980s, will diminish – even though they will remain substantial drivers of the national economy. In formulating their business strategies in China, EU companies must anticipate these changes in economic geography. The precise implications of such changes will vary, depending on the sector, the business model and the extent to which a particular company's business activity is integrated into global or regional supply chains or, alternatively, is aimed at domestic markets.

### Sectorial analysis

The commercial implications of expected changes during the 12FYP period will vary across different sectors. On the basis of this chapter's analysis, we identify five policy drivers, each of which has its own sectorial implications: industrial and urban development, innovation, energy efficiency and the environment, domestic consumption, and improved livelihoods and welfare. Their impact on various sectors of the Chinese economy is summarised in Table 3.2, though not all sectors are equally accessible to European investors (the Chinese government indicates the extent of its willingness to accept such involvement by placing sectors in one of four categories in order to show whether foreign investment is 'permitted', 'encouraged', 'restricted' or 'prohibited').[76]

## Education

### Headline content

Major educational objectives under the 12FYP are: comprehensive development of education at all levels; promotion of 'equality' in education; promotion of 'well-rounded' education, including physical and moral education; and intensified reform of the educational system.[77] Stated targets include raising gross enrolment in pre-school and secondary school education to 85 and 87 per cent, respectively; and increasing government spending on education to 4 per cent of GDP by 2012. Efforts will also be made to make nine-year compulsory education universal and to strengthen vocational education, especially in order to meet the needs of agriculture.

The 12FYP also commits itself to improving the quality of higher education[78] and to increasing the pace of development of 'world-class' and 'high-quality' universities, namely Chinese universities capable of competing on the highest level with those outside China. In promoting the university sector, the Programme emphasises 'key disciplines', notably those in S&T. Elsewhere in the Programme, reference is also made to the priority need for universities to produce specialists in order

**Table 3.2** Overview of sectorial implications of the 12FYP

| Policy driver (12FYP) | Sectorial targets and economic implications |
|---|---|
| Industrial and urban development | • Urbanisation, city planning, urban transport<br>• Infrastructure development (including water treatment)<br>• Transport and logistics<br>• Agriculture: irrigation, food safety |
| Innovation | • Technology (especially that which enhances the competitiveness of Chinese industry)<br>• Education, training and human resource development<br>• Research and development |
| Energy efficiency and the environment | • The seven 'strategic emerging industries': new-generation IT, energy efficient/ environmentally friendly, alternative energy, biotech, high-end manufacturing, new materials and alternative energy automotives<br>• Energy-saving and environmentally friendly businesses, including low-carbon technologies or models, and more efficient use of traditional forms of energy<br>• Pollution reduction (nitrates, sulphates, etc.)<br>• Negative impact on inefficient and environmentally degrading industries |
| Domestic consumption | • Service industries: finance, modern logistics, hi-tech and business services<br>• Tourism, sports, education and human resources<br>• Retail and consumer goods<br>• Cultural industries |
| Livelihoods and welfare | • Public services, especially healthcare-related industries<br>• Public housing<br>• Pension and welfare management<br>• Rural livelihoods, including financial services |

*Source*: Authors' Own.

to overcome 'critical shortages' of personnel in crucial areas such as biotechnology, new materials, aeronautics and astronautics, international business, energy and resources, equipment manufacturing and agricultural science and technology. Other designated priority disciplinary focuses include education, culture, law, pharmacology, health and social work.[79]

## China's educational policies: risks and challenges

Since the 1950s, literacy rates in China have risen dramatically, along with the proportion of children attending schools. Increasing numbers of students have participated in overseas undergraduate and, especially, postgraduate training. Between 1978 and 2010, the number of students enrolled in overseas postgraduate courses increased from 10,934 to 1.54 million, new enrolments rising from 10,708 to more than 538,000.[80] Young Chinese regard high-quality education as one of the most important prizes available to them, benefiting them and also their children. In the importance it attaches to extending educational opportunities, the 12FYP implicitly recognises the dangers if educational opportunities are perceived to be unequally distributed, especially in rural areas.

There is increasing excess demand for university places among young people, and it will become more and more difficult to accommodate students at the university of their choice, jeopardising China's commitment to quality assurance in higher education.

Whereas a decade ago a foreign university degree was something to which only the brightest students could aspire, there is now a widespread feeling that only those who lack the qualifications to be admitted to a top Chinese university seek to study overseas. The irresponsible attitude of some foreign universities, which have admitted large cohorts of Chinese students without sufficient regard for their quality, has helped to reinforce this perception. This issue could disrupt relations between European and Chinese universities. Nor can it be said that one alternative adopted by several European universities, that of setting up a branch campus in China, is the answer (some universities that have followed this course have experienced difficulties). It is possible that the influx of undergraduate students coming to universities in EU Member States from China has peaked.

## Implications for the EU

Education features prominently in the *EU 2020* economic and social goals. The EU and China share a number of concerns in formulating an educational policy that seeks to facilitate the establishment of an 'innovative country' (China 12FYP) or an 'innovation union' (*EU 2020*). The goals of inclusivity, improved quality, the creation of a skills base in science and technology and the enhancement of entrepreneurship are all elements that the two sides have in common. On the basis of initiatives that are already under way, there is much scope for dialogue and exchanges on governance issues in education.

There is great scope too for recruitment of Chinese postgraduate students by EU Member State universities – above all, in all areas of S&T, business studies, international relations and in niche areas such as environmental studies. But although there is strong interest among Chinese students in applying to EU universities' Master's and PhD programmes, it has been much more difficult to persuade European students to study in China. Language and cultural issues, a lack of familiarity with China's university system and the attitudes of potential European employers to the value of Chinese postgraduate university degrees have all played a part in this.

The next section of this chapter addresses research exchange and collaboration between individuals and institutions in China and the EU.

## Science, Technology and Innovation

### Headline content

The 12FYP's broad goal is to upgrade China's capabilities in indigenous research and innovation in S&T and to speed up the construction of an 'innovative country'.[81] To this end, China's investment in R&D is intended to increase from 1.8 per cent to 2.2 per cent of GDP between 2010 and 2015. This follows China's 'Medium to Long-Term Plan for Science and Technology' for 2006 to 2020, published in 2006. The Programme draws particular attention to the need to upgrade the innovation capabilities of enterprises, and encourages 'leapfrog advances in key areas', affirming the state's determination to continue to play a leading role in guiding and shaping the evolution of the innovative economy.

The 12FYP material covers:

- *Promoting major breakthroughs in science and technology*: It reaffirms the dual commitment to basic research and 'frontier technology' and calls for 'top-ranking achievements', especially in the physical sciences, life sciences, space science, earth sciences and nanoscience and technology. The need to link advancements in science and technology with the upgrading of industry is explicitly stated.
- *Speeding up the establishment of a technological innovation system, with enterprises as the key players*: The goal is 'an enterprise-centred, market-oriented and industry-education-research integrated technology innovation system' with enterprises as the main players in R&D input. Strategies include enhancing the S&T support provided by government to enterprises; encouraging large-scale enterprises to invest in R&D; increasing the motivation of research institutes and universities to carry out innovation; and setting up strategic innovation alliances among enterprises, research institutes and universities. A programme will also be instituted specifically to assist SMEs with innovation.
- *Strengthening the construction of science and technology infrastructure*: The Chinese government seeks to reinforce and develop its existing S&T infrastructure, with a view to enhancing capacities for innovation. The intention is to build on existing platforms for basic, 'frontier' and generic research in science and technology, to support the creation of technology-service platforms directed at enterprises and to establish technology centres within enterprises. The government has committed itself to building new national science centres and State Key Laboratories in core disciplines and strategic high-tech fields and also national engineering laboratories in key areas of industrial technology. Such developments should complement one another, and the principles of open access and sharing, and efficient utilisation, will be observed.
- *Strengthening policies to support science and technology innovation*: Here the emphasis is on strengthening financial and fiscal policies designed to support innovation in enterprises and on the industrialisation of research results. Such policies include tax incentives to support technological progress (for

example, an additional deduction for R&D spending by enterprises) and improvement in the evaluation and reward system for S&T results. They also include a range of commitments on intellectual property management: improvement in IPR laws and regulations, stricter enforcement and protection, the establishment of a technology property rights exchange and the promotion of technological standards in conjunction with IPR.

## Policy implementation

Looked-for breakthroughs in particular areas of science will be achieved through the provision of additional state funding through existing channels: money from the so-called '863' (National High-tech Research and Development Programme) and '973' (Key Basic Research Programme) programmes and other sources, distributed by the Ministry of Science and Technology (MOST), the Chinese Academy of Sciences (CAS) and the Natural Science Foundation of China (NSFC). These funds will be allocated to targeted projects in areas of research deemed important by the three bodies in discussion with the government.

Central to setting up a 'technology innovation system' with enterprises as the key players is likely to be the response of research institutions and individuals not now directly tied to industry to much more routine collaboration through strategic innovation alliances. Precisely how these alliances will work in practice remains to be seen. Achieving them is the desired outcome within the organisational scope of central government, although the programme to assist SMEs will require local knowledge and input, and may be devolved to local administrations.

In addition to removing roadblocks and anomalies in the existing system, strengthening S&T infrastructure will primarily require the establishment of 'technology centres' in suitable enterprises – both state-owned and private – and technology 'service platforms' aimed at enterprises. The principles of 'sharing', 'open access' and 'efficient utilisation' of technology suggest an intellectual property culture that may be inimical to Western practice, but is entirely consistent and rational in a context in which the State continues to play a key economic role.

The fourth goal focuses on financial and fiscal policies to support innovation in enterprises and the commercialisation of research. Introducing tax deductions for money spent by enterprises on R&D smacks of a market-based approach, but the proposal to evaluate and reward enterprises for S&T achievements is strongly reminiscent of former command economy practices. Success in tightening and enforcing legislation to protect intellectual property will ultimately depend on the effectiveness of the law courts.

The Chinese government faces risks and challenges in its efforts to formulate and implement policy for STI. Some of them derive from existing structures and inherited S&T issues; others arise from the 12FYP's new emphasis on 'innovation' and on 'enterprises' as the agents of R&D.

- ▷ Established structures are not sufficiently flexible, and there is a degree of tension between relevant bodies about the boundaries of their respective areas of responsibility.
- ▷ Postgraduate researchers who travel abroad do not always return to China, despite appeals to their patriotism and financial and other inducements; and at home, highly qualified young people frequently change jobs.
- ▷ Unresolved issues of intellectual property, and the copying of patents and the theft of intellectual property are still major concerns. The policy of 'indigenous innovation' may protect 'home-grown champions' and undermine rights of (foreign) IP developers,[82] though the increasingly common practice of well-established *Chinese* state-owned and private enterprises defending their intellectual property vigorously in the courts may presage a change in IP culture.
- ▷ Because of the way in which China's private sector has expanded during the past two decades, it is difficult to see how enterprises will be at the heart of the new 'innovation' agenda. China's entrepreneurial genius has been geared to the mass production of relatively low-technology consumer goods made to suit foreign tastes and using cheap labour. Turnover is rapid, profits come quickly and entrepreneurial skills have focused on merchandising and marketing, not on science, high technology or engineering. Except perhaps in ICT, there are almost no *privately owned* Chinese companies that routinely engage in high-tech in-house research.

▷ Nor does the 12FYP make provision for an effective market-based mechanism likely to encourage the private sector to change its ways. The tax deduction for expenditure by enterprises on R&D may help enterprises (mainly SOEs) already engaged in significant R&D activity. But it offers little to those whose activities do not require high technology or use technologies that can be more cheaply or more readily secured abroad through licence, joint venture or outright purchase.

China's attempt to achieve technological 'catch-up' is a very recent initiative and has coincided with a global revolution in information and communications technology, as well as in transport, both of which have benefited China, largely on the basis of low-tech exports manufactured with cheap labour. The Chinese government may decide that moving up the technology ladder is too important to leave its realisation to the market, especially if, as seems likely, it seeks ultimately to retain the capacity *in extremis* to act self-sufficiently. In short it is likely that the State and the Chinese Communist Party will continue to direct research and development for the foreseeable future. 'Innovation' should therefore be understood as relating to production goals broadly set by the State rather than to 'commercialisation', as in the West.

## Implications for the EU: STI in the 12FYP and in EU 2020

In science and technology, as in other areas of activity, the EU faces a conceptual problem in its efforts to promote itself in China. For some interlocutors, the fact that each Member State within the EU has its own approach to science, technology and innovation is a source of confusion. This apparent disadvantage could be turned into an advantage through the use of a phrase, such as 'shared values, diverse approaches', that emphasises the multiplicity of solutions the EU has to offer to problems that, as the Chinese themselves see, are pressing issues for both sides. There are a number of points relating to STI that the Europe 2020 Strategy and China's 12FYP have in common.

Linking academic research in S&T more directly to the needs of commercialisation is at the heart of the strategy to achieve 'smart growth'. *EU 2020* seeks to enhance the R&D environment and to raise combined public and private investment in R&D to 3 per cent of EU GDP by 2020. It also seeks to create an 'Innovation Union' as one of the seven 'flagship initiatives' of the Programme.

Among the 'action points' identified by the EC are:

- ▷ completing the European Research Area (ERA) to deliver the S&T research that necessarily precedes innovation, in order to promote common approaches to quality assurance, the mobility of researchers and the cross-border operation of funding agencies;
- ▷ focusing EU funding instruments on 'Innovation Union' priorities, thereby reinforcing industry-driven priorities;
- ▷ promoting the European Institute of Innovation and Technology as a model of innovation governance in Europe, so as to encourage a stronger role for entrepreneurship; and
- ▷ enhancing access to finance for innovative companies through collaboration with the European Investment Bank, national bodies and private capital.

Another *EU 2020* proposal is that 'Innovation Partnerships' should be set up to address specific challenges shared across the EU and 'where there is a large new market potential for EU businesses'. EU companies will increasingly confront Chinese high-tech enterprises head on in their efforts to develop projects requiring substantial investment, and China has national goals to secure strategic technologies, and to fill gaps. There is therefore benefit in a concerted approach by EU Member States to undertake projects jointly *with* China rather than in opposition to it, whether in research or in the commercialisation of technology. The International Thermonuclear Experimental Reactor (ITER) fusion reactor programme, a project involving both research and manufacture at a very high level of technology, is one very successful example of EU-China collaboration.

Recent significant progress towards facilitating closer collaboration between the two sides has focused mainly on the S&T prerequisites to the later stage of 'innovation/commercialisation'. Important positive developments include the publication in 2009 of a paper on 'China-Europe Research Collaboration as a Strategic Policy Priority',[83] as well as the establishment in 2010 of the ERA's Strategic Forum for International S&T Cooperation (SFIC), in which much attention is focused on China. Subsequently, an SFIC task force on 'priority setting' for relations with China was set up, and, after a visit to China by two SFIC experts, a report on ways of furthering S&T cooperation was published.[84]

## Issues of Sustainability: Energy and the Environment

Although China has been criticised for its position on climate change and for the environmental consequences of its remarkable reform-led growth since 1978, concern about the scale of environmental degradation and pressure on scarce resources, including energy, was a consistent theme of the Hu Jintao-Wen Jiabao administration. In recent years, the threat posed by climate change has been recognised. In 2008 the former State Environmental Protection Administration was upgraded to full ministerial status under the name of the Ministry of Environmental Protection (MEP) and the State Council issued China's first 'White Paper on Climate Change'. Meanwhile, research on sources of alternative energy has been intensified; and even though China has not subscribed to international emission reduction targets, it has set its own targets for the reduction in carbon intensity in energy use.

The 12FYP includes 10 chapters that address related issues,[85] which fall into two main categories: energy and the environment. Its advocacy of development sustainability is stronger than in any previous FYP:

> We will uphold the development of a resource-conserving and environmentally friendly society ... while accelerating the transformation of our pattern of economic development. We will ... implement ... the policy of conserving resources and protecting the environment, conserve energy, reduce greenhouse gas emissions, develop a circular economy, popularise low-carbon technology, actively respond to climate change.'[86]

### Energy

#### *Headline content*

The 12FYP sets out a wide range of energy initiatives, all of which offer opportunities for collaboration between China and the EU. The Programme's main thrust is to improve energy efficiency and to promote a low-carbon development strategy:

**Energy efficiency**
- ▷ to promote the use of diversified and clean-energy sources;
- ▷ to optimise the layout of energy development;
- ▷ to strengthen the construction of energy transmission lines;
- ▷ to strengthen energy conservation management; and
- ▷ to enhance and enforce energy conservation standards.

**Low-carbon development strategy**
- ▷ to develop a circular economy and to formulate low-carbon technologies;
- ▷ to implement exemplary projects of carbon dixoide use in the petrochemical industry; and
- ▷ to control greenhouse gas emissions.

**Energy security**
- ▷ to guarantee adequate supplies of energy to meet growth requirements

### *Contextualisation and interpretation*

The energy industry in China was for many years highly fragmented. In 2010, however, a new energy body was established. This was the National Energy Commission (distinct from the National Energy Administration under the NDRC – in effect the NEC's bureaucracy), which is responsible for drafting national energy plans, reviewing energy security and coordinating international cooperation on energy matters. It is still too early to assess the impact of this institutional initiative on the implementation of China's energy policies.

The 12FYP provides for an increasing use of non-fossil fuels, to reach 11.4 per cent of the primary energy mix by 2015 (Table 3.3 has some historical data). Despite the rise in the use of non-fossil fuels, heavy reliance on coal is bound to continue, although efficiency in its use will be enhanced through the application of new clean-coal technology. 'Smart grid' technology will also be developed in order to improve the efficiency and

**Table 3.3** China's energy consumption, 2005–10*

| Energy source | Consumption (million tonnes, standard coal equivalent) | | | | | |
|---|---|---|---|---|---|---|
| | **2005** | **2006** | **2007** | **2008** | **2009** | **2010** |
| Coal | 1,671 (70.8) | 1,839 (71.1) | 1,994 (71.1) | 2,049 (70.3) | 2,159 (70.4) | 2,304 (70.9) |
| Oil | 467 (19.8) | 499 (19.3) | 527 (18.8) | 533 (18.3) | 549 (17.9) | 536 (16.5) |
| Natural gas | 61 (2.6) | 75 (2.9) | 93 (3.3) | 108 (3.7) | 120 (3.9) | 140 (4.3) |
| Hydro, wind and nuclear power | 160 (6.8) | 173 (6.7) | 191 (6.8) | 224 (7.7) | 239 (7.8) | 270 (8.3) |

*Figures in brackets show each sector's share of total energy consumption.

*Source*: *Zhongguo tongji zhaiyao*, 2011, p. 141.

**Table 3.4** Energy consumption targets for 2015

| | **Planned consumption (2015)** | **Planned reduction (2015)** |
|---|---|---|
| Coal | 4,000 m. tonnes | n.a. |
| Oil | 500 m. tonnes | n.a. |
| Natural gas | 250 bn $m^3$ | n.a. |
| Hydro | 284 GW | n.a. |
| Wind power | 90 GW | n.a. |
| Solar power | 10 GW | n.a. |
| Nuclear power | 40 GW | n.a. |
| Grid | 1,470 GW | n.a. |
| Energy intensity per unit of GDP | n.a. | 16% |
| Carbon intensity per unit of GDP | n.a. | 17% |

*Note*: Information provided by the Energy and Climate Change Section, British Embassy, Beijing, from material publicly available.

reliability of China's power transmission systems. China is also developing nuclear power reactors, though after the Fukushima nuclear disaster in Japan, there was a temporary stay on approval of new plants. Table 3.4 has some targets for 2015.

There are three categories of issue around implementation of the 12FYP energy policies:

1. *Energy ministries and organisations*[87]
   Strategic policies decided by the National Energy Commission must be implemented through these organisations, all of which have ministry status.
2. *Energy consumers*
   The industrial sector accounts for about two-thirds of demand and many industrial users are major SOEs. But domestic and commercial users' share of energy consumption is rising rapidly, especially, under the impact of accelerating urbanisation, in major cities. These claimants' activities affect the efficient implementation of central policies that seek to promote energy efficiency and low-carbon solutions, and also pose technical challenges to the distribution of ever larger supplies of power.
3. *Research activities*
   Research into renewable energy sources (wind and solar power, hydropower, biomass, geothermal and wave energy) is carried out by State Key Laboratories and other research units under MOST, the CAS and a series of dedicated new 'national energy and research centres', as well as through international collaborative projects such as the EU-NDRC Clean Energy Research Centre and the BP-Tsinghua Alternative Energy Research Centre, both at Tsinghua University in Beijing. Other projects, many with an international dimension, are exploring carbon capture and storage and other low-carbon solutions still using coal as the primary energy source.

A challenge lies in the vested interests of fossil fuel ministries and organisations in the 'fossil-fuelled growth status quo'. There has been an underlying conflict between 'developmentalists' and 'environmentalists'. The former have advocated growth at any price, while the latter have increasingly warned that the economic and social threat posed by continued growth, based mainly on fossil fuels, could ultimately destabilise the country. The 'environmentalist' view is inherent in 12FYP energy policy proposals.

The low price of coal, the high cost of low-carbon solutions and greater reliance on market mechanisms to fulfil China's energy goals also pose challenges. For many years, the existence of enormous coal reserves kept the price of energy artificially low. But against the background of resource pressures and rail freight bottlenecks, the introduction in recent years of coal imports has made China more susceptible to the vagaries of fluctuations in international market prices.

For this reason, as well as because of growing concern about carbon emissions, experiments have been undertaken in recent years whereby some consumers have had to pay significantly higher prices for coal and other sources of primary energy. For their part, industrial users have been charged a premium for renewable or low-carbon sources of energy in order to help fund further R&D in this area. Such developments demonstrate the Chinese government's willingness to resort to market and other mechanisms in order to help meet its energy policy goals.

### *Implications for the EU*

The *EU 2020* programme features energy and the environment, and contains a strong commitment to 'sustainable growth'. There is clear congruence with the 12FYP and considerable scope for upgrading EU and Member State engagement in this area, as Europe has enormous expertise across a great variety of energy and sustainability technologies. Existing initiatives include joint research into clean coal and other low-carbon solutions, exchanges on wind and wave power, establishing joint laboratories, funding institutes to promote research into all forms of renewable energy, as well as commercial projects of technology transfer and consultancy. In addition, discussions have taken place on governance issues involved in the transition to a low-carbon future.

## Environment

There are also overlaps in terms of environmental policy goals between the EU, its Member States and China, which offer strong collaborative opportunities. Headline themes of the 12FYP are:

**Climate change**
- ▷ to control greenhouse gas emissions;
- ▷ to enhance China's capacity to adapt to climate change; and
- ▷ to engage in international cooperation on climate change.

**Creation of a 'green' economy**

- ▷ to develop a circular economy, based on 'cyclic' production and resource recycling;
- ▷ to promote 'green' consumption; and
- ▷ to strengthen the policy framework and technological support for environmental affairs.

**Environmental pricing policy**

- ▷ to rationalise resource pricing;
- ▷ to reform environmental protection charges; and
- ▷ to introduce market mechanisms in support of trading resources and environmental property rights.

**Other environmental aspects**

- ▷ to reduce pollution emissions;
- ▷ to protect against environmental risks;
- ▷ to strengthen environmental monitoring and supervision; and
- ▷ to enhance environmental governance.

**Ecology**

- ▷ to put in place ecological safety barriers;
- ▷ to strengthen ecological protection and governance; and
- ▷ to establish an ecological compensation mechanism.

**Water conservancy and disaster prevention**

- ▷ to increase water supplies through water diversion and other construction projects;
- ▷ to enhance flood control capacity; and
- ▷ to strengthen the prevention and control of natural disasters.

### *Contextualisation and interpretation*

On climate change, commitment to reduce GHG emissions and energy intensity has potential implications across all areas of productive activity. To bring about the profound changes outlined in the 12FYP will require the nurturing of a consensus among all parties involved in implementing the new policies. Similarly, the 12FYP's 'green' economy goal of extensive recycling of materials and what in the West would be described as a 'cradle-to-cradle' approach to production[88] will be fulfilled only through a cooperative approach involving many ministries and other organisations, both government and private.

Successful implementation of 12FYP measures designed to address other environmental problems – for example, pollution, resource conservation, the incidence of natural disasters, ecological preservation and the loss of bio-diversity – will require unprecedented commitment by those responsible for governance in those areas and the establishment of an appropriate regulatory framework and implementation of capacity-building across sectors and government departments. The 12FYP's reference to market mechanisms notwithstanding, the role of central and local government in encouraging and facilitating the pursuit of a 'green' economy is likely to be significant.

### *Energy and environment: risks and challenges*

*Climate change:* China signed the 1997 Kyoto Protocol, but on the basis of the principle of 'common but differentiated responsibilities', which permitted it as a developing country to avoid committing itself to specific targets for reductions in GHG emissions, and these have not been included in the 12FYP. The challenges of implementing measures to counteract climate change include fragmented structures for energy supply and distribution, growth-orientated priorities of many local enterprises and officials (although some one hundred cities are reported to have applied for inclusion in the national pilot scheme for low-carbon cities),[89] and the relative weakness of the Ministry for Environmental Protection.

*The 'green' economy:* Although references to a 'green' economy in the 12FYP mostly relate to a *recycling* agenda, this is not, however, synonymous with a 'green' economy. A genuine 'green' economy should not only embrace environmentally conscious practices – evidenced by the sustainable production of a high proportion of output – but also facilitate a shift to a pattern of production in which a major focus is manufacture and the application of devices that will ultimately generate a sustainable lifestyle. From such perspectives, China's challenge is to find a way of achieving this transition as part of its strategic macroeconomic endeavour to shift from the production of relatively low-tech goods for export towards the production of higher-tech items for both domestic use and export markets. Two impressive examples of progress in this direction are the manufacture and use of solar panels and wind turbines (China is the world's largest producer of both).

### *Implications for the EU*

Following the EU-China Summit in 2005, the two sides established the EU and China Partnership on Climate Change. Its aims are to develop advanced zero-emissions coal technology based on carbon capture and storage, to reduce the cost of key energy technologies and to promote their deployment and dissemination.[90] The partnership has funded three specific projects: the Clean Development Mechanism (CDM) Facilitation Project (2007–10); the EU-China Energy and Environment Programme (EEP) (2002–9); and the EU-China Cooperation on Carbon Capture and Storage (CCS).[91]

The core of these projects has been technology transfer by European companies. However, some on the Chinese side apparently feel that the relevant European commercial companies have been preoccupied by the profitability of the projects to the neglect of the potential public benefit to China resulting from reduced carbon emissions. Some European companies have been concerned about the perceived threat to their intellectual property as a result of collaboration. We do not subscribe to these criticisms in their entirety, but they highlight issues that need close attention. European companies should acknowledge both a European 'common purpose' in EU-funded projects and the diplomatic objective of securing a productive long-term relationship with China.

The EU's interpretation of a 'green' economy goes beyond the 'recycling' envisaged under China's 12FYP. Still, the potential for technology transfer from the EU to China may be more limited than might have been expected: China is already among the world leaders both in solar technology and production and in the design and manufacture of wind turbines. The scope for engagement is more likely to lie in the direction of ongoing dialogue on the ways and means of achieving a 'green' economy. On other dimensions, such as the pollution of water and soil by hazardous substances, the protection of endangered species and the preservation of bio-diversity, many Member States have already been engaged with China for some years in projects of joint research with direct practical application.

In sum, all the environmental issues that China faces, subsumed in the sustainability objectives of the 12FYP, offer scope for constructive collaboration between the EU and China.

## Conclusion

The content of the 12FYP underlines major reasons why Europe should seek to maintain strong ties with China over a broad range of activities, given China's size, economic growth, engagement with the global economy, growing role in international affairs, and crucial impact on sustainable development.

This analysis of the 12FYP underlines China's growing influence as a global player, derived from the success of a reform strategy that possesses its own 'Chinese characteristics'. From this perspective, far from being an exemplar of the triumph of liberal democracy or market economics, China's experience in the past three decades has defined itself. The recent global financial crisis has underlined the wisdom, as seen from Beijing, of China following its own path while serving as a warning of the essential fragility of Western development models. Beijing's *Weltanschauung* will continue to reflect its own view of history, its own values and its own ranking of priorities. Economic and social developments *within* China are likely to be more powerful catalysts for change than pressure from EU negotiators, which their Chinese counterparts may interpret as coercion. Further, bringing pressure to bear in areas, such as human rights, where the EU has little hope of achieving significant progress threatens to jeopardise progress in those areas (social welfare, improvements in material living standards, resource conservation, climate change and environmental enhancement etc.) where its impact promises to be more positive.

A recurring theme in some Western media is the threat allegedly posed by China's rise. All too often, these arguments ignore the historical perceptions and experiences that have shaped Chinese leaders' views of the country's place in the world. For the purposes of this chapter, we should bear in mind that China poses no military 'threat' to Europe. Nor is it an exporter of international terrorism. Its sphere of influence is primarily East and Southeast Asia where it seeks to protect its borders and to safeguard oil exploration projects in the South China Sea. It also aspires to develop a second line of defence through a naval presence in the Indian Ocean and potentially in the Pacific. But in neither case are European interests directly involved – something that promises to benefit the EU in its engagement with China.[92]

Europe is not the only region that seeks to benefit from China's continued growth and its increasing engagement in the global community. In the coming years, the EU must face up to an increasingly competitive environment. In addition, however, there are many areas in which Europe must expect to face growing competition from *within* China. This is symbolised by three trends identified in a 2011 EIU report:[93]

- ▷ China's ascent of the value-added ladder will see its domestic export producers emerge as serious competitors in 'core product markets' of developed countries;
- ▷ non-OECD countries are set to become the main source of demand for China's exports, further eroding the export market shares of Western countries;
- ▷ the formerly dominant role of foreign-funded firms in driving China's export growth is giving way to domestic Chinese enterprises.

The scenario depicted here captures important dimensions of change that are under way in China. However, we would counsel caution, as fundamental to China's ascent of the value-added ladder is rapid technological advance. As this chapter has shown, upgrading STI is one of the core priorities of the 12FYP. But transforming China into an 'innovative country' cannot be accomplished within a single FYP period. In 2010 its R&D spending (*c.*US$105.8 billion) was only 20 per cent higher than the previous year's combined R&D spending of the top five global *firms* in each of just five industrial categories (aerospace, electronics and electrical equipment, pharmaceuticals and biotechnology, software and computers, and technology hardware and equipment).[94] Even if foreign-funded firms' contribution to exports is declining, they remain dominant in China's high-tech sector: for example, they still account for around 90 per cent of exports of high-technology goods. Foreign-invested enterprises also account for more than one-third of all employment of high-tech workers and for around 40 per cent of scientists and engineers.[95] In short, the process of China's technological catch-up is set to continue for many more years, during which the potential contribution of European companies, as well as multinational companies elsewhere in the world, promises to be no less significant than in the past.

China's Twelfth Five-Year Programme sets out authoritatively and comprehensively the thinking of China's leadership about its national development trajectory in the foreseeable future. For the EU and EU Member States, the Programme provides clear signposts to the opportunities that will be available for engagement. We conclude that the Programme document sets out a vision of China's future which is not a mere exercise in rhetoric. A minority of the targets set out in the Twelfth Five-Year Programme are binding, and their fulfilment (or otherwise) will determine the future career trajectories of many officials. Most targets are, however, aspirational. If any of them, binding or aspirational, are left unfulfilled at the end of the 12FYP period, they will likely be carried over into the next five-year planning cycle, lending durability to China's strategic vision. Nor should the strong continuities of policy that it shares with the Eleventh Five-Year Programme be interpreted as evidence of the document's weakness. Rather, they serve to highlight areas in which previous goals have not been fulfilled and emphasise consistency of purpose. The shift from an ethos of growth maximisation to one of development sustainability represented a change in mindset by the generation of leaders under Hu Jintao and Wen Jiabao. It was a compelling response to serious systemic challenges, social and environmental as much as economic, that had emerged from more than two decades of reform. That logic has shaped the development strategy of both the 11FYP and the 12FYP.

This chapter has highlighted a number of broad priority goals set out in the 12FYP. They include:

▷ reduced GDP growth targets, intended to accommodate a more sustainable pattern of economic and social development;
▷ a reduction in regional and sectorial inequalities in the distribution of income, wealth and opportunity;

- ▷ enhancement of capacity-building in key areas of high-tech manufacturing;
- ▷ intensified research and development in targeted enterprises; and
- ▷ pursuit of low-carbon and no-carbon energy solutions in order to mitigate climate change.

We believe that these policy goals are logical responses to some of the most pressing problems that China faces at its current stage of development, many of which have their origins in the rapid growth and rising prosperity that have characterised China's development under reform, as well as in its emergence on the global stage. These factors have brought China closer to EU Member States, with which – in varying degrees, depending on its European comparator – it shares common aspirations and common problems. Thus, some of the 12FYP goals match those contained in *EU 2020*, the creation of a 'smart, sustainable and inclusive economy'. To this end, it is committed to expanding employment, promoting innovation, enhancing education and putting in place a more socially inclusive society. It also seeks to address issues, such as energy security and climate change, that transcend European boundaries. All these aspirations resonate with China's development ambitions, and are stimuli for dialogue and exchanges between China and the EU. As it happens, they also afford significant commercial opportunities for European companies.

In recent years, Chinese delegations to the EU and its Member States have also made clear their interest in learning more about European approaches to social insurance – health, pension and medicare provision. Enhancing social welfare is an important part of China's vision of sustainable development, and it features prominently among the goals of the 12FYP. Here is one area in which the EU should engage with China and assist in facilitating economic rebalancing through the reallocation of household resources from savings to spending.

Both sides have long recognised science and technology to be at the heart of bilateral cooperation. S&T collaboration will play a critical role in determining the success of the 12FYP in promoting industrial upgrading through the rapid expansion of strategic emerging industries and in addressing urgent environmental and energy challenges. In this process, the EU and Member States are well placed to make an even more significant contribution than they have already. No less important is the need for realism in recognising that deficiencies in IPR protection remain a serious problem and that China itself is seeking to become a 'strategic competitor in high-tech sectors'.[96]

Successful implementation of the proposals set out in the 12FYP will generate important, though gradual, changes in the spatial dimensions of the Chinese economy. The dominant economic role played by coastal regions and their great urban agglomerations (for example, the Lower Yangtze and Pearl River Delta regions) will persist. However, the emergence of new regional growth nodes and urban centres of economic activity will be an important feature of economic change in coming years. As long as associated infrastructural (transport) and logistical (retail distribution) challenges can be overcome, new commercial opportunities will be forthcoming from these geographical changes. With this is mind, we would strongly argue that the EU should give careful consideration to extending its representation in China.

Finally, implicit throughout this chapter is an awareness of the unique nature of EU governance. Grasping this has been a challenge for Chinese officials working on how best to deal with Europe. For the EU, it has been a constraint, limiting its ability to coordinate policy against the background of differing strengths and interests among Member States. In some cases, Beijing has been quite willing to exploit such differences in its own interests; in others, it has opted in favour of dealing bilaterally with individual Member States. In order to minimise the fallout from EU governance, it is incumbent on the EU and its Member States to act together consistently.

## Notes

This is a substantially edited version of the original ECRAN paper (see http://www.euecran.eu/), which included more material on the policy implications of the 12FYP for the EU.

1. *Zhonghua Renmin Gongheguo guomin jingji he shehui fazhan di shier ge wunian guihua gangyao* [Outline Twelfth Five-Year

Programme for National Economic Social Development of the People's Republic of China] (hereafter referred to as *Gangyao*) (Beijing: Renmin chubanshe, March 2011). The English Section of the Central Document Translation Department of the Central Compilation and Translation Bureau published an official translation of the 12FYP in Beijing called *Twelfth Five-Year Plan for National Economic and Social Development of the People's Republic of China* (hereafter CDTD, *Twelfth Five-Year Plan*) (Beijing: Central Compilation and Translation Press, 2011). References in this chapter are given to both the Chinese and the English-language versions of the 12FYP, but direct quotations from the 12FYP are from CDTD.

2. *Xiaokang* is the aim of delivering a reasonable standard of living right across the country, with a GDP per capita target in the order of US$10,000.
3. *EU2020* is the EU's growth strategy for the decade to 2020. See http://ec.europa.eu/europe2020/index_en.htm.
4. The focus is economic and social development, though there are some references to politics; see CDTD, *Twelfth Five-Year Plan*, Ch. 54, 'Develop Socialist Democratic Politics', pp. 219–20 and *Gangyao*, pp. 136–7.
5. See Cindy Fan, 'China's Eleventh Five-Year Plan (2006–2010): From "Getting Rich First" to "Common Prosperity"', *Eurasian Geography and Economics*, vol. 47, no. 6 (2006), pp. 718–19.
6. See World Bank, Poverty Reduction and Economic Management Unit, East Asia and Pacific Region, 'Mid-term Evaluation of China's 11th Five-Year Plan', Report No. 46355-CN, 18 December 2008, available at http://www-wds.worldbank.org/external/default/WDSContentServer/WDSP/IB/2009/03/12/000334955_20090312072154/Rendered/PDF/463550Midterm00YearPlan0finalreport.pdf (accessed on 18 June 2011).
7. Hu Angang has described this as 'the largest policy consulting and research activity conducted anywhere in the world', *China Daily*, 11 April 2011.
8. Li subsequently replaced Wen Jiabao as premier in March 2013.
9. See *Zhonggong Zhongyang guanyu jueding guomin jingji he shehui fazhan de shier ge wunian guihua de jianyi* [Proposal of the CCP Central Committee on the Twelfth Five-Year Guidance Programme for National Economic and Social Development] (Beijing: Renmin chubanshe, October 2010).
10. See *Gangyao*.

11. By comparison, *realised* GDP and per capita GDP growth under the 10FYP were 9.6 per cent and 8.9 per cent per annum respectively (in constant price terms).
12. The point has been well made that 'China's system is good [at] meeting output goals, but less so at delivering structural change' (Tom Miller, 'NPC 2011 – A man, a plan, a Congress – Premier Wen's policy promises', GaveKalDragonomics, DragonWeek, 8 March 2011, p. 2 (available online only by subscription).
13. See *China Daily*, 2 March 2011: 'the nation still faces great challenges, including its economic reliance on investment and exports, its unbalanced development between urban and rural areas, and a widening wealth gap.'
14. NBS statistics show that China's merchandise trade with all three countries reached a record level in 2010. See NBS, *Zhongguo tongji zhaiyao*, 2011, p. 71.
15. In his seminal 1954 article ('Economic development with unlimited supplies of labour'), W. Arthur Lewis showed how the transfer of cheap surplus labour from agriculture could be used to drive industrial growth in a nascent capitalist sector without bringing undue pressure to bear on industrial wages. Only when the reservoir of surplus farm labour begins to be exhausted (i.e., when the 'Lewis turning point' is reached) would competition for labour precipitate an increase in industrial wages.
16. More than half of all 12FYP targets are binding, compared with little more than one-third in the 11FYP.
17. The 12FYP contains two new pollution targets, relating to reductions in pollution from ammonia nitrogen and nitrogen oxides.
18. See also Barbara Finamore and Michael Davidson, 'China's Twelfth Five-Year Plan: Energy and Environment Positioned Strategically', *China-US Focus*, 29 March 2011, available at http://www.chinausfocus.com/energy-environment/china%E2%80%99s-twelfth-five-year-planenergy-and-environment-positioned-strategically/ (accessed on 1 July 2011).
19. Longer-term plans call for the corresponding figure to reach 15 per cent by 2020.
20. The seven industries contributed 2 per cent of China's GDP in 2010. See KPMG Advisory (China) Limited, 'China's 12th Five-Year Plan: Overview', available at http://www.kpmg.com/CN/en/IssuesAndInsights/ArticlesPublications/

Publicationseries/5-years-plan/Documents/China-12th-Five-Year-Plan-Overview-201104.pdf (accessed on 2 July 2011).

21. Namely new energy sources (e.g., nuclear, solar and wind power and biomass energy); energy conservation and environmental protection; new-generation information technology [IT] (Internet and mobile communication, network convergence etc.); biotechnology (e.g., bio-agriculture, bio-pharmaceuticals, bio-medical engineering products); new materials, including rare earth and semiconductor materials); high-end equipment manufacturing (e.g., aerospace, telecommunications, remote sensing and high-speed rail transport); and new-energy car industry (CDTD, *Twelfth Five-Year Plan*, Ch. 10., esp. Table 5, pp. 48–9 and *Gangyao*, Box 5, pp. 32–3).
22. For example, writing about the 12FYP 'Proposal', submitted to the CCPCC in October 2010, a senior analyst suggested that the Programme 'breaks no new ground, and provides little concrete guidance'. Barry Naughton, 'What Price Continuity?', *China Leadership Monitor*, No. 34, Hoover Institution, Stanford University, February 2011, p. 3, available at http://media.hoover.org/sites/default/files/documents/CLM34BN.pdf (first accessed on 27 June 2011).
23. The logic of China's pursuit of more sustainable development has been strengthened by the global recession.
24. For more on the 38 changes to the draft, see Hong Kong, *Ta Kung Pao*, 14 March 2011, available at http://www.takungpao.com/news/china/2011-03-14/625544.html (accessed on 15 March 2011).
25. *China Daily*, 14 February 2011.
26. See, for example, Patricia Adams, 'Private sector is being squeezed out as "the state advances"', *Financial Post*, 26 June 2011, available at http://opinion.financialpost.com/2011/06/23/nationalizing-china/#more-15670 (accessed on 29 July 2011).
27. To give just one example: under the 12FYP in the priority healthcare sector, barriers to private investment will be further reduced and private investment will be a major driver of expanded healthcare services.
28. The full text is at http://news.xinhuanet.com/english2010/china/2011-03/15/c_13779521_8.htm (accessed on 26 July 2011).
29. The material in this sub-section is a shortened version of Robert Ash, 'China's Consumer Revolution: Winners and Losers', prepared for the International Relations and Security Network

(ISN), Eidgenössische Technische Hochschule Zürich and published as an ISN Insight, 28 June 2011. The entire text of the original can be found at http://www.isn.ethz.ch/isn/Current-Affairs/ISN-Insights/Detail?lng=en&id=130359&contextid734=130359&contextid735=128317&tabid=128317&dynrel=4888caa0-b3db-1461-98b9-e20e7b9c13d4,0c54e3b3-1e9c-be1e-2c24-a6a8c7060233.

30. *Zhongguo tongji zhaiyao*, 2011, p. 36. The same source shows aggregate final consumption spending (i.e., household plus government expenditure) to have fallen from 62.3 per cent to 47.4 per cent in the same period.
31. CDTD, *Twelfth Five-Year Plan*, Ch. 3 ('Principal Targets'), p. 12 and *Gangyao*, p. 8: 'over the next 5 years, the major economic and social development goals are ... [to raise] the ratio of household consumption to GDP ...'.
32. CDTD, *Twelfth Five-Year Plan*, Ch. 4 ('Policy Orientation'), pp. 17–18 and *Gangyao*, p. 12.
33. NBS household survey data show that in 2010 the urban savings rate was 30 per cent while the corresponding figure for rural residents was 26 per cent (*Zhongguo tongji zhaiyao*, 2011, pp. 104–5).
34. The 12FYP commits the government to providing free nine-year compulsory education, including the provision of free accommodation in boarding schools in rural areas, and to increasing financial support for pre-school education. Measures are also in place to provide free secondary vocational education for rural students as well as for urban students from poor backgrounds and those studying agriculture. CDTD, *Twelfth Five-Year Plan*, Ch. 30 ('Raise the Level of Basic Public Services'), Table 17, pp. 140–2 and *Gangyao*, Box 17, p. 89.
35. CDTD, *Twelfth Five-Year Plan*, Table 19, p. 164 and *Gangyao*, Box 19, p. 105 (see also p. 94).
36. See Xinhua News Agency, 30 June 2011 (http://news.xinhuanet.com/english2010/china/2011-06/30/c_13958711.htm (accessed on 4 August 2011).
37. 'China takes measures to deal with aging problem', *People's Daily Online*, 11 October 2010, available at http://english.peopledaily.com.cn/90001/90776/90882/7162523.html (accessed on 4 August 2011). The experience of more developed, higher-income countries suggests that there are large dividends from targeting older consumers, especially for pharmaceutical producers and healthcare providers.

38. Morgan Stanley, 'European Corporates and China's Mega-transition', Morgan Stanley Blue Paper, 29 October 2010, available at http://www.morganstanley.com/views/perspectives/China_Files_APac.pdf (accessed on 1 August 2011).
39. China's consumer credit spending is projected to rise from a mere 10 per cent of total consumption expenditure in 2010 to 40 per cent in 2020. The resultant increase in purchasing power will be further boosted by higher wages and lower savings. (Ibid., p. 7). A major expansion in online shopping, as broadband access widens, is also expected during the 12FYP period.
40. The data are from *Zhongguo tongji zhaiyao*, 2011, p. 39. The further inference is that during the same period, the share of those of working age in the total population increased from 61.5 per cent to 74.5 per cent.
41. Ma Jiantang (NBS Director), 28 April 2011 (http://news.xinhuanet.com/english2010/china/2011-04/28/c_13849795.htm) (accessed on 5 October 2011).
42. CDTD, *Twelfth Five-Year Plan*, Ch. 36, p. 160 and *Gangyao*, p. 102.
43. One source has estimated that by the mid-2020s, the treatment of obesity-related heart disease and diabetes among the Chinese elderly could cost the government up to 9 per cent of GDP. See Somnath Chatterji et al., 'The health of aging populations in China and India', *Health Affairs*, vol. 27, no. 4 (2008), cited in the US Population Reference Bureau, 'Today's research on Aging: Program and Policy Implications', Issue 20, July 2010, available at http://www.prb.org/pdf10/TodaysResearchAging20.pdf (accessed on 30 July 2011).
44. See CDTD, *Twelfth Five-Year Plan*, Table 19, pp. 163–4 and *Gangyao*, pp. 104–5.
45. 'Working age' for the regularly employed means between the ages of 16 and 59 for men and between 16 and 54 for women.
46. The NBS shows urban unemployment to have been at 4.1 per cent in 2010 (*Zhongguo tongji zhaiyao*, 2011, p. 46). There is, however, a strong consensus that official figures are significant underestimates and that unemployment in Chinese cities is at least twice as high as that figure.
47. See Stephen S. Roach, 'China's 12th Five-Year Plan: Strategy vs. Tactics', Morgan Stanley, April 2011, available at http://www.morganstanley.com/im/emailers/inst/pdf/China_12th_Five_Year_Plan.pdf (accessed on 1 August 2011).

48. Even if this target is fulfilled, the tertiary sector's share of total employment will remain modest compared with that of developed countries, where the corresponding figure averages about 65 per cent.
49. CDTD, *Twelfth Five-Year Plan*, Table 19, p. 163 and *Gangyao*, p. 104. In the first half of 2011, minimum wages in 18 provinces, regions and cities rose by 13–28 per cent. Janet Zhang, 'China Economic Outlook', GaveKal Dragonomics, August 2011 (available online only to subscribers).
50. In 2010, the average urban disposable income was 3.22 times higher than the average rural net income (*Zhongguo tongji zhaiyao*, 2011, p. 104).
51. CDTD, *Twelfth Five-Year Plan*, Ch. 6, p. 27 and *Gangyao*, p. 19.
52. Though the 'Develop the West' initiative (*xibu da kaifa*) was launched under the administration of Jiang Zemin and Zhu Rongji.
53. See CDTD, *Twelfth Five-Year Plan*, Chs 18–20 and 79–93 and *Gangyao*, pp. 51–61.
54. The delineation of these regions by province/municipality/autonomous region is as follows: East – Beijing, Tianjin, Shanghai, Hebei, Jiangsu, Zhejiang, Fujian, Guangdong, Shandong and Hainan; Northeast – Liaoning, Jilin and Heilongjiang; Central – Shanxi, Anhui, Jiangxi, Henan, Hubei and Hunan; West – Inner Mongolia, Shaanxi, Gansu, Qinghai, Ningxia, Xinjiang, Chongqing, Sichuan, Guangxi, Guizhou, Yunnan and Tibet. This demarcation derives from the various mega-region policy frameworks, designed to 'Develop the West', 'Revive the Northeast' and 'Raise up the Central Regions', that were launched at different times since 2000.
55. See, for example, 'Tax discounts in western regions to continue', *South China Morning Post*, 6 August 2011.
56. CDTD, *Twelfth Five-Year Plan*, Section XII, Ch. 50, pp. 209–10 and *Gangyao*, pp. 130–1.
57. See Tim Summers, *Yunnan – A Chinese Bridgehead to Asia: A case study of China's political and economic relations with its neighbours* (Chandos, 2013).
58. The process of urbanisation is relevant to a wide range of policies and trends, including demographics, industrialisation and public service provision for migrant workers, etc., touched on elsewhere in this chapter.
59. According to the National Bureau of Statistics, GDP growth in 2010 was 14.2 per cent and 13.8 per cent respectively in western

and central China, compared with 12.3 per cent in eastern provinces. Faster growth in inland regions builds on a trend that has already been in evidence for several years. See Tim Summers and Doris Ma, 'Is China's growth moving inland?', Asia Programme Paper, Chatham House, 2009.

60. The Boston Consulting Group has predicted that the number of MACs could rise from 148 million in 2010 to 415 million by 2020 (cited in Bloomberg, http://surviveinchina.com/china-middle-class-and-affluent-consumers-may-triple-in-10-years-bloomberg/) (accessed on 15 August 2011).
61. These paragraphs are based on Section XII of the 12FYP (chapters 50–3). There is also material on 'national defence' (Section XV, or chapters 59–60, of the 12FYP), which is beyond the remit of this chapter. See next section for consideration of material concerned with global trade and investment.
62. For example, see Hu Jintao's speech at the 17th Party Congress in 2007 for an exposition of some of these themes. Although there has been talk about the possible emergence of a 'G2' of China and the United States, Premier Wen Jiabao made it clear that China was not interested in the development of such a structure. 'Wen: China disagrees to so-called G2, calling for effort to fight protectionism', *People's Daily*, 18 November 2009 (http://english.peopledaily.com.cn/90001/90776/90883/6817072.html).
63. 'The world should not fear China', Li Keqiang, *Financial Times*, 9 January 2011.
64. 'Revisionism' refers to a foreign policy approach that seeks to change the way the current international system is structured, in contrast to a 'status quo' approach, which supports the maintenance of the existing system.
65. This was made clear at the December 2010 Third Meeting of the EU-China High-level Economic and Trade Dialogue (Memo 10/698, available at the website of the European Commission). See, for example http://europa.eu/rapid/pressReleasesAction.do?reference=MEMO/10/698&format=HTML&aged=0&language=EN&guiLanguage=en.
66. As we comment in Section VIII on the commercial implications of the 12FYP, the EU's share of FDI into China and trade with it has been in decline since the 1990s.
67. Data from the EC. See http://ec.europa.eu/trade/creating-opportunities/bilateral-relations/countries/china/(accessed on 26 July 2011).

68. Ibid.
69. See Song Zhe, 'China's five-year plan is an opportunity for Europe', the full text of which can be found at http://www.europeanvoice.com/article/imported/china-s-five-year-plan-is-an-opportunity-for-europe/70821.aspx (accessed on 26 July 2011).
70. For reasons of space we do not consider Hong Kong and Macao.
71. The high premium placed on consumption in the 12FYP alongside China's continuing economic growth means that servicing the domestic Chinese market will become an ever more important part of foreign businesses' investments and exports into China.
72. See especially Section XII of the 12FYP (Chs 50–3), 'Create a Win-Win Situation: Raise the Levels of Opening Up'. CDTD, *Twelfth Five-Year Plan*, pp. 209–16 and *Gangyao*, pp. 130–5.
73. The policy implications of 'openness' are not confined to foreign trade and investment, and the focus of this section is deliberately formulated in the phrase 'openness to the outside world / foreign countries' (*duiwai kaifang*).
74. In 2009, China's outward FDI totalled US$56.29 billion, compared with US$90.03 billion of inward FDI. At the end of 2009, the stock of outward FDI totalled US$245.76 billion, of which Europe accounted for a mere 3.5 per cent (US$8.68 billion). NBS, *Zhongguo tongji nianjian*, 2010, p. 257.
75. See, for example, Tan Copsey and Isabel Hilton, 'Greening China: Outlook for European SMEs', Spring 2011, available at http://www.friendsofeurope.org/Portals/13/Documents/Reports/UC_Policy-Briefing_Greening-China_web.pdf (accessed on 24 July 2011).
76. Our thinking here has been helped by an analysis conducted by McKinsey, 'What China's 12th Five-Year Plan means for business', July 2011, https://www.mckinseyquarterly.com/Economic_Studies/Productivity_Performance/What_Chinas_five-year_plan_means_for_business_2832, accessed 15 August 2011.
77. See CDTD, *Twelfth Five-Year Plan*, Ch. 28 ('Accelerate Educational Reform and Development'), pp. 128–32 and *Gangyao*, pp. 82–5.
78. In 2009, China had 2,305 universities, of which 1,090 were universities offering full undergraduate courses. The remaining 1,215 were described as 'colleges with specialised courses'. *Zhongguo tongji nianjian*, 2010, p. 759.
79. CDTD, *Twelfth Five-Year Plan*, Ch. 29 ('Cultivate a Large Contingent of High-Quality Personnel'), p. 134 and *Gangyao*, pp. 86–7.

80. *Zhongguo tongji zhaiyao*, 2011, p. 167.
81. CDTD, *Twelfth Five-Year Plan*, Ch. 2 ('Guiding Principles'), p. 10 and *Gangyao*, p. 7.
82. Richard P. Suttmeier and Xiangkui Yao, 'China's IP Transition: Rethinking Intellectual Property Rights in a Rising China', Special Report, No. 29, National Bureau for Asian Research, Seattle, Washington, USA, July 2011.
83. The chapter was compiled by Denis Fourmeau, Deputy Counsellor, Science and Technology Section, EC Delegation, Beijing.
84. Manfred Horvat and Svend Remøe, 'Background Report on Steps towards Developing Strategies for S&T Co-operation with China', September 2010, available at http://www.minedu.fi/export/sites/default/OPM/Tapahtumakalenteri/2011/05/Approaching_China_liiteet/ApproachingxChina_BackgroundxReport_rev__2_.pdf (accessed on 2 September 2011). Recommendations are outlined in the original unedited ECRAN paper.
85. The most important chapters are Ch. 11 ('Accelerate the Reform of Energy Production and Use'); Ch. 21 ('Actively Respond to Global Climate Change'); Ch. 22 ('Strengthen Resource Conservation and Management'); Ch. 23 ('Vigorously Develop a Circular Economy'); Ch. 24 ('Intensify Environmental Protection'); Ch. 25 ('Promote Ecological Protection and Repair'); and Ch. 26 ('Strengthen the Construction of Systems for Water Conservation and Disaster Prevention and Mitigation'). On environmental and resource-related pricing issues, see Ch. 49; and on related governance issues, see Ch. 61.
86. CDTD, *Twelfth Five-Year Plan,* Ch. 2 ('Guiding Principles'), p. 11 and *Gangyao*, p. 7. A circular economy is taken in this chapter to mean one in which waste, both biological and industrial, is recycled and turned into inputs.
87. The bodies under the supervision of the new National Energy Commission that have a major role in energy production and distribution are the State Electricity Regulatory Commission, the State Administration of Coal Mine Safety; the Ministry of Water Resources; the Ministry of Land and Resources; the China National Petroleum Corporation; Sinopec; and the State Grid Corporation of China. See Lan Xinzhen, 'Who'll turn on the lights?', *Beijing Review*, 29 November 2007.
88. The paradigm originated in the work of William McDonough and Michael Braungart. See their *Cradle to Cradle: Remaking*

*the Way We Make Things*, North Point Press, 2002. See also Pan Yue, 'The harmonious and environmentally conscious society', in Yang Dongping (ed.), *China Environment Yearbook*, vol.2 (CASS) (Leiden: Brill, 2008), pp. 55–7.

89. Professor Porter's interview at CASS, Institute for Urban and Environmental Studies, Beijing, 1 August 2011.
90. See *The EU-China Partnership on Climate Change: Bilateralism Begetting Multilateralism in Promoting a Climate Change Regime?* Mercury E-paper No. 8, December 2010 at http://www.mercury-fp7.net/fileadmin/user_upload/E-paper_no__8_2011.pdf (accessed on 27 July 2011).
91. The CDM involved dialogue, policy research and capacity-building. The EEP focused on the development of plans to strengthen EU-China cooperation in carbon capture and storage. The CCS seeks to achieve cooperation in developing, deploying and transferring clean technologies to China, to improve energy efficiency and to promote the transition to a low-carbon economy. It is intended to lead to the construction by 2020 of a 'commercial-scale, demonstration, coal-fired power plant supplied with CCS technologies'.
92. See also Ibid., p. 29.
93. Economist Intelligence Unit (EIU), 'Heavy Duty: China's Next Wave of Exports', 2011.
94. These are crude calculations, based on the GDP estimate for 2010 given in *Zhongguo tongji zhaiyao*, 2011, divided by the yuan-dollar exchange rate from the same source (Ibid., pp. 20 and 66). Even so, they suggest the scale of the technological challenge facing China. Detailed R&D spending in 2009 by the top 1,050 global firms in 41 industrial categories is available from the UK government's Department of Business Innovation and Skills and can be downloaded in full at http://webarchive.nationalarchives.gov.uk/20101208170217/http://www.innovation.gov.uk/rd_scoreboard/?p=31) (accessed on 7 September 2011). Of the 25 firms from the five industrial categories, just five had their headquarters in EU Member States: one Finnish firm; one French firm; and three German firms. Switzerland was the only other European country represented (with pharmaceutical firms).
95. Edward S. Steinfeld, *Playing Our Game: Why China's Rise Doesn't Threaten the West* (Oxford: Oxford University Press, 2010), p. 161.
96. Ibid.

# 4 China's Rulers: The Fifth Generation Take Power (2012–13)

*Michael Dillon*

## Preamble

As the Seventeenth Central Committee of the Chinese Communist Party, met for its sixth Plenary Session in Beijing on Saturday 15 October 2011, optimistic commentators predicted the dawn of a new era of profound political change. In anticipation of the leadership changes planned for 2012 and 2013, there was a rush to publish books in Chinese (mostly in Hong Kong) on the emerging leadership and the selection process, sources that have been underused in English-language accounts of China's leadership.

The fifth generation 'core leadership' of the CCP was approved formally at the meeting of the Eighteenth National Congress of the Party which opened on 8 November 2012. The government appointments of Xi Jinping and Li Keqiang as respectively President and Premier, known for several years, were then confirmed at the Twelfth National People's Congress (NPC) which took place from 15–17 March 2013. The spectacular and unexpected dismissal of Bo Xilai as Chongqing Party Secretary in March 2012 disrupted arrangements for the Eighteenth Party Congress but the published timetable – that it would be held in the second half of 2012 – was adhered to.[1]

## Change and Continuity

Radical or fundamental political change in China is far from inevitable but it is unlikely that the CCP's 62-year-old monopoly of government can remain unchanged indefinitely in the wake of the country's extraordinary economic development. The CCP is not willing to permit independent organisations to represent the aspirations of emerging social groups and has every intention of retaining the current system of one-party control. A statement issued on 1 July 2011 during celebrations of the ninetieth anniversary of the CCP's foundation made it clear that Western-style multi-party democracy was not considered suitable for China's 'national conditions' and could even precipitate a repeat of the 'chaos and factionalism' of the Cultural Revolution. It claimed that 30 years of economic growth proved that the CCP had the welfare of the people at heart and guaranteed its legitimacy.[2]

The new leadership of the CCP is determined that future political change will remain under its control. Central control by the Party collapsed briefly in the early stages of the Cultural Revolution (1966–7) but this was rapidly remedied by military intervention and the reconstruction of the CCP in 1969. Since the death of Mao Zedong in 1976, and especially since the final retirement of Deng Xiaoping in 1992, political change has been institutionalised; the leadership intend that the risks and conflict associated with the uncertainty of succession should be a thing of the past.[3] While the process of selecting the new top leadership is still opaque and restricted to the inner circle of the CCP's Politburo and Organisation Department, in recent years the results have been made known and the names of preferred candidates publicised well in advance – five years – although only indirectly. The successful candidates have usually been unknown outside China. They are typically drawn from the pool of provincial governors and Party secretaries, but also include other senior Party functionaries and state officials, and are known within the CCP.[4] There is a determination to avoid the appointment of one dominant individual – another Mao or Deng and especially not a 'Chinese Gorbachev'.

The key question for China's future is whether political change can be confined within the 80 million-strong Party (with reserves of over 20 million applicants annually and probably 75 million in the Communist Youth League – CYL[5]) or whether non-Party organisations will be permitted to play a role. For the foreseeable future, the CCP will play the leading role. It is not a monolith: factional differences and conflicts are key drivers in the development of policy, yet there is no open acknowledgement that these factions even exist. Indeed they are not factions in the Western sense as they do not have distinctive political platforms or manifestos. They are patronage groups operating on the basis of personal loyalty and are based in regions or in influential organisations such as the Communist Youth League.

Since the death of Mao in 1976 and the move towards a more open economic system, discussions on the history of the Communist Party have also become more open and the role of reform-minded individuals who were defeated politically by Mao is being re-examined. This has a direct impact on the current leadership changes as some of the key candidates appear to draw on the tradition of these reformers.[6]

Zhou Enlai (1898–1976), whose political position was always difficult to characterise, is considered by some to have been the first significant reformer after the foundation of the PRC. He was the first powerful advocate of the 'four modernisations', for which Deng Xiaoping is often given credit, although Zhou remained close to Mao and did not press for political reform. Deng Xiaoping, who for all his enthusiasm for economic reform was a conservative on the question of political reform, developed Zhou's economic agenda. However it is Hu Yaobang, Zhao Ziyang and – arguably – Wen Jiabao who have been seen as the standard bearers of political reform. It would not be accurate to describe these people as 'liberal' or even 'pro-democracy' but they do personify a current within the CCP that has been willing to articulate the need for political reform. The precise nature of their reform strategy has not been openly articulated because of the resistance of conservative elements within the Party. The reformist current has been gaining ground in recent years but, since the forced retirement of Hu Yaobang in 1987 after accusations that he was too indulgent with student demonstrators against corruption, and the dismissal of Zhao Ziyang for his opposition to the use of force against Tiananmen demonstrators in June 1989, senior political figures – with the exception of Wen

Jiabao – have been reluctant to identify openly with this current. However many appear to associate themselves with Hu's legacy, including both Xi Jinping and Li Keqiang.[7]

On Wednesday 18 January 2012, Hu Yaobang's eldest son, Hu Deping, convened a forum on political reform on the twentieth anniversary of Deng Xiaoping's 1992 'southern tour', the mission during which Deng finally secured support for his reform policies. At this meeting, academics, retired public servants and relatives of former senior Party and government officials heard Hu Deping, an economist who chairs the Chinese National Chamber of Commerce and Industry, commend the way in which protests in the village of Wukan in Guangdong had been handled. He argued that the time was right to extend Deng's 'opening and reform' to political reform.[8]

Access to the higher positions within the CCP and the government is by a combination of bureaucratic progression and personal connections. Appointments to the leadership are made initially on the basis of rank order in the hierarchy of the *nomenklatura* [*zhiwu mingcheng biao* 职务名称表]. As the use of the Russian term suggests, it emulates the system that existed in the Communist Party of the former Soviet Union; it is managed by the CCP's Organisation Department.[9] Individuals rise in status and authority on the basis of their rank and with the availability of positions, but their progress is modified by personal, historical or factional connections, which can increase or reduce chances of promotion. Like all personnel matters within the CCP, this is not a transparent process. Those at the apex of the political structure have typically arrived there through an ascending spiral of successive rotations between central and provincial Party and government appointments. Most high-ranking officials have served as provincial Party secretary or governors in the regions: hardship postings in the deprived and problematic northwest (Tibet, Xinjiang, Gansu) attract particular esteem. Overseas experience and knowledge are not valued in the same way.

## Senior Political Appointments

Party appointments at the highest level are formally approved at the five-yearly National Congresses of the CCP which take place in the autumn. Government posts are ratified at the annual meeting of the National People's Congress in the following spring. Although it is always possible for appointments previously announced to be revoked, the expectation is that they will be confirmed. There is a broad consensus that conflict should be confined within the Chinese Communist Party and its decision making bodies – the CC and the Politburo – and that in public the CCP should present a united front, in line with the Leninist practice of 'democratic centralism'.[10]

The current system of replacing the collective leadership is designed to maintain maximum political stability while preventing the ossification of the power structures and allowing for the routine renewal of senior personnel as the older generation retires. The intended outcome of this arcane process is that the change in personnel will not precipitate dramatic changes in the direction of policy.

Bitter struggles for position and power within the Party are based on political commitment and differing views of China's political direction as much as on personal ambition. Official consensus masks deep and divisive conflicts and some commentators have argued that within the superficially unruffled Hu-Wen administration there was a 'dangerous and unpredictable' [*fengyun xian'e* 风云险恶] mood. The leadership transition of 2012–13 was planned as smooth and seamless but the shocking downfall of Bo Xilai indicates that serious conflicts remain.[11]

Interest focuses primarily on candidates for the top two positions, the assumption being that 'the fate of the Party and the state is in the hands of one or two individuals'. This is the direct opposite of the wish of Deng Xiaoping that the future of China should depend on a collective leadership and that there should be no appointments for life. Appointments are for fixed terms and strong or charismatic leaders are distrusted but the two senior appointments remain the most important.[12]

Starved of the level of inside information that is available in democratic societies, Chinese and Western commentators have been obliged to speculate on the views of candidates and their policies. Two provincial leaders seen as probable new entries to the Politburo Standing Committee, Wang Yang and Bo Xilai were characterised as offering diametrically opposed models of development – the Guangdong and Chongqing models. Wang

Yang promoted a 'Happy Guangdong' campaign to appeal to an emerging middle class that was presumed to have 'a stronger appetite for political participation and rights protection'. The Chongqing Party Secretary, Bo Xilai, ran a campaign for 'red culture', marked by nostalgic television programmes and the singing of revolutionary songs harking back to the 1950s and 1960s.[13]

## Political Generations in China

The successive leaderships of the CCP are now expressed in terms of political generations. Mao Zedong, Deng Xiaoping and Jiang Zemin respectively were the first three: the identification of these as separate 'generations' is retrospective, although the press began to refer to Jiang as the 'core of the third generation' while he was still in power.

The fourth generation leadership team of Hu Jintao (President of PRC, General Secretary of the CCP, and Chairman of the CCP and PRC Central Military Commissions) and Premier Wen Jiabao has worked effectively, in spite of persistent rumours of serious conflict and some obvious differences of personality. They had previously worked together in Gansu Province during the 1980s which may have strengthened this relationship.

The 'core leadership' of the fifth generation was elected at the Eighteenth CCP National Congress towards the end of 2012 and their government posts were formally confirmed at the meeting of the NPC in March 2013. Xi Jinping replaced Hu Jintao as President and CCP General Secretary. Li Keqiang became Premier, succeeding Wen Jiabao. On the level below, the membership of the Standing Committee of the Politburo was reduced from nine to seven and in addition to Xi and Li, the members are Zhang Dejiang, Yu Zhengsheng, Liu Yunshan, Wang Qishan and Zhang Gaoli.

## CCP Factions and the Succession Process

With a total of over 80 million members, and a complex national organisation the CCP is not surprisingly riven by internal conflicts although these are usually concealed. Names for factions or patronage groups within the CCP include the Communist Youth League and 'cliques' based on Shanghai and the universities of Qinghua and Beijing. The best known are the 'princelings' (*Taizidang*), descendants of former senior officials, a category so large that it can hardly function as a faction. The others are based on local origins, education or social connections and have effectively replaced pre-Cultural Revolution factions based on service with field armies in the civil war of 1946–9.

The usefulness of factions as a guide to the workings of the CCP and specifically to promotions to the Politburo Standing Committee is questionable. The possibility of cooperation between factions on senior appointments limits their usefulness to analysts and a number of successful leaders, notably Xi Jinping, command loyalties that cross factional boundaries. The analysis of Chinese politics based on factions must be complemented by detailed historical and biographical studies which reveal the complexity of these relationships.

The commonly used factional names do not reflect the serious political differences that exist within the CCP. One tendency, the 'internal democrats' [*dangnei minzhu pai* 党内民主派] or the 'internal democratic liberals' [*dangnei minzhu ziyou pai* 党内民主自由派], is rarely acknowledged, although its voice can be heard through journals, including the monthly *Yanhuang chunqiu* 炎黄春秋 (Spring and Autumn Annals of the Emperors Yan and Huang), which combines political comment, historical analysis and reminiscences of Hu Yaobang and other reformist icons.[14]

## Key Issues

The main domestic policy issues that faced the incoming leadership concerned the speed of economic growth and ways of dealing with its social consequences, particularly inequality, conflicts over rural development and corruption. It has long been accepted that there is an informal social contract between the CCP and the people of China: as long as the Party delivers prosperity and continuing economic growth, the people will turn a blind eye to the lack of democracy. It is not usually possible to identify policy differences on any of these issues with specific individuals within the leadership because of the insistence on democratic centralism. The background of the new fifth generation leadership is similar to that of its predecessor, so over-optimistic expectations of a new and more liberal political era cannot be justified. None of the leadership has worked or studied abroad, with the exception of Zhang Dejiang (a North Korea specialist) so there is no significant international experience.[15]

### Corruption and rural protests

The new leadership, like their predecessors, are committed to eradicating corruption: the greatest problems are at the grass-roots level and peasant discontent at land seizures for development. The standoff between the villagers of Wukan in Guangdong Province and local officials between September and December 2011, following the death of a popular village leader in police custody, is one of tens of thousands of 'mass incidents' that have erupted in China in recent years. These protests are fragmented responses to local grievances. Attempts to link them have been crushed at the outset.

China has a well-established system of elections for village representatives. It is a structure that could be used to develop rural democracy, but only the names of candidates approved by the local branch of the CCP usually appear on the ballot paper and independent candidates have been harassed and obliged to withdraw. Protestors in Wukan demanded representative government and concessions were made after the intervention of Wang Yang, the Governor of Guangdong Province, a candidate for the Politburo Standing Committee. Some independent candidates were then elected by secret ballot but their authority remains in question.[16]

## Key Players

### Third generation

#### *Jiang Zemin*

Jiang Zemin (85) was the surprise candidate for the CCP leadership after the military suppression of the Beijing Democracy

Movement on 4 June 1989. He managed demonstrations in Shanghai successfully and Deng Xiaoping chose him to replace Zhao Ziyang, who was dismissed for being too sympathetic to the demonstrators. Derided for his awkward 'Three Represents' theory and poor performance in public, he nevertheless paved the way for the broadening of CCP membership to include the business community.[17]

Jiang retired as General Secretary of the CCP in 2002 to make way for Hu Jintao and the fourth generation but he did not finally relinquish his last appointment as Chairman of the State Central Military Commission until March 2005. He remained a shadow member of the fourth generation, a position strengthened by his leadership of the 'Shanghai faction' within the CCP. His position was undermined by the enforced retirement, in October 2007, of his protégé, Zeng Qinghong, who had been seen as a potential future Party chief.[18] Jiang operated behind the scenes and although the power of the 'Shanghai faction' has waned, his support in the leadership elections carried some weight.[19]

## Fourth generation

The fourth generation, which followed Jiang's drawn-out retirement between 2002 and 2005, emerged from a new process of selecting the top leadership, a process that was secretive but was clearly based on intense lobbying by factional and other interest groups within the most powerful Party organs.

### *Hu Jintao*

Hu Jintao (69), who succeeded Jiang as President in 2003 is a classic product of the 'double burden' system of technological education and political training that has produced most of the CCP leadership. He graduated from Qinghua (Tsinghua) University in Beijing as a hydroelectric engineer. He worked in water conservancy and power and his key political postings were to Gansu and Tibet, where he was CCP Secretary and responsible for the imposition of martial law. He also served as head of the Central Party School and is the senior member of the Communist Youth League faction, having served as First

Secretary of the CYL, which he still cultivates, from 1984–5. He was recalled from Tibet in 1992 to become a member of the Politburo Standing Committee and became President in 2003. His reserved public manner is the approved style for a Party head and his pronouncements concentrated on theoretical and general policy issues, notably 'scientific development', China's 'peaceful rise' and 'harmonious' society. He made a point of strengthening his power base in the military after Jiang Zemin's retirement from the Central Military Commission in 2005 but also continued with Jiang's strategy of recruiting more business leaders to the CCP. Hu relinquished power in March 2013, including the chairmanship of the Central Military Commission (in contrast to Jiang), and any continuing involvement in political life has been discreet.[20]

### *Wen Jiabao*

Wen Jiabao (69) was the most popular of the fourth generation leadership and certainly the most consciously populist. He trained as a geologist and spent part of his career in Gansu with Hu Jintao. He achieved national prominence working for China's 2001 World Trade Organisation (WTO) application. He was associated with the reformists Hu Yaobang and Zhao Ziyang and accompanied Zhao during his fateful 1989 visit to the hunger strikers in Tiananmen Square. He publicly associated himself with victims of the Wenchuan earthquake in May 2008 and dramatically rose from his sick bed to visit the scene of the Wenzhou train crash near in July 2011. He criticised official corruption and incompetence and openly espoused democratic values but was criticised for hypocrisy.

Wen Jiabao made speeches at home and abroad calling for political reforms: he appears to be a lone voice but has not been silenced. Hu Jintao refrained from backing Wen and both Wu Bangguo, the head of the National People's Congress, and Zhou Yongkang, who controls security policy for the CCP but was under investigation for corruption in 2013, rejected the possibility of meaningful political reform.

In January 2011, Wen met petitioners in Beijing and heard their complaints of maladministration and injustice, the first time a state Premier had done this since 1949. A tribute to the reformer

Hu Yaobang written by Wen for the journal *Beijing Literature* on the twenty-first anniversary of Hu's death was praised. His call for 'political restructuring' and institutional change was repeated at the end of the National People's Congress in March 2011 and on 25 March he made a speech to the State Council demanding an increased emphasis on fighting corruption.[21]

## Fifth generation

### *Xi Jinping*

Of all the candidates for promotion in the new round of leadership changes, Xi Jinping's position as the President-in-waiting in succession to Hu Jintao was always the most secure, especially after he was appointed as second in command of the Central Military Commission in October 2010. At the Seventeenth Party Conference in 2007, Xi Jinping had emerged as the crown prince, apparently put forward by Jiang Zemin and Zeng Qinghong with the intention of countering Hu Jintao's protégé, Li Keqiang, and pushing Li into the number two position. Xi was acceptable to many of the old guard because of his political pedigree. His father was Xi Zhongxun (1913–2002), a former CCP guerrilla leader in Shaanxi, Party elder and founding father [*yuanlao*元老] of the PRC who served as Deputy Prime Minister from 1959 to 1962. Xi Zhongxun had been persecuted and purged on Mao Zedong's orders in 1962, because of his tenuous association with a novel, *Liu Zhitan*, which appeared to play down Mao's role as a guerrilla leader. The older Xi was imprisoned and not fully rehabilitated until 1978 although he then served as Governor and Party Secretary of Guangdong Province. He is reputed to have been a mentor to both Hu Jintao and Wen Jiabao. Xi Jinping, also maintained good relations with Hu Jintao and this might have contributed to his preferment.[22]

## Factional allegiance

Xi is usually described as a 'princeling' [*taizidang*] faction member but he also has a Shanghai background. 'Princelings', mostly the sons and daughters of previous senior leaders, have acquired the reputation of being arrogant and corrupt but Xi Jinping has been described as the 'princeling' with the common touch [*zui you pingmin qinghuai de taizidang* 最有平民情怀的太子党. Xi does not like people to mention the 'stars in the political firmament' [*zhengtan mingxing* 政坛明星] – family backgrounds of senior cadres – and if anyone 'violates this prohibition' he becomes somewhat heated and flushed with anger. He maintains a distance between himself and other 'princelings' as memories of his father's political downfall when Xi Jinping was only ten years old, taught him that his father's generation had brought disaster on his own family and he should be wary of their descendants.[23]

## Rustication at the end of the Cultural Revolution

In 1969 when he was barely 16 years old, Xi Jinping was sent to the Liangjiahe (Liang Family River) Production Brigade in the Wen'anyi Commune which is in Yanquan County in northern Shaanxi as part of a school agricultural labour group. Recalling this many years later, he observed that,

> For almost a whole year I did not rest at all unless I was actually ill. In rain and wind I chopped up hay for fodder in a cave and at night I watched over the animals. I took the sheep out to pasture and did all kinds of jobs and at that time I would carry 200 jin (100 kilos) of wheat one my shoulders for ten *li* (5 kilometres) along a mountain road without shifting it from one shoulder to the other.

He was unable to cook for himself and preferred studying so one of the villagers prepared his meals. In 1994 when he was a senior Party official in Fujian he helped with medical expenses that this villager could not afford. Together with almost 30,000 other Beijing students who had been rusticated, he joined the CCP in Yan'an in January 1974 and became the first to become Party secretary of a Production Brigade branch. He was then approved as a 'Worker-Peasant-Soldier Student' and enrolled in the chemical engineering department at Qinghua University from 1975–9.

### *Rise to power*

Xi Jinping was relatively unknown when he was assigned to the post of Secretary of the Shanghai Party Committee in March

2007, after the dismissal and imprisonment for 18 years of Chen Liangyu who had been convicted of the misuse of social security funds. This was a brief sojourn for Xi as he was appointed to the Politburo Standing Committee that October and was replaced in Shanghai by Yu Zhengsheng (who joined the Politburo Standing Committee in 2012). When Chinese Central Television profiled the 2007 Standing Committee, they contrasted the bespectacled Li Keqiang, always willing to discuss and explain policies, with Xi Jinping, 'either lost in thought or listening attentively'. In October 2007 at a discussion on 'scientific development' (Hu Jintao's signature theory) at the Seventeenth Party Congress that lasted over two hours, Xi did not make a speech and at the question and answer session with the media afterwards only made general comments, avoiding any detailed policy issues. The Beijing correspondent of the Korean Daily, *Chosun Ilbo*, noted that Li Keqiang grasped the microphone and was willing to answer question after question but Xi 'just adopted the classic pose of inclining his head and listening'.

Xi had powerful supporters within the Party hierarchy, particularly He Guoqiang, who until October 2007 was head of the Central Organisation Department [*zhongzubu* 中组部], which controls the *nomenklatura* system of appointments and promotions. He Guoqiang subsequently became the head of the Central Commission for Discipline Inspection [*zhongjiwei* 中纪委] which targets corruption inside the Party and can make or break political careers. When Xi was appointed to lead Shanghai, He Guoqiang praised him unstintingly as 'politically strong and with a high level of ideology and policy' [*zhengzhi shang qiang, you jiaogao de sixiang zhengce shuiping* 政治上强，有较高的思想政策水平] and complimented him on his experience, leadership style, work methods and commitment to democratic centralism, as well as his honesty, concern for the masses and his ability to bring people together.

## *Xi's early career*

When Xi Jinping graduated in 1979 he became secretary to Geng Biao, a former ambassador and future Minister of Defence, who at the time was a member of the Politburo, Vice-Chairman of the State Council and Secretary General of the Central Military

Commission in whose offices Xi worked in Zhongnanhai. When Xi was appointed Vice-Chairman of the Central Commission in 2012 this had been his only military experience, essentially a political role although technically he was a serving officer.[24]

From 1982 to 1985 he was Deputy Secretary and then Secretary of the CCP Committee of Zhengding County in Hebei Province. In 1985 he was transferred to Fujian Province where he was to spend seventeen and a half years. He took up his new posts as deputy mayor of Xiamen and member of the local CCP Standing Committee on his thirty-second birthday. In contrast to his father's career, his progress was smooth and after three years he had advanced to the post of CCP Secretary of the prefectural-level city, Ningde, south of Fuzhou. In 1990, still only 37 years old he became Party secretary of Fuzhou City and chairman of the municipal people's congress. During his time in Fuzhou he was noted for his lack of interest in prestigious construction projects and in particular for his opposition to the new Fuzhou airport during the provincial airport boom of the 1990s.

In 1995 he also took on the role of Secretary of the Fujian Provincial Party Committee and two years later became an alternate member of the CCP Fifteenth Central Committee. In 1999, at the age of 46, he was appointed Deputy Party Secretary and Deputy Governor and Acting Governor of Fujian Province. The following January he was formally adopted as Fujian's Governor but was transferred rapidly to the neighbouring province of Zhejiang as Deputy Party Secretary. Xi Jinping emerged from his provincial appointments with a reputation for incorruptibility.

In 2002 on the eve of the CCP Sixteenth Congress there were rumours that Xi Jinping was on the verge of being admitted to the Politburo. This did not materialise, but he was elected as a full member of the Central Committee and Zhejiang Party Secretary, replacing Zhang Dejiang who had been promoted to membership of the Politburo and CCP Secretary of Guangdong Province. The following year Xi was appointed chairman of the people's congress in Zhejiang Province.

People who knew Xi well reported that in 2002 when he was transferred from Fujian to Zhejiang this had already vastly exceeded his own expectations of his prospects as he thought he might be sent to Shaanxi, a much less prestigious posting. He assiduously cultivated the local leadership of the Zhejiang region by travelling widely and visiting as many counties as possible. Even allowing for the hyperbole of the official media it is clear that he had acquired a reputation for working tirelessly on behalf of his province and not enriching himself. One paper referred to his 'two planks' [*liang ban* 两板] 'boss during the day, hard bed at night' [*baitian zuo laoban, wanshang shui diban* 白天做老板,晚上睡地板]. Xi's reputation and political standing also benefited from the success of the Zhejiang economy which was regarded by many outsiders as a model for provincial development. He is credited personally for building on an existing strong private sector of small businesses to develop industry and external investment and for promoting the integration of the economies of the Yangtze Delta provinces. This strategy was so highly regarded that he led a Zhejiang delegation to Shanghai to report on it in March 2003 and spoke again on the same topic in November 2006, giving him the opportunity to demonstrate that his vision went beyond the purely provincial.

### *Peng Liyuan*

Xi Jinping's first wife was Ke Lingling, the daughter of China's ambassador to the United Kingdom from 1978–83, Ke Hua, but they divorced after three years. Xi and his second and current wife, Peng Liyuan, were introduced by friends when he was deputy mayor of Xiamen and married in 1987 although her parents were unhappy about the consequences of her marrying into the political hierarchy. Peng did not have a political background but was already well known as a singer of traditional folksongs and appears regularly on television. She had joined the PLA at the age of 18, her career developed through military song and dance troupes and she was a civilian member of the PLA, reputedly with a military-equivalent rank of Major-General. Her military connections have been useful to Xi and he took every opportunity to visit military units near his political bases in Fujian and Shanghai. After the announcement of his promotion, many photographs of Peng Liyuan appeared, glamorous in PLA uniform as well as in civilian clothes, and this further increased his popularity. Xi and Peng have often lived apart, which has led to speculation that they have separated, but physical separation is common for many professional couples in contemporary China.

## Shanghai and the Politburo Standing Committee

Xi Jinping was transferred to Shanghai to replace the disgraced Chen Liangyu. Among the reasons for this move were his 22 years' experience working on the east coast and his interest in integrating the economies of the Yangtze Delta. He also had a reputation for cleaning up corruption and reforming official practices. His approach was low-key and his factional allegiances were ambiguous so he had few obvious opponents. At a time when the 'Shanghai faction' was in retreat and the 'Communist Youth League (CYL) faction' was unpopular for being overbearing and arrogant, Xi Jinping was a useful compromise candidate.

He Guoqiang made it clear that Xi's move to Shanghai had been made on the basis of the 'overall national interest'. The significance of this remark would become apparent at the Seventeenth CCP Congress in October 2007 when Xi Jinping was elevated to the Politburo Standing Committee, apparently with the full support of Hu Jintao who may have wished to demonstrate that the higher echelons of the CCP were not entirely dominated by the CYL Faction. By this promotion, Xi appeared to have overtaken the 'two Lis' of the CYL Faction, Li Keqiang and Li Yuanchao (Head of the CCP Organisation Department since 2007 in succession to He Guoqiang). His ranking at No. 6 in the Politburo after the Seventeenth Congress marked him out as the likely leading figure in the post Hu-Wen administration. The Shanghai post automatically qualified Xi for a seat on the Politburo at the Seventeenth Congress and it was assumed that he would remain in Shanghai for a decent interval before being moved to Beijing. In the event, he was appointed to the Politburo Standing Committee within six months which meant that he could not remain in charge of Shanghai.

## Connections: Hu Yaobang, Hu Jintao and Xi Jinping

The tortuous path that brought Xi Jinping to power was influenced, not only by the political past of his father, Xi Zhongxun, but also by the legacy of Hu Yaobang, the reform-minded CCP Secretary General, and earlier head of the Communist Youth League who was forced from power in 1987 and whose death on 5 April 1989 led to demonstrations that were the immediate precursor of the 4 June Democracy Movement. Xi's background demonstrates the power of complex interpersonal ties rather than simple factional links in Chinese politics.

President Hu Jintao was a protégé of Hu Yaobang, who made a point of spending the Spring Festival with him in Guizhou in February 1986. This was partly to support Hu Jintao but Hu Yaobang could also assess progress in China's poorest province. Hu Jintao greatly admired and respected Hu Yaobang and after his mentor's death in 1989, visited his grave in Gongqing, Jiangxi to pay his respects. Hu Jintao was acutely aware of how highly Hu Yaobang thought of Xi Zhongxun and his political integrity and championed Xi Jinping, although he did not give his 'imperial endorsement' [*qin dian* 钦点] to any specific successor at the Seventeenth CCP Congress in 2007.

Hu Jintao frequently called for greater 'democracy within the Party' [*dangnei minzhu* 党内民主] although he did not publicly back Premier Wen Jiabao's more strident demands. Li Datong, the managing editor of *Freezing Point* [*Bingdian* 冰点], a weekly supplement published by *China Youth Daily*, argued (before he was dismissed and his publication temporarily suspended in January 2006) that China was moving from autocracy towards democracy and that internal Party democracy was the first step.[25] He suggested that 'nomination by the leadership' [*you lingdao timing* 由领导提名] was being replaced by 'everything could be changed by voting' [*you toupiao neng gaibian yiqie* 有投票能改变一切]. This might have been over-optimistic but probably represented the aspirations of many younger members of the CCP: votes within the Party play an increasingly important role in decision making.[26]

The Central Organisation Department carried out a survey by questionnaire among 20 per cent of the leading officials in Shanghai and members of the National People's Congress and CPPCC, a total of 2,000 people; it found overwhelming support for Xi. Reuters cited sources that Xi had gained the majority of votes in inner Party elections from the regions, and other sources indicated that he had obtained 90 per cent of the votes in the first ballot in Shanghai and that he had unanimous support from the heads of Party committees [*dangwei shounao* 党委首脑]. His reputation within the Party was that of a virtuous official and he was said to 'embody the traditional Chinese virtues of filial piety, respect for elders and caring for the young' and to have a clean record which was invaluable at a time when concern about official corruption was high on the Party's agenda.[27]

It is tempting to link this evaluation of Xi to his father's track record of 'pursuing the ideals of democracy and freedom' [*zhui-qiu minzhu ziyou linian* 追求民主自由理念] as well as 'reform and opening' and therefore to the reformist current exemplified by Hu Yaobang and Zhao Ziyang. However, in the light of the political fate of Hu, Zhao and their supporters it is hardly surprising that Xi and others might choose to keep their reformist powder dry and place economic development and political stability ahead of democracy, at least in public.

Xi Jinping's cautious public pronouncements before 2012 concentrated on familiar themes of the Hu and Wen administration such as measures to combat corruption and the promotion of 'harmonious economic development' [*jingji hexie fazhan* 经济和谐发展], appropriate behaviour for a Party leader in waiting. He also warned about demonstrations in the universities and demanded tighter management of educational institutions in the run-up to the 2012 Party Congress to ensure 'harmony and stability'. This does not prevent some commentators from hoping that he is a closet democrat who plays his cards very close to his chest and may permit political reform during the second half of his term in power once the influence of conservatives of the older generation has waned.[28]

Insiders have revealed that in March 2007 when Xi Jinping went to Shanghai to take up his post as Secretary of the Municipal Party Committee he was met with 'sugar-coated bullets' [*tangyi paodan* 糖衣炮弹]. On 28 March the Shanghai Municipal Committee Hospitality Department took him to a detached 'British style' three-storey house at South Xiangyang Road which was over 800 square metres in area with a garden. Regulations limit the floor area of accommodation for provincial level officials to 250 square metres and even members of the Politburo are not supposed to have more than 300 square metres. It was reported that Xi went into his luxury home, took one look and walked out saying that it should be used as a convalescent home for elderly cadres. It is not possible to verify this account but it raises interesting questions: was this the normal treatment for a new Party secretary; did the officials misread Xi's reputation and his likely response; were they trying to entrap this sea-green incorruptible? On another occasion when Xi was due to visit Hangzhou his subordinates had arranged for a private train to take him there from Shanghai but Xi insisted on travelling by road. Relatives of his who had business interests in Shanghai reportedly moved their businesses elsewhere when he became Party secretary to forestall any possible criticism. Although similar stories are routinely published to indicate the positive qualities of officials, they tend to support his reputation for old-fashioned frugality and unwillingness to be compromised by corrupt practices.[29]

### *Li Keqiang*

Li (56) was born in Dingyuan County in eastern Anhui in 1955. His father was a low level CCP cadre at the county level. Li joined the CCP in 1976 and studied in the Faculty of Economics at Beijing University, where he was an in-post research student [*zaizhi yanjiusheng* 在职研究生] and graduated with the equivalent of a BA in Law and a PhD in Economics. In 1974, at the age of 19, he was sent to live in the Damiao Commune Brigade in Fengyang County, Anhui as part of the 'rustication' [*xiafang* 下放] programme as the Cultural Revolution was wound down. Fengyang, although a backwater, became celebrated in 1978 after the decision to end the People's Commune system there and replace it with individual household contracts in one of its villages, Xiaogang. Within two years, Li had become the secretary of the Damiao Production Brigade Party committee. He is remembered by older residents of Damiao as a resourceful young man who moved stones to help build his own accommodation as there was nowhere else for him and his colleagues to live. He became secretary of the local Communist Youth League branch and joined the CCP while he was in the village. Anecdotes of his experiences as a young man are remarkably similar to those of Xi Jinping.

### Beijing University and Communist Youth League

Li left Damiao in March 1978 after passing the revived entrance examinations to Beijing University (Beida). He was part of the energetic and determined first cohort to enter the

Law Department after the Cultural Revolution. Li Keqiang is believed to have entertained liberal ideas during his student years and had an interest in 'legal culture', under the influence of Gong Xiangrui (1911–1996), an academic lawyer who had studied at the London School of Economics in the 1930s and this has encouraged hopes that Li might champion greater openness and democracy. Li became secretary of the Communist Youth League branch at Beijing University and this began his move away from a possible academic career, for which he had seemed destined, into politics.[30]

The intellectual ferment at Beijing University in the late 1970s had a lasting effect on Li and he acquired a lifelong respect for learning and books. Beida has a political inferiority complex and there is a popular saying that can be translated on one level as, 'Great world for Qinghua, Beida is a wasteland', because Qinghua graduates dominate the leadership. In the nine-man Seventeen Politburo Standing Committee of 2007, there were three Qinghua alumni, Hu Jintao, Wu Bangguo and Xi Jinping. Li Keqiang from the 'Beida wasteland' had joined the Standing Committee but there were others in the full Politburo (Li Yuanchao and Bo Xilai). In the provinces at Deputy Governor level and above (and therefore eligible for Politburo status in the future) Beida alumni already outnumbered those from Qinghua by 57 to 37. The balance of Party factions was changing.[31]

Li owes his rise to power primarily to his association with the Communist Youth League (CYL), the recruiting ground for CCP members. He remained at Beida after graduating in 1982, ran the university's CYL, joined the CYL Standing Committee, and headed its Universities Department and National University Liaison Committee. Wang Zhaohua, the head of the CYL Central Organisation Department nominated him to the CYL Eleventh Congress and he was also elected to the CYL Central Committee Standing Committee.

This was Li Keqiang's fast track entry to the political world and a concrete example of the operation of patronage in selecting leading cadres. In May 1993, after almost ten years in the CYL Secretariat, Li, at the age of 38, became First Secretary of the CYL for a five year period. He had not neglected his academic development, taking his Master's degree in the Beida Faculty of Economics and completing a PhD there in 1995.

### *Henan Province*

In 1997 at the Fifteenth CCP Congress Li Keqiang was elected to the CC. He was transferred from the CYL Secretariat to Henan Province in June 1998 as Deputy Secretary of the Party committee of the province and later appointed deputy, then acting Governor and within six months had become Governor in his own right. At the conclusion of the Sixteenth Party congress in 2002 he was also elevated to the position of Henan Party Secretary and the following year became Chairman of the Standing Committee of the Henan People's Congress. Establishing such a suite of powerful positions in one of the provinces is a *sine qua non* for potential senior leaders of the CCP.

A series of unpredictable events in Henan and difficulties in dealing with complex political relationships in the province left him politically bruised. Li had left his family behind in Beijing to shield them from the inevitable political socialising and moved to Zhengzhou, the provincial capital, on his own. He acquired a reputation for declining invitations to banquets that had no connection with his official role and dined simply, alone or with his private secretary.

Two serious fires occurred soon after his appointment as Governor. Seventy-four people died in Jiaozuo City on 29 March 2000 while watching a film and a further 309 people perished on 25 December 2000 when fire took hold of a dance hall in the city of Luoyang. Since Li had only been Governor for a short time he avoided any direct blame for these disasters and attended personally to direct operations. The death toll (second highest in a fire since 1949) and the revelation that the local fire brigade had warned that the building was unsafe reflected badly on the provincial government. Li Keqiang accepted responsibility and wrote to the central government offering his resignation but it was not accepted. The effects of these fires and a series of mining disasters taxed him mentally and physically between June 1998 and 12 December 2004 when he left Henan to take up new challenges in Liaoning Province.

Other political headaches included the scandal of contaminated noodle flour and the popularity of Falungong. Worst of all was the wilful neglect by local medical authorities of the illegal sale of blood which led to an unprecedented epidemic of HIV and AIDS. The commercialisation of blood supplies had begun before Li arrived in Henan, probably as early as 1992, but he was severely criticised for the news blackout and cover-up which might have exacerbated the outbreak. He enforced a clampdown on illegal sales, established a network of model blood-collection stations and visited one of the worst affected areas, Wenlou Village in Shangcai County, three times. The newly installed central administration led by Hu Jintao and Wen Jiabao was beginning to make a serious commitment to deal with China's HIV/AIDS problem at the national level. Li publicly shook hands with AIDS sufferers, announced free medical treatment and met AIDS activists (who had previously been silenced by the authorities) to discuss the problem of AIDS orphans and treatment. The timing suggests that he might have been waiting for a change of heart at the Party centre before he acted. At the beginning of 2004 he organised work teams of his own officials to go to the 38 worst affected villages to give 'help and support'. The official media claimed that by 2004 the HIV/AIDS epidemic had been brought under control and that the number of AIDS-related deaths had fallen significantly.

Commentators differ on Li's effectiveness in developing the economy of Henan. He promoted agricultural production and the processing of agricultural products and Henan certainly became known for famous brands of foodstuff, but critics argued that the 'cities of the central plains' were not well-managed and had difficulty attracting investment. Although not all of these problems were the result of Li's policies he was the top man [*yibashou* 一把手] at the time and much of the blame fell on him.[32]

## *Liaoning Province*

The morning after his formal send off from Henan Li flew to the Liaoning provincial capital of Shenyang and at 3.30 that afternoon gave his 'appointment speech' [*jiuye jiangyan* 就业讲演] to a meeting of Liaoning's leading cadres. He was introduced at the conference by Li Jingtian, deputy director of the CCP's Central Organisation Department, and himself a former CYL official, on behalf of the central leadership in Beijing. Li Jingtian's speech at the meeting can be seen as an endorsement and appraisal of Li Keqiang. It praised the new Party secretary's achievements in his previous post, failed to mention the problems that had beset him and emphasised his open and democratic style of work and the close alignment of his ideas with those of the leadership in Beijing.

Liaoning is one of north-eastern China's traditional industrial heartlands, known for oil and mining industries and with an impressive record of growth in GNP. Its Party and government hierarchy also has a track record of supplying members of the highest CCP bodies, notably the three Lis of Liaoning in the second half of the 1980s – Li Tieying (President of the Chinese Academy of Social Sciences, 1998–2003, and vice-chairman of NPC Standing Committee 2003– ), Li Guixian (President of the Bank of China, 1988–93) and Li Changchun (Member of the Standing Committee of the Politburo 2002– ) – not to mention Bo Xilai (CCP Secretary of Chongqing, 2007–12). Liaoning could be seen as another fast track to the top. However, Liaoning faced severe economic and social challenges, mostly stemming from the move away from the planned economy and state owned enterprises, the resulting pension burden and changes in development strategies. Li Keqiang made full use of the state's policies of revitalising the Northeast, which were initiated under the Hu – Wen administration, to improve the living standards of local people.[33]

In Liaoning, Li found a major project with which he could be publicly associated – the shanty town districts [*penghu qu* 棚户区]. These were temporary constructions in declining mining areas, originally erected in the 1960s for mine and factory workers but taken over by the poor and destitute. In a television interview with the well-known presenter Wang Xiaoya, Li vowed that he would transform the shanty town districts if it was the last thing he did [*zaguo maitie* 砸锅卖铁]. He quoted Archimedes and argued that his fulcrum to change the shanty towns was the CCP Centre and the power of the people but the shanty towns also functioned as a fulcrum for his own rise to power. He was able to raise substantial funds from the State Development Bank to build new housing for 1,200,000 people. Redevelopment started in 2005 and by 2007 relocation was well under way. Li was praised for solving this long-standing problem but it was possible only because of his powerful connections with the centre. He included an account of this programme in his report on the economic revitalisation of Liaoning to the Seventeenth CCP Congress on 17 October 2007.[34]

On the eve of the 2007 Spring Festival, Wu Bangguo, Chairman of the Standing Committee of the 10th NPC visited Liaoning. Premier Wen Jiabao followed hard on his heels, his second visit to Liaoning in three years, in an unusual show of support for Li Keqiang's policies. Lee Kuan-yew, the elder statesman and 'Minister Mentor' of Singapore also visited the province and Lian Zhan, Chairman of the Taiwan Guomindang spent four days in Henan in 2007 and commented on Li Keqiang's contribution to the economic progress of the province.[35]

However there were more disasters that affected Li Keqiang's standing in Liaoning and his political prospects, especially an explosion at a dance hall in which 25 people died. Because some occurred during the 'two meetings' (NPC and the CPPCC) in Beijing which Li was attending, this brought them to the attention of a wider public. Li ordered officials in Liaoning to make a full report to the media, deftly avoiding criticism of any cover-up. He travelled to the scene and assumed control of the rescue operations, avoiding criticisms from the relatives. This effective crisis management won him approval but, on the orders of the Central Propaganda Department, there was also a ban on criticism of Li in the media. The leadership wished to protect the reputation of the man who was about to join their ranks.

### *Rise to power*

As a student Li Keqiang had set out the essential prerequisites for a successful official: serve the masses but be assertive when necessary; intellectual organisation and political vision; and a sense of justice and loyalty. Some Beida contemporaries, including the dissident Wang Juntao, had doubts about his ability, believing that Li suffered from typical Beida academic aloofness and might not be able to handle the Party machinery. Wang Juntao also pointed to former high fliers from the 'liberal' or 'reformist' wing of the CCP, notably Hu Yaobang and Zhao Ziyang, who had been forced out of office.

On the eve of the Seventeenth CCP Congress, Xi Jinping suddenly emerged to seize the top Party post from Li's grasp, a position that was maintained at the Eighteenth CCP Congress in the autumn of 2012.[36] In 2009, a source close to the State Council (but admittedly also close to Li's rival, Bo Xilai) argued that Li Keqiang was very lucky to have got as far as he had and some commentators in China and Hong Kong argue that he is not up to the job. The political and news magazine *Kaifang* [开放] 'revealed' in July 2010 that Li's abilities had been called into question at the highest level within the Party and that he might even be moved to take the chairmanship of the National People's Congress, an important position but not as politically sensitive as that of Premier. Li Keqiang succeeded to the premiership in 2013 as planned: after Bo Xilai's political demise, stability was the top priority.[37]

## Fifth Generation leadership and Politburo Standing Committee

As expected the appointments of Xi Jinping and Li Keqiang to the two most senior posts were confirmed. Appointments to the Politburo Standing Committee were much less predictable, especially as the new Standing Committee was reduced from nine to seven seats which left room for only five additional members in addition to Xi (Ranking No. 1) and Li (No. 2). This is assumed to be the result of horse trading to achieve a factional balance after Bo Xilai was ruled out of membership.

### *Zhang Dejiang (No. 3)*

Vice-Premier Zhang Dejiang (66) was considered an outside candidate but secured the top appointment after Xi and Li. Zhang graduated in Korean from Yanbian University in Yanji, the capital of China's ethnic Korean region in Jilin Province, and studied economics at Kim Il-sung University in Pyongyang. Although his background indicates a key role in negotiations with North Korea, Zhang's principal responsibilities are liaison with the National People's Congress. He is thought to be close to Hu Jintao and the Communist Youth League.[38]

### *Yu Zhengsheng (No. 4)*

The father of Yu Zhengsheng (67) joined the CCP in 1932 and was rumoured to have been married to Jiang Qing. His background is in electronic engineering, ballistic missile control systems and research administration. His early political roles were as mayor in the cities of Qingdao and Yantai in Shandong Province. In 1992 his brother Yu Qiangsheng, a senior official in the Ministry of State Security, defected to the United States. He later served as Party Secretary of Hubei Province and then on the staff of Deng Xiaoping's respected economic adviser Zhu Rongji when Zhu ran Shanghai between 1987 and 1991. Yu joined the Politburo in 2002 and succeeded Xi Jinping as CCP Secretary in Shanghai after the Seventeenth CCP Congress in 2007.

Yu Zhengsheng survived his brother's defection because of his close connections with Deng Xiaoping's family, in particular Deng's eldest son Deng Pufang. Deng Pufang's Kanghua Development Corporation became embroiled in a tax evasion controversy during an anti-corruption drive. Yu wound it up with minimum collateral damage to the Deng family and became their informal representative in internal CCP politics. His age and experience is a useful counterweight in a relatively young Politburo Standing Committee and a stabilising presence in the wake of the Bo Xilai debacle. He also chairs the Chinese People's Political Consultative Conference.[39]

### *Liu Yunshan (No. 5)*

The former Head of the CC Propaganda Department, Liu (66) now controls the powerful Central Secretariat and is also President of the Party School. He was initially a reporter and public relations specialist and his political career began in Inner Mongolia where he was born in 1947 and worked for over 20 years. His family roots are in Shanxi Province. He was a conservative and authoritarian head of the CCP Propaganda Department and is known to favour tighter controls on dissent and the media. He is closely associated with the Communist Youth League and through this with Hu Jintao, the retiring President.[40]

### *Wang Qishan (No. 6)*

Wang Qishan (63) was CCP Secretary of Hainan, ran the China Construction Bank from 1994–1997 and was Mayor of Beijing before his election to the Politburo in 2007 and then promoted to Vice-Premier with responsibility for the economy, finance and energy in March 2008. A historian by training with publications on the early Republican period, he is noted for his financial expertise and promotion of China's stock exchanges, as well as having been Zhu Rongji's gatekeeper during Zhu's premiership from 1998–2003. His political style is remarkable for its openness and he is regarded as a safe pair of hands and a useful trouble-shooter who can be relied on in a crisis: his nickname is 'firefighter' so he was given a Fire Department helmet when he visited New York City in January 2011. Wang has been deemed a 'princeling' but also flippantly as a member of the 'son-in-law faction'. His wife Yao Mingshan is the daughter of Yao Yilin who was a First Vice-Premier from 1988 to 1993. Wang successfuly managed the Guangdong banking crisis in 1998, the SARS crisis in 2002 and the 2008 Olympic Games and participated in the US-China Strategic and Economic Dialogues in 2009, 2010 and 2011.[41]

### *Zhang Gaoli (No. 7)*

Ranking last in the Standing Committee but also serving as First Vice-Premier, the former Tianjin Party Secretary is an economic development specialist who was considered an outsider before the Eighteenth Party Congress. He maintains a very low profile – some have called him invisible – but is understood to have been a protégé of Jiang Zemin. His appointment is seen as a success for the remnants of Jiang's Shanghai faction although Zhang never held a post in Shanghai. His early career was spent in Guangdong Province including the Shenzhen Special Economic Zone and then in State Council posts with responsibility for economic development and energy policy.[42]

## Outside the standing committee

### *Li Yuanchao (Vice-Premier)*

Li Yuanchao (61) is a mathematician and economist who served as CCP Secretary of Jiangsu Province and headed the Party's powerful Organisation Department from 2007. He became Vice-President in the 2012/13 transfer of power but did not gain a Standing Committee seat. He was responsible for commissioning a major internal report from the Party Building Institute, in collaboration with the Shanghai Party School and Shandong University, on the international experience of communist parties, to see what lessons could be learnt for 'the construction of our party', possible pointers to political reform.[43]

### *Wang Yang (Vice-Premier)*

Wang Yang (57) moved from Chongqing in 2007 to be Secretary of the CCP Committee in Guangdong Province and Bo Xilai's high-profile campaign against organised crime in Chongqing was interpreted partly as a criticism of his rival. Wang's policy of a more open and tolerant Guangdong encouraged supporters of reform in contrast to Bo Xilai's call for a return to 'red culture'. After the Wukan protests, Wang clamped down on protestors and the media in Guangdong to demonstrate his toughness but he did not achieve the expected seat on the Standing Committee.[44]

### *Bo Xilai and the transfer of power*

Bo Xilai (62) was a member of the Politburo and the CCP Secretary of Chongqing Municipality but his historic powerbase was in China's Northeast where he was Mayor of Dalian and Governor of Liaoning Province. He is deemed to be a member of the 'princeling' faction as the son of Bo Yibo, one of Deng Xiaoping's closest allies in his later years. Bo Xilai was regarded as both a dark horse and a loose cannon and he made no secret of his political ambitions. Some commentators wondered whether Xi Jinping could work with Bo Xilai as Bo Yibo and Xi Zhongxun had clashed. There is no evidence that Xi Jinping was instrumental in the downfall of Bo Xilai but it is unlikely to have distressed him unduly.

Bo moved to Chongqing as Governor in January 2007 and became CCP Secretary in November 2007, replacing his great rival Wang Yang who was transferred to Guangdong. Bo consolidated his position in Chongqing by bringing in his former colleague from Liaoning, Wang Lijun, as Deputy Mayor in 2008 to run his campaign against triad ('black') gangs. This campaign was controversial because of allegations of corruption, abuse of civil rights and even torture. However it was eclipsed by the 'red culture' campaign: during the spring and summer of 2011, television programming in Chongqing was dominated by 'red' subjects and Bo's officials encouraged the singing of revolutionary songs and the sending of students to the countryside to learn old-fashioned (Maoist) values. These two campaigns – the 'red' and the 'black' – were linked in the media and were endorsed by members of the senior leadership in Beijing including Wu Bangguo, the Chairman of the National People's Congress.

On the ground in Chongqing in October 2011 there was little evidence of 'red culture'. The National Day edition of *Chongqing wanbao* (*Chongqing Evening News*) published on 1 October carried stories about Bo Xilai with his photograph but these were in connection with improved rail travel and (ironically in the light of what later transpired) a meeting with former US President George H.W. Bush. There was no mention of 'red culture'.[45]

In February 2012 Wang Lijun stayed overnight at the United States consulate in Chengdu, the Sichuan provincial capital. He was apparently trying to defect with damaging information about Bo and other senior Party leaders but was taken away by officials of the Ministry of State Security.

Bo was dismissed as Party Secretary of Chongqing on 15 March with the unanimous approval of the Politburo Standing Committee and his membership of the Central Committee and the Politburo were suspended on 10 April. It transpired that Bo's wife, Gu Kailai, was responsible for the death of Neil Heywood, a British businessman and associate of the Bo family, whose body had been found in a Chongqing hotel room in November 2011. Gu was sentenced to death, suspended for two years, in August 2012 and the following month, Wang, with whom she had an emotional entanglement, was imprisoned for 15 years for associated offences.

Bo Xilai was tried for corruption and abuse of power in August 2013. He mounted a spirited and robust defence against all the charges during a hearing that was reported in unprecedented detail. A guilty verdict was announced on 22 September and he was sentenced to life imprisonment on the bribery charges and to lesser terms for embezzlement and abuse of power. The sentence, which is subject to appeal, was harsher than any commentators had predicted. This may reflect displeasure at his failure to plead guilty and the waning of support for him within the CCP. The

Bo Xilai affair continues to haunt the new leadership: Bo's most powerful ally, Zhou Yongkang, who had responsibility for state security in the Politburo Standing Committee until the autumn of 2012, is under investigation for corruption and the cases of others close to Zhou are under review.[46]

## Notes

1. An earlier but longer version of this paper was published by ECRAN in 2012 before the changes were announced. The author is grateful to Krzysztof Szumski, former Ambassador of Poland to the People's Republic of China for sharing his insights on the leadership changes and also to the anonymous reviewers for ECRAN and Kerry Brown of Chatham House and the University of Sydney.
2. *Xinhua* via *South China Morning Post* 3 July 2011.
3. Deng relinquished his final official position as Chairman of the Central Military Commission in 1989, but his continuing authority was evident from the impact of his 'southern tour' in 1992.
4. It can be assumed that senior military officers and officials of the intelligence services, among others, will have some input into the selection process but there is no reliable information on this.
5. 73.496 million *China Daily* 5 April 2007.
6. Details of the discourse on party reform and the legacy of Hu Yaobang and others can be found in successive issues of the critical journal *Yanhuang chunqiu* (*The Spring and Autumn Annals of the Emperors Yan and Huang*).
7. Supporting evidence is provided in the detailed accounts of the careers of Xi and Li below. Detailed information on Deng Xiaoping's attitude to political reform will be found in Michael Dillon *Deng Xiaoping: a political biography* London: I.B. Tauris, 2014 (forthcoming).
8. *South China Morning Post* 20 January 2012; Hu Deping *Zhongguo weishenme yao gaige: siyi fuqin Hu Yaobang* (*Why China needs reform: remembering my father Hu Yaobang*) Beijing: Renmin chubanshe, 2011, pp. 86–129 and passim.
9. John P. Burns 'China's nomenklatura system' *Problems of Communism,* September–October 1987, Volume XXXVI pp. 36–51; John P. Burns (ed.) *The Chinese Communist Party's*

*Nomenklatura System* Armonk, NY and London: M.E. Sharpe, 1989.

10. Waican bianji bu 外参编辑部 (Editorial Department of Waican Magazine) *Zhong Gong shibada zhi zheng* 中共十八大之争 (The struggle for Chinese Communists' Eighteenth Congress) Hong Kong: Waican Publishers, 2011, p. 92.
11. Shi Hua 史华 *Hu Wen weiji* 胡温危机 (*TheHu Wen crisis*) Hong Kong: Hong Kong Cultural Press, 2004, p.15.
12. Tan Tian 谭天*Shiba da qian de xiaoyan* 十八大前的硝烟 (*Smell of Cordite before the Eighteenth Party Congress*) Hong Kong: New Culture Press, 2010, pp. 16–17.
13. Qiu Feng, Unirule Institute of Economics (independent think tank in Beijing) quoted in Louisa Lim '"Cake theory" has Chinese eating up political debate', NPR, 6 November 2011; Tania Branigan 'China's leaders break ranks in readiness for new dawn' *Guardian* 26 November 2011.
14. There are interesting parallels with the factional structure of the Japanese Liberal Democratic Party, raising the question of whether East Asian cultural factors play an important role. The LDP, a conservative party, held power in Japan almost without interruption from 1955 until 2009. Although it has acknowledged factions, these are based on the patronage of powerful individual politicians and it is difficult to determine any real differences of political ideology between them. The LDP and CCP have little in common politically but both insist on governing by consensus and ensuring that disputes and policy differences are hammered out in private.
15. Shi Hua 史华 *Hu Wen weiji* 胡温危机 (*The Hu Wen crisis*) Hong Kong: Hong Kong Cultural Press, 2004, pp. 4–7.
16. *South China Morning Post* 8, 10 March 2012.
17. In a *speech at the Sixteenth CCC Congress in November 2002* Jiang had argued that the CCP should be 'a faithful representative of the requirements in the development of advanced productive forces in China, the orientation of the advanced culture in China, and the fundamental interests of the broadest masses of the people in China'.
18. Wen Yu 'Zeng Qinghong: A potential challenger to China's heir apparent' *China Brief*, volume, 3, issue 10, 2001.
19. Willy Lam 'National People's Congress maneuvers: Jiang on top' *China Brief*, volume 3, no. 5, 2004; *South China Morning Post* 31 October, 5 December 2011, 21 April, 10 May 2012; Shi

Hua 史华 *Hu Wen weiji* 胡温危机 (*The Hu Wen crisis*) Hong Kong: Hong Kong Cultural Press, 2004, pp. 17–24.

20. 'Not much will change under China's next leaders' Willy Lam *China Post* Taiwan 13 May 2010; Willy Lam 'Hu's state visit exposes rift in Chinese foreign policy', *China Brief*, volume 11, no.2, 28 January 2011; *South China Morning Post* 19 January, 16 April, 6 May 2012.
21. Yu Jie 余杰*Zhongguo yingdi: Wen Jiabao* 中国影帝：温家宝 (subtitled in English *China's Best Actor: Wen Jiabao*) Hong Kong: New Century Press, 2010. Yu Jie, a high profile dissident, was unable to publish this in China and was interrogated and brutally treated by the police for criticising Premier Wen; *South China Morning Post* 26 January, 28 January, 13 February, 6 April, 9 May, 28 July, 3 November, 18 November 2011, 19 January 2012; BBC News 14 March 2011; Ian Johnson 'Rumblings of reform in Beijing?' *New York Review of Books*, 20 October 2010.
22. Tan Tian 谭天 *Shiba da qian de xiaoyan* 十八大前的硝烟 (*Smell of Cordite before the Eighteenth Party Congress*) Hong Kong: New Culture Press, 2010, pp. 8–9, 17–18. *Xinhua*; *BBC News* 18 October 2010.
23. *Duowei Times* Beijing correspondent.
24. *Xinhua* 18 October 2010.
25. Susan Shirk *China: Fragile Superpower* Oxford: Oxford University Press, 2007, pp. 79–80, 92, 94.
26. An experimental poll of 370 members and alternate of the Central Committee was held in May 2012 to assess the popularity of possible leadership contenders. *South China Morning Post* 8 June 2012.
27. In the voting for membership of the Central Committee in 1997 he had finished last and joined the committee as an alternative member only. However this can be seen as a protest against 'princelings' in general rather than a reflection on Xi's popularity or suitability.
28. Wu Ming 吴鸣 *Xi Jinping zhuan: Zhongguo xin lingxiu* 习近平转：中国新领袖 (*Biography of Xin Jinping: China's new leader*) Hong Kong: Hong Kong Cultural Press, 2010, pp. 287–325 for an account of Xi Jinping in Zhejiang and his relations with Zhang Dejiang.
29. Xia Fei et al. 夏飞*Taizidang he gongqingtuan: Xi Jinping PK Li Keqiang* 太子党和共青团: 习近平 PK 李克强 (*Crown Prince Party and Communist Youth League Faction: Xi Jinping competes with*

*Li Keqiang*) Hong Kong: Mirror Books, 2007, pp. 89–122. There is a more complete account of Xi's life and career in Wu Ming 吴鸣 *Xi Jinping zhuan: Zhongguo xin lingxiu*习近平转：中国新领袖 (*Biography of Xin Jinping: China's new leader*) Hong Kong: Hong Kong Cultural Press, 2010, pp. 13–15 and passim. This account is copiously illustrated and there are no major disagreements about the broad outline of his political career. See also *Waican bianji bu* 外参编辑部 (Editorial Department of Waican Magazine) *Xi Jinping mianlin de tiaozhang* 习近平面临的挑战 (The challenge facing Xi Jinping) Hong Kong: Waican Publishers, 2011, pp. 83–91, 342–7 and passim. Geoff Dyer 'The People's Princeling', *Financial Times*, 23 October 2010; *South China Morning Post* 14, 21, 22, 29 December 2011, 17, 23, 25 January 2012, BBC News 24 January, 14, 17 February 2012.

30. Xia Fei et al. 夏飞 *Taizidang he gongqingtuan: Xi Jinping PK Li Keqiang* 太子党和共青团: 习近平 PK 李克强 (*Crown Prince Party and Communist Youth League Faction: Xi Jinping competes with Li Keqiang*) Hong Kong: Mirror Books, 2007, pp. 131–163; Alice Miller 'The Preparation of Li Keqiang' *China Leadership Monitor* 31, Stanford: Hoover Institution, Winter 2010; Chris Buckley 'China premier-in-waiting schooled in era of dissent' *Reuters* 28 October 2011; Zhao Lei *'Beida falüxi 'huangpu yiqi' neibanren'* 北大法律系'黄埔一期'那班人 The "Graduates of the First Class of the Huangpu Academy": The Students of the First Post-Cultural Revolution Class at the Law Department of Beijing University, *Nonfang zhoumo* (*Southern Weekend*) June 7, 2007.

31. *Da Qing shijie bei dahuang* [大清世界北大荒] also means 'the great northern wastes of the Qing dynasty world'. Xia Fei 夏飞 et al. *Taizidang he gongqingtuan: Xi Jinping PK Li Keqiang* 太子党和共青团: 习近平 PK 李克强 (*Crown Prince Party and Communist Youth League Faction: Xi Jinping competes with Li Keqiang*) Hong Kong: Mirror Books, 2007, pp. 131–163.

32. Xia Fei et al. 夏飞 *Taizidang he gongqingtuan: Xi Jinping PK Li Keqiang* 太子党和共青团: 习近平 PK 李克强 (*Crown Prince Party and Communist Youth League Faction: Xi Jinping competes with Li Keqiang*) Hong Kong: Mirror Books, 2007, pp. 131–163. For the 2008 celebrations of the thirtieth anniversary of the Fengyang reforms, see www.fengyang.gov.cn; *People's Daily* 27 December 2000. Pierre Haski *Le sang de la Chine: quand le silence tue*, Paris: Grasset, 2005.

33. *Xinhua* 8 September 2004; Zhiyue Bo 'The Sixteenth Central Committee of the Chinese Communist Party: formal institutions and factional groups' *Journal of Contemporary China* (2004), 13(39), May, pp. 223–256. Bo identified Li Keqiang as the best connected member of this Central Committee.
34. *China Daily*; *english.cpcnews.cn/92375/6284736.html*Cached.
35. *People's Daily* 15 May 2006; *China Daily* 14, 21 February, 9 March 2007.
36. Xia Fei et al. 夏飞 *Taizidang he gongqingtuan: Xi Jinping PK Li Keqiang* 太子党和共青团: 习近平 PK 李克强 (*Crown Prince Party and Communist Youth League Faction: Xi Jinping competes with Li Keqiang*) Hong Kong: Mirror Books, 2007, pp. 131–163.
37. Personal communication, Beijing 2009; Waican bianji bu 外参编辑部(Editorial Department of *Waican* Magazine) Zhong Gong shibada zhi zheng 中共十八大之争 (*The Struggle for the Chinese Communist Party's Eighteenth Congress*) Hong Kong: Waican Publishers, 2011, pp. 92–3; *Kaifang* 6, 2010. The careers of some of these rivals are outlined below; *South China Morning Post* 19 March 2012.
38. Willy Wo-Lap Lam *Chinese Politics in the Hu Jintao era: new leaders, new challenges* New York: M.E. Sharpe, 2006, pp. 19–20; *South China Morning Post* 19 June 2012.
39. Jia Yumin贾玉民 Di Wudai Zhonggong shiba da zhujue 第五代中共十八大主角 (Fifth Generation: Leading players in the CCP Eighteenth Congress) Hong Kong: Mirror Books, 2010, pp. 262–3 and 263–95 passim. Willy Lam 'Jockeying for position intensifies among candidates for the Politburo Standing Committee' *China Brief*, volume 11, issue 20, 28 October 2011; Benjamin Lim 'China princeling emerges from defection scandal' *Reuters*, 19 June, 2007. Yu Minsheng (another brother of Yu Zhengsheng) and Deng Pufang were at primary school together and Deng and Yu Zhengsheng may have known each other at university though Deng is one year older; *South China Morning Post* 23 May 2012.
40. Jia Yumin贾玉民Di wudai Zhong gong shibada zhujue 第五代中共十八大主角 (Fifth Generation: Leading players in the CCP Eighteenth Congress) Hong Kong: Mirror Books, 2010, pp. 323–35.
41. Jia Yumin贾玉民 Di Wudai Zhonggong shibada zhujue 第五代中共十八大主角 (Fifth Generation: Leading players in the

CCP Eighteenth Congress) Hong Kong: Mirror Books, 2010, pp. 129–162; *China Daily* 5 November 2011.

42. Jia Yumin贾玉民 Di wudai Zhong gong shibada zhujue 第五代中共十八大主角 (Fifth Generation: Leading players in the CCP Eighteenth Congress) Hong Kong: Mirror Books, 2010, pp. 295–321.
43. Jia Yumin贾玉民 *Di Wudai: Zhonggong shibada zhujue*第五代中共十八大主角 (Fifth Generation: Leading players in the CCP Eighteenth Congress) Hong Kong: Mirror Books, 2010, pp. 98–128; Li Cheng 'China's Two Li's: Frontrunners in the Race to Succeed Hu Jintao' *China Leadership Monitor*, no. 22, 5 October 2007; *Financial Times* 30 September 2009.
44. *South China Morning Post* 27 December 2010, 9 June 2012.
45. Waican bianji bu 外参编辑部(Editorial Department of Waican Magazine) Xi Jinping mianlin de tiaozhang 习近平面临的挑战 (The challenge facing Xi Jinping) Hong Kong: Waican Publishers, 2011, pp. 159–66. *South China Morning Post* 13 April, 20 April, 28 May, 30 June, 2 July, 9 July, 14 October, 2011; Eric Li 'Chongqing Rising' *South China Morning Post* 1 December, 2011, 6, 7, 10, 18 March 2012; *Chongqing Evening News* 1 October 2011. These observations are informed by the author's visit to Chongqing in October 2011.
46. *China Daily* 15 March 2012; *South China Morning Post* 18 March, 25, 26 May, 4 June 2012; Ian Johnson 'A Chinese Murder Mystery' *New York Review of Books* 7 June 2012.

## Bibliography

Branigan, Tania 'China's leaders break ranks in readiness for new dawn' *Guardian* 26 November 2011.

Cheng, Li *China's Leaders: the New Generation* Lanham: Rowman and Littlefield, 2001.

*Feng Chongyi* 'Charter 08, the Troubled History and Future of Chinese Liberalism' *The Asia-Pacific Journal*, 41-5-10, 11 October 2010.

Gao Tian 高天 (ed.) *Zhong gong diliudai*中共第六代 (*Chinese Communist Party: The Sixth Generation*) Hong Kong: Hong Kong Cultural Press, 2010.

Jia Yumin贾玉民Di wudai Zhong gong shibada zhujue 第五代中共十八大主角 (Fifth Generation: Leading players in the CCP Eighteenth Congress) Hong Kong: Mirror Books, 2010.

Johnson, Ian 'A Chinese murder mystery' *New York Review of Books* 7 June 2012.

Ma Ling 马玲*Wen Jiabao xin zhuan*温家宝新传 (*New Biography of Wen Jiabao*) Hong Kong: Mingbao, 2008.

Nathan, Andrew J. and Bruce Gilley *China's New Rulers: The secret files* New York: New York Review of Books, 2003 (2nd edition).

Shi Hua 史华*Hu Wen weiji*胡温危机 (*TheHu Wen crisis*) Hong Kong: Hong Kong Cultural Press, 2004.

Tan Tian 谭天*Shiba da qian de xiaoyan*十八大前的硝烟 (*The Smell of Cordite before the Eighteenth Party Congress*) Hong Kong: New Culture Press, 2010.

Waican bianji bu 外参编辑部(Editorial Department of *Waican* Magazine) Zhong gong shibada zhi zheng 中共十八大之争 (The Struggle for Chinese Communists' Eighteenth Congress) Hong Kong: Waican Publishers, 2011.

Waican bianji bu 外参编辑部(Editorial Department of *Waican* Magazine) Xi Jinping mianlin de tiaozhang 习近平面临的挑战 (The challenge facing Xi Jinping) Hong Kong: Waican Publishers, 2011.

Wu Ming 吴鸣*Hu Jintao xin gongliie e*胡锦涛新攻略 (*Hu Jintao's New Attack*) Hong Kong: Hong Kong Cultural Press, 2007.

Wu Ming 吴鸣*Xi Jinping zhuan: Zhongguo xin lingxiu*习近平转：中国新领袖 (*Biography of Xin Jinping: China's new leader*) Hong Kong: Hong Kong Cultural Press, 2010.

Xia Fei et al. 夏飞*Taizidang he gongqingtuan: Xi Jinping PK Li Keqiang*太子党和共青团: 习近平PK 李克强 (*Crown Prince Party and Communist Youth League Faction: Xi Jinping plays Li Keqiang*) Hong Kong: Mirror Books, 2007.

Yi Ming 伊铭*Hu Wen xin zheng*胡温新政 (*New Politics of Hu and Wen*) Hong Kong: Mirror Books, 2003.

Yu Jie 余杰*Zhongguo yingdi: Wen Jiabao* 中国影帝：温家宝(subtitled in English *China's Best Actor: Wen Jiabao*) Hong Kong: New Century Press, 2010.

# 5 Social Unrest in China

*Lynette H. Ong and Christian Göbel*

## Introduction

Social unrest is on the rise in China. Few incidents of public demonstrations, disruptive action or riots occurred in the 1980s, but the 1989 student protests in Tiananmen Square marked a turning point. In 1993, there were already 8,700 'mass incidents' recorded. By 2005, the number had grown tenfold to 87,000. Unofficial data estimated by a researcher at Tsinghua University suggests that there were 180,000 incidents in 2010.[1] These figures could easily be interpreted as signs that the days of the Chinese Communist Party's (CCP) rule are numbered. However, the number of media outlets has proliferated since the 1990s; and with that, the incentive to report on eye-catching stories has increased. In comparing these incidents with the protests that toppled several authoritarian regimes during the Arab Spring of 2011, a number of significant differences emerge. The scale of most protests in China is much smaller. Protestors are usually a homogenous group, such as peasants, taxi drivers, migrant workers or homeowners. Mobilisation across social groups, an important precondition for system-threatening collective action, is therefore largely absent. Further, despite rising unrest, the death toll in such activities remains low.

Most important, few of these protests are aimed at toppling the regime, even though popular uprisings can do so, as evidenced in the Arab Spring. Interestingly, rising incidents of social unrest do not correlate with a decrease in the legitimacy of the CCP's one-party rule.[2] Although local officials are heavily criticised for their incompetence and corruption, few people are in favour of regime change.

If it is not a sign of an impending regime change or even of a major legitimacy crisis, what does social unrest in China signify? In this chapter, we argue that social unrest should be seen as a form of participation – as a means to communicate specific grievances in the hope that local government or the central authorities will address them. Two issues are at stake here: grievances and participation. Although scholars and politicians tend to focus on the former, the latter deserves equal attention. In fact, rising incidents of unrest might not be the result of mounting grievances but of changing forms of participation. The growth of information and communication technology (ICT) in China has brought about improved availability of information on issues at the heart of people's well-being, such as food quality and environmental pollution. It has also improved the ability of protestors to learn from the success or failure of previous initiatives, and to communicate their grievances and strategies.

In simple terms, the increase in occurrences of social unrest is likely the result of exploitation of material interests of disadvantaged groups, the inadequacy of formal channels of communication combined with greater opportunities for and falling costs of instigating or participating in social unrest.

As we will also show, this does not make social unrest innocuous. If the number of protests continues to rise, the perception that grievances are not being adequately addressed may translate into opposition to the regime. Even more likely is a scenario in which security forces overreact, protests spiral out of control, isolated protests link up with each other and large-scale riots are answered with massive repression. Realising these dangers, the Chinese government has begun to address the grievances underlying social unrest. It is also investing considerable resources in improving its ability to control, repress and prevent unrest, while some formal channels for communicating grievances are being improved.

This report sheds light on the forms, manifestations and root causes of social unrest and its role in the political system. It also analyses various strategies of the Chinese government for mitigating and countering protests. The section 'The Changing Nature of Social Unrest' examines definition, forms, distribution and development of social unrest in China. The next section 'Issues Leading to Grievances' analyses the root causes of rising unrest.

The study is based on English- and Chinese-language sources comprising official documents, newspaper reports, statistical yearbooks and scholarly publications as well as data and observations gathered in several weeks of fieldwork in Guangzhou (in February 2010), Shenzhen, Shenyang, Chongqing (in 2003 and 2004), Hefei (in December 2011) and Beijing.

## The Changing Nature of Social Unrest

Escalating incidents of social unrest do not indicate an impending collapse of one-party rule in China. They signify instead the desire of an increasingly complex society to take part in the allocation of political and material values. As formal channels of participation fail to meet this need, informal channels such as demonstrations, protests and riots are chosen.

### Evidence of social unrest

Social unrest is a sensitive subject in Chinese politics, which makes gathering evidence for it an arduous if not impossible task. This sensitivity is rooted at least partly in traditional philosophies of statecraft. Confucianism is still very influential even today, and some observers argue that the Chinese leadership is increasingly basing its claim to legitimacy on a Confucian world view. A central concept in Confucianism is the Mandate of Heaven or the divine approval to rule over others. It commits the ruler to justice and morality and is withdrawn from despots and tyrants. In this worldview, natural disasters and social unrest are seen as indicators that rulers are losing their divine mandate.[3] Mencius, one of the most important philosophers of the Confucian school, extended this idea to justify the overthrow and even killing of tyrants. Thus Confucianism allows people to protest against despotism. Not incidentally, the Chinese characters for 'revolution' (*geming*) translate as 'change of mandate'. Arguably, the passive component (social unrest as a sign of loss of mandate) and its active counterpart (overthrowing a tyrant) can reinforce each other, as large-scale social unrest might affirm people's belief that their protests are justified and even sanctioned by higher powers.

As a consequence, the Chinese government puts great effort into controlling and framing information on popular unrest.

A lack of reliable and consistent data makes it difficult to draw definitive conclusions about the size and regional distribution of social unrest. Until 2005, the Ministry of Public Security issued official annual figures on the number of incidents of social unrest. Even though these figures were probably biased downwards, they illustrate a clear rise in protest activities. Incidents of social unrest rose at an alarming rate, from 8,700 in 1993 to 87,000 in 2005. No data were released for the first few years of the 2000s, and the Ministry of Public Security stopped issuing such data altogether after 2005. Informal estimates based on newspaper reports, hearsay and other unconfirmed sources suggest a further increase in occurrences of social unrest. A more commonly cited figure is 180,000 incidents in 2010 put forward by the researcher Sun Liping at Tsinghua University. However, an estimate by another Chinese scholar even suggests that there were 230,000 incidents in 2009.[4]

These figures hide more than they reveal. Varying definitions underlie this official data, which makes a comparison of trends over time a complicated task. During the 1990s, social unrest was officially classified under 'mass incidents' (*qunti shijian*). This was changed to 'public order disturbances' (*raoluan gonggong zhixu*) in the 2000s. The Chinese authorities have never properly defined what these terms mean. However, it appears that 'mass incidents' are defined with reference to the number of participants. According to the Jiangsu provincial government, 'important mass incidents' involve between 1,000 and 5,000 people and 'extraordinary mass incidents' include more than 5,000 participants. Following the same logic, incidents involving fewer than 1,000 people are also considered 'mass incidents'; but they are just not 'important' or 'extraordinary'. As for 'public order disturbances', the definition is characterised by the nature of the event rather than by the number of participants. It includes provocation or troublemaking, gambling, running underworld criminal organisations, obstruction of official business, mob fighting, delaying the delivery of mail, holding mass orgies, computer hacking, making and selling fake police uniforms, forging identity cards, burning national flags and corpse desecration.[5]

Nor is there information about the regional distribution of these protests. Because a lack of available official data has led to reliance on media reports for information, the steep increase in the number of incidents since 2005 could be the result of more media reporting of social unrest than before. This could reflect the prevalence of commercially minded media vying for readership and the consequent efforts to investigate and report stories that were previously neglected. Also, the growth of ICT makes it easier for journalists to find out about such incidents and more difficult for the Ministry of Propaganda to keep them secret from the public.

## Social unrest as a form of participation

What are the existing channels for Chinese citizens to participate in politics? We distinguish six forms of participation in China, which can be classified as legal, grey zone and illegal.[6] See Table 5.1.

Most of the legal forms of participation mentioned here are aimed at influencing political programmes and are therefore not suitable for addressing specific grievances. This is especially the case for elections and most other forms of institutionalised participation. They are of limited appeal to protestors because they are spatially restricted and non-responsive (such as village elections and neighbourhood self-governance), very exclusive (such as most institutionalised forms of participation) or tightly regulated (such as the activities of registered social organisations). However, the mechanisms described here are not a one-way street: increased social unrest has prompted central and local authorities to improve some of these channels, but not enough so far to dissuade people from taking to the streets.

Social networking, i.e. participating in politics through personal networks, is different, however. Although it is far more suitable for addressing specific grievances, it is problematic when political or material benefits accrue only to those who have invested in such a network. In other words, social networking is also very exclusive, but in a different way from participation in political parties or mass organisations. In order to be successful in politics or business in China, personal contacts with influential individuals need to be established. Friends and existing contacts have to be rewarded as go-betweens in facilitating such contacts, and the new contacts are showered with expensive gifts

**Table 5.1** Forms of political participation in China

| Legal | Grey zone | Illegal |
|---|---|---|
| **Citizen participation**<br>Elections at the village and neighbourhood level | **Social networking**<br>(Establish and employ close personal and social relationships)<br>Clan networks<br>Nepotism<br>Patronage<br>Other kinds of informal relations | **Popular resistance**<br>Illegal demonstrations<br>Strikes<br>Refusal to pay taxes<br>Foot-dragging<br>Forming clandestine organisations |
| **Institution-orientated participation**<br>Membership of CCP or other parties<br>Delegate in national or local legislatures or consultative conferences<br>Membership of mass organisations<br>Engaging in registered social organisations | n.a. | **Political violence**<br>Violence against property or persons |
| **Problem-specific participation**<br>Letters to the editor<br>Visits and complaints<br>Contacting functionaries<br>Legal demonstrations | n.a. | n.a. |

*Source*: Thomas Heberer, *Einführung in die politischen Systeme Ostasiens: VR China, Hong Kong, Japan, Nordkorea, Südkorea, Taiwan* [Introduction to the Political Systems of East Asia: PR China, Hong Kong, Japan, North Korea, South Korea, Taiwan], 2008. (Wiesbaden: VS Verlag), p. 85.

or even cash. In addition, such networking involves hosting lavish banquets, which can add up to a large sum.[7]

The tools for problem-specific participation have received much attention in the literature, but their usefulness in overcoming grievances remains the subject of intense debate. This is especially true for 'letters to the editor' (*xinfang*) and legal demonstrations. Letters of complaint sent to newspapers are evaluated, bundled and presented to the authorities in unpublished compendiums, and they are often not printed for public consumption. Thus although they feed into political agenda-setting, they almost never lead to concrete action by the authorities. The usefulness of legal demonstrations is equally limited, simply because it is almost impossible to gain a permit to demonstrate about the sensitive issues that most grievances represent. Contacting individual functionaries is just as futile, for similar reasons.

Analysts have devoted much attention to the system of 'letters and complaints'. This enables citizens to file complaints, either in writing (*xinfang*) or as part of a visit (*shangfang*) to specialised complaint offices in central and local ministries.[8] As Carl F. Minzner points out, 'in the absence of open political and legal channels, petitioning is one of the main methods by which Chinese citizens challenge and participate in the official decisions that affect their lives'.[9] Thus scholars perceive the xinfang system as a means to empower disadvantaged groups, a 'safety valve' for political tension[10] and an 'alarm system' for the central authorities.[11] But as the authorities act upon only a small proportion of complaint letters filed, most petitioners favour personal visits to complaint offices to written complaints. However, the increased influx of complaints to Beijing has led the central government to put a lid on this form of participation.[12]

## The role of ICT

The Internet has also become a virtual space where contentious politics takes place. Incidents with sensational images can go viral and capture international media attention in a short time. ICT has become a medium for netizens to air their grievances and to rally the public to stage physical protests. To a certain extent, it has become a form of check-and-balance against official misconduct. Also, topics discussed in the virtual forum may be picked up by print media and television, which acts as a further check on official behaviour.

China's gradual development towards a knowledge-based economy has direct and immediate consequences for the nature and frequency of social unrest. It confronts the government with a dilemma. On the one hand, as it draws much of its legitimacy from economic growth, becoming a knowledge-based economy is crucial to maintaining the country's competitiveness in world markets. This transformation requires the political elites and the population at large to have improved access to all kinds of information. On the other hand, enhanced access to information can also undermine the legitimacy of an autocratic government such as China because it enables people to obtain and disperse sensitive information and to organise resistance against dictatorship.

ICT has grown rapidly in China. While it accounted for only 38 per cent of China's research and development (R&D) expenditure in high-technology industries in 1997, the figure went to more than 60 per cent in 2011. In absolute terms, R&D expenditure on ICT has increased from Rmb 1.2 billion (EUR 150 million) to Rmb 48.7 billion (EUR 6 billion) in that period.[13] At the same time, the central government is actively promoting popular access to ICT.[14] China has the largest number of Internet users and the largest mobile phone market in the world today.

As of June 2013, there were nearly 591 million Internet users in China. Fewer than 5 per cent of China's population in 2002 went online but more than one-third did in the early 2010s, of which 65.5 per cent accessed the Internet through their mobile phone. Additionally, Internet use is no longer confined to young, male and educated residents of China's rich coastal provinces as it used to be. It has now reached all segments of the population.[15] These include migrant workers, whose potential to ignite social unrest is a matter of grave concern to the central government. As part of this development, Twitter-equivalent platforms such as Sina Weibo and QQ Weibo, which enable real-time sharing of texts, images and videos, have redefined the media landscape in China.

Microblogs (*weibo*) enjoy great popularity among ordinary citizens and also journalists, lawyers and advocacy activists. For instance, the number of people using microblogs reached 274 million at the end of 2012.[16] Microblogs are an important channel for discussing controversial social issues, anger-venting about injustice, linking like-minded people and obtaining first-hand information on current events, protests and disasters that are not reported in the traditional media. This has limited the government's ability to control the flow of information about sensitive events. As it is very difficult for the propaganda authorities to prevent accounts of government malfeasance from leaking to the general public through microblogs, they are forced to also allow the conventional media to report on those events.

The widespread adoption of microblogs has helped to spread awareness of mass incidents caused by official misdemeanours that would otherwise have remained unknown and isolated. In some instances, public outrage against official misbehaviour has caused the government to take remedial action. The Internet is becoming a means of ensuring official accountability and enforcing the rule of law in that respect, even though it has not inspired political revolution in China or toppled the authoritarian regime as it has done in the Arab countries.

In September 2010, three people in Jiangxi province set themselves on fire after forced evictions by the local government in order to make way for a public transport project. When family members of the victims attempted to travel to Beijing to lodge a petition, they were obstructed at the airport in the provincial capital, Nanchang. Using their mobile phones, they petitioned journalists for help. The event then sparked a huge public outcry. Two local Party officials came under investigation and were subsequently removed from their position. The victims were also given financial compensation.[17] In another case, public criticism of the safety record of the much-publicised high-speed railway, particularly through the sharing of photos in social media, has prompted the authorities to re-evaluate the ambitious project and scale it down.[18]

The Internet, particularly social media, has also become a means of rallying people for physical protest. In the Dalian and Xiamen cases against the construction of toxic PX chemical plants, calls for protest, mounted on Internet forums and communicated via microblog platforms, helped to mobilise a large number of demonstrators.[19] In early 2011, the Arab Spring-inspired 'Jasmine Revolution' in China was initiated by postings on microblogs such as Twitter and Boxun. It was severely clamped down on by the authorities before it caught fire.

## Classifying social unrest

Modernisation of Chinese society has led to diversification of protest activities. The official classification of social unrest activities is far from satisfactory because it conflates different forms of collective action as well as being ideologically biased. This highlights the need to classify popular protests along more dimensions than its current definition does. We suggest six dimensions: geographical location; motivations for protests; strategies of protest; degree of organisation; the degree of homogeneity of protest crowds; and ethnic protest.

Protests in China have shifted from events happening mostly in rural areas to both rural and urban areas. The issues at stake have diversified, and formal channels of communication have not kept up with diversifying expression of grievances. In the 1990s, peasant resistance against excessive and illegal taxation by rural governments used to dominate the social unrest scene. After the rural tax reform in the early 2000s, which abolished illegal rural taxes, an increasing number of protests are recorded in peri-urban and urban areas. Increasingly, residents in these areas are engaging in popular resistance in order to express their grievances about a range of issues affecting their livelihood, such as expropriation of land and residential property for development, job losses from factory closures and also rising fuel prices, which have incited unrest among taxi drivers. Social resistance, which used to be staged by the underprivileged, such as retrenched workers and peasants, is now an increasingly common means of expression for the middle class too. The other causes of unrest, which will be discussed below, include environment-related disputes, labour disputes over owed wages and appalling working conditions, urban housing issues and conflicts related to ethnic groups. As a general rule, urban protests are more dangerous to the regime than rural protests because news spreads faster in urban areas and hence they are more difficult to contain.

On motivations driving public protests, there are protests seeking redress for grievances, anger-venting incidents and anti-system protests.[20] Examples of redress-seeking incidents include occupational groups such as farmers fighting to keep their land, untrained workers protesting against loss of jobs, taxi drivers resisting rising fuel prices, homeowners or students complaining of unfair treatment and migrant workers striking or even taking their own lives for higher wages and better working conditions.

Of increasing significance are 'anger-venting incidents', a term coined by the Chinese scholar and social critic Yu Jianrong. The term denotes incidents reflecting deep-seated anger that has been brewing for some time and is vented when seemingly minor incidents occur. Their participants, usually in excess of 10,000, have no relationship with the victims of the incidents. Modern communication tools such as short text messaging and the Internet often aid the mobilisation of protestors. They sometimes engage in extremely violent behaviour, usually directed at local officials.[21]

In June 2008, as many as 30,000 people participated in a riot in Weng'an County in Guizhou province in which police cars were overturned and burnt and the Public Security Bureau building was set on fire. The incident was triggered by an incident of no direct significance to the protestors. Weng'an is a mineral town. In exploiting mineral resources and building hydropower stations, thousands of residents had been adversely affected in the previous few years. The local authority had forced many to relocate, often without much consultation and with only minimum financial compensation. Underground criminal gangs, often in collaboration with local officials, were also prevalent and active in Weng'an. Local Party leaders colluded with mine owners and gang leaders in running of mining businesses and in coercing local residents to comply with the government's instructions. Corruption was therefore rife. Local residents had clashed with the police and the local government prior to this incident. Public order was poor and the crime rate was high. Gangs had even penetrated the local schools and instigated gang-related violence.[22] Given this background, when a 16-year-old girl was sexually abused and killed by perpetrators allegedly connected with local officials and her uncle was subsequently beaten up for launching an investigation, as many as 30,000 Weng'an residents took to the streets, vandalising local government properties in their demand for justice.

The Weng'an incident was not an isolated case. In July 2008, more than 100 migrant workers stormed government buildings and destroyed police cars in a county in Guangdong province. The incident was triggered by the alleged abuse and murder of a migrant worker who was a taxi driver when he refused to pay Rmb 200 (€25) 'protection money' to village officials.[23] And in December 2010, mourning for a boy in Zhangjiagang in Jiangsu province also turned violent. More than 1,000 people clashed with riot police when a five-year-old died after an injection at a local hospital. The incident highlighted the tension and distrust between citizens and local hospitals and the local government apparatus at large and showed the public's sympathy for the victim.[24] A peculiar social phenomenon is the ability of these seemingly minor incidents to act as a force for mobilising thousands of people not directly involved in them to mount collective action. It reflects a deeply rooted feeling of injustice widely shared by many strata of Chinese society.

Although protests that are aimed 'against the system' happen infrequently, they are the most dangerous to the regime. For instance, the 1989 student demonstrations in Tiananmen Square, which started as protests against political corruption and favouritism, turned into calls to topple the Communist Party. Another example is the 'Jasmine Revolution' in 2011, which called for a democratic revolution in the wake of the Arab Spring. Most important in this category is ethnic unrest, which we will turn to later.

The three major types of protest strategy are peaceful demonstrations, disruptive action and violence. Each of these strategies serves different objectives. Peaceful demonstrations are less risky for protestors than the other two strategies but are probably less likely to succeed. One of the authors of this paper examined such demonstrations in the central business district of Guangzhou. Protest leaders repeatedly urged the participants to maintain public order, to refrain from destroying public property and not to disrupt traffic.[25]

Risk aversion is not the only reason why protestors often choose peaceful demonstrations. Protestors frequently seek the support of higher-level administrations and the media, but cannot enlist help if they are labelled a threat to public security. The participants in such protests tend to present their activities as lawful. They also see themselves as partners of the central government in reining in local abuses of power, fighting corruption and strengthening the rule of law. Kevin O'Brien and Lianjiang Li have termed this class of protest 'rightful resistance'.[26]

Disruptive action involves activities that disrupt daily life, such as blocking roads and thoroughfares. It often follows from unsuccessful petitioning or repression of peaceful demonstrations. However, it can also be a strategy employed by occupational groups, such as bus or taxi drivers, who are well positioned to cause disorder. Examples include the large-scale strikes by taxi drivers in Chongqing and Sanya in November 2008.[27]

Riots frequently happen in, but are not restricted to, minority provinces such as Tibet and Xinjiang or in poor provinces such as Guizhou and Anhui. Often they are responses to events that spark moral outrage, for example the previously mentioned attempted cover-up of the rape of a teenage girl by a local government-related perpetrator.

Another dimension of protest concerns how they are organised. In China, it is illegal to form an organisation without prior approval from the relevant authorities. If someone is being convicted as the organiser of a major demonstration, he will likely have a long prison sentence. In order to protect the organisers operating in the background, participants in protests often claim that their protest is spontaneous.

Given popularisation of ICT, protest organisers can now learn from the success and failure of their own activities as well as those of others. As a general rule, well-organised protests are more sustainable than unorganised ones, and the tactical employment of ICT can serve to surreptitiously coordinate protestors and to outsmart government censorship. Organisers of such activities are therefore more difficult to detect, which increases the cost to the government of maintaining stability.

The demonstrations in Guangzhou described earlier provide a good example of organisational learning in collective action. In a protest against irregularities in a redevelopment programme, protestors reacted to the arrest of some of their organisers by imposing a division of labour among themselves. The protest leaders took great care not to be seen at the protest site and delegated activities from behind the scenes. A division of labour was also imposed between men and women, old and young, employed and unemployed. We observed that it was predominantly elderly people, many of them women, who carried out the protests following an initial wave of arrests.[28] Young men are the principal wage earners, whom no family can afford to do without, whereas older people have less to lose, command some respect and are therefore less likely to be imprisoned. During this protest, an informal rule was imposed by which each family in the village had to send at least one representative to the demonstrations. Usually the burden fell on the women of the family, especially if they were unemployed and their children had left home.

External allies are another factor that influences the sustainability and, by extension, the impact of a protest on social stability. As mentioned above, lawful protests often seek the attention of the media, as the protestors know that the authorities are more likely to intervene in their favour if their grievances are reported in the press. Lawyers who boldly take up cases that motivate people to engage in further acts of social unrest are another popular ally. It is important to note here that protestors often do not welcome foreign support, because the government tends to interpret it as an attempt to undermine domestic order. The involvement of foreign actors can lead to unusually harsh jail sentences for protestors and thus needs to be undertaken with great care. Deep contextual knowledge, respect for Chinese counterparts and sensitivity to their particular situation are preconditions for this risky kind of intervention.

A further dimension of social unrest is the degree of homogeneity of protest crowds. Homogeneous protest crowds, such as occupational or status groups, indicate that issue-specific grievances are at stake. These are frequently easier to address than broader or more far-reaching demands such as for democratisation or social justice. Also, crackdowns on such groups are less likely to lead to larger protests if the population at large does not identify with the protestors or their demands. By contrast, social unrest may become widespread if organisers are able to reach beyond their core group and mobilise other social groups for solidarity.

A good example is the riots in Wukan, a village in southern China where more than 3,000 villagers demonstrated against illegal land grabs in late 2011. The local police responded with a massive show of force, which triggered further demonstrations in the following months. Subsequently, four suspected organisers were incarcerated by the police.[29] The death in custody of one of the suspects outraged villagers, which helped to mobilise more supporters. The unrest gained in intensity and became a movement against corrupt relations between business and politics in the locality.[30] Had this been a taxi drivers' strike, monetary concessions could have been made to address, for example, declining profits because of increasing petrol prices. In contrast, the protestors in Wukan criticised the general lack of quality in China's (local) governance. Instead of making monetary concessions only, the provincial leadership saw itself compelled to make political changes. It is easy to see how this could lead to popular demands for more far-reaching reforms, eventually questioning one-party rule itself.

The demonstrations at Tiananmen Square in 1989 provide another illustration of the potency of heterogeneous protest crowds. These demonstrations were initiated by students, and later were joined by workers and then members of all social groups. Such events are more likely to pose a threat to the regime's legitimacy than issue-specific unrest. The heterogenisation of protest crowds can lead to broader demands, which in turn can mobilise more followers. A tipping point is reached when protestors' demands go beyond specific issues and pose a threat to the regime's legitimacy.

The ethnic dimension of social unrest deserves additional attention, even though the danger of ethnic protest to regime stability stems from two factors discussed earlier. Despite being united by their ethnicity, protest crowds encompass a wide array of social groups (heterogeneity) and their protests are frequently 'against the system'. Uighur and Tibetan protestors routinely deplore the political supremacy of the Han Chinese and often demand independence from China. However, it would be erroneous to conclude that separatism is always the root of such protests. Many Tibetans and Uighurs resent being disadvantaged vis-à-vis people of Han ethnicity, who enjoy a privileged status in minority regions. Han Chinese often regard minorities and their culture as inferior to their own culture.[31] They tend to enjoy better employment opportunities, not least because high wages are often an incentive for them to move to a place that they are not accustomed to.[32] Thus ethnic grievances have an economic as well as an ethnic component. Often, social unrest in minority regions starts with an 'anger-venting incident', a relatively small incident that can ignite a large-scale protest that reflects the Han versus ethnic minority tension.

Another type of ethnic protest, such as the widely publicised incidents in Lhasa in March 2008[33] and in Urumqi in July 2009,[34] is more comprehensive and organised. They also involve separatist political agendas. Nevertheless, in both cases, there was an underlying negative sentiment against the other ethnic group that had been brewing for some time. 'Anger-venting' and 'anti-system' incidents can be difficult to discern, especially because the former often evolves into the latter: well-organised separatist groups can use 'anger-venting protests' as a vehicle to organise pro-independence activities, often aided by activists operating from abroad. In contrast to unrest in non-minority regions, protests in Tibetan, Uighur and Mongolian areas are seen by the regime as a serious challenge to its right to rule. Accordingly, unrest in minority areas is quelled swiftly and with a large show of force; activists are punished severely and police presence is prominently visible.

## Issues Leading to Grievances

In this section, we examine the grievances that lie at the heart of social unrest. Contrary to popular belief, the rising incidence of unrest is not directly correlated with economic growth rates. It arises instead from land disputes, environmental degradation, labour conflicts and ethnic strife and is rooted in the institutional structure of central–local relations and the authoritarian nature of Chinese politics.

### Social unrest and economic transformation

There is a popular belief that social unrest intensifies when growth slows down, that grievances accumulate and translate into social unrest. If this belief is correct, China will be able to keep the lid on unrest as long as it maintains its growth. However, we find no evidence of a direct relationship between growth and unrest. As we will argue, unrest is a function of increased incentives and opportunities for protest and of growing impatience from people who have not benefited from economic growth.[35] This implies that the government has to take measures in addition to maintaining economic growth in order to tackle social unrest.

Figure 5.1 suggests that the relationship between growth and unrest is not straightforward. During the 1990s, the economic growth rate and the number of incidents of unrest seemingly trended in opposite directions: while economic growth rates declined, the number of 'mass incidents' rose. But when the economy grew in the 2000s, the number of incidents also increased.

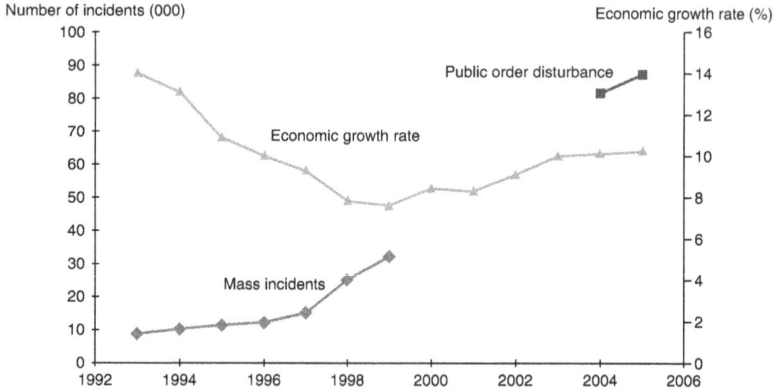


Figure 5.1 **The number of social unrest incidents vs economic growth rates, 1993–2005**

*Source*: Ministry of Public Security for data on 'mass incidents' and 'public order disturbances' and China's Statistical Yearbook.

## Immediate grievances or causes of unrest

Land disputes are a primary cause of social unrest, and account for 65 per cent of all cases as Yu Jianrong has found.[36] In some instances, local governments expropriate land illegally, sometimes in collusion with real estate developers in order to avoid sharing land sale proceeds with higher-level governments. In other cases, they fail to consult the citizens affected or force them to vacate their properties against their will. In most instances, the compensation offered by local governments to affected residents is minimal and is considered grossly inadequate. Worse still, there is an increasing trend that local governments are hiring local mafia to force villagers to comply with their demands and to carry out forced land expropriations and seizures.[37]

Land-related social unrest is happening in peri-urban and urban areas. In peri-urban areas, local officials expropriate farmland in order to transfer land-user rights from farmers to real estate developers or private individuals. These transfers happen mostly in urban fringes where there is a demand for urban and/or industrial expansion, for which land is a requisite resource. In urban neighbourhoods, land disputes occur when local governments seek to tear down older residential areas in order to make way for profitable office space or expensive apartment complexes.

The environment is another leading cause of social unrest. Often for the reason of increasing their tax revenue, local governments acquiesce to hosting polluting factories or plants that violate environmental regulations. This results in the loss of crops, endangered livestock and serious public health concerns. There are estimated to be more than 450 'cancer villages' in China. This term describes villages with an extraordinarily high number of cancer patients where water contamination from local factories is often the leading cause of the disease.[38] Affected villagers often gather to cause disturbance at polluting factories and gain attention from local governments and the media.

Some villagers have successfully engaged the non-governmental organisation (NGO) community to help them advance their cause, though this is still rather uncommon. Green Anhui, a student-founded environmental NGO, played an instrumental role in the success story of 'Qiugang', an Oscar-nominated documentary that depicted how a village of 2,000 people in the Huai River basin in Anhui province triumphantly forced the chemical factories that had been polluting their water sources and had caused many cancer-related deaths to shut down their operations. The green NGO advised villagers on evidence gathering and capturing media coverage in order to fight and eventually win their case.

Another type of environmental protest has less to do with a direct adverse environmental impact and more to do with the growing aspirations of the middle class. This type of protest happens in large cities, where the population has a high-income level. In August 2011, some 12,000 people in Dalian, a coastal city in Liaoning province, took to the streets in protest against the city government's decision to host a chemical plant. They were worried that a leak in a storage tank could cause a disaster akin to the Fukushima disaster in Japan.[39] This threat is not immediate, unlike the 'cancer village' incidents. In 2007, a similar protest took place in Xiamen, another affluent coastal city, in Fujian province. It involved close to 20,000 participants demonstrating against a petrochemical plant.[40] In this case, the residents' concerns had as much to do with falling property prices as with the harmful environmental consequences of the plant's construction. These protests reflect certain post-modern values of protestors, which emerge only when society has reached a certain post-subsistence level of economic development. They should be differentiated from subsistence- or survival-based resistance and from environment-related resistance in the countryside.[41]

Labour-related protests are also on the rise in China. Most of them involve migrant workers employed in factories in coastal cities who demand higher wages and better working conditions. Some of them also complain of wage arrears by employers. In the face of labour shortages, some employers, for example Foxconn and Honda, have responded by raising wage rates and improving working conditions.[42]

Labour protests organised by laid-off state-owned enterprise (SOE) workers were frequent in the late 1990s and early 2000s, when those enterprises underwent restructuring and privatisation. As a result of this restructuring, many workers lost their jobs, once considered 'iron rice bowls' under the planned economy. In a knock-on effect, retrenched workers also lost their entitlements to medical care and pension benefits. These despairing workers were typically middle-aged or close to retirement and had difficulty finding a new job. They had few options but to take to the streets. These protests were typically large-scale, involving hundreds or thousands of enterprise workers.

### Institutional causes

Most if not all of these social protests are directed at local governments rather than the central government. The motive for local officials' behaviour is their revenue imperative, created by economic and political institutions. Institutional incentives make it necessary for local officials to maximise revenue collection that comes at the expense of citizens. In order to finance targeted development projects, local officials do not stop short of illicit taxation.

In the 1980s, China went through fiscal decentralisation, which empowered provincial and lower-level governments to collect and retain tax revenue. Sub-national governments were also made responsible for financing the provision of public goods and services to local residents. Faced with declining revenue levels, the central government introduced a fiscal recentralisation policy in 1994 called the 'tax-sharing system'. The policy recentralised major sources of tax revenue, for example value-added tax, to the central government while local governments' expenditure responsibilities were left largely unchanged. As a consequence of this reform, only 46 per cent of tax revenue now accrues to sub-national governments, even though they are responsible for 77 per cent of public expenditure. The World Bank has called China the most decentralised country of all in terms of expenditure responsibility,[43] and sub-national governments there are under systemic pressure to increase revenue collection in order to meet their expenditure obligations.

The imperative to augment revenue drives local governments to seek income growth by increasing extra-budgetary income and off-budget funds. This income is independent of the formal tax system and is not subject to sharing with higher-level governments. The late 1990s and early 2000s saw a rise in arbitrary taxes, administrative fees and fines collected by townships, such as agriculture-related retained funds (*tiliu*) and fees (*tongchou*), township and village levies and various surcharges, fees and funds for education and other local infrastructure projects. While supplementing grassroots governments with much-needed revenue, these fees and fines aggravated 'peasant burdens' and became a leading source of rural discontent.[44]

Revenue constraints in general impose institutional pressure on sub-national governments to attract real estate and construction developments, from which they can derive land-related income. Since the 1990s, land-related revenue has risen to become the single most important revenue source for sub-national authorities. This has given rise to the term 'fiscalisation of land' (*tudi caizheng*) in China, referring to the management of land resources by government authorities for the purpose of generating fiscal income.[45] This income includes budgetary revenues, such as taxes collected from manufacturing and services industries, as well as extra-budgetary revenues, namely land conveyance fees.

Local governments' imperative to augment tax revenue also explains why they are likely to condone factories and enterprises that violate environmental standards and labour laws. This is particularly the case in a county or township where the company contributes the predominant share of the local government's tax revenue. Closing down the factory that pollutes the drinking water source for local residents may be equivalent to cutting off the lifeline of local government.

The Communist Party cadre evaluation system, which rewards local government officials for local economic and industrial development and for tax revenue collection, is another major institutional reason for the surge in local government-initiated land transactions. Land development, with its concomitant real estate and construction activities, brings various taxes and other benefits greatly valued by the evaluation system to local government officials.

The cadre responsibility system was instituted by the CCP in the late 1980s as an instrument for the central leadership to exercise control over lower-level cadres. But not all cadres' performance targets are created equal. They are divided into three categories, reflecting their significance in the eyes of the central government. One is 'priority targets with veto power' (*yipiao foujue*), such as maintaining social order. However, achieving 'priority targets' does not guarantee career advancement: it is a necessary but not sufficient condition for a successful career in the CCP. The other two categories are 'hard targets' (*ying zhibiao*) and 'soft' or 'ordinary' targets (*yiban zhibiao*). 'Hard targets' are quantifiable binding targets, such as tax renminbi collected or the local economic growth rate. 'Soft targets' are non-binding targets more difficult to measure and quantify, for example education and healthcare provision and cultural and social development. The 'hard targets' are the determining factors in leading cadres' careers: those who score high on these binding targets are politically and financially rewarded; those with a dismal performance have stagnating careers and will receive no bonus. The 'hard targets' thus command far more attention and effort from cadres than 'soft targets'.

Besides fuelling local economic growth and bringing in fiscal income, land development is usually accompanied by mega-scale construction projects such as public squares, highways, railways, airports and economic development zones, which are highly visible 'political accomplishments' (*zhengji gongcheng*). From the perspective of cadre evaluation, these ostentatious physical achievements are much more likely to score points with political superiors than 'softer' accomplishments such as increased provision of basic education and healthcare, even though the latter may be more vital for a locale's long-term development.

In effect, the fiscal and cadre evaluation systems reinforce each other in creating and sustaining the revenue imperative. Promoting local economic growth and augmenting fiscal revenue become *political* as well as *economic* necessities for local leaders. They need to meet these necessities not only to advance their political career but also to ensure the sheer economic survival and functioning of the local government.

## Institutional failure to address grievances

The above analyses explain why local officials' behaviour contributes to social unrest but they do not account for what happens when citizens have grievances. In line with our argument, Murray Scot Tanner, a long-time observer of social unrest in China, argues that social protests arise when economic, social and political development produces new demands, but socialist democratic and legal institutions fail to keep up with this change. Frustration spills over into the streets when citizens either have not yet learnt how to voice their demands (e.g. they do not yet fully understand their legal rights) or the institutional avenues for voicing demands are 'underdeveloped' or 'clogged'.[46] This view echoes our earlier contention that social unrest erupts when citizens lack legitimate institutional channels through which to air their grievances and thus that they are forced to make themselves known through other means, for example illegal assemblies, marches and demonstrations.

Growing awareness of rights, legal knowledge and assertiveness notwithstanding, Chinese citizens still face an uphill battle in filing lawsuits against government officials. Despite the promulgation of the Administrative Litigation Law in 1989, the analogy of throwing an egg against a stone (*yiluan jishi*) is often used to describe an act of suing the politically powerful. Ordinary citizens face a range of hurdles in seeking justice through administrative litigation. There are legal restrictions on whom citizens can sue and Party secretaries and committees have legal immunity. Separating the Party and the government is tricky; and local authorities can sometimes use this lack of separation between the Party and the state to deflect lawsuits.[47] Local authorities can also prevent the local court from accepting cases by other means, for instance by forbidding them to accept lawsuits on politically sensitive issues, namely land confiscation, forced evictions and excessive financial burdens. The fact that the Party secretary of a locality has power over the appointment and promotion of local judges suggests that their rulings are far from independent of the Party.

Once a case is successfully filed, the local Party secretary can often influence or intervene in court decisions. The fact that local judges are ranked lower than local Party leaders in the Party hierarchy does not help in warding off administrative interference. Local leaders can press the court to delay hearings until the plaintiffs voluntarily give up, as protracted cases can drain plaintiffs' financial resources, energy and time. Even when a plaintiff has successfully won a lawsuit, court rulings can go unexecuted, as local officials can simply ignore them. Filing a lawsuit against local governments deters some citizens for fear of retaliation.[48] Given the low odds of filing and winning a lawsuit, many citizens decide to take their grievances to the streets instead.

## The State's Responses to Social Unrest

### State actors and social unrest

To understand the state's responses to social unrest, it is necessary to discuss three relevant actors: the central government, local government and the security apparatus. The central and local governments have different goals and objectives, and thus they may respond differently to the same incident. Even though the police are accountable to the local Party committee and government, their respective objectives are not necessarily identical at all times.

Traditionally, Chinese policy analysts adopt the view that the role of security forces in a developing country whose priority is economic development is to contain protests and to prevent popular demands from overwhelming the state's ability to govern.[49] Policing is conducted by several kinds of police. The most important police force is the People's Armed Police (*wujing jingcha*, PAP), a paramilitary force subordinate jointly to the Ministry of Public Security and the Ministry of Defence. The PAP is responsible mainly for China's domestic security, which includes quelling riots, maintaining law and order and responding to emergencies. Subordinate only to the Ministry of Public Security is the Public Security Service (*gong'an jingcha*), which is in charge of local policing, criminal investigation, counterterrorism and the control of residence. In recent years, quasi-police forces hired by city governments (*chengguan*) have assisted these forces in their actions.

In the years immediately after the Tiananmen Square protests of 1989, the regime engaged in a strategy of quick suppression and/or quelling demonstrators with force. But as the number of 'mass incidents' grew over time, the authorities recognised that moderate levels of protest are inevitable and they adopted instead a 'permissive strategy of containment and management'.[50] This more sophisticated and nuanced strategy means that the government has allowed non-violent and low-key protests to be staged while professional policing of protests is maintained in order to ensure that they do not get out of control or turn violent. Instead of pre-empting all protests like it used to do, the security apparatus now employs coercive forces selectively in cases of mob violence, looting or attacks on government property. Officers are encouraged not to make mass arrests when unrest occurs but to gather intelligence, intensify policing and quietly detain protest leaders when crowds have dispersed.

The provision of local security has been decentralised. The CCP Central Committee passed a resolution for the improvement of public security in 2003 that has resulted in an increase in the quantity and quality of grassroots security organs: police substations (*paichusuo*) at the village and neighbourhood level.[51] Their number grew from 37,978 in 1990 to 52,000 in 2004. A similar trend can be observed of PAP forces, which increased from 680,000 in 1978 to 1.43 million in 2004.[52]

The role of the local security forces in handling popular protests is complex. Like all local agencies, they are subject to demands and orders from local Party and government leaders, on the one hand, and from their functional superior, the Ministry of Public Security, on the other. Local Party committees, however, are in charge of police budgets and the appointment of personnel, making them the more powerful of the two bosses. In addition, the police may become sympathetic to the cause of the protestors.

The security forces must tread a fine line between being too harsh or too soft on protestors.[53] They are sometimes caught in a 'catch-22' situation: they may be defying orders from local Party bosses if they refuse to take swift action against protestors, but they may suffer official punishment or popular revenge if they apply the force needed to restore order.

Another factor that influences policing is the quality of the security forces. As local governments are required to finance the larger part of their security expenditure from their own budget, the police tend to be ill-trained, especially in poor localities. By contrast, policing capabilities tend to be much better in wealthier places. In rich and poor localities alike, the *raison d'être* of the police is to maintain regime stability rather than to solve crimes. For this reason, ordinary citizens often regard the police with suspicion. Given the renewed focus on maintaining stability (*weiwen*), officials tend to employ police units against protestors, petitioners and other groups that might prevent local administrations from meeting the rather strict stability targets prescribed from above. In addition, massive police forces are occasionally deployed in national and local 'strike hard' campaigns against drug trafficking, prostitution, gambling and organised crime.

Drawing on media coverage of large-scale incidents (those involving more than 500 participants) from 2003 to 2009, Tong and Lei analyse local government responses to 248 cases of social unrest. The responses are classified into four categories: 'tolerance', 'accommodation', 'discipline of local officials' and 'application of force'.[54] Sixty per cent (152 of 248) of the cases were 'tolerated' by local governments. These were cases that did not specifically target the state and in which local officials typically tried not to get involved. These incidents included labour disputes with foreign companies, anti-Japan student demonstrations and student protests against school administration. Another 29 per cent (72 of 248) of cases were 'accommodated' by local government: protestors were usually given monetary compensation. These cases were more common in prosperous than in poorer locales, where local authorities could ill afford to provide compensation. Examples include protests by war veterans, land disputes and labour disputes with SOEs.

Local officials were disciplined by higher-level governments in 8 per cent (20 of 248) of the cases considered. Each of those cases involved one of the following situations: (1) a large number of people had taken part in the protests; (2) the protestors had assaulted government institutions; (3) deaths and injuries had occurred; (4) the incident occurred on the eve of an important public event, e.g. the Olympic Games and National Day; and (5) the protest had evolved into a mass riot.[55] In these cases, local officials were seen to have mishandled the incidents, and discipline was deemed necessary to appease the public. Central or local government used force in only 4 per cent (10 of 248) of the cases. The preconditions for the application of force were the occurrence of (1) politically motivated protests, (2) attacks on police officers and (3) violent acts, such as killing, burning and looting. Ethnic riots, such as those in Lhasa and Urumqi in the late 2000s, also fall into this category that sees the use of force in cracking down protestors.

## 'Social management' as a comprehensive strategy against unrest

As we have argued, local government's responses to social unrest are often subject to local variations and generally lack coordination by the central government. A recent strategy aims to rectify this shortcoming. At the annual session of the National People's Congress in March 2011, the improvement of 'social management' (*shehui guanli*) was high on the agenda. It was also featured in a speech by President Hu Jintao in February 2011.[56] Hu specified eight measures to address 'social management'. They fall into four categories: alleviating inequality and social hardship; heightened indoctrination; decentralisation of service provision; and improving public security. In combination, these measures are aimed at removing the various sources of public grievances, improving popular attitudes towards the regime, outsourcing social control and keeping social unrest in check.

Despite numerous speeches and official documents, the concept of 'social management' still remains rather vague. However, what is certain is that the priorities and importance the central leadership attaches to it reflect its concern with the rise in the number of 'mass incidents'. The central leadership also recognises the type of growth that China has pursued – in Wen Jiabao's words, 'unbalanced, uncoordinated, and unsustainable' – have inevitably resulted in social conflicts.

'Social management' may be a misnomer for what the central leadership has in mind and the policies that have thus far been implemented. Much of it is aimed at 'controlling' society, rather than 'managing'. Since 2008, the central government has increased its measures to influence public attitudes towards it by means of propaganda and indoctrination. The news media is under stricter control than before. The central government sees the media now as a means by which to guide public opinion. Concurrently it has stepped up its efforts to indoctrinate politicians and the general population through political education and propaganda campaigns. This applies not only to patriotic education in schools, for example, but also to larger government involvement in the field of culture. Thus the Twelfth Five-Year Programme envisions a larger role for the government in the production of popular entertainment such as films, literature and art.[57]

The other important element is improved public security. Government outlays for public security have increased dramatically, and official documents make clear that a powerful security apparatus will be the centrepiece of the government's social management efforts. According to official statistics, in 2011 the Chinese government spent more on internal security (USD 111 billion (€90 billion)) than on national defence (USD 106 billion (€86 billion)). The rationale of this effort is not to improve crime-fighting capabilities but to increase control over society in order to maintain political stability.

However, there is a great deal of variation among internal security budgets of local governments.[58] Figure 5.2 contrasts economic development and public security outlays for all provincial governments. It shows that the provinces fall into three rough clusters: poor minority provinces with large public security budgets; rich coastal provinces with large outlays; and some provinces where level of development and relative size of the public security budget correlate. The variation is striking: Gansu province spent only 4.6 per cent of its budget on public security in 2010 but the corresponding figure for Guangdong was nearly 9 per cent.

This subnational budget is used for decentralising and augmenting the local police force, as well as for technological upgrading. In particular, the Chinese government has invested heavily in creating large-scale databases hosting personal data of

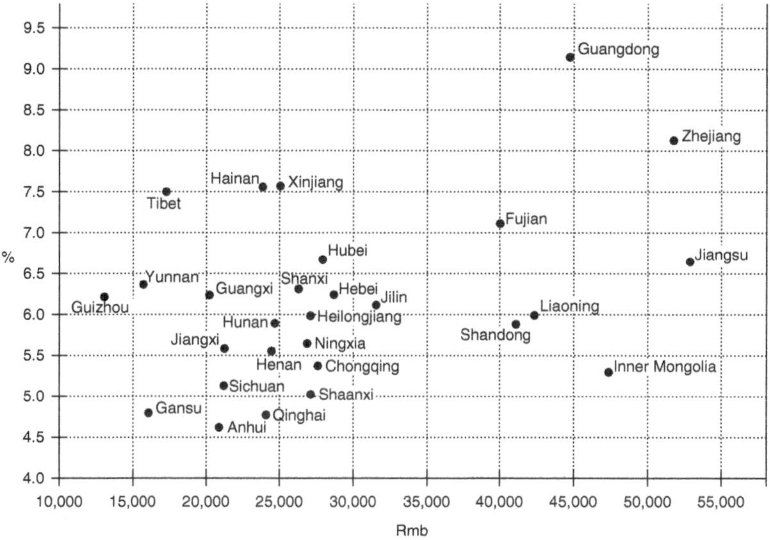


Figure 5.2 **Public security outlays as a percentage of budget (%) vs Gross Regional Product (GRP) per capita (Rmb), 2010**

*Source*: Calculated from *China Statistical Yearbook 2011*. GRP/capita for Beijing, Shanghai and Tianjin is so high that if they were included in the graph, the other provinces would be compressed into an illegible cluster. GRP/capita and public security expenditures for the three cities are Beijing: Rmb 75,943 (EUR 9,529)/6.66 per cent; Tianjin: Rmb 72,994 (EUR 9,159)/6.17 per cent; and Shanghai: Rmb 76,074 (EUR 9,545)/5.67 per cent.

the population[59] and in improving its rapid-response capacities at all levels.[60] Investments in high-technology surveillance systems largely explain the comparatively high public security expenditures of Guangdong province. China now possesses the largest network of closed-circuit television cameras in the world, with more than 10 million cameras being installed in 2010 alone.[61]

## Conclusions

Our central argument is that social unrest will continue to grow but will not pose an immediate threat to the regime. Nevertheless, there is a danger that localised protests will escalate and that containing unrest will result in intensification of repression. The probable future trend of social unrest in China is that it is likely to occur more frequently. Local officials, who are still subject to revenue imperatives, are unlikely to change their behaviour of maximising income for organisational and personal gains. There has been some debate among the central leadership about de-emphasising GDP growth in cadre evaluation, but it does not seem prepared as yet to compromise the pursuit of GDP growth for other social objectives.

In addition, social unrest will grow unabated because the political and judicial systems have failed to allow the aggrieved to redress their concerns. The central government has restricted access to existing institutional channels for anger-venting and expression of grievances. Furthermore, making local stability a key criterion in cadre evaluation provides an incentive for local officials to prevent people from using the letters and complaints system. This is an unintended outcome of the central government policy. As formal institutional channels fail to allow distressed citizens to seek justice for their grievances, public demonstrations and protests become a venue for venting anger and gaining sympathy for their causes.

Improved access to information and communications technology enables broad segments of the Chinese population to obtain and disperse information critical of the regime as well as to better organise and coordinate protests. As a result, there are now greater incentives to air grievances outside legal channels while the costs of doing so have fallen.

To what extent does growing social unrest pose a threat to the stability of the Chinese leadership? In the age of modern technology, popular resistance has the potential to catch fire and spread very quickly. This challenges the ability of the authorities to suppress public sentiment or to appease the aggrieved. The Chinese leadership is fully cognisant of this risk, which explains why it is spending more on maintaining domestic public security than on military defence.

Notwithstanding this, escalating popular resistance is not capable of toppling the regime, for three reasons. First, more protests may not signify the rise of 'rights consciousness', as Western observers have come to understand. Elizabeth Perry of Harvard University once argued that Chinese conceptions of 'rights' are more akin to 'economic rights' – those of attaining subsistence (*shengcun*) and development (*fazhan*) – which are rooted in the thinking of the ancient philosopher Mencius.[62] As Perry notes, 'when Deng Xiaoping initiated his reforms, in sharp contrast to Gorbachev in the Soviet Union, he talked not of *glasnost* (political openness) or of *perestroika* (restructuring) but of *xiaokang* (economic comfort).'[63] These 'rights' are of a different order from the Western concept of individual civil rights or civil liberty, which are more antithetical to the power of the state. Under the conception of 'economic rights', political legitimacy stems from the state's ability to deliver prosperity and economic goods to society. In this respect, the political legitimacy of the Chinese state is more appropriately described as its 'performance legitimacy'.

Second, the central authority has a propensity to intervene before an incident gets out of hand. Our analysis suggests that the central or provincial governments will step in and punish local officials when incidents pose a threat to their political legitimacy. Based on this logic, concessions will be offered to protestors before the 'tipping point'.

Third, the ability of the central and local governments to handle social unrest is steadily improving. They have invested in modernising police stations, training public security forces and purchasing state-of-the-art surveillance technology. Riot police are becoming increasingly skilled at crowd control, and even minor threats to stability are quickly answered with massive police deployments. As a result, governments at all levels have become more technically sophisticated in recent years. Communication on the Internet and by mobile phone is strictly controlled in order to prevent the distribution of content considered detrimental to social stability. Also, critics of the regime and suspected ringleaders of anti-government activities are under permanent surveillance and are subject to arbitrary arrest.

Unfortunately, repression has proven to be more expedient than intervention or co-optation. Increased budgetary allocations have also created an inherent organisational interest in maintaining and possibly increasing the flow of monetary resources towards public security agencies. Similar to the military apparatus, a growing public security sector will seek to justify its existence by exaggerating threats and lobbying for increased repression.

## Notes

1. Tom Orlik, 'Unrest on Rise as Economy Booms', *Wall Street Journal*, 26 September 2011, http://online.wsj.com/article/SB10001424053111903703604576587070600504108.html (accessed on 26 September 2011).
2. John James Kennedy, 'Maintaining Political Support for the Chinese Communist Party: The Influence of Education and the State-Controlled Media', *Political Studies*, vol. 57 (2009), pp. 517–36.
3. Elizabeth Perry, 2002. *Challenging the Mandate of Heaven: Social Protest and State Power in China* (Armonk, NY: M.E. Sharpe).
4. Zhu Zhaogen, '*Xunzhao Zhongguo zhenggai de "jin yaoshi"*' (Searching for the 'Golden Key' to China's Political Reform), *Lianhe zaobao*, 14 October 2010. http://source.takungpao.com/news/10/10/14/_IN-1314137.htm (accessed on 16 January 2012).
5. For an interesting discussion of the definitions, see by Roland Soong's blog: http://my.opera.com/PRC/blog/show.dml/581789 (accessed on 14 December 2011).
6. This concept is based on Thomas Heberer, *Einführung in die politischen Systeme Ostasiens: VR China, Hong Kong, Japan, Nordkorea, Südkorea, Taiwan* (Introduction to the Political Systems of East Asia: PR China, Hong Kong, Japan, North Korea, South Korea, Taiwan), 2008. (Wiesbaden: VS Verlag), p. 85.
7. Mayfair Mei-hui Yang, 1994. *Gifts, Favors, and Banquets: The Art of Social Relationships in China* (Ithaca, NY: Cornell University Press).
8. For a comprehensive overview, see Carl F. Minzner, 'Xinfang: An Alternative to Formal Chinese Legal Institutions', *Stanford Journal of International Law*, vol. 42 (2005), pp. 1–92 as well as Zhang Yonghe and Zhang Wei, *Lintong xinfang: Zhongguo jiceng xinfang wenti yanjiu baogao* (Letters and Complaints in Lintong: A Research Report on Letters and Petitions at China's Grassroots), 2010. (Beijing: *Renmin chubanshe*).
9. Minzner, 'Xinfang: An Alternative to Formal Chinese Legal Institutions', p. 84.
10. Yongshun Cai, 'Managed Participation in China', *Political Science Quarterly*, vol. 119, no. 3 (2004), pp. 425–51.
11. Peter Lorentzen, 'Regularized Rioting: Informational Mechanisms in an Authoritarian State', paper presented at the

Political Economics Student Conference at the National Bureau of Economic Research, 29 April 2005, http://www.stanford.edu/group/peg/Papers%20for%20call/lorentzen_pescfinal%5B1%5D.pdf_(accessed on 16 January 2012).

12. Lianjiang Li, Minxing Liu and Kevin O'Brien, 'Petitioning Beijing: The High Tide of 2003–2006', *The China Quarterly*, vol. 210 (2012), pp. 313–34.
13. People's Republic of China, Ministry of Science and Technology, *Zhongguo keji tongji shuju* (China Science and Technology Statistics) (various years), available at http://www.sts.org.cn/sjkl/kjtjdt/index.htm (accessed on 16 January 2012).
14. People's Republic of China, National Development and Reform Commission, *Zhonghua renmin gongheguo guomin jingji he shehui fazhan si shierge wu nian guihua gangyao (2011–2015)* (Twelfth Five-Year Guidelines for the National Economic and Social Development of the People's Republic of China (2011–2015)], Xinhua News Agency, 16 March 2011, http://news.xinhuanet.com/politics/2011-03/16/c_121193916.htm (accessed on 16 January 2012).
15. China's Internet Network Information Center, Twenty-sixth Statistical Report on Internet Development in China (July 2010), http://www.cnnic.cn/uploadfiles/pdf/2010/8/24/93145.pdf (accessed on 16 January 2012).
16. Tian Ying and Han Miao, 'New Media Elevates Traditional Media Stories', Xinhua News Agency 25 September 2011, http://news.xinhuanet.com/english2010/china/2011-09/25/c_131159136.htm (accessed on 17 January 2012).
17. Jessica Colwell, 'Jiangxi Authorities Sacked After Nail House Self-Immolation Incident: Shanghaiist', *Shanghaiist*, 12 October 2010, http://shanghaiist.com/2010/10/12/authorities_sacked_in_self-immolati.php (accessed on 3 December 2011).
18. David Bandurski, 'All Eyes on China's New High-Speed Rail – China Media Project', *China Media Project*, 13 July 2011, http://cmp.hku.hk/2011/07/13/13764/ (accessed on 3 December 2011).
19. Jiangtao Shi, 'The People have Spoken', *South China Morning Post*, 20 August 2011.
20. Ying Xing, *'Qi' yu kangzheng zhengzhi. Dangdai Zhongguo xiangcun shehui wending wenti yanjiu* (Emotions and Contentious Politics in Rural China), 2011. (Beijing: *Shehui kexue wenxian chubanshe*).

21. Joseph Fewsmith, 'An "Anger-Venting" Mass Incident Catches the Attention of China's Leadership', *China Leadership Monitor*, no. 26, 2 September 2008, http://www.hoover.org/publications/china-leadership-monitor/article/5673_(accessed on 17 January 2012).
22. Buzhi Ding, 'Weng'an, bu'an de xiancheng' (Weng'an, an 'Unsafe' County Seat), *Nanfang Zhoumo*, 10 July 2008, http://www.infzm.com/content/14365 (accessed on 14 December 2011).
23. Fiona Tam, 'Hundreds Riot Over Suspicious Death of Taxi Driver', *South China Morning Post*, 19 July 2008.
24. Pinghui Zhuang, 'Mourning for Boy Erupts into Violence', *South China Morning Post*, 7 December 2010, http://topics.scmp.com/news/china-news-watch/article/Mourning-for-boy-erupts-into-violence (accessed on 26 November 2011).
25. Field research conducted in Guangzhou, February 2010. See Xianwen Kuang and Christian Göbel, 'Sustaining Collective Action in Urbanizing China', *The China Quarterly* 216 (forthcoming, December 2013).
26. Kevin O'Brien and Lianjiang Li, 2006. *Rightful Resistance in Rural China* (Cambridge, New York: Cambridge University Press), pp. 1–22.
27. Ming'ai Zhang, 'Mass Unrests Shock China', *China.org.cn*, 1 December 2008, http://www.china.org.cn/china/features/content_16880561.htm (accessed on 16 January 2012).
28. See Kuang and Göbel, 'Sustaining Collective Action in Urbanizing China'.
29. Michael Wines, 'Chinese Protestors Seek Return of Villager's Body', *New York Times*, 18 December 2011, http://www.nytimes.com/2011/12/19/world/asia/wukan-protestors-seek-return-of-xue-jinbos-body.html (accessed on 16 January 2012).
30. Malcolm Moore, 'Wukan Siege: First Crack in the Villagers' Resolve', *Daily Telegraph*, 15 December 2011, http://www.telegraph.co.uk/news/worldnews/asia/china/8959080/Wukan-siege-First-crack-in-the-villagers-resolve.html (accessed on 16 January 2012).
31. Dru Gladney, 'Representing Nationality in China: Refiguring Majority/Minority Identities', *Journal of Asian Studies* vol. 53, no. 1, pp. 92–123.
32. Michael Webber, *Making Capitalism in Rural China*, Cheltenham and Northampton, NH: Edward Elgar, 2012, Chapter 8.

33. The protests by monks started in Lhasa, Tibet descended into rioting, burning, looting and killing in the Tibetan capital. The protests also spread to other Tibetan populated areas in Qinghai, Sichuan and Gansu, and attacks on Chinese embassies worldwide. While the Chinese government accused the Dalai Lama of instigating the incidents, the Tibetan Spiritual Leader claimed that they reflected widespread discontentment against Han rule.
34. The ethnic riots broke out on 5 July 2009 in Urumqi, Xinjiang resulted in clashes between the Uighurs, Han Chinese and riot police, which resulted in hundreds of deaths, and a few thousands injuries.
35. This is consistent with the classic theoretical prediction in sociology about the timing of revolution and societal needs. See James Davies, *American Sociological Review*, vol. 27, no. 1 (1962), pp. 5–19.
36. 'Rural land disputes lead unrest', *China Daily*, 11 June 2010. http://www.chinadaily.com.cn/business/2010-11/06/content_11511477.htm (accessed on 25 October 2011).
37. Kathy Le Mons Walker, 'From Covert to Overt: Everyday Peasant Politics in China and the Implications for Transnational Agrarian Movements', *Journal of Agrarian Change*, no. 8 (2008), p. 473.
38. Liu Lee, 'Made in China: Cancer Villages', *Environment Magazine*, March–April 2010, http://www.environmentmagazine.org/Archives/Back%20Issues/March-April%202010/made-in-china-full.html (accessed on 25 November 2011).
39. Christina Larson, 'The New Epicenter of China's Discontent', *Foreign Policy*, 23 August 2011, http://www.foreignpolicy.com/articles/2011/08/23/the_new_epicenter_of_china_s_discontent?page=full (accessed on 25 November 2011).
40. Edward Cody, 'Text Messages Giving Voice to Chinese', *Washington Post*, 28 June 2007, http://www.washingtonpost.com/wp-dyn/content/article/2007/06/27/AR2007062702962.html (accessed on 17 January 2012).
41. Tong and Lei, 'Large-scale Mass Incidents and Government Responses in China', pp. 487–508.
42. Rob Gifford, 'Momentum Builds behind Chinese Workers' Protests', *NPR*, 24 September 2010, http://www.npr.org/templates/story/story.php?storyId=130078240 (accessed on 25 November 2011).

43. World Bank, 2002. *National Development and Sub-national Finance – A Review of Provincial Expenditures* (Beijing: Poverty Reduction and Economic Management Unit, East Asia and Pacific Region, The World Bank), pp. 27–47.
44. Thomas P. Bernstein and Xiaobo Lü, 2003. *Taxation without Representation in Contemporary Rural China* (New York, NY: Cambridge University Press).
45. China Land Survey Planning Institute, '*Woguo xianxing caizheng tizhixia de tudi liyong*' (The Use of Land in China's Fiscal System), *Zhongguo tudi* [China Land], vol. 7 (2006), pp. 4–7.
46. Murray Scot Tanner, 'Rethinking Law Enforcement and Society', in Neil J. Diamant, Stanley B. Lubman and Kevin J. O'Brien (eds), 2005. *Engaging the Law: State, Society, and Possibilities for Justice* (Stanford, CA: Stanford University Press), p. 203.
47. Kevin J. O'Brien and Lianjiang Li, 'Suing the Local State: Administrative Litigation in Rural China', in Diamant, Lubman and O'Brien (eds), *Engaging the Law*, pp. 31–53.
48. Ibid., p. 41.
49. Murray Scot Tanner, 'China Rethinks Unrest', *The Washington Quarterly*, vol. 27, no. 3 (2004), p. 147.
50. Ibid.
51. Fan Peng and Yi Junjian, '*Difangfenquan, shehui fanzui yu guojia qiangzhi nengli zengzhang – jiyu gaige shiqi Zhongguo gong'an caizheng jingfei fazhan de shizheng fenxi*' [Decentralization, Crime, and the Increase in the Law Enforcement of the Chinese Government], *Shijie jingji wenhui* (World Economic Papers), 2009, no. 2, pp. 99–120.
52. Ibid.
53. Murray Scot Tanner, *Unrest in China.*
54. Tong and Lei, 'Large-scale Mass Incidents and Government Responses in China', pp. 487–508.
55. Ibid., p. 503.
56. Hu Jintao, '*Hu Jintao zai sheng bu ji zhuyao lingdao ganbu shehuiguanli ji qi chuangxin zhuanti yantaoban kai banshi shang fabiao zhongyao jianghua qiangdiao zhazhashishi tigao shehuiguanli kexuehua shuiping jianshe Zhongguo tese shehu-izhuyi shehui guanli tixi*' (In his Important Opening Speech at the Meeting of the Leading Ministry-Level Provincial Cadres on the Issues of Social Management and Social Management

Innovation, Hu Jintao Stresses [the need to] Diligently Improve the Scientific Level of Social Management [and to] Establish a Socialist Social Management System with Chinese Characteristics], *Renmin Ribao*, 20 February 2011, p. 1.

57. National Development and Reform Commission, '12th Five-Year Guidelines'.
58. Calculations based on *China Statistical Yearbook*, various years.
59. Hu Jintao, 'Important Opening Speech'.
60. China Information Technology, a Chinese NASDAQ-listed company, is developing an ID card for migrant workers, who are deemed a 'risk' group. The card will store biographical and employment data of the worker and will be traceable via satellite. Combining geographical positioning systems and geographical information systems, security departments will be able to monitor the movement of individuals in real time and intervene if members of this 'risk' group assemble in sensitive locations. It is no coincidence that the public security departments of rich cities in southern China are among the main customers. See http://www.chinacnit.com/en/detail.php?article_id=908 (accessed on 16 January 2012) and http://www.chinacnit.com/cn/page.php?column_id=286 (accessed on 16 January 2012).
61. Loretta Chao and Don Clark, 'Cisco Poised to Help China Keep an Eye on Its Citizens', *Wall Street Journal*, 5 July 2011, http://online.wsj.com/article/SB10001424052702304778304576377141077267316.html (accessed on 16 January 2012).
62. Elizabeth J. Perry, 'Chinese Conceptions of "Rights": From Mencius to Mao – and Now', *Perspectives on Politics*, vol. 6, no. 1 (2008), pp. 37–50.
63. Ibid., p. 41.

# 6 Untapped Trilateralism: Common Economic and Security Interests of the European Union, the United States and China

*Bates Gill and Andrew Small*

## Untapped Trilateralism

In many respects, we live in a tripolar world. The European Union, the United States and the People's Republic of China rank first, second and third respectively in gross domestic product (GDP) in the world, and together account for nearly 54 per cent of global GDP.[1] They are the three largest traders in the world and their total imports and exports account for 36 per cent of all global merchandise trade.[2] The members of the EU, China and the US account for more than 67 per cent of global military spending. In 2006–10, the US, China and just four EU countries (France, Germany, Greece and the United Kingdom) accounted for nearly 72 per cent of the global trade in major conventional weapons.[3] The three parties' combined populations make up about 30 per cent of the world's 7 billion inhabitants. They are jointly the three largest emitters of greenhouse gases, with more than 56 per cent of total global emissions.[4]

The three engage in an increasingly complex range of activities, from summits to sectorial dialogues to intensive interaction among their respective business sectors, civil society institutions and private citizens. Although transatlantic relations have a long-standing history of political, economic, allied military, cultural and people-to-people engagement, there has been a particularly strong increase in interaction with China and interdependence between the three players in just the past decade or two.

Since 2003, when the EU and China formally established a 'comprehensive strategic partnership', the two sides have created more than 50 sectorial dialogues covering the full spectrum of their bilateral relationship: trade and financial affairs, environment, energy, education, culture and language training, customs cooperation, food, consumer and labour safety, agriculture, civil aviation, space cooperation, domestic regional policy, employment and social affairs, and civil society. The European Commission established the Policy Dialogue Support Facility between 2007 and 2011; it is intended to further strengthen exchanges between EU and Chinese officials across the range of policy dialogue issues.

Since the late 2000s, the EU and China have set up two senior-level forums: the High-Level Economic and Trade Dialogue (established in 2008) and the High-Level Strategic Dialogue (established in 2010). At the Fourteenth EU-China summit in February 2012, it was announced that a 'people-to-people dialogue' would be established in order to complement the two dialogue mechanisms. In addition to these interactions, the EU and China engage in a range of regularised meetings of their respective political directors, officials and experts (and also at the ambassadorial level) on Asia-Pacific affairs, international security and non-proliferation.

The United States and China also engage in a wide range of official relations that have intensified and deepened with time.[5] The latest ones are the Senior Dialogue (on political and security issues), held six times between 2005 and 2008; the Strategic Economic Dialogue, held five times between 2006 and 2008; and the Strategic and Economic Dialogue, initiated by the Obama administration and held annually since 2009. The US and China have an ongoing but irregular set of military-to-military exchanges and dialogues between officials of their respective defence and armed forces establishments.

In addition, the EU, the US and China have intensifying trilateral or bilateral official interaction across the full range of international and regional multilateral institutions, from the United

Nations and its institutions to organisations such as the World Bank, the Association of Southeast Asian Nations (ASEAN) Regional Forum (ARF), the Asia-Europe Meeting process, the Asia-Pacific Economic Cooperation forum, the G20 meetings and so on. With the ever-growing degree of non-governmental business, scientific, cultural and people-to-people exchanges among the EU, the US and China – the level of interaction and interdependence has never been greater in this triangular relationship.

Yet despite intensifying interactions, a greater degree of joint purpose and collaborative response remains elusive. This point becomes all the more important in today's world of shifting power dynamics between East and West, the global financial crisis and economic downturn, particularly in the EU and the US, and the rise of players such as China. With these trends comes the diffusion of responsibility and capability for action, even as the agenda for action becomes more complex in nature and global in scope.

## Common Economic and Security Interests

### Introduction

As major world players with a global presence, the EU, the US and China share a range of interests. Many of these shared interests they proclaim publicly, often in the form of joint US-China, EU-China and EU-US bilateral summit communiqués or in joint statements and documents emerging from larger multilateral forums of which they are members and/or observers, for example the United Nations and the ARF. These statements present joint interests in a very broad way, as in the case of the joint press communiqué of the Fourteenth EU-China summit in February 2012, which stated:

> [I]n an ever changing and increasingly inter-dependent world where their interests become more closely intertwined, [the EU and China] should strengthen their interaction and cooperation to better meet the opportunities and challenges in the new bilateral, multilateral and global framework.[6]

At the summit, the two sides agreed to deepen dialogue and exchanges on global issues, including cyber-security and climate change.[7] In strikingly similar themes, the joint US-China presidential summit statement of January 2011 declared:

> The United States and China agreed to advance cooperation to: counter violent extremism; prevent the proliferation of nuclear weapons, other weapons of mass destruction, and their means of delivery; strengthen nuclear security; eliminate infectious disease and hunger; end extreme poverty; respond effectively to the challenge of climate change; counter piracy; prevent and mitigate disasters; address cyber-security; fight transnational crime; and combat trafficking in persons …
>
> [They] recognized the vital importance of working together to build a cooperative economic partnership of mutual respect and mutual benefit to both countries and to the global economy.[8]

As these statements underscore, the list of areas in which the EU, the US and China purport to share common interests is lengthy and complex, as it should be. Given the numerous areas in which their interests overlap, this brief report cannot provide a comprehensive exploration of all relevant issues. Instead, it will examine three broad areas of joint interest – economic matters, political-security affairs and emergent transnational issues; and within each of them it will delve into prominent sub-issues.

## Common economic interests

### *Interdependence, financial stability and burgeoning trade and investment*

China, the EU and the US are the world's three largest economic blocs and are also very interdependent. Although China has been the only one of the three to maintain strong economic growth through the global financial crisis, this was not a result of any 'decoupling'.[9] China is at the centre of a network of supply chains in Asia that performs a vital role for all three economies.[10] Trade flows have burgeoned – from US$121.5 billion in bilateral trade with the US and US$77.6 billion with the EU when China joined the World Trade Organisation (WTO) in 2001 to

US$456.8 billion and US$480.9 billion respectively in 2010. The explosion of the Chinese consumer market, increasing by US$300 billion in 2010 and potentially by as much as US$500 billion in 2012, has also turned it into a major new source of export growth for leading European and US industries.[11] More recently, Chinese overseas direct investment (ODI) has started to play an important role of its own, and is projected to run as high as US$2 trillion in Western economies by 2020.[12]

Several changes have placed China at the heart of decision-making processes in global economic management that were once the preserve of the Western powers. Among the most important of them are the shift of the locus of decision-making from the G8 to the G20; the beginning of a readjustment of both the voting shares and the allocation of senior positions at international financial institutions; and the prominent role occupied by China in the Doha Development Round of negotiations at the WTO. Nevertheless, these institutional adjustments still lag behind the reality of Chinese economic power. With more than US$3 trillion in foreign exchange reserves and a growing ability to deploy resources during a period when much of the Western world is going through a painful period of debt reduction, the weight of China's position at the top table far outstrips its formal role.

China has also played a helpful role in dealing with the eurocrisis. It has offered political and rhetorical support for the European Financial Stability Facility (EFSF) and issued statements of confidence in various distressed European economies. Many observers have suggested that China would or should be a major purchaser of bonds issued by the EFSF; but while China has made purchases, it has not invested on a large scale.[13] China has also undertaken 'buying trips' in both Europe and the United States – a familiar practice in Chinese commercial diplomacy but now on a much grander scale. Deals amounting to some €16 billion were signed during Hu Jintao's visit to France in November 2010,[14] and US$45 billion dollars' worth of deals was concluded during his state visit to the United States in January 2011.[15] China's apparent willingness to make large investments in EU Member States during austerity conditions, whether the purchase of Greek ports or an offer from China's sovereign wealth fund to put money into UK infrastructure projects,[16] has received much publicity.

The image of China supporting Europe in its hour of need is a potent one, especially as the US has so far been unwilling to provide additional financing to the EFSF through the International Monetary Fund. But its support has still largely been on the margins – Chinese investment in the EU amounts to around 0.2 per cent of total inflow – and to date, the reaction in both the United States and Europe has been ambivalent. Although there has been enthusiasm about China bailing out failing companies, such as Sweden's Volvo, there has also been suspicion about state-subsidised firms taking public procurement contracts and purchasing European companies being used as a back-door method of acquiring technology, as well as objections to the absence of Greenfield investments.

To be sure, the economic agenda between China and the EU and China and the US has a number of problems, and they are increasing. Both Europe and the United States have a list of concerns, among them violations of intellectual property rights (IPR), market access barriers for their companies, 'indigenous innovation' policies, state subsidies for Chinese companies, the deliberate undervaluation of the Chinese currency and, as a result, spiralling bilateral trade deficits. On the multilateral front, the shared commitment to addressing genuine crises in a constructive way was very much in evidence through the worst moments of the financial crisis.[17] But the G20 has since struggled to reach substantive agreements and the WTO has been virtually deadlocked. China's policies are far from the only reason for this – note the failed green room talks in Geneva in 2008[18] and disputes over rebalancing issues in Seoul in 2010 – but it has tended to act as a blocking force rather than as one of the powers seeking to drive agreements forward. For the EU and the US, the result is an economic policy agenda with China that is increasingly focused on problem management; and much of the positive agenda, of further trade liberalisation, is now largely being constructed *around* China.

China has complaints of its own. It is still subject to embargoes on arms exports from both Europe and the United States and to a broader set of restrictions on dual-use technology exports. It also objects to being treated as a non-market economy, a status that enables anti-dumping charges to be brought against it more easily, even though under the terms of its WTO accession protocol it will acquire market economy status automatically in 2016.[19] It has successfully brought WTO cases itself, notably against the US imposition of both anti-subsidy and anti-dumping duties. And Chinese policymakers have also made their own critiques of US and European economic behaviour – from low savings rates in the US to the seemingly limited willingness of the West to learn lessons from the Asian financial crisis of the late 1990s. But ultimately, in view of the balance of trade being so heavily in China's favour and the relative openness of the US and European economies, those objections have come much more strongly from China's economic partners.

### *Long-standing problems*

The business climate for international companies has worsened; China's need to pull in foreign investment has diminished and its disposition towards tilting the playing field in favour of state-owned enterprise (SOE) champions has become further entrenched, much to the detriment of both its own private sector and Western companies. US and European companies were willing to put up with the difficulties of operating in China in the hope that they would be able to reap the dividends of the world's largest market further down the line. But in a number of sectors, this has begun to look like a false promise.

Second, the theft of intellectual property is becoming an increasing threat to the core business and competitive advantage of Western companies. Technology transfer arrangements and intellectual property theft at the higher end poses a threat to Western companies not only in the Chinese market but also in other overseas markets, including the home market for some of the companies in question. High-speed rail is one highly visible example: European and Japanese companies now face new competition from Chinese companies whom they accuse of stealing their core technologies.

A third long-standing concern has been the call for China to 'rebalance' its domestic economy in the direction of greater consumption. This has two intertwined components: internal and external balances. Externally China has run large and rising surpluses, becoming a major creditor to indebted countries and accumulating vast currency reserves. Internally its economy is disproportionately dependent on investment and exports and it has excessive savings levels and the lowest share of private consumption of any major economy.

But rebalancing has been on the table in China for so long, at least since 2004, that there are serious questions as to whether the Chinese government possesses the political will or the wherewithal to push through the necessary measures. The global economic crisis has reinforced these tendencies, weakening the hand of China's economic reformers (who were hardly in the ascendancy anyway) and prompting a stimulus package that has further entrenched the role of the state in China's economy.[20]

The impact of these developments extends beyond the economic realm. Business lobbies in the US that previously played a major part in keeping the US-China relationship on track, not least by moderating the protectionist measures advocated by certain pockets of the US Congress, are professedly no longer willing to play that role.[21]Debates in the US about broader China policy do not have that buffer any more.

In sum, when defining the shared interests of the EU, the US and China in the economic realm, it is impossible to ignore the context of growing bilateral tension and the diminishing belief among policymakers that there is a genuinely shared agenda on global trade and economic issues. At the same time, the benefits of economic cooperation are clear, and they call for a reinvigorated agenda, albeit modest, to foster greater mutually beneficial outcomes. The concluding sections to this report will explore the opportunities and limits of this approach.

## Common security interests

### *Regional conflicts, tensions and instability*

Beijing remains a strong proponent of traditional understandings of sovereignty and the sanctity of the internal affairs of states. These views arise from China's historical experience of colonialism and from contemporary national self-perceptions fed by its economic success in recent years. They remain deeply held by Chinese leaders and strategists and profoundly shape Beijing's interests and actions regarding regional conflicts, instability and tension.[22]

Nevertheless, China's leaders have begun to recognise the importance for its interests of stability in areas around its periphery and farther afield. As a result, China has come to demonstrate a more constructive and active approach towards the global challenges of regional conflicts and instability and of failing states, and in the process there has been more convergence of its interests with those of the US and the EU in a number of instances.

China has come to accept a more prominent role for the UNSC and region-based multilateral security organisations in dealing with failing states and regional instability. It has also become more active itself in placing people and materiel in harms' way in order to help mitigate regional security challenges, and it increasingly has done so by developing a less rigid approach to questions of sovereignty and intervention.

For example, Beijing voted in favour of UNSC resolutions in early 2011 that imposed sanctions upon Libya and then did not oppose UNSC resolution 1973, which ultimately authorised 'Member States ... acting nationally or through regional organisations or arrangements ... [to] take all necessary measures ... to protect civilians and civilian populated areas under threat of attack' in Libya.[23]

Official Chinese positions and policies have evolved from support for groups associated with insurgencies and terrorist activities in the 1970s to conducting activities to counter extremist violence and terrorism both at home and abroad since the late 1990s.[24] A part of this shift can be explained by the fact that China itself has become the target of violent extremist activity, including incidents widely viewed as terrorist action, both outside and inside China. For example, three Chinese citizens died in the destruction of the World Trade Center towers in September 2001; and between 2001 and 2004, a further 56 Chinese civilians were killed in suicide bombings and other terrorist acts in nine separate incidents in Israel, Kyrgyzstan, Sri Lanka, Pakistan, Laos and Afghanistan.[25] China has also faced violent extremist activity within its own borders; prior to the 2008 Beijing Olympics, China claimed to have disrupted several terrorist plots, meanwhile, violent separatist activities among Uighur groups in its far western province Xinjiang persist.

Seeing links between Islamic separatist movements and groups outside China, Beijing took steps in the late 1990s and especially the early 2000s to cooperate bilaterally and multilaterally with other governments. In June 2001, for example, China joined Russia and four Central Asian states, Kazakhstan, Kyrgyzstan, Tajikistan and Uzbekistan, in establishing the Shanghai Cooperation Organisation (SCO). Its founding charter declared the intention to combat the 'three evil forces: terrorism, separatism and extremism'. In the early 2000s, China also moved to establish cooperative counterterrorist ties with the US as well as the EU. This cooperation has included regular consultations, intelligence sharing, disruption of terrorist financial networks and unified positions as expressed in UNSC resolutions and as co-signatories of UN conventions and other international agreements aimed to counter terrorist activities.[26]

China has also sent 10 separate missions of escort ships to the Gulf of Aden since early 2009 in order to cooperate with (but to operate formally independent from) established multinational counter-piracy operations in the region. According to Chinese sources, in the three years of this involvement, Chinese naval vessels have escorted some 4,411 Chinese and foreign commercial vessels while providing protection as well to World Food Programme shipments.[27]

One of the most interesting demonstrations of Beijing's more flexible and constructive approach to questions of regional conflict, instability and tension is its growing support of UN peacekeeping operations. Its contribution to UN peacekeeping remained between 50 to 100 peacekeepers from 1993 to 2002 but then expanded rapidly to 2009 to reach its present level of about 2,000 personnel deployed. Most Chinese troops deployed with UN peacekeeping operations provide engineering, transport or medical support. But China began to deploy police (to East Timor) in 1999; and as of 31 December 2011, it had 71 police deployed in Haiti, Liberia, South Sudan and Timor-Leste. It also had 40 military experts in seven UN missions.[28] According to China's defence white paper published in 2011, Chinese peacekeepers have 'built and repaired over 8,700 km of roads and 270 bridges, cleared over 8,900 mines and various explosive devices, transported over 600,000 tons of cargo across a total distance of 9.3 million km, and treated 79,000 patients'. The white paper notes that as of the end of 2010, China had sent 17,390 military personnel to 19 UN peacekeeping operations, nine of whom had lost their life in the line of duty.[29]

Another area where China's approach to regional conflicts and instability is changing concerns the protection of Chinese citizens abroad. According to recent research, the number of Chinese citizens working abroad hovered at around 5 million in 2011, a number that will continue to grow. Moreover, the number of Chinese travelling abroad as tourists or on other short-term travel has grown from only 10 million in 2000 to 60 million in 2012. It will reach some 100 million by 2020. The issue of protecting its nationals took an especially high profile in 2011 and 2012: China evacuated a total of 48,000 of its nationals from Egypt and Libya during the uprisings there in 2011 and from Japan after the March 2011 tsunami and nuclear disaster, a number five times larger than the total evacuations of Chinese citizens in the previous 30 years. Thirteen Chinese merchant sailors were murdered on the Mekong River in northern Thailand in October 2011, some two dozen Chinese workers were kidnapped by Sudanese rebels in late January 2012 and about the same numbers of Chinese workers were reportedly kidnapped in the northern Sinai about a week later.

The decision-making process and logistics involved in citizen protection overseas will probably demand a more adaptable response from Beijing to the dangers posed to its nationals by the instability of states and regions abroad.[30]

In sum, as China's global dependence grows, it will be increasingly in its interests to leverage its power and influence in ways that protect and promote those interests, however distant. This will include areas where the US, the EU and EU Member States also have significant economic, political and security interests, as in Africa, the Middle East, Southwest Asia and on the high seas. As such, the three sides will experience both conflict and convergence on matters of regional security. In a current example, China's continuing reluctance to support tougher measures against Syria reflects Beijing's persistent wariness about intervention, particularly when led by the West. The challenge ahead is to broaden the areas of cooperation while narrowing the potential for confrontation. The concluding section of this study will discuss the possibilities and pitfalls of doing so.

*Arms control and non-proliferation*

Beijing has come to see a common interest with the majority of the international community in working to stem the proliferation of weapons of mass destruction (WMD)-related materials, technologies and systems and to prevent the emergence of new nuclear-armed states.[31] China's efforts to promote non-proliferation have been demonstrated most clearly by its own national policies.

At the global, bilateral and domestic levels, often in stark contrast to its policies in the 1970s, 1980s and early 1990s, China has taken significant action to support, implement and adhere to international non-proliferation norms and commitments. At the global level, China acceded to the Convention on Physical Protection of Nuclear Material in 1989, joined the Nuclear Non-proliferation Treaty (NPT) in 1992 and has since joined or sought membership in the major supply-side non-proliferation regimes: the Zangger Committee (joined in 1997); the Nuclear Suppliers Group (joined in 2004); the Missile Technology Control Regime; and the Wassenaar Arrangement. China joined with other UNSC members in April 2004 to unanimously endorse resolution 1540, which obliges Member States 'to refrain from supporting by any means non-State actors from developing, acquiring, manufacturing, possessing, transporting, transferring or using nuclear, chemical or biological weapons and their delivery systems'.[32]

Through a series of bilateral agreements with the United States in the mid- to late 1990s, China cut off or significantly curtailed its missile- and nuclear-related cooperation with Iran and Pakistan. At Washington's urging, and in recognising the potential vulnerability of its ports to destabilising commodity flows, especially nuclear weapons and related materials, China also joined the US-led Container Security Initiative (CSI) in 2003. CSI is operational in three Chinese ports, Hong Kong, Shenzhen and Shanghai, and involves US-China cooperation in the identification of high-risk containers, the pre-screening and evaluation of containers and the use of non-invasive technologies to screen containers moving from Chinese to US ports.[33]

To be sure, there are questions about the extent of shared interests between China, on the one hand, and the US and EU, on the other hand, on a number of proliferation issues. These questions arise from two important sources. First, Chinese individuals and companies allegedly continue to engage in proliferation activities in contravention of Chinese law and China's international commitments. According to US intelligence sources, for example, 'entities ... in China continue to sell technologies and components in the Middle East and South Asia that are dual use and could support WMD and missile programs.' In addition, 'Chinese entities – including private and state-owned firms – continue to engage in WMD-related proliferation activities. ... Chinese entities continue to supply a variety of missile-related items to multiple customers, including Iran, Syria, and Pakistan.'[34]

Second, Beijing has been criticised for not doing enough to prevent North Korea from acquiring and testing a nuclear device and for not agreeing to even tougher measures against Teheran. Beijing has also been criticised for continuing significant trade with and investment in Iran and North Korea, including a marked intensification of economic and also political relations with North Korea in 2010 and 2011, some of which could contribute to sanctions-evading activities by North Korea.[35] There also appears to be growing distance between the US and EU positions regarding Iran and that of China. In January 2012, for example, in response to Teheran's announcement that it had begun to enrich uranium at its underground facility at the Fordow military base, the EU agreed to impose tougher economic sanctions on Iran, including the prohibition of oil imports from the country. But the Chinese foreign ministry said that this was 'not a constructive approach'.[36]

With regard to arms control, there remains a separation of interests between China and the United States. As members of the NPT, the US, China and the EU Member States are all committed in principle to nuclear disarmament, according to Article 6 of the treaty. The United States, China, France and the United Kingdom are all signatories of the Comprehensive Test Ban Treaty (CTBT); but of these four, only the latter two have also ratified the treaty. Nonetheless, all four have abided by a de facto moratorium on nuclear testing, even though the treaty has not formally entered into force. EU Member States, the US and China are also signatories of the Chemical Weapons Convention and the Biological and Toxin Weapons Convention.

But the strategic relationship between the US and China, not least concerning the role of nuclear weapons and deterrence, remains uncertain and problematic. It results from frequently divergent interests between the two on arms control matters. For example, the 13-year stalemate at the Conference on Disarmament – is traceable to continuing differences between the US and China. At bottom, Beijing's concerns about further nuclear disarmament measures, such as ratifying the CTBT or negotiating a binding FMCT, are rooted in its fundamental interest in maintaining a viable retaliatory capability for its nuclear arsenal in the face of what it views as the overwhelming nuclear and conventional strike capability of the US (and, to a lesser degree, that of Russia). It is this concern about the reliability of its nuclear deterrent that generates Beijing's opposition to strategic missile defences on the part of the US and its allies – another significant difference between the two on fundamental arms control matters. Thus although President Barack Obama's April 2009 call in Prague for a nuclear-weapons-free world, and some subsequent disarmament steps by the US, were greeted with widespread enthusiasm in Europe, they received only a tepid and sceptical 'wait-and-see' response from China.[37]

Differences in interests over arms control matters also exist between the EU Member States and the US, between the EU and China and among EU Member States as well.

In the conventional weapons realm, the EU Member States strongly supported the negotiation of a robust and enforceable arms trade treaty (ATT), but China and the US were initially much less enthusiastic. In December 2006, the UN General Assembly vote on resolution 61/89, 'Towards an Arms Trade Treaty: establishing common international standards for the import, export and transfer of conventional arms', China abstained, the United States voted against and all EU Member States voted in favour. With the advent of the Obama administration, the US has engaged constructively in the preparatory committee (PrepComm) and the ad hoc intergovernmental meetings in advance of the July 2012 UN conference to negotiate an ATT. China has also become more active in these meetings.

During the July 2011 PrepComm, the P5 members of the UNSC issued a joint statement which suggests greater solidarity among the positions of the US, China and some EU Member States. But although all EU Member States would like China and the US to sign and ratify an ATT, there is concern in some quarters that the price for Chinese agreement will be too high: a watering down of criteria and the adoption of a narrow scope with regard to arms and activities to be covered by an ATT. Furthermore, US insistence on the treaty being adopted by consensus has also been seen as an opportunity for sceptical states to prevent the treaty text from being agreed for adoption, and then there is the prospect that US ratification of even a limited ATT would be likely to face overwhelming opposition in the US Senate. Even within the EU, there is disgruntlement among some members with France and the UK for negotiating on the P5 statement.

Finally, the EU arms embargo on China exposes differing interests among the EU, China and the US. The embargo was imposed in response to the Chinese crackdown on demonstrators in Tiananmen Square in June 1989. It remains in place, in part on human rights grounds but also as a result of pressures from both outside and inside the EU not to take measures that could assist in China's military modernisation. The US has made clear that it opposes lifting the EU arms embargo. On the other hand, China has consistently insisted that the embargo is unfair and belittles the concept of a 'strategic partnership'. According to European reports, High Representative Catherine Ashton presented a foreign and security policy strategy paper at the December 2010 EU Summit that stated that the 'current arms embargo is a major impediment to developing stronger EU-China cooperation on foreign policy and security matters' and that the EU 'should assess its practical implication and design a way forward.'[38] No concrete steps have since been taken in this direction, in part owing to opposition from within the EU and from the United States.

In considering the common interests of the EU, the US and China on matters of non-proliferation and arms control, a very mixed picture emerges. At the high level of official declaratory policy, there appears to be a strong convergence of interests. But on closer examination of near-term tactical interests and policies, the three often have divergent approaches.

## Common Action: Imperatives and Impediments

### Imperatives for common action

The range of shared economic and security interests between the EU, the US and China arise from a mix of at least three underlying forces which are likely to continue in the medium to long term as a largely positive impetus towards common interests and action. First, the forces of globalisation – advances in communications that richly facilitate interaction and create enormous mutual benefit for millions of persons from the EU, the US and China as a result of travel, commerce and enhanced connectivity – generate real interdependences and a greater degree of shared economic and security interests.

Second, the remarkable trajectory of China over the past three decades has in itself been a force for bringing the EU, the US and China closer together on economic and security issues. Chinese leaders, in seeking to realise China's re-emergence as a major power, have recognised that to do this successfully requires a stable internal and external environment in order to access the much-needed inputs of capital, technology and know-how. And that in turn demands a constructive and peaceable approach to the outside world. For their part, the leaders of the EU and the US recognised early on the strategic value, both from an economic and a security perspective, of seeking to integrate, not isolate, a waking China. Many government and non-governmental observers of relations with China have encouraged China to emerge as a 'responsible stakeholder'.[39] China's performance in the wake of the global financial crisis and economic recession in the late 2000s is indicative of China's growing presence in world affairs and integration into the international system.

Third, and most recently, globalisation's downsides – are another factor that has generated a greater sense of common economic and security interests among the EU, the US and China. The economic and security challenges posed by mobile, violent extremism, including terrorism, or by illicit trafficking of weapons have been of concern for many years. But newer and urgent challenges, including potential pandemics, cyber-attacks and well-organised transnational criminal activity, have become more and more problematic in a globalising world. These types of challenge, some new, some less so, are all the more problematic as they are facilitated by the very openness of a globalised world even as they threaten to disrupt the stable functioning of the global flows of people, goods, technologies, information and services that underpin and sustain the modern world.[40]

These three forces provide a powerful impetus for the EU, the US and China to recognise common interests and to work together in practical ways to build a common sense of purpose while cooperatively addressing shared challenges. Whether old or new, these impediments threaten to forestall and perhaps foreclose cooperation among the EU, the US and China precisely when the uncertainties of shifting geopolitical power dynamics, growing transnational risks and other national, regional and global challenges demand a greater degree of common purpose and action.

## Impediments to common action

### *A changing world*

A long-standing assumption in the EU and the US – that by fostering the forces of globalisation to engage and integrate a rising China, a more open, pluralistic and democratic China will one day emerge – has come increasingly into question. This has been especially true as Chinese authorities in the past five years have stepped-up their efforts to stifle political and religious discontent while seeking to tighten access to independent sources of information. For many Chinese leaders, the interflow of people, information and ideas that comes with globalisation has not necessarily been a good thing to the degree that it contributes to delegitimising one-party rule in the country. It is also increasingly clear that globalisation and China's rise have disproportionately benefited some and not benefited others, as evidenced by the growing income gap between rich and poor, between the cities and the countryside and between China's coastal east and its inland provinces. On the other hand, for many citizens in the EU and the US, and particularly those hard hit by recession, a rising China in a globalising world is seen not as an opportunity but as a challenge and even a threat.

In some high-profile and troubling cases, China appears to be a source of problems rather than solutions. Late 2011 and early 2012 saw a number of statements from very senior US officials pointing for the first time in a public way to China as a major source of illicit and hostile cyber activities. In late October 2011, the US Office of the National Counterintelligence Executive, under the Office of the Director of National Intelligence, outlined in an extensive declassified document how 'Chinese actors are the world's most active and persistent perpetrators of economic espionage.'[41] This point was soon underscored by the director of the Central Intelligence Agency, who told Congress that among state actors posing cyber threats to the US, 'China and Russia are of particular concern.'[42] In a *Wall Street Journal* opinion piece, three recently retired and high-ranking US officials went further, saying that the 'Chinese government has a national policy of economic espionage in cyberspace.'[43] There are numerous reports of China-sourced hacking, thievery and disruptions against US and European government and corporate facilities.[44] Tens of billions of dollars' worth of intellectual property, as well as military-technical secrets, are said to be taken from Europe and the US (and others) by Chinese cyber thieves and cyber spies. Whether or not these exfiltrations can be ultimately attributed to official Chinese policy, cyber-security will become an increasingly contentious issue in US-China and EU-China relations.

In a more open and globalised world, concerns also arise about China as a source of other problems, such as infectious outbreaks of disease regionally and around the world. The most troubling instance to date involved the severe acute respiratory syndrome outbreak, starting in Guangdong province in China. The Chinese government initially sought to cover it up, but it eventually resulted in 8,096 illnesses and 774 deaths worldwide.[45] The possible spread of other infectious diseases from China (and elsewhere), such as avian and swine influenza subtypes, to which humans may have little to no immunity, continues to worry the global community. Avian influenza A (H5N1) – its first outbreak affecting humans was in Hong Kong in 1997; and since 2003, it has killed 346 persons in 15 (mostly Asian) countries – has recently reappeared in China, causing two known deaths in late 2011 and early 2011.[46] Of particular and increasing concern in China is the growing prevalence of multidrug-resistant and extensively drug-resistant TB.[47] Inadequate health conditions, preventive measures and treatments in China contribute to this problem, and they all require greater investment from the Chinese government.

As China has become more globalised, broadly considered a positive development for it and the world, problems have arisen regarding it as a transit point for illicit and destabilising transactions and commodity flows. For example, in March 2007, a bank in the Chinese territory of Macao, Banco Delta Asia, was identified by the US Department of the Treasury as facilitating financial transactions, including money laundering and passing counterfeit US currency, for North Korea. US companies and financial institutions were ordered to sever relations with the bank. Also worryingly, a 2011 report by the UNSC committee established to monitor compliance with resolutions 1718 and 1874 found that a 'neighbouring third country', widely understood to be China, served as a transshipment point for ballistic missile-related items between North Korea and Iran.[48]

The outlook for trilateral economic relations in the following 20 years has significantly shifted. There is a still-tentative recovery in Europe and the United States; a China that now has 61 companies in the Global 500 and is a major source of ODI in its own right; a shift to the G20 as the principal economic conclave; and a shift away from the WTO framework towards bilateral and multilateral trade deals. Chinese companies seeking to become global MNCs risk facing market access and investment restriction issues, largely as a result of conditions in their home market. China will be dealing with countries that, although they have a greater need for external injections of capital, also have a more acute focus on economic 'fairness' and reciprocity than when there was a rapidly growing economic pie.

The trade game is changing too. There has long been a danger that the WTO would be weakened if it went two decades without concluding a new round, and none of the 'new' issues that have emerged in global trade since the Uruguay round have been incorporated into WTO mechanisms. China has a greater stake than most countries in ensuring that disputes continue to be managed through the WTO and in holding off the threat of protectionism. But there is a growing risk that the WTO's authority will be eroded in the coming period. The US and the EU are starting to move towards a framework in which the trade agenda is once again driven by deals between the advanced economies. This is epitomised by the new trade arrangements being envisaged (or in some cases actively agreed) between members of the old General Agreement on Tariffs and Trade 'quad' of the EU, the United States, Canada and Japan. It is evident in the TPP and in the EU's web of new FTAs in Asia – the EU-Korea FTA is the most comprehensive trade deal that Europe has ever concluded – and it is also the main thread in proposals for a multilateral deal on services among a broader group of developed economies. If China thought that its accession to the WTO in 2001 meant that it was now 'in the club', it could find that frustration with how the club is working means that newer, more exclusive ones will emerge.

### *Bilateral ties*

In addition to such potential global-level impediments and concerns, the three bilateral relationships involved in this triangle – EU-China, US-China and EU-US relations – all retain their own internal impediments that will constrain a greater degree of common purpose and common action across the trilateral relationship. Perhaps the greatest impediments will arise in US-China relations, but the other bilateral ties have persistent problems too.

The EU-China relationship has made significant strides in the past decade, declaring a 'strategic partnership' in 2003, expanding interaction to some 50 sectorial dialogues, establishing a high-level security and foreign policy dialogue in 2010 and becoming critically important trading partners of one another. But it still struggles to realise greater potential and it lacks strategic momentum. The EU, as it struggles in the wake of the financial crisis, has not cohered as a strategic actor. And as China's domestic political reforms remain stalled, these expectations have increasingly come into question in Beijing. Nor have expectations in the EU about relations with China met their hoped-for promise. China has fared poorly in a range of issues that matter to European politicians, publics and the private sector: respecting human rights and religious freedoms, addressing environmental degradation and climate change, promoting fair trade and protecting intellectual property. This is reflected in polling data in Europe, which indicate a downturn of favourable views towards China since the mid-2000s.

A poll by the German Marshall Fund taken in mid-2011 shows a diversified degree of favourable and unfavourable opinion towards China in EU Member States. On average in 12 EU Member States, less than half the respondents (47 per cent) had a favourable opinion of China, and a roughly similar proportion of respondents saw China as an economic threat (41 per cent) versus an economic opportunity (46 per cent).[49]

US-China relations face an even more difficult set of impediments to identifying bilateral, let alone trilateral, common interests and action. Since the mid-1990s in a range of security questions, for example, US official policy, elite views and public opinion have entertained increasing worries about China, whether in relation to Taiwan, weapons proliferation, espionage, cyber-attacks and Chinese relations with regimes of concern to the US from Iran to North Korea to Zimbabwe. The Chinese too have worries; Chinese leaders, strategists and citizens forcefully express their views about US 'hegemony', 'bullying' and 'containment' of China and about the US undermining Chinese security through its support for Taiwan and other activities such as conducting military surveillance missions close to Chinese shores.

An abiding concern among Chinese leaders and elites, that the US seeks to delegitimise the Chinese Communist Party and ultimately foster political change in China through 'peaceful evolution', has become all the more acute as a range of political grievances come to the fore in China in the context of a broader political awakening of citizenries around the world. These long-standing issues of mistrust between the two sides have only deepened as China has grown in economic and military strength and as the US has worked to reinvigorate its alliance relationships and presence in the Asia-Pacific, most recently cast in terms of a 'pivoting' towards the region.

US-China relations are deepening in many respects, and the political leaderships are seeking to build more constructive ties, but those relations appear to be strategically ambivalent at best and, at worst, they risk veering into a more confrontational relationship in the longer term. This ambivalence is expressed in polls taken both in the US and in China. Polling by the Gallup organisation in early 2012 found that although about two-thirds of those Americans polled would term China either as 'friendly' or an 'ally', only 42 per cent were prepared to give a favourable opinion of China. And of those adults who said that they closely follow the news about China, 54 per cent had an unfavourable view of the country. In a 2012 Gallup poll commissioned by the *China Daily*, almost 80 per cent of Americans surveyed said that 'lack of trust' was the biggest obstacle to improved US-China relations.[50]

Polling in China gives similar data. According to polling conducted by the BBC World Service in 2011, when opinion around the world towards the US was improving, China was the only country that registered an increase in negative views, with 53 per cent of Chinese respondents expressing a negative opinion towards America, up by 9 percentage points from 2010. In another survey over this period, Chinese who felt that the US took Chinese interests into account fell from 76 per cent to 57 per cent.[51]

A survey carried out in seven major Chinese cities in February 2012 found by a large margin that 'hegemonism' is the first thing to come to mind to Chinese respondents when talking about the US. About 63 per cent of Chinese respondents said their impression of the United States had worsened owing to the NATO intervention in Libya in 2011 and to stepped-up Western pressure on Syria in late 2011 and early 2012; and 42 per cent said that their impression of the US had worsened owing to the US-led 'global war on terrorism'.[52]

While EU-US relations have improved very much since the early-2000s, there remain frustrations that impede more robust transatlantic bilateral and trilateral cooperation. Internal bureaucratic struggles have impacted the effectiveness of both the High Representative for Foreign Affairs and Security Policy and the European External Action Service, calling into question the EU's abilities as a unitary actor (which has further been speculated over since the 2009 Eurozone crisis). Meanwhile, America's struggles with internal divisiveness have paralysed its economic and political fronts which constrains its ability to act abroad and engage with its European partners more effectively.

The movement of the centre of world economic and political gravity towards Asia, and specifically China, also presents challenges to the future of the transatlantic partnership, including

EU-US relations. It reflects a long-standing recognition of the growing economic, political and military influence of key countries in the region such as China, India, Indonesia and others and their impact on the US as a Pacific nation. Meanwhile, EU Member States increasingly look to Asia for greater engagement, including economic and financial partnerships. In 2011, 49 per cent of those surveyed in Spain, 48 per cent in Germany, 47 per cent in the UK and 47 per cent in France said that China is the world's leading economic power – figures up significantly in 2009.[53]

Recurrent misgivings and suspicions over the possibility of lifting the EU arms embargo on China add to these challenges. Overall, views in the EU and the US about one another are good but not overwhelmingly favourable. For example, the 2011 German Marshall Fund survey noted above found that EU and US respondents were of similar minds when looking at the state of EU-US relations. Of those surveyed in 12 EU Member States, more than 45 per cent felt that relations were 'good', compared to 42 per cent in the US.[54]

### *Domestic concerns*

In addition to these global and bilateral impediments to common action, domestic challenges will cause the three players to be predominantly inward-looking in the near to medium term and to be constrained by these challenges from undertaking bold, cooperative international action.

China faces the greatest domestic challenges, and they have been described in detail elsewhere.[55] Those problems arise in many respects from the country's economic success, but they are further exacerbated by a brittle political system fearful for its legitimacy and often unresponsive to heightened socio-economic demands and expectations. Resource problems pose growing threats to people's health and livelihood. Endemic corruption and growing income gaps between rich and poor, between urban and rural residents and between the country's east and its inland provinces foster disgruntlement and nagging questions among the disenfranchised about China's future. Unrest and popular dissatisfaction across a spectrum of issues – land use, labour rights, product and industrial safety, ethnic and religious identity, and political dissent – is on the rise. The ability of these disaffected persons to voice their protest has increased with the spread of new communications and media technologies, aggravating local and national authorities' worries about social stability and how to maintain it.

At a fundamental level, China's long-term growth and sustainability will depend on tough choices by the Fifth Generation of leadership in 2012 about how to transform its growth model from investment to consumption and from energy-intensive use to cleaner and more efficient energy use, all the while absorbing and meeting the needs of tens of millions of persons flocking to burgeoning new urban areas.

Leaders in the EU and the US confront less daunting but nonetheless arduous long-term problems that will keep their focus on the home front as well. Assuring stricter financial oversight and fiscal responsibility, maintaining internal political and bureaucratic coherence, integrating new Member States, immigration, demographic trends such as ageing, and enhancing societal security and resilience within EU borders will remain of pre-eminent importance to its leaders. Likewise, American leaders will be preoccupied with economic and fiscal recovery, but in a context of political divisiveness and stalemate beyond the 2012 elections. Basic socio-economic and socio-political challenges for the US – fiscal deficits, unsustainable social benefits, developing smarter and greener energy sources, a weakening infrastructure, healthcare reform, renewed investment in education for a twentieth-century workforce and a sensible immigration policy – will demand a serious readjustment of political and financial priorities in order to focus on domestic affairs.

These imperatives for the EU and the US will not exclude proactive policies on the international scene: indeed, many solutions to internal challenges must be found through international engagement. But those challenges will vitiate the willingness and ability of EU and US leaders to engage with each other and with China, as well as to take bold trilateral initiatives.

## Conclusions: Ways Forward for Collective Action

The difficulty is in identifying cooperative actions that the three can genuinely and jointly embrace, implement and sustain together. These cautious recommendations are rooted in a realistic appreciation of the constraints on such trilateralism and of the power of bilateral ties – EU-US, US-China and EU-China – to achieve meaningful results in promoting common economic and security interests. The EU can play a critical linchpin role in fostering greater trilateral partnership, purpose and action on the global stage. But to do so, it will need to substantially step up its strategic engagement with the burgeoning power dynamic of the Asia-Pacific region.

The EU must:

- **Avoid the establishment of a formal trilateral structure and instead make better trilateral use of extant multilateral mechanisms.**
  Support from China or the US for such a formal mechanism is unlikely. China is more likely to engage actively in multilateral institutions such as the SCO, the emergent BRICs process, the East Asia Summit, the G20 group or the UNSC. It is also likely that the US would prefer to work more directly with China on a bilateral basis. Even so, some trilateral discussions between the EU (as well as EU Member States), China and the US should be fostered within established multilateral channels such as the UNSC, the G20 and the ARF. The critical challenge for the EU is to be taken more seriously as a principal player by China and the US in Asia and on other regional and global issues.
- **Focus on economic engagement as the most promising area for trilateral cooperation.**
  All three sides share common defensive interests: averting an upsurge in protectionism; maintaining the centrality of the WTO and its dispute-settlement mechanisms; and, perhaps most important, keeping an open door to investment. Constructive cooperation can be sustained and deepened: by strengthening close cooperation between central banks; identifying and expanding areas of economic and development cooperation in third areas, such as the 'New Silk Road' strategy for Afghanistan; coordinating to address threats to global energy markets; and expanding China's role in and contribution to international financial institutions.

▷ **Intensify the focus on economic 'rebalancing' and its benefits for China.**
A qualitative shift in the direction of building a consumption-led economy in China would not provide a magic bullet solution to all sources of tension between China and its partners – IPR problems and government procurement issues, for instance, are not attributable to rebalancing alone – but it would take much of the heat out and potentially even open up the possibility of a more serious joint plan of action for revitalising the global economy led by the EU, the US and China.

A systematic effort to readjust the way that capital and resources are allocated in the Chinese economy is imperative: reforming banks' lending practices (notably, negative real deposit rates for households), reducing SOEs' ability to retain earnings; acknowledging the more efficient private sector and continuing the appreciation and internationalisation of the renminbi.

▷ **Explore possibilities for alliances with progressive economic thinkers.**
Today the EU's and the US's bilateral approaches to China should visibly establish and reinforce a sense of common cause with the beneficiaries and advocates of reform in China itself. The most important battles will be domestic ones in China, and US and European actions should be tailored to reward reformist choices.

The World Bank's China 2030 report,[56] which lays out an ambitious roadmap for structural reform, green development, innovation and reform of the fiscal system, was devised in close collaboration with the Development Research Center of China's State Council and Ministry of Finance. It indicates the kind of detailed reform agenda that some leading figures in the Chinese government are prepared to pursue with their international partners. External encouragement from the US and Europe should be combined with support of efforts of this sort, and should be careful not to undermine it.

▷ **Reinvigorate and elevate EU-US economic and security consultations on Asia and China.**
Official transatlantic dialogue on Asia and China, which enjoyed a brief period of relatively senior-level activity in the

mid-2000s, has drifted and become less consequential. A renewed effort in this direction made in talks between US and EU officials in January 2012 is a welcome step and should be sustained at a high level.

Those discussions would include closer coordination on economic and trade strategy between the EU and the US vis-à-vis China. Any approach could be pursued in parallel with a form of economic hedging. This would involve expanding and deepening EU and US ties with other 'like-minded' countries in their relationships with China and constructing an international economic and trade architecture that is robust enough to deal with a problematic Chinese stance but attractive enough for China to want to be a part of it. To achieve this, it is important that Europe and the US should work together to ensure that their trade policies in Asia are mutually reinforcing. In practice, the dual opportunity of access to the European and US markets makes the rewards for countries willing to make the necessary trade-offs and reforms all the greater. China too is seeking investment in Western markets rather than simply selling goods there; EU-US leverage can be exercised through coordinating access to these markets and contracts. The net result – a strong set of complementary bilateral and multilateral agreements with China's neighbours – will have a substantial impact on China's own choices. As President Obama stated: 'We're organizing trade relations with countries other than China so that China starts feeling more pressure about meeting basic international standards'.[57]

However, closer transatlantic consultations should avoid the impression of 'ganging up' on China. Taken to such an extreme, the consultations could easily result in Chinese responses that could negate the outcomes that they aim to achieve.

▷ **Devote greater attention in EU-US-China interactions to next-generation interests at the nexus of economics and security, with a priority on challenges related to energy, the environment, regional stability and cyber-security.**

In the security realm, some of the greatest challenges facing the EU, the US and China are those threatening the global commons and the open, productive flows of goods, capital and information that support and sustain modernising societies. Chinese leaders and policymakers already recognise the problems such challenges present, especially as their country becomes more globally open and integrated.

The three have a very strong interest in coordinating and combining resources to address environmental and energy resource challenges not only in China but also around the globe. A particularly encouraging development in this regard is the deepened counter-piracy cooperation among the EU, the US and China, as in the Gulf of Aden. Concerted efforts to deepen cooperation in this area would probably be welcomed in Beijing.

The EU and the US share a common interest in exchanging notes and practices for dealing with China-sourced cyber threats. But they also should work in concert, and with China, to underscore trilaterally shared interests as increasingly wired societies and economies to combat cyber fraud, larceny, intellectual property theft, child pornography, human trafficking and other abuses of cyberspace. The three sides will struggle to find the right balance between 'openness' and 'security' and to develop productive forms of cooperation across their respective government and private sectors.

▷ **Invest much greater resources to strengthening its position in the trilateral dynamic, particularly on security issues.**

The EU must strive to become a much greater contributor in the burgeoning power dynamic of the Asia-Pacific with a more consistent, regularised and high-level presence there. Of especial importance are its relationships with China but also with Australia, India, Indonesia, Japan, South Korea and Taiwan and its institutional relationships with ASEAN and the ARF. Establishing FTAs with regional partners beyond South Korea to include India, Malaysia, Singapore, Vietnam and even Japan and the United States would be another component of a greater EU engagement with the Asia-Pacific.

But the EU should also step up its role on security issues of concern to China and the US, both in Asia and in areas closer to its borders. China and the US will generally look favourably upon effective EU action, including in the military sphere, to help bring greater stability to regions around Europe's periphery, particularly in sub-Saharan Africa and the Horn of Africa. The EU's experience and capacity in promoting security through civilian assistance in post-conflict and post-disaster situations is another valuable asset that can be leveraged in various cooperative ways to enhance security cooperation with China and the US.

An overemphasis in EU-China relations on government-to-government ties needs to be balanced by other, non-governmental forms of exchange and understanding. The announcement at the February 2012 EU-China summit of a people-to-people dialogue, to complement the existing Economic and Trade Dialogue and the Strategic Dialogue, is a welcome step in this direction.

As a collection of Member States, the EU already faces enormous challenges in putting forward coherent EU-wide policies that promote bilateral EU-US and EU-China relations and meet EU interests but also promote the possibilities for trilateral cooperation. Nevertheless, the pragmatic and effective pursuit of such policies, while challenging, would place the EU in a much stronger position as a principal actor on the global stage.

## Notes

1. This figure is for 2010 and is in purchasing power parity terms. International Monetary Fund, *World Economic Outlook Database*, September 2011 edition, accessed at: http://www.imf.org/external/pubs/ft/weo/2011/02/weodata/index.aspx (27 December 2011).
2. This figure is for 2010. World Trade Organization Press Release, *World Trade 2010, Prospects for 2011*, Press/621, 7 April 2011, accessed at: http://www.wto.org/english/news_e/pres11_e/pr628_e.htm (12 December 2011).
3. On their military spending, see *SIPRI Yearbook 2011: Armaments, Disarmament and International Security* (Oxford: Oxford University Press, 2011), Tables 4A.1 and 4A.2 (the figures are for 2010). On arms trade, see *SIPRI Yearbook 2011: Armaments, Disarmament and International Security* (Oxford: Oxford University Press, 2011), Tables 6A.1 and 6A.2.

4. This figure is based on data for 2005 and 2009. See World Resources Institute, Climate Analysis Indicators Tool, accessed at: http://cait.wri.org/cait.php?page=yearly and International Energy Agency, *$CO_2$ Emissions from Fuel Combustion: 2011 Highlights*, accessed at: http://www.iea.org/co2highlights/ (12 December 2011).
5. A recent comprehensive look at contemporary US-China relations is Robert G. Sutter, *US-Chinese Relations: Perilous Past, Pragmatic Present* (Lanham, Maryland: Rowan & Littlefield, 2010). For an overview focusing on US-China government-to-government and other policy community exchanges, see Bates Gill, *Meeting the Challenges and Opportunities of China's Rise: Expanding and Improving Interaction between American and Chinese Policy Communities* (Washington, DC: Center for Strategic and International Studies, 2006).
6. Council of the European Union, *Joint Press Communiqué of the 14th EU-China Summit*, Beijing, China, 6474/012 (Presse 50), 14 February 2012.
7. José Manuel Durão Barroso, President of the European Commission, *Statement by President Barroso following the 14th EU-China Summit*, Press point, Beijing, 14 February 2012, accessed at: http://europa.eu/rapid/pressReleasesAction.do?reference=SPEECH/12/94&format=HTML&aged=0&language=EN&guiLanguage=en (28 February 2012).
8. The White House, Office of the Press Secretary, *US-China Joint Statement*, 19 January 2011, accessed at: http://www.whitehouse.gov/the-press-office/2011/01/19/us-china-joint-statement (29 December 2011).
9. For an exhaustive look at the continued interdependence of China and its Western trading partners, see Premachandra Athukorala, 'Production Networks and Trade Patterns in East Asia: Regionalization or Globalisation?', *Asian Development Bank Papers, no. 56*, August 2010, accessed at: http://aric.adb.org/pdf/workingpaper/WP56_Trade_Patterns_in_East_Asia.pdf (15 March 2012) and Soyoung Kim, Jong-Wha Lee, and Cyn-Young Park, 'The Ties that Bind Asia, Europe, and United States', *Asian Development Bank Papers, no. 192*, February 2010, accessed at: http://www.adb.org/Documents/Working-Papers/2010/Economics-WP192.pdf (15 March 2012).
10. For analysis of the growing centrality of China to Asian supply chains, see, for instance, Adil Mohommad, Olaf

Unteroberdoerster and Jade Vichyanond, 'Asia's supply chain: implications for rebalancing', *Vox EU*, 12 June 2011, accessed at: http://voxeu.org/index.php?q=node/6637 (3 March 2012).

11. Gordon Brown, *Beyond the Crash: Overcoming the First Crisis of Globalisation* (London: Simon & Schuster, 2010), p. 152.
12. Rhodium Group, 'An American Open Door? Maximizing the benefits of Chinese Foreign Direct Investment', 4 May 2011, accessed at: http://www.rhgroup.net/reports/an-american-open-door-maximizing-the-benefits-of-chinese-foreign-direct-investment (15 March 2012). It should be noted, however, that the US and Europe are each other's number one destination and source of foreign direct investment by far and that the level of Chinese ODI in the US and Europe pales against the levels of transatlantic direct investment flows, which reached more than €2 trillion by 2010, compared, for example, to the two-way investment stocks between the EU and China of about €64 billion in 2009. *European Union – Background: EU-US Summit*, Washington, DC, 28 November 2011. See also Daniel S. Hamilton and Joseph P. Quinlan, *The Transatlantic Economy 2011: Executive Summary* (Washington, DC: Johns Hopkins University School of Advanced International Studies, 2011).
13. Testimony to the U.S.-China Economic and Security Review Commission, 'China, the eurozone crisis and transatlantic cooperation', 19 April 2012, p. 2, accessed at: http://www.uscc.gov/hearings/2012hearings/written_testimonies/12_4_19/Small.pdf (25 October 2012).
14. 'French firms seal lush deals during visits by China's Hu', *France 24*, 5 November 2011, accessed at: http://www.france24.com/en/20101104-chinese-sign-trade-deals-with-french-giants-sarkozy-jintao-paris-areva-total-airbus (10 March 2012).
15. 'China Agrees to $45 billion in US export deals', *Voice of America*, 19 January 2011, accessed at: http://www.voanews.com/english/news/Hu-Faces-Day-of-Rich-Ceremony-Tough-Talk-114193599.html (15 March 2012).
16. 'China eyes UK infrastructure investment to boost growth', British Broadcasting Corporation, 27 November 2011, accessed at: http://www.bbc.co.uk/news/business-15914102 (27 February 2012).
17. See, for example, Henry M. Paulson, *On the Brink: Inside the Race to Stop the Collapse of the Global Financial System* (New York: Business Plus, 2010), pp. 18, 273.

18. Paul Blustein, 'The Nine-Day Misadventure of the Most Favored Nations: How the WTO's Doha Round Negotiations Went Awry in July 2008', The Brookings Institution, 5 December 2008, accessed at: http://www.brookings.edu/articles/2008/1205_trade_blustein.aspx (26 February 2012).
19. This has been challenged in a recent article. See Bernard O'Connor, 'Is China a Market Economy?', *Vox EU*, 27 October 2011, accessed at: http://www.voxeu.org/index.php?q=node/7345 (1 March 2012). But most experts consider the 2016 deadline to be real. Note, for example, Christian Tietje and Karsten Nowrot, 'Myth or Reality? China's Market Economy Status under WTO anti-dumping law after 2016', *Policy Papers on Transnational Economic Law*, December 2011, accessed at: http://telc.jura.uni-halle.de/sites/default/ files/telc/PolicyPaper34.pdf (25 February 2012).
20. Michael Pettis, 'Chinese Consumption and the Japanese "Sorpasso"', *China Financial Markets*, 10 August 2010, accessed at: http://www.carnegieendowment.org/2010/08/10/chinese-consumption-and-japanese-sorpasso/b04 (15 February 2012).
21. 'China to lose ally against US trade hawks', *Financial Times*, 21 March 2010, accessed at: http://www.ft.com/intl/cms/s/0/97b29e4e-351c-11df-9cfb-00144feabdc0.html#axzz1phNYQU8C (22 March 2012).
22. On Chinese approaches to issues of sovereignty and intervention, see Allen Carlson, *Unifying China, Integrating with the World: Securing Chinese Sovereignty in the Reform Era* (Palo Alto, CA: Stanford University Press, 2005); Allen Carlson, 'China's Approach to Sovereignty and Intervention', in Alastair Iain Johnston and Robert Ross (eds), *New Directions in the Study of China's Foreign Policy* (Palo Alto, CA: Stanford University Press, 2006), pp. 217–41; and Bates Gill, *Rising Star: China's New Security Diplomacy* (Washington, DC: Brookings Institution Press, revised edition, 2010), especially Chapter 4.
23. United Nations Security Council, S/RES/1973 (2011), 17 March 2011. China, along with Brazil, Germany, India and Russia, abstained on this resolution.
24. See Bates Gill and Melissa Murphy,'China's Evolving Approach to Counterterrorism', *Harvard Asia Quarterly*, vol. 9, Winter/Spring 2005, pp. 21–32.

25. This data is revised and updated from David M. Lampton and Richard Daniel Ewing, *The U.S.-China Relationship Facing International Security Crises: Three Case Studies in Post-9/11 Bilateral Relations* (Washington, DC: Nixon Center, 29 January 2004), accessed at: http://www.cftni.org/index98ce.html?action=publications (15 February 2012).
26. For example, see Office of the Spokesman, US Department of State, 'U.S.-China Counterterrorism Sub-Dialogue', 22 September 2009, accessed at: http://www.state.gov/r/pa/prs/ps/2009/sept/129485.htm (15 February 2012); Council of the European Union, *10th China-EU Summit, Beijing, 28 November 2007, Joint Statement*, 16070/07 (Presse 279), Brussels, 28 November 2007. But in the joint press release of the Thirteenth and fourteenth EU-China summits, in 2010 and 2012 respectively, there is no mention that countering terrorism was discussed. Council of the European Union, *13th EU-China Summit Joint Press Communiqué*, 14577/10, Presse [267], Brussels, 6 October 2010 and Council of the European Union, *Joint Press Communiqué of the 14th EU-China Summit*, Beijing, China,6474/012, Presse 50, 14 February 2012.
27. 'Chinese naval escort squads to Somali waters escorted 4,411 vessels in three years', Xinhua, 11 January 2012, accessed at: http://eng.chinamil.com.cn/news-channels/china-military-news/2012-11 01/12/content_4766489.htm (22 January 2012).
28. UN Department of Peacekeeping Operations, 'Troop and Police Contributors', accessed at: http://www.un.org/en/peacekeeping/resources/statistics/contributors.shtml (22 January 2012).
29. *China's National Defense in 2010* (Beijing: State Council Information Office, March 2011), section IV.
30. On the issues and challenges of protecting Chinese nationals abroad, see Mathieu Duchatel and Bates Gill, 'Protecting Chinese Citizens Abroad: What Next?', *PacNet Newsletter*, 6 February 2012, accessed at: http://csis.org/publication/pacnet-9-protecting-chinese-citizens-abroad-what-next (15 February 2012) and Andrew Erikson and Gabe Collins, 'China's New Challenge: Protecting Its Citizens Abroad', *Wall Street Journal*, 10 February 2012, accessed at: http://blogs.wsj.com/chinarealtime/2012/02/10/chinas-new-challenge-protecting-its-citizens-abroad/ (15 February 2015).
31. China's changing policies and practices regarding non-proliferation are documented and analysed in Evan S. Medeiros,

*Reluctant Restraint: The Evolution of China's Nonproliferation Policies and Practices, 1980–2004* (Palo Alto, CA: Stanford University Press, 2007); Wendy Frieman, *China, International Arms Control, and Nonproliferation* (London: Routledge Curzon, 2004); and Gill, *Rising Star*, especially Chapter 3.

32. From the website of the UNSC Resolution 1540 Committee, accessed at: http://www.un.org/sc/1540/ (22 January 2012).
33. See the website for the Container Security Initiative, accessed at: http://www.cbp.gov/xp/cgov/trade/cargo_security/csi/ (22 January 2012).
34. *Unclassified Report to Congress on the Acquisition of Technology Relating to Weapons of Mass Destruction and Advanced Conventional Munitions Covering 1 January to 31 December 2010*, March 2011, accessed at: www.fas.org/irp/threat/wmd.htm (22 January 2012).
35. See Bates Gill, *China's North Korea Policy: Assessing Interests and Influences*, United States Institute of Peace Special Report, July 2011, accessed at: http://www.usip.org/publications/china-s-north-korea-policy (22 January 2012).
36. 'China says EU ban on Iran oil not "constructive"', Reuters, 26 January 2012, accessed at: http://www.reuters.com/article/2012/01/26/china-iran-idUSL4E8CQ46H20120126 (28 January 2012). It was later reported that Chinese oil imports from Iran had decreased in late 2011 and early 2012, but primarily as contractual leverage to secure better commercial terms from Iran. See, for example, Guy Chazan and Javier Blas, 'China cuts Iranian oil imports, says IEA', *Financial Times*, 10 February 2012, accessed at: http://www.ft.com/intl/cms/s/0/a9fcc826-53d4-11e1-9eac-00144feabdc0.html#axzz1mXW6zBqQ (16 February 2012) and Judy Hua and Alex Lawler, 'China buys up Saudi, Russian oil to squeeze Iran', Reuters, 7 February 2012.
37. On recent Chinese approaches to nuclear arms control and disarmament, see Bates Gill, *China and Nuclear Arms Control: Current Positions and Future Policies*, SIPRI Insights on Peace and Security, no. 2010/4 (April 2010), accessed at: http://www.sipri.org/research/security/china/research/nuclear (28 January 2012).
38. See Andrew Rettman, 'Ashton pragmatic on China in EU foreign policy blueprint', *EU Observer*, 17 December 2010, accessed at: http://euobserver.com/884/31538 (29 January 2012).
39. Robert B. Zoellick, 'Whither China: From Membership to Responsibility?', remarks to the National Committee on

US-China Relations, 21 September 2005, accessed at: http://www.ncuscr.org/recent-remarks-and-speeches (22 February 2012). See also Thomas J. Christensen, 'The Advantages of an Assertive China', *Foreign Affairs*, vol. 90, no. 2 (March/April 2011), pp. 54–67; Bates Gill and Michael Schiffer, 'A Rising China's Rising Responsibilities', in Michael Schiffer and David Shorr (eds), *Powers and Principles: International Leadership in a Shrinking World* (Lanham, MD: Lexington Books, 2009), pp. 99–124.

40. Dr Tomas Ries, *The Global Security Environment 2030 and Military Missions* (unpublished manuscript), Department for Strategic and Security Studies, Swedish National Defence College, 17 October 2010.
41. Office of the National Counterintelligence Executive, *Foreign Spies Stealing US Economic Secrets in Cyberspace: Report to Congress on Foreign Economic Collection and Industrial Espionage, 2009–2011*, October 2011, p. i, accessed at: http://www.ncix.gov/publications/reports/fecie_all/index.html (22 February 2012).
42. In this testimony on major threats to the United States, cyberthreats appeared after terrorism and proliferation. See James R. Clapper, *Unclassified Statement for the Record on the Worldwide Threat Assessment of the U.S. Intelligence Community for the Senate Select Intelligence Committee*,31 January 2012, p. 7, accessed at: http://www.dni.gov/ (22 February 2012).
43. Mike McConnell, Michael Chertoff and William Lynn, 'China's Cyber Thievery is National Policy – and Must Be Challenged', *Wall Street Journal*, 27 January 2012. McConnell was Director of the National Security Agency (1992–6) and Director of National Intelligence (2007–9); Chertoff was Secretary of Homeland Security (2005–9); and Lynn was Deputy Secretary of Defence (2009–11) and Undersecretary of Defence (1997–2001).
44. See an abbreviated compilation of open-source examples in Jamie Metzl, 'China and Cyber-Espionage', December 2011, accessed at: http://asiasociety.org/policy/strategic-challenges/china-and-cyber-espionage?gclid=CLGD_ZOWg60CFRDHKgodAllaTA (22 February 2012). On a major intrusion, attributable to China, into thousands of secret files related to the US F-35 Joint Strike Fighter programme, see David Fulghum, Bill Sweetman and Amy Butler, 'Internet Hacking Drives Up Pentagon Costs: F-35 and classified programs victimized by

network intrusions', *Aviation Week & Space Technology*, 6 February 2012, p. 30.

45. Deaths from SARS occurred in Canada, China, France, Malaysia, the Philippines, Singapore, South Africa, Taiwan, Thailand and Vietnam. In addition, non-fatal cases were diagnosed Germany, India, Indonesia, Italy, Kuwait, Mongolia, New Zealand, Ireland, Romania, Russia, South Korea, Spain, Sweden, Switzerland, the United Kingdom and the US. See World Health Organization, 'Summary of probable SARS cases with onset of illness from 1 November 2002 to 31 July 2003', accessed at: http://www.who.int/csr/sars/country/table2004_04_21/en/index.html (22 February 2012).
46. Deaths reported to the World Health Organization (WHO) resulting from H5N1 infection in 2011 and early 2012 also occurred in Bangladesh, Cambodia, Egypt, Indonesia and Vietnam. See World Health Organization, 'Cumulative number of confirmed human cases of avian influenza A (H5N1) reported to WHO', accessed at: http://www.who.int/influenza/human_animal_interface/H5N1_cumulative_table_archives/en/index.html (23 January 2012).
47. World Health Organization, 'Global Tuberculosis Control 2011', accessed at: http://www.who.int/tb/publications/global_report/en/index.html (23 January 2012).
48. See *Report of the Panel of Experts Established Pursuant to Resolution 1874 (2009)* (May 2011), p. 40, accessed from the website of the National Committee on North Korea: www.ncnk.org/resources/publications/55808872-UN-Panel-of-Experts-NORK-Report-May-2011.pdf (22 January 2012).
49. German Marshall Fund of the United States, *Transatlantic Trends: Key Findings 2011*, Charts 8 and 11, accessed at: http://trends.gmfus.org/transatlantic-trends/key-findings/ (22 January 2012).
50. See Cheng Guangjin and Chen Weihua, 'Survey reveals positive public attitudes', *China Daily*, 10 February 2012.
51. 'Views of US Continue to Improve in 2011 BBC Country Ranking Poll', *BBC World Service Poll*,7 March 2011, accessed at: http://www.worldpublicopinion.org/pipa/articles/views_on_countriesregions_bt/680.php (22_February 2012) and 'US Consideration of Other Countries' Interests', *Pew Global Attitudes Project*, accessed at: http://www.pewglobal.org/database/?indicator=4&country=45 (23 February 2012).

52. This data is drawn from a *China Daily*-Horizon Research Group poll taken in late 2011. It was reported in Cheng Guangjin and Chen Weihua, 'Survey reveals positive public attitudes', *China Daily*, 10 February 2012.
53. Pew Research Center, *China Seen Overtaking US as Global Superpower*, Global Attitudes Project, 13 July 2011.
54. *Transatlantic Trends*, Chart 5.
55. See, for example, Susan Shirk, *China: Fragile Superpower: How China's Internal Politics Could Derail Its Peaceful Rise* (Oxford: Oxford University Press, 2008).
56. *China 2030: Building a Modern, Harmonious, and Creative High-Income Society*, The World Bank and the Development Research Center of the State Council, People's Republic of China, 27 February 2012, accessed at: http://www-wds.worldbank.org/external/default/WDSContentServer/WDSP/IB/2012/02/28/000356161_20120228001303/Rendered/PDF/671790WP0P127500China020300complete.pdf (2 March 2012).
57. Transcript, Third Presidential Debate, 22 October 2012, accessed at: http://www.npr.org/2012/10/22/163436694/transcript-3rd-obama-romney-presidential-debate (25 October 2012).

# 7 China's Food Security: Is it a National, Regional or Global Issue?

*David Norse, Yuelai Lu and Jikun Huang*

## Introduction

The maintenance of high levels of food security (with over 95 per cent self-sufficiency in grains is a policy that was officially introduced in 1996 and has been implemented thereafter) is a political imperative in China, but not a physical or economic issue now nor in the period to 2030 and probably longer. Supply projections by the Centre for Chinese Agricultural Policy (CCAP) and FAO projections suggest that on average China could continue to be self-sufficient for rice and wheat until 2030. Only soya bean and maize imports for livestock feed will continue to rise. Soya bean and maize imports may increase from the current nearly 60 Mt to 100Mt and to 30 Mt per annum respectively by 2030, which will require a major yet feasible expansion in production in its traditional sources (USA, Brazil and Argentina) or new ones. But this will not be an economic issue. Such imports will require a minute fraction (considerably less than 1 per cent) of China's more than £2 trillion foreign exchange reserves (using an exchange rate of 9.5 yuan to the £ here and elsewhere in the chapter).

But the long-term average food security situation hides a number of local and global issues regarding sustainability of agricultural production in China and particularly because of:

(a) inconsistences in the official statistics for recent cereal production and the current supply and demand situation;

(b) resource mismanagement (loss of good cropland to urban and industrial development; non-point pollution of land and water and high greenhouse gas (GHG) emissions) that require substantial shifts in national policies and great improvements in the implementation of such policies by local governments. The latter may be aided by pressures from environmental and land reform lobby groups that are pushing for policies favourable to sustainable intensification rather than unsustainable high productivity;

(c) the knock-on effects of Chinese food purchasers on world market prices if China is forced to make large imports during severe droughts or other extreme events. They could easily outbid less affluent and food insecure developing countries. To date this has not been an issue because of China's policy of maintaining very large carry-over stocks of grain and of boosting irrigation – about 70 per cent of the grain land is irrigated (and therefore less drought prone) and it accounts for an even greater share of production. However, both of these favourable factors need to be supported by policy changes if they are to continue their important food security roles.

Consequently this chapter undertakes three tasks. First, to provide an overview of the current and future food security situation in China, and the structure of food production. Second, to review the role of central and local government in the maintenance of food security. And finally, it assesses the global and EU implications of China's future food security, and the evolving role of OECD based agro-industrial companies in the modernisation of China's food chain.

## China's Past, Present and Future Food Supply and Demand

### Past and current food production and supply situation

Growth of the food and agricultural sector has been impressive in China since the policy reforms of the late 1970s. Compared to 1970–1978 when agricultural GDP increased by 2.7 per cent annually, the growth during the initial reform period (1978 to 1984) was 7.1 per cent (Table 7.1). Although during the later reform periods the annual growth rates slowed down to around 4 per cent or so in real terms, they were sustained for over 25 years.

Production growth occurred in all sub-sectors of food and agriculture in both the early and late reform periods. Between 1978 and 1984, production of grain, including cereal, sweet potato, potato, soy and other beans, increased 4.7 per cent annually (Table 7.1). The sown area did not change during this time[1] so yield growth accounted for nearly all growth in grain production. Cash crops and animal sector, in general, and the production of specific commodities, such as cotton, edible oils, vegetables, fruit, meats and fishery, grew even faster than grains throughout the reform era (Table 7.1). This was primarily because of freer markets and greater public investment in agriculture.

High growth of food production has kept pace with or exceeded growth in demand for most of the last 30 years with

**Table 7.1** The annual growth rates (%) of China's agricultural economy, 1970–2010

| | Pre-reform | Reform period | | | | |
|---|---|---|---|---|---|---|
| | 1970–78 | 1979–84 | 1985–95 | 1996–00 | 2001–05 | 2006–10 |
| Agricultural GDP | 2.7 | 7.1 | 4.0 | 3.4 | 4.3 | 4.5 |
| Production | | | | | | |
| Grain[a] | 2.8 | 4.7 | 1.7 | −0.7 | 1.1 | 2.5 |
| Cotton | −0.4 | 19.3 | −0.3 | −1.9 | 5.3 | -0.9 |
| Oil crops | 2.1 | 14.9 | 4.4 | 5.6 | 0.8 | 2.7 |
| Fruits | 6.6 | 7.2 | 12.7 | 10.2 | 21.0 | 5.9 |
| Meats (pork/beef/poultry) | 4.4 | 9.1 | 8.8 | 6.5 | 4.9 | 2.3 |
| Fishery | 5.0 | 7.9 | 13.7 | 10.2 | 3.6 | 3.9 |
| Planted area: | | | | | | |
| Vegetables | 2.4 | 5.4 | 6.8 | 9.8 | 3.1 | 2.0 |
| Orchards (fruits) | 8.1 | 4.5 | 10.4 | 2.0 | 2.4 | 8.1 |

a: Grain includes cereal, sweet potato and potato, soya and other beans in China.

*Source*: Authors' estimates based on data from *National Bureau of Statistics of China* (NBSC), 1985–2011.

the exception of soya beans since the late 1990s. China was a net exporter of food for most of the past 20 years (Figure 7.1) and for the deficit commodities other than soya beans the net trade has generally been *c.* 1 per cent or less. Thus, with the exception of soya beans, the 95 per cent grain self-sufficiency target has not been breached and food security has not been an issue.

While China's accession to the World Trade Organization (WTO) in 2001 has often been considered as a turning point in its relationship with the world, in fact China's open door policy started much earlier.[2] In the process, China has turned itself from an isolated and inward looking country into one of the world's great trading nations, including in the area of agricultural trade. Total agricultural exports since the 1978 reforms have exceeded imports as shown in Figure 7.1 but this aggregate picture hides the important shift in the composition of trade that China has experienced over the past two to three decades. Accession to the WTO facilitated shifts in the pattern of China's agricultural trade rather than directly changing it. Consequently, net exports of *land-intensive bulk commodities*, such as grains, oilseeds and sugar crops, have fallen faster and exports of higher-valued, more *labour-intensive products*, such as horticultural and animal products (including aquaculture) have risen faster.[3] In other words, after China joined the WTO, it began to export more of those commodities in which it has a comparative advantage and import

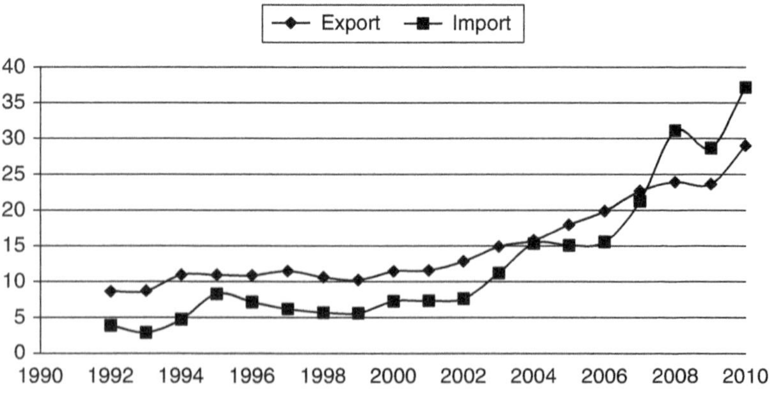


Figure 7.1 **Food Trade: export and import (billion EUR) in 1992–2010**
*Source*: Calculated based on UNCOMTRADE data.

more of those for which it has less or no advantage. This has improved farmers' income and household food security.[4]

However, although physical availability has not been an issue, rising food prices have become a major political concern and particularly food price inflation. The government of China (GOC) acts quickly and comprehensively to ensure that the latter does not rise to levels that harm low-income consumers or puts pressure on wages in the manufacturing and service sectors. Pork and vegetable prices are particularly sensitive because they account for a high proportion of food purchases and often vary significantly between seasons.

## Major drivers of food demand

The GOC started to limit population growth in the mid-1950s, and measures were progressively tightened leading to the 'one child per family' policy in 1978. It requires all couples except those from ethnic minorities to restrict themselves to having only one child. This policy has progressively reduced the role of population growth as the major driver of food demand. By 2010 the annual growth rate had declined to about 0.5 per cent and by 2030 it will be close to zero. Consequently population growth no longer has significant implications for food security, although the ageing of the population will have a positive impact by reducing average per capita food demand.

Since 1978 income growth and urbanisation have increasingly become the main drivers of food demand.[5] Per capita income growth in real terms has averaged at 9.7 per cent and 7.1 per cent in urban and rural areas, respectively, in 2000–2010.[6] Urban population share has increased from 19 per cent in 1980 to more than 50 per cent in 2011. These changes have brought about substantial shifts in food consumption patterns with decline in demand for staple foods (rice, wheat and coarse grain such as maize and root crops for food), increases in demand for vegetables, fruit, livestock products and feed grains (Figure 7.2), and substantial differences between higher income urban consumers and poor rural consumers. An increasingly important factor in this change in food consumption patterns is the proportion of food eaten away from home.[7] In Beijing, for example, about 45 per cent of meat consumption occurs away from home as does a high percentage of bean, fish and drink consumption.[8]

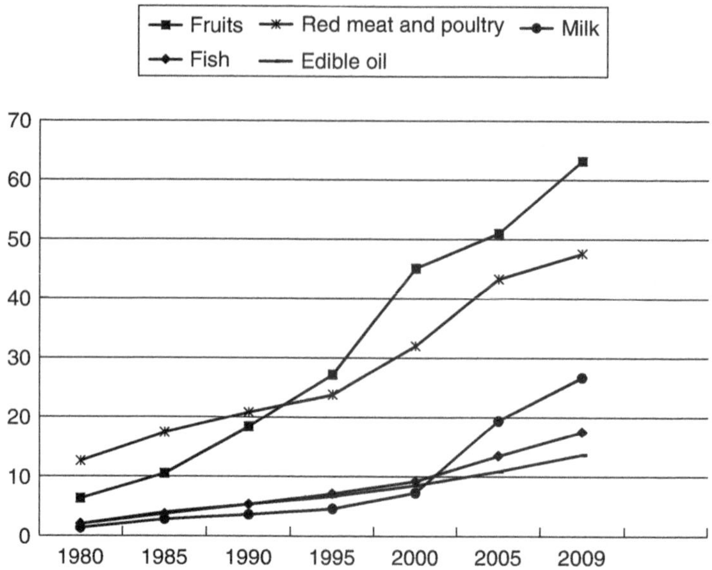


Figure 7.2 **Per capita consumption of meat, milk and other non-staple foods (kg per year)**

*Source*: CCAP's food demand and supply balance database.

China's agriculture has responded to these shifts in consumption patterns through both structural and technological change, and generally has met domestic needs without any serious threats to food self-sufficiency targets or food security (see 'Major drivers of food production' below). However, there are increasing concerns about China's ability to meet long-term food demand (see 'Global and Regional Implications of China's Future Food Security' below), and that these demands may endanger food security of other low-income developing countries or increasingly link China's food security to global food security.[9]

## Major drivers of food production

Prior to the policy reforms of 1978, the expansion of food output was largely driven by the need to ensure national grain security for the growing population as this was the primary focus of national agricultural policy. Food production was expanded mainly through reclaiming new land for cultivation, substantial expansion of irrigation infrastructure, and adopting improved crop varieties.

The following three decades saw the increasing dominance of two drivers (a) income growth and urbanisation as drivers of both qualitative and quantitative changes in food demand as discussed above and (b) agricultural productivity growth and the increasing use of agricultural inputs. The former led to changes in agricultural production structure in response to new market opportunities and shifts in the marginal profitability of different crops leading to the declining importance of rice and wheat and the growing importance of cereals for livestock feed and fruit, vegetables and livestock products for direct consumption.[10]

There have been several major factors driving agricultural productivity growth. In the early reform period (1979–2004), agricultural productivity increased by about 50 per cent,[11] driven primarily by socio-economic policies, namely the household responsibility system (HRS) that allocated the collective owned land equally to individual farmers and gave them control and income rights in agriculture, and market liberalisation.[12] However, since then, technological change has been the primary engine of agricultural productivity growth.[13]

Public agricultural R&D was the major contributor to China's growth in agricultural productivity and to food security. It tripled between 1990 and 2010, and in terms of staff numbers the public research system is the largest in the world with >65 per cent of the staff working in the crops sector and particularly on rice, wheat and maize. Consequently, average cereal yields and total factor productivity in the crops sector grew by 2–3 per cent between 1980 and 2010, though with important issues regarding the fall in partial factor productivity of nitrogen fertiliser (see Figure 7.4 and related discussions). Private investment started to grow in the 2000s,[14] and is now about one-quarter of the size of public R&D though generally it is not in areas important to food security. This R&D played a critical role in development of high yielding crop varieties (particularly cereals) that have been responsible for about 30 per cent of the incremental production over the past 20–30 years, and made an appreciable contribution to food security in other Asian countries through south-south technology transfer.

The full benefits of this R&D have not been realised because of continuing weaknesses in public extension systems, the provision of technical advice to farmers and in vocational training. Various reforms have been introduced but much more needs to be done including development of pluralistic extension systems and making full use of the private sector and farmer professional associations. The fundamental role of R&D in ensuring long-term food security is recognised by the GOC's No. 1 Document for 2012[15] which focuses on innovation in agricultural science and technology. The key objectives for future R&D include raising agricultural output, resource use efficiency and labour productivity; strengthen agricultural extension services; and promote training and education in rural areas.

The investment in irrigation and transport infrastructure has also contributed to China's agricultural productivity. Irrigation has played a critical role in establishing the highly productive cropping systems in China.[16] The proportion of cultivated area under irrigation increased from 18 per cent in 1952 to a level at which about half of all cultivated land had been irrigated since the early 1990s.[17] Irrigated land now accounts for about 70 per cent grain area and 80 per cent of grain production.[18] Water management reform stimulated by rising water scarcity has been helping to increase the efficiency of water use in north China.[19] Transportation and market infrastructure have also improved remarkably since the early 1990s. These actions have not only improved market access for farmers, reduced transport costs for production inputs and commodities, and given China an efficient and well integrated food market,[20] but have also raised the return to farmers at the farm gate and facilitated agricultural structural changes.

Last but not least, the use of off-farm production inputs has increased considerably, particularly synthetic nitrogen fertiliser and modern crop varieties, which were responsible for 50–60 per cent of the incremental growth of agricultural production from the mid-1970s onwards.

But most of these developments have involved a number of perverse or relatively ineffective subsidies that have grown from c. £10.5 million in 2002 to over £10.5 billion in 2010. The production of nitrogen fertilisers is heavily supported by perverse energy subsidies (£2.5 billion in 2007), and secondarily by storage and transport subsidies, which artificially lowers prices to farmers and encourages overuse. The largest subsidies go directly to farmers to encourage grain production but are administered in such a way that they are more an income transfer to farmers than specific incentives to raise yields and production.[21]

However, these positive features carry with them some other unfavourable characteristics. First, it can be argued that the growth in crop output for much of the reform period has also largely been from the intensification of production. Thus the intensification of production has involved higher and higher applications of conventional synthetic fertilisers (Figure 7.3) rather than more technologically advanced smart fertilisers such as slow-release formulations (that are >5 per cent of the market). The situation for livestock production has some similarities to the crops sector, with part of the increased output stemming from the use of modern compound feeds and improvements in livestock breeds. However, much of the intensification has been associated with structural change involving backyard pig, poultry and dairy production being replaced by the much larger units employing substantially different management practices which could have significant positive implications for the environment because of better waste management.[22]

Second, this pattern of intensification has had a number of negative consequences for food security. First, average partial factor productivity of fertiliser at the national level has declined though total factor productivity has increased.[23] There have been substantial falls in fertiliser use efficiency (Figure 7.4) partly related to the overuse (by 30–50 per cent) and mismanagement of nitrogen fertiliser.[24] Similarly, water use efficiency is also low; the national average WUE is only about 45 per cent. In addition excessive irrigation, especially for covered intensive vegetable production, has accentuated the decline in fertiliser efficiency.[25] These negative impacts will have affected food security in two main ways. First, they will have raised food production costs, contributed to food price inflation and reduced food purchasing power. Secondly, they will have reduced yields through acidification and other forms of soil degradation and increased pest attacks.[26]

It follows from the above that a new agricultural development strategy is needed if these negative consequences of the present model are not to undermine future food security. The GOC has

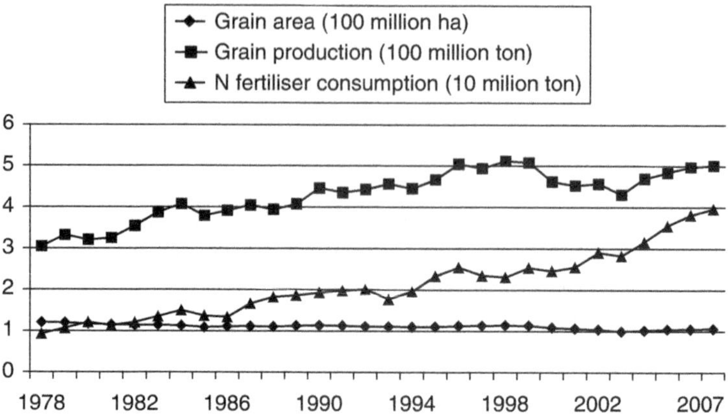


Figure 7.3 **Grain production, synthetic nitrogen fertiliser inputs and cropped area 1978–2007**

*Source*: NSBC (2011) China Statistical Yearbook 2011, (China Statistics Press, Beijing).

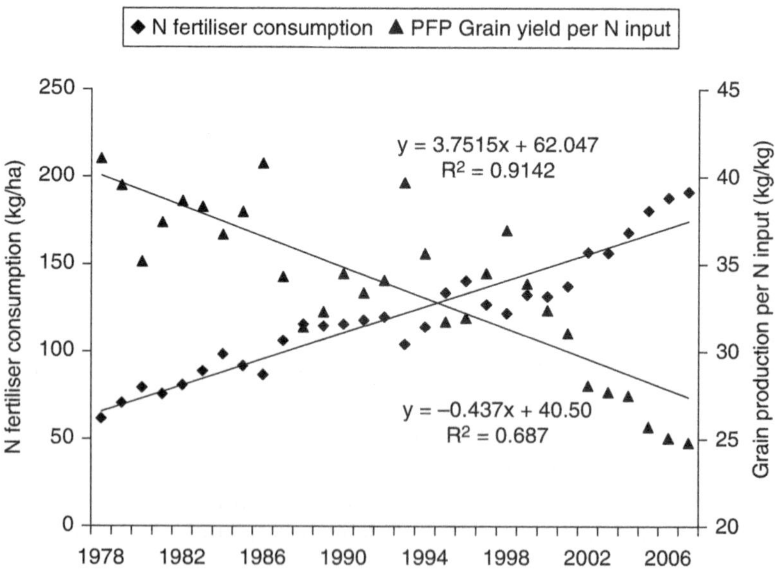


Figure 7.4 **Decline in fertiliser use efficiency since 1978**

*Source*: D. Norse (2011) Greater food security and a better environment through improved nitrogen fertilizer management, SAIN Policy Brief No 2.

already taken some steps to move on to a low carbon resource efficient pathway[27] but more needs to be done to raise crop and livestock yields and achieve sustainable intensification. The policy and technological options for doing this are considered in section 'Feed use efficiency' below.

## Future prospects

### *Introduction*

Some early commentators were unduly pessimistic about China's ability to feed itself. Lester Brown (1995),[28] for example, projected that China's grain import needs would rise 155 Mt in 2010, 256 Mt in 2020 and 369 Mt 2030. He argued that these would distort world trade and prevent other developing countries meeting all of their food import needs. Alexandratos (1996)[29] showed clearly that this pessimism was unfounded and based on weak data and inappropriate assumptions. More recently, representatives of international agencies and other observers were forecasting the need for major grain imports in 2011, because of widespread droughts earlier that year. The reality has been quite different although uncertainties in the official statistics still hamper analysis. Net grain imports in 2010 were only c. 3 Mt, and this was largely maize for livestock feed, and grain production in 2011 was the highest ever. Much of the pessimism of the earlier projections stemmed from different assumptions about China's supply potential (particularly land and water resources and prospects for technological change) rather than growth in grain demand[30] while the more recent pessimism regarding the impact of the 2011 drought on wheat production can be attributed to a lack of allowance for China's agro-climate complexity and the GOC's ability to quickly give farmers greater incentives to increase production. Lastly, the validity of some recent projections can be questioned because of their extreme assumptions about changes in consumption patterns as discussed in section 'Projected demand to 2030 – food, feed and net exports' below.

Future prospects will continue to be shaped by policy choices that primarily affect production, for example, biofuel and GM crop policies and investment in R&D. However, it may also be influenced by changes in demand if (a) the GOC decides to discourage livestock consumption patterns that pose health risks to people and the environment, and/or (b) consumers switch to healthier diets.

## Projected demand to 2030 – food, feed and net exports

Demand will continue to be driven by growth in population, incomes and urbanisation (as discussed earlier). Population growth will have virtually no effect by 2030 although there will be impacts from the ageing of the population. Income driven changes in consumption preferences will also slow down.

Direct demand for cereals will follow the pattern of the past 30 years with per capita demand for rice, wheat and other food grains being virtually flat by 2030 following recent trends (Figure 7.5). It will require nearly zero increases in production (see 'Projected production' below) with no significant food security implications.

The growth of indirect demand for cereals is less certain. The main uses are for livestock feed, food processing (particularly

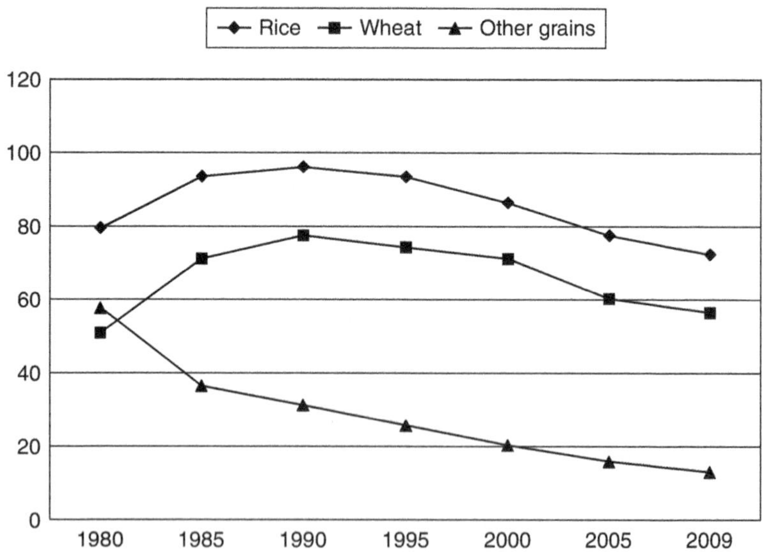


Figure 7.5 **Per capita grain consumption (kg/person)**
*Source*: CCAP's food demand and supply balance.

starch), and for alcoholic beverages which are all income driven. These projections assume that their use for biofuels will continue to be restricted (as discussed later). The largest use is for feed (about 36 per cent of total demand), and its future demand is subject to two major uncertainties: first, regarding the growth of per head demand for livestock products and second, about the growth in livestock productivity and especially about future gains in feed use efficiency and feed demand,[31] which will be discussed in section 'Projected production' below.

Results from the National Food Survey[32] show that the growth in per head adult meat consumption appears to have started to slow down from the early 1990s during a period of high urbanisation and income growth, but the survey does not include food consumption away from home which has been growing considerably since the 1990s as discussed earlier. By 2009, consumption levels in rural areas were rising towards urban levels and those in cities, towns, and suburbs were converging. Moreover, the impact of income growth on meat consumption was substantially reduced. Similar shifts in consumption patterns were apparent for milk and eggs.[33] Looking ahead to 2030 and beyond, CCAP results suggest that rural meat consumption per capita will continue to rise until 2035 but at a declining rate. Growth in urban meat consumption will continue until 2025. But with population growth becoming negative after 2030 and the ageing of the population, total meat demand will start to level off by 2030 and then decline slowly.

It seems possible, therefore that the per head demand for livestock products projected by some analysts may be too high. For example, IFPRI's baseline projection gives meat consumption levels in 2030 of about 70 kg per head, and c. 35 kg if people adopt a healthier low meat diet.[34] These projections are in strong contrast to the food survey data that suggest that actual meat consumption levels of high income adults had levelled out in 2009 at about 37 kg, but this does not include consumption away from home so the total intake could be about 60 kg which is similar to FAO's latest estimate of 65 kg.[35] Even if one allows for (a) the differences between the NFS data which is for actual meat consumption and the IFPRI data that uses dressed carcass weight divided by population, and that (b) the NFS average consumption estimate is for adults as opposed to IFPRI's average for the whole population, it still seems likely that meat demand in 2030 could be less than the 136 Mt projected by Masuda et al.[36] and closer to the 93 Mt projected by CCAP for 2020/21 and the 104 Mt projected by FAO for 2030 (Table 7.2).

These uncertainties about the demand for meat, milk and eggs have substantial implications for total feed demand, imports of coarse grains and soya beans and food security. In addition, there are uncertainties about growth rates for technological and management improvements in livestock production to raise feed use efficiency. Past improvements in these two factors have been modest[37] and have not achieved the large potential gains in feed use efficiency that are feasible by 2030. The MOA's twelfth FYP for livestock development and feed industry development both mention raising feed/grass/crop residue use efficiency, but do not set specific targets.

## Projected production

The projections in Table 7.2 assume the continuation of present policies and no appreciable impact of climate change on average national food production. They suggest that China has the

**Table 7.2** Current and projected production (Mt)

| | CAPSiM – CCAP | | OECD-FAO | | FAO | |
|---|---|---|---|---|---|---|
| | **2010/11** | **2020/21** | **2008/10** | **2020** | **2005/07** | **2030** |
| Rice | 195.8 | 170 | | | 183 | 196 |
| Wheat | 115.2 | 103 | 114 | 116 | 105 | 117 |
| Coarse grains | 208.7 | 274 | 177 | 210 | 157 | 202 |
| Maize | 177.2 | 223 | | | 148 | 190 |
| Oilseeds | 47.4 | 53 | 56 | 65 | 15 | <20 |
| Soya bean | 15.1 | 18 | 16 | | | |
| Sugar | 14.4 | 16 | 12 | 18 | 14 | 19.5 |
| Beef and mutton | 8.0 | 12 | | | >9 | 16.5 |
| Beef | 4.6 | 7 | 6 | 7 | 5.9 | 11.5 |
| Pork and poultry | 58.7 | 81 | | | 59 | 77 |
| Pork | 45.8 | 57 | 49 | 62 | 45 | 62 |
| Milk | 37.5 | 79 | 40 | 59 | 36 | 59 |

*Source*: Simulation results from CAPSiM 2012, CCAP, OECD-FAO (2012), and unpublished FAO data.

capacity to remain broadly self-sufficient for the next 10 to 20 years for most food commodities and achieve a high level of food security from domestic resources (Table 7.3). The major exceptions are coarse grains (primarily maize), oilseeds (primarily soya bean), milk products and possibly sugar.

There are differences in the estimates of Huang et al.[38] and FAO estimates for the production and self-sufficiency ratios (SSRs) for sugar and beef which are part demand related (see 'Resource constraints and policy challenges' below) but also a reflection of the uncertainties about resource allocation. In the early 2000s, the GOC decided that it was beneficial to allow more land, labour and other resources to be shifted from the production of cereals and soya bean to vegetables and higher-value crops and also out of agriculture, because this shift need not endanger the production of staple foods and basic food security. This opened the way for greater imports of soya bean and more recently of maize and sorghum[39] and this is likely to continue (see Figure 7.6 and section 'Global and Regional Implications of China's Future Food Security').

This allocation issue will continue to shape production throughout the projection period and beyond. Some recent policy decisions on this issue, for example, on biofuels, GM crops, and sugar, could shift the production pathway away from that suggested by Huang et al. and FAO.

**Table 7.3** Past and projected self-sufficiency levels (per cent)

| | CAPSiM, CCAP | | | FAO | |
|---|---|---|---|---|---|
| | **2010** | **2020** | **2025** | **2005/07** | **2030** |
| Rice | 100.1 | 100.5 | 101 | 100 | 101 |
| Wheat | 99.2 | 99 | 99 | 101 | 102 |
| Coarse grains | 99.1 | 92.4 | 90 | 107 | 97 |
| Oilseeds (vegetable oils for FAO) | 49.0 | 41 | 40 | 53 | 45 |
| Sugar | 90.0 | 90.4 | 88 | 94 | 93 |
| Beef and mutton | 99.5 | 97 | 96 | 100 | 100 |
| Pork and poultry | 99.9 | 98.5 | 98 | 100 | 98 |
| Milk | 98.1 | 91.5 | 90 | 99 | 97 |

*Source*: As Table 7.2.

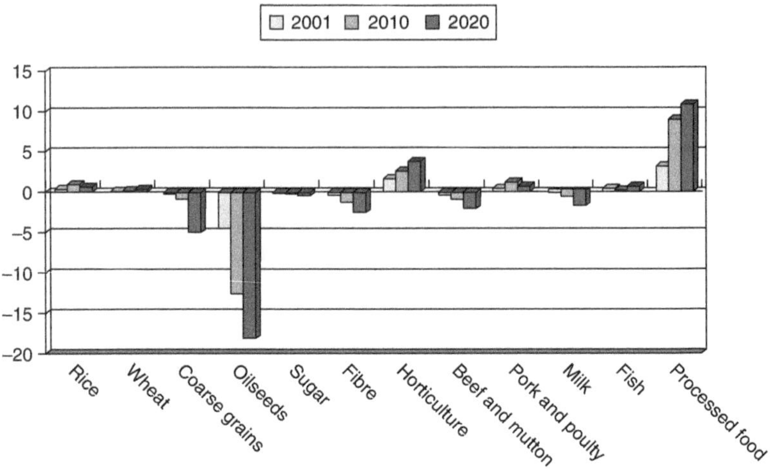


Figure 7.6 **China's net export of agriculture and food (billion EUR) under baseline in 2001–2020**

In 2007, the GOC prohibited the expansion of bioethanol production from cereals above the levels allocated at that time. Consequently, the potential competition between cereals for food or feed and those for bioethanaol production will be prevented and any further expansion of biofuel production will have to be based on non-food crops grown on marginal land.[40] Thus earlier concerns that bioethanol production could threaten food security are no longer valid.[41]

The twelfth FYP sets a number of targets and investment decisions regarding the development and application of agricultural biotechnology, and the expansion of sugar production. Most of such targets set by the past two FYPs were achieved[42] and so it is reasonable to assume that could continue to be the case and affect self-sufficiency levels. The increased R&D in GM maize could increase self-sufficiency in 2025 by several percentage points though not eliminate the need for imports.[43] The Chinese Ministry of Agriculture has set a target of raising sugar production by 2 Mt over the duration of the plan,[44] and it is technologically feasible to continue this rate of expansion up to 2030, which would make China close to self-sufficient. However, (a) such a reallocation of cropland could take away land from food and feed production, (b) sugar beet and sugar cane may not be as profitable to farmers as other crops and (c) imported sugar could be cheaper.

A major factor affecting cereal production and imports will be progress or the lack thereof in raising feed use efficiency. This will be considered in next section.

### *Resource constraints and policy challenges*

*Cropland.* There are large uncertainties about the current area of cropland in part due to whether estimates are based on census data, which have been distorted in the past by local officials, or on remote sensing images. The main concern is the continuing loss of highly productive cropland to urban development and other non-agricultural uses given that less than 10 per cent of the land mass is suitable for crops and some two-thirds of this area is not of high potential productivity. The eleventh and twelfth FYPs have addressed this issue by stipulating that the area should not fall below 120 Mha compared with 130 Mha in 1996 when there was a substantial upward revision in the official cropland area estimates. However, some analysts argue that the area is already below 120 Mha or soon will be but there are large uncertainties in the data. For example, recent unpublished estimates from CAS and the Ministry of Land and Resources show that the total area of cultivated land did not decline during 1990–2010 and is now about 140 Mha but average quality or primary productivity of land has been falling.

It is generally agreed that:

(a) urbanisation will continue to be the main cause of good arable land loss and if this follows the pattern of the 1990s it could undermine food security. Moreover, the decline in average primary productivity of land will continue.
(b) some marginal cropland may be returned to pasture or forest through the grain for green or similar programmes but with limited implications for food security
(c) China has virtually no additional land to develop for crop production.

Although restrictions on land transfers from agriculture to other sectors have been placed on local governments these are not always applied. For example, any cropland which is transferred to non-agricultural uses is supposed to be balanced by an equal area of land reclamation elsewhere. This is seldom done in part because of perverse incentives, for example some local governments gain up to 50 per cent of their total revenues from land transfer fees.[45] In the short term at least the financial incentives for permitting land transfers seem likely to continue, and could pose a threat to food security unless productivity gains on the remaining land or food imports make up for the loss.

Some compensation for these losses could arise from land consolidation which is now a GOC priority and an increase in cropping intensity. Land consolidation could:

(a) increase the effective cropped area because of the removal of narrow roads, footpaths, paddy levées and other non-cultivated land which can account for 20 per cent of the gross cropland area;[46]
(b) allow greater mechanisation and other productivity enhancing changes that lower the unit costs of food production,[47] and raise fertiliser use efficiency (FUE)[48] with important environmental benefits as discussed below.

A number of analysts have concluded that the problem of land loss to non-agricultural uses will be compounded by land degradation from desertification[49] and soil erosion.[50] Though there is no doubt that desertification and soil erosion are serious in some areas, their impact on staple cereal production is limited. For example, the bulk of rice and wheat production is irrigated and grown on naturally level river flood plains or on land which has been levelled by farmers over many centuries. Such land is not prone to serious erosion. The same is true for much of the maize, soya bean and vegetable production.

*Labour resources.* They are and will continue to be an important constraint to agricultural growth but not a major or unmanageable challenge to food security. Two factors are of particular concern: first, the loss of labour to non-agricultural activities because of temporary or permanent out-migration without any or insufficient compensating increases in labour productivity through mechanisation and land consolidation (as discussed above) and second the progressive ageing of the active labour force such that a recent survey[51] in five important food producing provinces found that >65 per cent of those heavily engaged in farming were over 45 years of age and only 14 per cent were in the under 35 group. This situation is likely to deteriorate further by 2030 if current policies prevail with growing difficulties in hiring labour and maintaining high multiple cropping rates, and continuing use of sub-optimal crop management practices that reduce output growth, contribute to low fertiliser use efficiency and are unsustainable in the long-run. However, as discussed above in the context of the land constraint and in section 'Central and Local Government Context of Food Security Policies' regarding central and local government policies and practices, this constraint can be overcome by a combination of land consolidation, appropriate mechanisation and improved provision of technical advice and skills and the GOC is re-shaping its policies to implement these measures. Thus, labour force change can be considered more as an opportunity than a challenge, although rising wages could have negative impacts on labour-intensive products such as fruits and vegetables but not on commodities critical for food security commodities such as grains and edible oils.

*Irrigation.* Agriculture accounts for 65–70 per cent of total water use. Income and urban/industrial development driven demand for water could pose similar challenges to those regarding land, because irrigation plays a critical role in staple food security, vegetable production and some feed grain production. Irrigated land produces about 80 per cent of grain production[52] and with around 37 per cent of the maize and 80 per cent of the wheat area being irrigated when required.[53] Much of this irrigation is dependent on falling groundwater tables[54] but this is not the only challenge:

(a) Continuing urbanisation and income growth will increase competition for water.
(b) Groundwater depletion means that the energy cost of pumping will rise and with it the GHG emissions from the production and use of that energy – these emissions already account for about 3 per cent of agriculture's total GHG emissions.[55]
(c) Although water use efficiency (WUE) has risen in the past 10–20 years as a result of public investment in ditch and

canal lining, sprinkler irrigation, and so on, average irrigation efficiency is still only about 45 per cent.[56]

(d) Climate change is likely to have a negative impact on cereal production in some parts of China unless there are sustained improvements in agricultural technology.[57]

(e) Over irrigation adds to the low fertiliser use efficiency and non-point pollution challenges discussed below.

*Fertilisation use efficiency (FUE).* This has declined by about one-third since 1978 (Figure 7.4) with numerous negative environmental impacts on the local, national and global environment and particularly non-point pollution.[58] A series of GOC actions since 2000 in successive FYPs have failed to resolve the problem[59] which has complex origins that require integrated action by a number of ministries to improve advice to farmers and to help overcome the labour constraints of part-time farmers. For example, in 2007 four ministries – the Ministry of Science and Technology (MOST), the Ministry of Agriculture (MOA), the Ministry of Finance (MOF), and the State Administration of Grain signed collaboration agreements with major grain producing provinces to raise yields and lower negative environmental impacts through the application of improved science and technology. This appears to have had positive impacts on crop yields but not on FUE or on non-point pollution. Thus current staple food security is damaged by the reduction in yields caused by the overuse of nitrogen fertiliser[60] and long-term food security is placed at risk by soil acidification (see below) and unnecessarily high GHG emissions.

### Climate change

Earlier assessments of the impact of climate change on Chinese agriculture suggested that China's food security was seriously at risk. However, they were based on analyses that either were not sufficiently integrated or not spatially disaggregated enough to arrive at reliable conclusions. Some recent studies do not have such limitations, and use scenario analysis to explore uncertainties in key parameters and are therefore a better starting point for determining the risks of climate change for food security.[61]

They all conclude that climate change is not a serious threat to China's staple cereal production and food security over the next 20–40 years unless one adopts the unrealistic assumption that the GOC and farmers do not respond or adapt to climate change. In fact some scenarios suggest that climate change could have a small positive impact on food security but this would be much less than the positive impacts of measures to stop cropland loss or raise agricultural productivity. Although rice yields in the South of China might decline because of rising temperatures, production could shift to cooler provinces further north – a trend that is already well established. Average wheat yields are projected to be favoured by climate change up to about 2030 but possibly not thereafter. Maize yields may decrease but this could be counter balanced by yield increases from better crop management, conventional plant breeding and the introduction of GM maize. These increases should meet the direct demand for food grains and contribute to meeting feed grain demand.

### *Emerging threats*

Soil acidification of much of China's intensively cultivated land has doubled over the past 30 years and N fertiliser has contributed about 60 per cent of this[62] and affects cash crops more than cereals. Much of the acidification stems from the high inputs of N fertiliser rather than from acid rain, although ammonia emissions from fertiliser, manure and other livestock wastes may become of increasing importance. It can reduce crop yields, for example, by increasing the concentrations of toxic metals in soils. Control is possible but is labour intensive and costly.

Soil pollution by heavy metals is receiving greater emphasis in GOC policies because of food safety issues but the implications for staple food production are probably limited. The main problems seem to be on peri-urban farmland receiving sewage or waste water, or downwind of mining or industrial activities. These areas account for a relatively small proportion of the total arable area.

Low level ozone damage to crops may already be serious because concentrations in parts of China downwind of cities and industrial areas already exceed those known to cause yield loss in other countries.[63–65] Wheat and soya bean are particularly sensitive to ozone damage with losses of 4–15 per cent. The ozone arises largely from urban transport pollution and with the growing urbanisation and transport growth the area at risk is likely to widen, but it remains an under researched issue that is not reflected in GOC priorities.

### *Feed use efficiency*

In general feed use is low in China, although there have been significant improvements in the past 5–10 years that were largely associated with the shift from small- to large-scale production. This is particularly important as regards the large intensive dairy units that are expected to be the main source of increased milk output in the future,[66] and in the pig industry which is the main user of feed grains.[67] For example, the average feed use efficiency in dairy farms is 25–30 per cent lower than in developed countries using the same breeds, and for pork production average feed conversion rates (kg feed/kg weight gain) are also much higher than in the EU although those for the best large operations are similar to the EU average. Consequently measures to raise feed use efficiency could have major benefits for food security, and the environment. The policy and technological responses required could be implemented in the next 5–10 years and have a substantial impact by 2020/30. They concern (a) the genetic improvement of livestock, which is currently partly constrained by GOC policies, for example, regarding the import of semen, and (b) the quality of the feed mix which is strongly influenced by the price of maize. These factors have important implications both for lower maize and soy bean imports and reduced livestock pollution of surface waters and emissions of ammonia and GHGs. State farms and commercial livestock enterprises are actively pursuing these options either alone or through joint ventures with OECD based companies.[68]

## Central and Local Government Context of Food Security Policies

### Evolution of food security and food security polices since the 1950s

China suffered from acute food insecurity during the 1950s and 1960s with average food consumption of only 2000 Kcal/

person/day and at times dropped substantially below this average because of droughts and pest outbreaks. Until the economic reforms of 1978, the GOC tended to focus on industrial development supported by cheap food and raw materials, and agriculture and food security were not given strong emphasis. The management of agricultural production was highly centralised under a command and control system with state imposed targets for local level production, unfavourable procurement prices, and tightly controlled marketing and trade. However, after 1979, the GOC started to introduce measures to ensure that poor agricultural growth did not endanger food security or hold back the development of the manufacturing and service sectors. As one of the Four modernisations (agriculture, industry, national defence, and science and technology), the rapid development of the agricultural sector in 1979–84 provided a fundamental base for the expansion of the industrial sector (Figure 7.7).

The first major action in 1979 was the introduction of the household responsibility system to provide incentive for individual farmers to expand and diversify agricultural production. This system allowed farmers to sell surplus produce grown on land allocated to them by the collective once they had met their centrally imposed quota for staple food (rice, wheat, maize, soya bean, edible oils) and livestock production. This led to the rapid increase in stable food productivity, which also enabled farmers to expand vegetables production six-fold between 1978 and 2010 and backyard pig production (which doubled between 1980–90) and is a clear indication of how rapidly Chinese farmers respond to price and market incentives.

The next major reform was in 1984 when the mandatory quotas were replaced by voluntary contracts for grain following a fall in net grain imports. Grain production expanded throughout the next 10 years, but did not keep ahead of per capita demand and food security targets. This led to another set of reforms to boost staple food production (by re-imposing the state compulsory quota system in most parts of China, higher procurement prices and technological improvements) and to further decentralise the management of food security by the introduction in 1995 of the 'Provincial Governor's Grain Bag Responsibility System'. The latter made provincial governors responsible for ensuring that grain production and stocks in their province met local

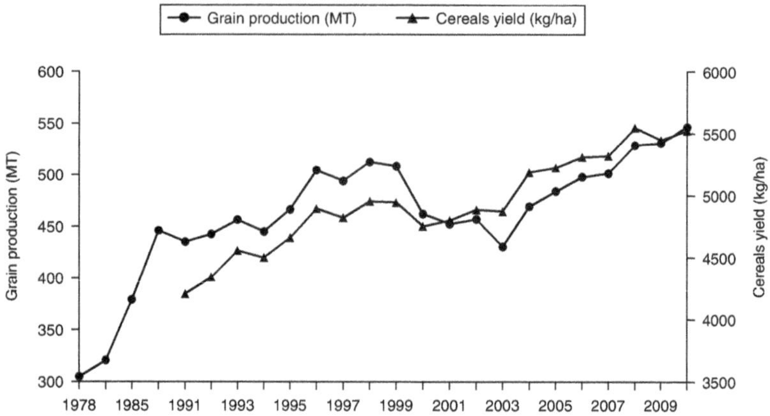


| | | | |
|---|---|---|---|
| Re-construction of the agricultural production system;<br><br>Implementation of households responsibility system (HRS);<br><br>State monopoly of grain purchase and marketing. | Reform on grain distribution system, demolished state monopoly for purchase and marketing of grain;<br><br>Establish multi-level grain reserve system;<br><br>1996 White Paper: Grains Issues in China – declared 95 per cent grain self-sufficiency;<br><br>Land Administration Law 1998 – Strictly protect basic farm land;<br><br>Ensure fertiliser supply by stabilise fertiliser and pesticides prices, subsidise fertiliser manufacture and transport. | Further perfect grain policies;<br><br>Stabilise HRS, encourage land use right transfer;<br><br>Grain Security incorporated in Agriculture Law | Direct payment of subsidies to farmers;<br><br>Implement floor price for rice and wheat;<br><br>Strengthen farm land protection;<br><br>Stabilise grain sown area, raise per unit yield, ensure food security;<br><br>Agricultural tax scrapped |

Figure 7.7 **Change in grain production, cereals yield and policy interventions**

*Source*: NSBC (2011) China Statistical Yearbook 2011, (China Statistics Press, Beijing).

needs and grain prices were relatively stable and high enough to encourage farmers to raise their grain output without increasing food price inflation for urban consumers. It was effective but carried a number of negative features. Regional comparative advantage and inter-provincial trade was suppressed and both grain storage costs and losses from storage pests rose.

Further reforms were introduced between 1995 and 2010 to provide a comprehensive policy framework (Table 7.4) and to improve the functioning of grain markets, the cost and efficiency of the grain reserve system,[69] and farm incomes by lowering or removing agricultural taxes. They have been effective in maintaining national food security, and contributing to global food security. Per capita grain production has exceeded demand together with substantial quantitative and qualitative improvements in dietary patterns. China was a net grain exporter for most of the past 20 years (see 'Medium and Long-Term Food Security Plan (2008–2020)' below), has provided food aid to other countries, and has avoided de-stabilising international markets by investing heavily in irrigation and using large carry-over stocks to offset the impact of droughts and other extreme events on domestic production (see 'Global and Regional Implications of China's Future Food Security' below).

Throughout the period 1950–2000 the focus of the national food production strategy was on maintaining 100 per cent self-sufficiency in all staple grains defined as rice, wheat, coarse grains, soya beans, pulses, potatoes and sweet potatoes.[70] However, towards the end of this period there was increasing discussion about the appropriateness of this definition because

**Table 7.4** Food security policy framework and action points

| Policies | Action points |
|---|---|
| Land Administration Law<br>Law on Land Contract in Rural Areas<br>Regulations on the Protection of Basic Farmland<br>Farmer Professional Association Law | Protection of arable land from other uses<br>Insist household responsibility system and allow land use right transfer |
| Scrap agricultural tax<br>Agricultural subsidies (for farmers purchase high quality seeds, farm machinery, fertilisers, fuel and other input); Floor price for rice and wheat purchase | Farmer income protection<br>Price stability |
| Provincial governor 'Rice Bag' responsibility<br>Establish major grain production zones with preferable /specific financial support | Ensuring grain supply and demand is balanced within the province |
| 95 per cent grain self-sufficiency<br>Multi-level food reserve system | Ensure food supply and reduce volatility |
| R&D: high yield varieties, water-saving technologies | Increase per unit productivity |

*Source*: Authors' Own.

of (a) the decreasing importance of potatoes and sweet potatoes in diets; (b) the increasing use of coarse grains and soya beans for livestock feed; (c) the impending entry of China into the WTO; and (d) the shortage of arable land. These discussions led to the decision to revise the food security target to 95–100 per cent self-sufficiency for cereals under normal conditions and opened the way for the expansion of soya bean imports.[71]

## Food security strategy in the twelfth FYP period and beyond

Entering its twelfth FYP period (2011–15), the GOC faces several challenges to maintain food security, including continued increase in food demand and decline in arable land. These were examined in section 'China's Past, Present and Future Food Supply and Demand' and the GOC has formulated responses to them on the basis of the following predictions for 2020:

- Per capita grain demand of 395 kg, and total demand of 572.5 billion kg
- Total food grain consumption of 247.5 billion ton, accounting for 43 per cent of total consumption; feed grain consumption of 235.5 billion ton, accounting for 41 per cent of total grain consumption
- Per capita edible oil consumption of 20 kg, and total demand of 29 million tons.

A number of strategic plans have been prepared that address the food security problem and in particular respond to the continued increase in food demand (in both quantity and quality, mainly driven by increased wealth and consumption patterns), the constraints in natural resource base (land, water), and to global food price inflation. These include the medium *and* long-term Plan for National Food Security (2008–2020); National Plan for Expansion of Grain Production Capacity by 50 million tons (2009–2020); The twelfth Five-Year Plan for National Economic and Social Development (2011–2015); and the twelfth Five-Year Plan for Agricultural and Rural Economic Development.

The present and future objectives of China's food security strategy are well presented in these documents. Maintaining 95 per cent grain self-sufficiency and 120 Mha of arable are the overarching targets. This means future food security has to rely on increased productivity per unit of land, water, fertiliser, and livestock feed; therefore, sustainable intensification is the key objective. These requirements are similar to those in other parts of the world, but the situation in China perhaps is more acute.[72,73]

### *Medium and Long-Term Food Security Plan (2008–2020)*

Prepared by the National Development and Reform Committee (NDRC), together with over more than ten ministries, the Medium *and* Long-Term Food Security Plan (2008–2020) (the Plan hereafter) outlines the objectives, tasks, and specific programmes for food security and provides the strategic framework for all actions and policy measures on food security leading to 2020.

**Objectives**

(i) Stabilise the grain-sown area and ensure that the arable land area is not less than 120 Mha in 2020.
(ii) Ensure China remains basically self-sufficient in grain and other major food. Maintain grain self-sufficiency at over 95 per cent.
(iii) Maintain a reasonable level of grain stocks and the proportion of wheat and rice should not be less than 70 per cent of the stock.
(iv) Establish a modern grain logistic system and reduce grain distribution costs.

#### The key actions

The Plan outlines a number of actions to safeguard China's future food security. These include increasing grain production capability, utilisation of non-grain food resources, international cooperation, further improve grain distribution systems, strengthen grain storage, logistics and process system and have recently been reviewed.[74]

### *The Twelfth Five-Year Plan for National Economic and Social Development (2011–2015)*

This is China's most comprehensive development plan which covers all the important sectors of social and economic development. It contains all of the main tasks and targets related to agricultural development and food security,[75] but faces some serious constraints.

### *Grain Law (draft for public comments, 2012)*

On 21 February 2012, the Legislative Affairs Office of the State Council released a draft of a new Grain Law to solicit public opinion. The purpose of the draft law is to promote grain production, safeguard the order of grain distribution and national grain security.

The draft law contains ten chapters and 97 articles, covering the following aspects of legislation:

- ▷ Market-oriented allocation of grain resources
- ▷ Safeguarding grain production
- ▷ Safeguarding grain distribution
- ▷ Safeguarding grain quality safety
- ▷ Grain regulation and reserve
- ▷ Support to and development of the grain industry
- ▷ The responsibility for grain security
- ▷ Supervision, inspection and accountability

## Institutional constraints to policy implementation

Formulation and implementation of food security policies involves different departments and sectors of central and local government. Consequently institutional barriers within government are often a constraint to the effective formulation and implementation of the policies.

### *Responsibilities of government departments*

There are two aspects of government department responsibilities that are or may become barriers to the implementation of agricultural and food policies, namely overlapping and divided responsibilities.

Overlapping responsibilities lead to inefficient management of resources. 'Nine dragons administer water' is a Chinese saying describing overlapping responsibilities of different parties that in the end can lead to a situation where no one takes responsibility; this situation is particularly true for China's water resource management where the responsibilities are scattered between several ministries (Table 7.5). This makes water pollution control more difficult, particularly non-point pollution control against which little progress has been made.

**Table 7.5** Complexity of government structures responsible for resource management and the food system: the case of water

| Ministry | Responsibilities |
|---|---|
| National Development and Reform Commission (NDRC) | Strategic planning |
| Ministry of Water Resources (MWR) | Water resource planning and development, flood control, drought relief, guidance on irrigation, drainage and rural water supply, watershed management and water-borne soil erosion |
| Ministry of Environmental Protection (MEP) | Environmental pollution prevention and control |
| Ministry of Agriculture (MOA) | Irrigation and the use of water for agricultural purposes, wetland development, fisheries |
| Ministry of Housing and Urban–Rural Development (MHRUD) | Waste water treatment and use of urban groundwater |
| Ministry of Land and Resources (MLR) | Monitoring and prevention of over-extraction and contamination of groundwater |
| Ministry of Health (MOH) | Water quality standards |
| Ministry of Transport | Water pollution control relating to the transport sector |
| Ministry of Finance | Finance of water development and water pricing |
| Ministry of Science and Technology (MOST) | Funding of R&D, e.g. on water use efficiency |

*Source*: Authors' Own.

The complexity of management structures is also an issue for the grain production, distribution, processing and consumption chain, with overlapping tasks being split between several ministries. For example, the NDRC is responsible for regulating the price of fertiliser and other production input materials, MOA is responsible for grain production; State Administration of Grain (SAG) is responsible for grain purchase, storage, distribution and macro control, and MOFCOM is responsible for international trade of agriculture products.[76] Each sector has its own capacity to make and implement related policies, and sometimes this may have conflicting consequences. For example, changes in production input prices and grain prices have a strong impact on farmers' incomes and therefore on the decisions about future grain production and farm input use.

The complicated and divided nature of departmental responsibilities is also apparent in the food safety governance system which suffers from serious difficulties for inspection, and enforcement. Some departments are linked vertically under the direct auspices of a higher level authority, while others are linked latterly at the same level of government, and commonly with each department being responsible for certain parts of whole food safety chain which makes coordination more difficult.

### *Perverse incentives to local government*

The key objective of preventing the arable area declining below 120 million is clearly set out in the national medium- and long-term food security plan as well as in the twelfth FYP. However, the implementation of policies to achieve this objective face great difficulties at all levels. For example, property sector development and infrastructure construction are the major driving force for China's rapid economic development. Local government regard these as key components of their strategy to achieve their political target – GDP growth. However, they are also the main reason for the loss of cropland. Table 7.6 shows approved land transfers for construction in the period of 2001–2008, two- thirds of construction land was transferred from agricultural and half was from arable land. Research on agricultural land conversion in 1989–2006 and shows 67 per cent of agricultural land converted to non-agricultural use was not justified nor necessary.[77] Moreover, local governments have come to rely on land transfers for a substantial

**Table 7.6** Approved land transfers for construction use (1000ha)

| Year | Total | Transferred from agricultural land | Transferred from cultivated land |
|---|---|---|---|
| 2001 | 167 | 110 | 840 |
| 2002 | 184 | 138 | 102 |
| 2003 | 421 | 2760 | 192 |
| 2004 | 285 | 1680 | 116 |
| 2005 | 351 | 253 | 170 |
| 2006 | 406 | 288 | 189 |
| 2007 | 413 | 274 | 177 |
| 2008 | 399 | 270 | 173 |
| 2011 | 612 | 411 | 253 |

*Source*: China Land Resource Statistic Yearbook, 2009; China Land Resource Bulletin, 2011.

part of their revenues so there is a perverse economic incentive for them to allow them.[78] Land transfer fees can account for 30–50 per cent of total sub-provincial government revenue.

## Future challenges for China's food security policies

The Chinese government has formulated a comprehensive policy framework and policy instruments to ensure future food security as discussed above. However, there are a number of alternative policy options which may help for future food security.

### *Reduction of self-sufficiency rate*

The grain White Paper published in 1996 was the first clear declaration by the GOC that the grain self-sufficiency rate should not be less than 95 per cent, and net imports should not be more than 5 per cent of domestic consumption. Maintaining 95 per cent grain self-sufficiency remains the overarching target for future agricultural and food policy. However, with changes in domestic supply and demand, and China's widening international cooperation for food and agriculture, there is a need to re-investigate the possibility of a reduction in the self-sufficiency rate.

### *Land consolidation and the rural social security system*

As briefly discussed in section 'China's Past, Present and Future Food Supply and Demand' there is a consensus that land consolidation will increase land use efficiency,[79] and it is an inevitable trend as more rural people move out to urban centres.[80] Slow progress in land consolidation is mainly due to concerns about social security for those who transfer their land use rights but later lose their off-farm earnings. Land use rights in rural China function as part of a social security safety-net. There are also concerns that agricultural land will be transferred to non-agricultural use. There is a need to develop policies to guide and regulate the process of land use transfer. A number of policy options are available to overcome the potential risks of land use rights transfer, include confirmation of household land use rights contract, subsidies and to grain production, and to improve the rural social security system.[81]

### *Healthy food consumption*

The overall nutrition improvement in China has been substantial. However, the increase in meat consumption, particularly in urban areas, has raised concerns about increased obesity and associated diseases. On the other hand, malnutrition is still common in many rural areas and among vulnerable groups of people. Consequently, future policies need to tackle the challenge of over consumption as well as malnutrition. In one sense China is better placed to meet this challenge than many developed countries because diets are still broadly rice, vegetable and white meat based with limited consumption of red meat and dairy products. However, a major public information campaign might be needed to limit a switch to high red meat diets and reduce obesity.

## Global and Regional Implications of China's Future Food Security

### Will China put pressure on global markets?

Given the size of China's population, its large total demand for cereals (540 Mt in 2010), and the relatively small size of the current world market, it is not surprising that some commentators have voiced concern that sudden large-scale grain purchases by China could destabilise global markets.[82] It happened in the early 1970s when the USSR secretly made large grain purchases on the US market following a severe drought. China's large purchase of wheat in 2003–4 had a similar impact but it is important to understand why these imports were needed. It was not because of the lack of production potential in China – it was mainly due to changes in the relative prices of grain and cash crops which favoured the latter. Wheat and rice production fell during 1998/99–2004 because of falling prices as a result of two major changes: (1) the decline in per capita consumption since about 2000 driven by rising incomes and urbanisation and (2) the decision by the GOC to lower the financial burden of maintaining large state grain stores. The GOC and local governments acted quickly to remove or lower these constraints and wheat production expanded during the rest of the decade and kept close to the 100 per cent self-sufficiency target.

It follows that this question must be considered comprehensively and dynamically. There are three main aspects to consider. First, will China's food security needs put pressure on global food markets? Second, will China's actions to protect its own food security help other developing countries to do the same? Third, and related to the previous question, will China's trade with and aid to developing countries improve their agricultural productivity and food purchasing power?

The question of whether China's food security needs put pressure on global markets is multi-dimensional. Component questions include:

(a) Has the long-term food demand and supply situation been projected in a sound manner?
(b) Can the food security and food self-sufficiency policies examined in the previous section continue to achieve China's goal of 95 per cent self-sufficiency in key commodities?
(c) Do other countries have the supply potential to meet China's food and feed import needs without putting unsustainable pressures on their own natural resources and world market prices?

The section 'China's Past, Present and Future Food Supply and Demand' of this chapter addressed component (a) and concluded that the long-term demand for food and feed has probably been over-estimated and China's production potential under-estimated. With respect to component (b) section 'Central and Local Government Context of Food Security Policies' concluded that the current policy framework contains much of what is required to maintain 95 per cent self-sufficiency for key commodities and that China's past responses to domestic and foreign supply shortfalls show that the GOC and Chinese farmers have the capacity to react positively and quickly to extreme events such as droughts and rising market prices.

Component question (c) may also be less of an issue than some analysts suggest. Taking maize and soya beans as potentially China's largest import requirements, it is illuminating to see how the current droughts in the USA have resulted in press comments about rocketing food prices and impending doom and more measured responses from farmers in the southern hemisphere who see a market opportunity. Brazil, Argentina and other South American countries have quickly expanded maize and soya bean production to help overcome any reduction in US exports. Moreover, this supply potential is not just a short-term one. CCAP,[83] USDA and OECD projections for 2020/2021 and FAO projections for 2030 all suggest that the traditional cereal and soya bean exporters have significant capacity to expand their exports. The remainder of this section provides supporting evidence for this conclusion, and examines the supply potential of non-traditional exporters.

*China's net food import needs in 2020/21 and 2030.* The CCAP, USDA, OECD and FAO projections are relatively consistent with each other (Table 7.8). They suggest that there are only three commodities where China's possible import needs account for more than 10 per cent of the projected world trade: soya bean (>60), maize (14–16 per cent) and sugar (>12 per cent). The only other notable import needs could be pork (up to 8 per cent) and dairy products (up to 8 per cent).

All of these incremental needs are within the supply capacity of China's traditional trading partners. China's soya bean imports rose from 13.9 Mt in 2001 to 54.8 Mt in 2010. This four-fold increase in imports was made possible by the rapid expansion of production in the USA and later in Brazil and Argentina without putting pressure on world market prices. China's projected incremental import needs for 2020/21 are 21–35 Mt (Table 7.7) compared with nearly 41 Mt for the last decade, which the traditional exporters seem well able to supply. The USA has relatively limited potential to expand exports – possibly by only 2–3 Mt,[84] although in the longer-term climate change may increase the area suitable for soya beans. Brazil, in contrast could increase exports by 40Mt[85] without the need for further deforestation.[86] A further 7 Mt could come from Argentina, and another 12 Mt from Uruguay, Paraguay and Bolivia.[87] Of course other countries will be increasing their import needs, notably India and SE Asian countries, but it is clear that traditional exporters have the capacity to meet these and those of China. In addition, a number of other countries have the capacity to expand production and become exporters once infrastructural and technological constraints are overcome (see later discussion).

The situation for China's maize import needs is similar to the above. China's 2020/21 requirements could be around 18–20 Mt (Table 7.7). Maize exports from the USA have been slowing down but they could still expand by about 15 Mt by 2020/2021.[88] The Ukraine and other Former Soviet Union (FSU) countries could export some 17 Mt per year by 2020/21, Argentina over 23 Mt and Brazil about 14Mt. Thus the global maize export capacity seems well able to meet China's needs and those of other developing countries, and as with soya beans there are countries in Africa which could become significant exporters in the long-term even though the overall picture might look bleak.[89]

China's long-term demand and supply for sugar raises more complex issues. First, it should be noted that some 65 per cent of demand is by the food processing sector, and part of this demand could be met by synthetic sweeteners and other sugar substitutes unless the GOC continues to restrict their use. Second, there is no consensus regarding the evolution of supply and demand. FAO projects 93 per cent self-sufficiency for 2030,[90] and Luke Matthews[91] projects near self-sufficiency in 2030 under a trend consumption growth scenario (2.2 per cent per annum). The latter is consistent with the twelfth FYP target of 3.1 per cent per annum growth in production and near self-sufficiency. However, his high growth scenario (4.4 per cent per annum) projects a 4–5 Mt deficit for 2030 which is close to the CCAP's CAPSiM estimates (Table 7.7) and those of the OECD[92] (5 Mt) which are based on the assumption that domestic production will be increasingly limited by water availability. The latter may be true but it is basically a question of GOC and farmer resource allocation. If the GOC decides to allocate R&D and capital resources to raising irrigation efficiency and crop productivity, and domestic prices are favourable to farmers, then near self-sufficiency is feasible.

But from a strategic point of view, the GOC may decide that it is more important to allocate these resources to maize production and accept higher soya bean and sugar imports.

Pork is the remaining import requirement that could be substantial, that is, potentially as much as 8 per cent of world trade (Table 7.7) although more recent estimates suggest the maintenance of near self-sufficiency. Given the close attention that the GOC gives to stable pork supply and prices and the good pig production potential, it is assumed here that there are no global food security risks associated with China's long-term pork demand. The same is also true for wheat and rice needs.

## China's food security and the potential for new food exporters

The above discussion on the future supply potential of traditional food and feed exporters showed that many of those in Latin America have the land resources and opportunities for raising crop yields to meet China's projected import needs. However, there are also many African countries that have substantial areas of land that are agro-climatically suitable for cereal and soya bean production but are constrained by poor crop distribution and marketing infrastructure, and by lack of access to fertiliser, improved seeds, other production inputs and technical advice. The potential land resources that are suitable for China's main deficit crops are substantial (Table 7.8), and in total are more than double China's arable area. Zambia alone has the supply potential to meet a substantial proportion of China's 2010–2020 incremental maize import needs.[93] Much of Zambia's c. 13 Mha

**Table 7.7** China's current and projected net exports (per cent of world trade) and Total World Trade (Mt)

| | CAPSiM, CCAP | | USDA | | FAO | | Projected world trade | |
|---|---|---|---|---|---|---|---|---|
| | 2010/11 | 2020/21 | 2010/11 | 2020/21 | 2005/07 | 2030 | USDA 20/21* | FAO 2030** |
| Rice | 0.23 | 0.6 | <0.1 | 0.55 | 0.76 | 2.4 | 45 | 54 |
| Wheat | –0.95 | –0.8 (<1 per cent) | 0 | –0.3 (<1 per cent) | 0.78 | 2.0 | 157 | 134 |
| Coarse grains | –2.96 | –22.5 | –2.5 | –21 | 5.1 | –5.5 | | |
| Maize | –1.44 | –20.4 (16 per cent) | –0.9 | –18 (14 per cent) | | –1.9 (2 per cent) | 131 | 108 |
| Oilseeds | –55.09 | –77.2 | | | –12.9 | –24 | | |
| Soya bean | –54.63 | –75.9 (54 per cent) | –52 | –87 (62 per cent) | | | 140 | |
| Sugar | –1.68 | –1.7 (3 per cent) | –1.5 | | –0.85 | –1.4 (<3 per cent) | | 54 |
| Beef and mutton | –0.04 | –0.29 | | | 0.12 | 0 | | |
| Beef | 0 | –0.08 (<1 per cent) | | | | | 8.5 | 8.7 |
| Pork and poultry | –0.01 | –1.25 | | | 0.32 | 0.6 | | |
| Pork | –0.09 | –0.30 (5–6 per cent) | –0.2 | –0.4 (7 per cent) | –0.14 | –0.42 (8 per cent) | 5.5–7.0 | >5 |
| Milk | –0.71 | –7.3 (8.5 per cent) | | | –0.52 | 2.0 | | 4.4 |

*All or just major exporters depending on the commodity.
** 110 countries.

*Source*: CCAP data base.

**Table 7.8** Sub-Saharan African countries with large potential for expanded crop production (Mha)

| | Current cropland * 2009 | Additional potential cropland** | Current as per cent of potential |
|---|---|---|---|
| Angola | 4.29 | 20 | 18 |
| Central African Republic | 2.04 | 11 | 16 |
| Chad | 4.33 | 16 | 23 |
| Congo | 0.5 | 15 | 3 |
| Democratic Republic of the Congo | 7.45 | 102 | 7 |
| Madagascar | 3.55 | 19 | 15 |
| Mozambique | 5.3 | 29 | 16 |
| Former Sudan | 20.39 | 36 | 36 |
| Tanzania | 11.5 | 14 | 46 |
| Zambia | 3.9 | 26 | 13 |
| Total | 52.8 | 282 | 19 |

*Arable land and permanent crops.

**Potentially available land outside nature reserves and other protected lands that are suitable or very suitable for at least one of following crops: wheat, maize, soya beans, sugar cane and oil palm.

*Source*: Based on data from Fischer and Shah, 2010.[94]

of land which could be available for expanded maize production is suitable for large-scale mechanisation, and the transport infrastructure is good partly thanks to China's investment in the road and rail network since the 1960s. However, yields are generally low except on the larger commercial farms, and there has been underinvestment in agricultural R&D and advisory services for many years which China is now helping to strengthen. It is quite feasible to triple or quadruple maize yields over the next 10–20 years, and produce some 10 Mt for export.

Similar potentials exist for other food and feed crops: rice in Angola although soil management problems may have to be overcome; soya beans in the Sudan, the DRC, Mozambique, Zambia and Angola but farmers have little experience; and sugar cane in the DRC and Madagascar. Such opportunities could be important to China's food security in terms of diversifying both politically and agro-climatically its sources of imports, and to global food security for similar reasons. In addition they are important to the farmers in these countries, particularly where they are providing a new cash crop for them, and to workers in the support industries throughout agriculture. These employment multipliers can have a substantial impact on food purchasing power and hence on food security. China is playing an active part in exploiting this potential but is not a significant contributor to the so-called land grab.[95]

## N-S and S-S technology transfer and food security

In China more formal contributions to technology transfer date back to the 1960s, for example, with the establishment of rice demonstration farms in Malawi. However, the most significant contribution, which has improved the food security of millions of people in Asia, was China's sharing of improved crop varieties and particularly hybrid rice through collaboration with the International Rice Research Institute. Hybrid rice varieties have higher yield potential than traditional ones, and from the early 1980s China played a significant role in passing these benefits to other South and East Asian countries. This was a key part of the green revolution. The relatively ad hoc technology transfers of the 1960–2000 period made an important contribution to global food security. These are likely to continue with potentially very significant advances becoming available for North-South (N-S), South-North (S-N) and South-South (S-S) technology transfer from China's highly successful rice and wheat breeding programmes and from its huge investment in biotechnology.[96] Moreover, since about 2004 these ad hoc transfers have been complemented by a more programmed approach to technology transfer through the FAO-China Strategic Alliance on South-South Cooperation, which is aimed particularly at raising agricultural productivity and food security.

## Implications of China's food security for the EU

These implications can be assessed in terms of:

(a) The role of the EU as a supplier of China's food and feed imports and technology needs.

(b) EU support to China's food security by helping to raise agricultural productivity and increase the efficiency and effectiveness of the food chain.
(c) EU-China collaboration on raising global food security and particularly in Sub-Saharan Africa.

## The EU as a supplier of China's food and feeds

The EU is already the fifth largest exporter of agricultural products to China though some of them are not essential to food security such as wines and spirits. In the longer term, however, the EU could provide some of China's wheat and barley imports although other low cost suppliers in the Russian Federation and the Ukraine may have greater comparative advantage. The situation for dairy products is different. The EU seems likely to continue to have surplus capacity and some cost-advantages so it could increase exports to China and particularly of processed higher-value added products. A number of EU companies are already well established exporters to China or domestic producers with local partners, for example, Friesland, Nestle and Parmalat. However, other OECD countries including the USA and New Zealand already have significant market shares.

## EU support to raising agricultural productivity and increasing the efficiency and effectiveness of the food chain

EU food and feed exports to China seems likely to play only a small role in China's future food security. However, its support to the implementation of China's food security policies could be critically important, first, by sharing the EU's well established public and private sector expertise in raising agricultural productivity, which will have secondary benefits to the EU's food security, and second, by increasing the efficiency and effectiveness of the food processing and marketing chain. For example, joint action on livestock and crop diseases could help to avoid the build up of epidemics and pandemics that in the past have caused serious reductions in cereal and meat supply, notably wheat rust and swine fever. EU support to raising fertiliser and feed use efficiency would benefit the EU and the world, because it will also help to reduce greenhouse gas emissions and mitigate climate change. Another important component of the productivity gains could be breed improvement through exports of breeding animals, semen and embryos, but here the EU faces strong competition from US companies that already have joint ventures with Chinese companies.[97] The private sector is already making an important contribution to the latter. AB Agri, for example, is helping raise the efficiency of China's livestock feed concentrates industry and of sugar production and processing. Supermarkets such as Carrefour and Tesco are helping raise the efficiency of the marketing chain, reduce storage wastes and improve food quality and safety. The main issue here is perhaps what the role, if any, of the Commission is in widening these private sector contributions.

## China's collaboration on raising global food security and particularly in Sub-Saharan Africa

EU-China collaboration on food and agriculture stretches back over 20 years but there are few tangible outcomes of any importance. Most of the major initiatives have been bilateral ones such as those with Denmark, France, Germany, the Netherlands, the UK and others, yet there are a number of food security challenges that are best tackled at the level of the EU 27, notably livestock and crop diseases, and food safety. The EU-China Dialogue launched in 2005 has helped to promote mutual understanding on the dominant issues confronting global food security. And the EU-China Cooperation Plan on Agriculture and Rural Development signed in June 2012 provides an appropriate framework for extending collaboration. These are supported by more focused structures, for example, (a) the EU-China Policy Dialogue Support Facility (PDSF) which could do much to share EU experience on agri-environment problems and policies, and (b) the Task Force on Food, Agriculture and Biotechnologies, which could be very important given the vast investments that China is putting in to biotechnology R&D.

There remains the question of how China and the EU can work together to improve food security in Sub-Saharan Africa. A number of EU countries have a long history of engagement with Africa. Some of them still provide a great deal of support both multi-laterally through the CGIAR and bilaterally. Denmark, for example, contributed a great deal in the past through well focused programmes for seed quality improvement and the development veterinary services. China and the EU could work together on such programmes.

## Vulnerability to national and international disasters and the implications for global food security

Responses to such risks have been an important component of GOC policies for many years and have been addressed at various points in this chapter. The risks are both natural and man-made, and can be internal and external in origin. The ones of greatest concern are: (a) natural droughts and floods within the range of past events; (b) man-made disasters, for example, increased flooding from deforestation and disruption of natural drainage systems, (c) climate change and increased frequency of extreme events notably droughts and floods; and pest and disease epidemics.

Risk (a) is a permanent feature of Chinese food production with weather induced losses in grain production occurring annually in one or more regions but normally offset by good production elsewhere.[98] It has been the main driver during the past 50 years or more of China's: (i) food self-sufficiency policies, (ii) high public investment in the expansion of the irrigated area and flood control and more recently in water conservation and improved water use efficiency, (iii) substantial public support for agricultural R&D since 1990 and (iv) heavy investment in food storage facilities, carry-over stocks and supply management mechanisms.

Risks (b) and (c) are addressed by one or more of the above measures but also through China's ecosystem management programmes for reforestation, vulnerable slope lands and wetlands, and her large and world class climate change modelling, monitoring, adaptation and mitigation programmes. These programmes have already made important contributions to food security and will continue to do so. They are complemented by policy shifts to encourage the expansion of food production in the North-East of China which seems likely to be favoured rather than endangered by climate change. In addition and well exemplified by the current situation, is China's geographical diversification of its grain suppliers (as discussed earlier) so that it is less vulnerable to drought in the USA which in recent years has been its main source of maize and soya bean imports.

Risk (d) is minimised by measures (iii) and (iv) for risk (a) but also by the comprehensive mechanisms discussed in section 'Major drivers of food production to prevent pest and disease epidemics'. They are particularly important for preventing livestock disease epidemics from becoming pandemic and causing major food supply disasters at the national and international level.

## Conclusions

The chapter has four key conclusions:

1. Ensuring China's food security to 2020–30 need not pose risks at the national, regional or global level.
2. In the main China could feed itself. It has the capacity to maintain a high level of self-sufficiency except in soya bean, maize and dairy products. However, this will require critical policy and technological changes to re-direct agriculture on to a sustainable growth path that minimises GHG emissions and other negative impacts on the environment.
3. China's net food imports in 2020–30 need not place an unsustainable burden on global agriculture, and could provide agricultural export opportunities for some countries in Sub-Saharan Africa.
4. The implications for the EU are modest but some member countries could make significant contributions to China's food security as a source of commodities, management expertise or technology.

China's net food imports in 2020–30 may be less than other assessments have estimated: firstly, because they over-estimated demand for meat per head, and secondly, they under-estimated the gains in feed use efficiency that are possible over the next 10–20 years and which would lower substantially the indirect demand for maize and soya beans.

The projected net imports of maize and soya beans in 2020–21 are 16 and 54 per cent respectively of projected world trade. Traditional exporters in North and South America can probably supply much of China's needs, and there are potential exporters in Sub-Saharan Africa that could also make an important contribution.

Maintaining high levels of self-sufficiency though technically feasible, particularly given China's substantial funding of agricultural R&D, will need major changes in GOC policies and farmers' practices which are currently unsustainable. The Medium and Long-Term Food Security Plan for 2008–2020 and the twelfth FYP contain some of the measures required. However, more needs to be done to re-direct agricultural subsidies to favour sustainability and tighten the regulatory environment to promote greater fertiliser, water and feed use efficiency.

The main opportunities for the EU are as a supplier of dairy products, a research collaborator for the control of livestock and crop diseases, a source of management expertise for improving the performance of the food production, distribution and marketing chain, and as partner in support to Sub-Saharan African and other developing countries for the sustainable expansion of their agriculture and improvement of their food security.

The longer-term situation is less clear. After 2030, food demand will be relatively stable because of a declining and ageing population, and only modest income related changes will occur in consumption patterns. Small gains in productivity should be able to meet much of the incremental demand and ensure food security. However, uncertainties regarding the impact of climate change on food production present a major challenge for China's long-term food security. It seems quite possible that lack of national and international action in the next 10–20 years to slow down global GHG emissions could seriously disrupt food production and agricultural trade after 2050 and result in widespread food insecurity.

Notwithstanding the latter uncertainties, the overall conclusion for 2012–2030 is that China can continue to meet most of its food security needs, and other countries could make up the balance without placing undue stress on their natural resources. Moreover, three GOC actions support the view that China's food situation poses no risk to global food security and in fact improves it: first, its progressive response to changing comparative advantage by increasing imports of soya bean and other land-intensive commodities, and boosting exports of labour-intensive crops, notably fruit and vegetables; second, through its maintenance of large grain carry-over stocks to buffer against natural disasters, and finally, its strong support for both domestic and developing country agricultural R&D and for S-S technology transfer.

## Notes

1. NSBC (2011) China Statistical Yearbook 2011 (China Statistics Press, Beijing).
2. J. Huang and S. Rozelle (2003) 'Trade Reform, WTO and China's Food Economy in the 21st Century', *Pacific Economic Review*, 8, 143–56.
3. J. Huang, S. Rozelle and M. Chang (2004) 'The Nature of Distortions to Agricultural Incentives in China and Implications of WTO Accession', *World Bank Economic Review*, 18, 59–84.
4. K. Anderson, J. Huang and E. Lanchovichina (2004) 'Will China's WTO Accession Worsen Farm Household Income?'*China Economic Review*, 15, 443–5.
5. J. Huang (2010) 'Sixty Years of China's Agricultural Development and Three Decades of the Reform Miracle: Institutional Innovation, Technological Advancement and Market Reforms', *Journal of Agrotechnical Economics*, 1, 4–18.
6. NBSC (2011) *Statistic Yearbook 2011*, China Statistical Publishing House, Beijing.
7. J. Bai, B. Wahl, B. Lohmar, and J. Huang (2010) 'Food Away from Home in Beijing: Effects of Wealth, Time and "Free Meals"'. *China Economic Review*, 21, 432–41.
8. J. Huang, J. Yang and S. Rozelle (2012) 'Changing Food Consumption Pattern and Demand for Agri-based Industrial Products in China: Implications for Southeast Asia's Agricultural Trade' in P.S. Intal Jr., S. Oum and M. J.O. Simorangkir (eds), *Agricultural Development, Trade and Regional Cooperation in Developing East Asia*, Economic Research Institute for ASEAN and East Asia (ERIA).
9. K. Morton (2012) 'Learning by Doing: China's Role in the Global Governance of Food Security', Working Paper 30, Research Center for Chinese Politics and Business.

10. J. Huang, J. Yang and S. Rozelle (2012) 'Changing Food Consumption Pattern and Demand for Agri-based Industrial Products in China: Implications for Southeast Asia's Agricultural Trade in: Ponciano S. Intal, Jr. Sothea Oum, and Mercy J.O. Simorangkir (eds), 2011, Agricultural Development, Trade and Regional Cooperation in Developing East Asia, Economic Research Institute for ASEAN and East Asia (ERIA).
11. J. Huang, R. Tao, Z. Xu, M. Liu and S. Rozelle (2011) 'China's Agricultural and Rural Development (1978–2008)', Cengage Learning Asia Pte. Led, 2011.
12. J. Y. Lin (1992) 'Rural Reforms and Agricultural Growth in China'. *American Economic Review*, 82, 34–51.
13. J. Huang, and S. Rozelle (1996) 'Technological Change: Rediscovering the Engine of Productivity Trowth in China's Agricultural Economy'. *Journal of Development Economics*, 49, 337–69.
14. K. Chen (2011) 'Foresight Regional Case Study R2. Agricultural R&D as An Engine of Productivity Growth: China'. Foresight. The Future of Food and Farming. Final Project Report. The Government Office for Science, London.
R.Hu, Q. Liang and J. Huang (2009) 'Private Agricultural Research Investments in China: Current Situation and Past Trend', *China Soft Science*, 7, 28–34.
15. *China Daily*, 2012, Scientific input to seed agriculture, 20 February 2012, http://www.chinadaily.com.cn/china/2012-02/02/content_14521995.htm.
16. J. Wang (2000) Innovation of Property Right, Technical Efficiency and Groundwater Irrigation Management in China, PhD thesis, Center for Chinese Agricultural Policy, Beijing.
17. NBSC (2001) Statistics Yearbook 2001, *China Statistical Publishing House*, Beijing.
18. J. Wang, S. Rothausen, D. Conway, L. Zhang, W. Xiong, I. Holman, and Y. Li (2012) China's Water-Energy Nexus: Greenhouse Gas Emissions from Groundwater Use for Agriculture. *Environmental Research Letters*, 7.
19. J. Wang, Z. Xu, J. Huang, and S. Rozelle (2005) 'Incentives in Water Management Reform: Assessing the Effect on Water Use, Production and Poverty in the Yellow River Basin', *Environment and Development Economics*, 10, 769–99.
20. J. Huang and S. Rozelle (2006) 'The Emergence of Agricultural Commodity Markets in China'. *China Economic Review*, 17, 266–80.

21. J. Huang, X. Wang, H. Zhi, Z. Huang and S. Rozelle (2011) 'Subsidies and Distortions in China's Agriculture: Evidence from Producer-level Data'. *Australian Journal of Agricultural and Resource Economics*, 55, pp. 53–71.
22. D. Chadwick (2012) 'Improving Manure Nutrient Management Towards Sustainable Intensification in China', SAIN Policy Brief No. 6.
23. S. Jin, H. Ma, and J. Huang (2010) 'Productivity, Efficiency and Technical Change: Measuring the Performance of China's Transforming Agriculture'. *Journal of Productivity Analysis*, 33 (3), 191–207; L. Hou, Y. Zhang, J. Zhan, and T. Glauben (2012) 'Marginal Revenue of Land and Total Factor Productivity in Chinese Agriculture'. *Journal of Geographical Sciences*, 22 (1): 167–78.
24. D. Norse (2011) 'Greater Food Security and A Better Environment through Improved Nitrogen Fertilizer Management, SAIN Policy Brief No. 2.
25. Y.P. Wei, B. Davidson., D. Chen and R. White (2009) 'Balancing the Economic, Social and Environmental Dimensions of Agro-ecosystems: An Integrated modelling Approach'. *Agriculture, Environment and Ecosystem*, 131, 263–73.
26. J. Guo, X. Liu, Y. Zhang, J. Shen, W. Han, W. Zhang, P. Christie, K. Goulding, P. Vitousek and F. Zhang (2010) 'Significant Acidification in Major Chinese Croplands', *Science* 327, 1008–1010.
27. R. Ash, R. Porter and T. Summers (2012) China, the EU and China's Twelfth Five-year Programme, Europe China Research and Advice Network, London.
28. L. R. Brown (1995) *Who Will Feed China? Wake-Up Call for a Small Planet* (Worldwatch Institute, Washington, DC).
29. N. Alexandratos (1996) 'China's Projected Cereals Deficits in a World Context'. *Agricultural Economics*, 15, 1–16.
30. S. Fan and M. Agcaoili-Sombilla (1997) 'Why projections on China's Future Food Supply and Demand Differ'. *Australian Journal of Agricultural and Resource Economics*, 41, 169–90.
31. P. Huffstutter and S. Niu (2012)'Insight: U.S. Barnyards help China Super-size Food Production'. Reuters. 20 April. Available at: http://www.reuters.com/article/2012/04/20/us-usa-china-food-idUSBRE83J05R20120420.
32. F. Zai (2011) 'Meat and Dairy Consumption Transition and Nutrition Transition in China', Presented at UK China Workshop

'*Consuming Livestock*: Food Security, Climate Change, Livelihoods and Animal Welfare', 7–8 June, 2011, Beijing.

33. Ibid.
34. S. Msangi and M.W. Rosegrant (2011) Feeding the Future's Changing Diets: Implications for Agriculture Markets, Nutrition, and Policy , 2020 Conference Paper 3, Leveraging Agriculture for Improving Nutrition and Health, 10–12 February 2011; New Delhi, India.
35. FAO (2012) Food and Agriculture Outlook 2015/30, FAO, Rome.
36. T. Masuda and P.D. Goldsmith (2010) 'China's Meat Consumption: An Income Elasticity Analysis and Long-Term Projections'. Poster prepared for presentation at the Agricultural and Applied Economics Association 2010 AAEA, CAES, and WAEA Joint Annual Meeting, Denver, Colorado, 25–27 July, 2010. National Soya bean Research Laboratory and University of Illinois. http://ageconsearch.umn.edu/bitstream/61601/2/Poster11972AAEA_MasudaGoldsmith20100503b.pdf.
37. H. Xiao, J. Wang, L. Oxley and H. Ma (2012) 'The Evolution of Hog Production and Potential Sources for Future Growth in China'. *Food Policy*, 37, 366–77.
38. J. Huang, J. Yang and S. Rozelle (2012) 'Changing Food Consumption Pattern and Demand for Agri-based Industrial Products in China: Implications for Southeast Asia's Agricultural Trade' in P.S. Intal Jr., S. Oum and M.J.O. Simorangkir (eds), Agricultural Development, Trade and Regional Cooperation in Developing East Asia.
39. China's US sorghum buys 'far bigger than thought'. Agrimoney.com – available at http://www.agrimoney.com/news/news.php?id=6118, accessed 5 August 2013.
40. H. Qiu, J. Huang, M. Keyzer and W. van Veen (2008) 'Policy Options for China's Bio-ethanol Development and the Implications for Its Agricultural Economy', *China and World Economy*, 16, 112–24.
41. H. Qiu, J. Huang, M. Keyzer, W. van Veen, S. Rozelle, G. Fisher, and T. Ernolieva (2011) 'Biofuel Development, Food Security and the Use of Marginal Land in China', *Journal of Environmental Quality*, 40, 1058–1067.
42. A. Hu and J. Liang ( 2011) 'China's Green Era Begins' in *China's Green Revolution: Energy, Environment and the 12th Five-Year Plan*, China Dialogue, http://www.chinadialogue.net/

UserFiles/File/PDF_ebook001.pdf, accessed on 18 October 2012.

43. J. Huang (2012) Views on China's Food Security and Trade, unpublished, Center for Chinese Agricultural Policy.
44. Ministry of Agriculture, 2012, 'The Twelfth Five Year Plan for Agricultural and Rural Economy'.
45. L. Guo, J. Lindsay and P. Munro-Faure (2008) 'China: Integrated Land Policy Reform in a Context of Rapid Urbanisation', *Agricultural and Rural Development Notes: Land Policy and Administration*, issue 36. (World Bank, Washington DC).
46. J. Liu, M. Liu, H. Tian, D. Zhuang, Z. Zhang, W. Zhang, X. Tang, and X. Deng (2005) 'Spatial and Temporal Patterns of China's Cropland during 1990–2000: An Analysis Based on Landsat TM Data'. *Remote Sensing of Environment*, 98, 442–56.
47. S. Tan, N. Heerink, G. Kruseman and F. Qu (2008) 'Do Fragmented Land Holdings Have Higher Production Costs? Evidence from Rice Farmers in Northeastern Jiangxi Province, P.R. China'. *China Economic Review*, 19, 347–58.
48. S. Feng, N. Heerink, R. Ruben, and F. Qu (2010) 'Land Rental Market, Off-farm Employment and Agricultural Production in Southeast China: A Plot-level Case Study', *China Economic Review*, 21, 598–606.
49. R. F. Ash (2011) Feeding Billions: Food Security in China, ISN Security Watch. Available at www.isn.ethz.ch/Digital-Library/Articles/Detail/?lng=en&id=127105ý.
50. V. Smil (1996) 'Environmental Problems in China: Estimates of Economic Costs'. East-West Center, Honolulu, Hawaii.
51. C. Carter, F. Zhong and Jing Zhu (2012) 'Advances in Chinese Agriculture and Its Global Implications'. *Applied Economics and Policy*, 34 (1): 1–36.
52. L. Jin and W. Young (2001) 'Water Use in Agriculture in China: Importance, Challenges, and Implications for Policy'. *Water Policy*, 3 (3), 215.
53. USDA (2011) 'China Peoples Republic, Grain and Feed Annual'. GAIN Report No CH1014 USDA Washington, DC.
54. W. Xiong, D. Conway, E. Lin, Y. Xu, H. Ju, J. Jiang, I. Holman, and Y. Li (2009) 'Future Cereal Production in China: The Interaction of Climate Change, Water Availability and Socio-economic Scenarios', *Global Environmental Change*, 19, 34–44.

55. Ibid.
56. P. Wu, J. Jiming Jin and X. Zhao (2010) 'Impact of Climate Change and Irrigation Technology Advancement on Agricultural Water use in China', *Climatic Change*, 100, 797–805.
57. As note 54.
58. D Norse (2005) 'Non-point Pollution from Crop Production: Global, Regional and National Issues'. *Pedosphere*, 15, 499–508.
59. MEP (2010) 'Technical Guideline on Environmental Safety Application of Chemical Fertilizers', National Environmental Protection Standard, HJ555-2010.
60. D. Norse (2011) 'Greater Food Security and a Better environment through Improved Nitrogen Fertilizer Management', SAIN Policy Brief No. 2.
61. Though none of the global circulation models they use can satisfactorily examine the impact of an increase in frequency of extreme events nor do the assessments give adequate consideration to the impact of climate change on livestock production.
62. J. Guo, X. Liu, Y. Zhang, J. Shen, W. Han, W. Zhang, P. Christie, K. Goulding, P. Vitousek and F. Zhang (2010) 'Significant Acidification in Major Chinese Croplands', *Science* 327, 1008–10.
63. As note 58.
64. S. Wilkinson, D. Mills, R. Illidge and W.J. Davies (2011) 'How Is Ozone Pollution Reducing our Food Supply?', *J. Experimental Botany*, 63, 527–36.
65. X. Wang, W. Manning, Z. Feng and Y. Zhu (2007) 'Ground-level Ozone in China: Distribution and Effect on Crop Yields', *Environmental Pollution*, 147, 394–400.
66. Feed Conversion Efficiency for Livestock Producers in China: Implications for Feed Ingredient Demand and the Production of Livestock Products. A Feport by the Center for Chinese Agricultural Policy, Chinese Academy of Sciences in conjunction with Bunge China Research.
67. As note 37.
68. S. Nuiping (2012) 'Factbox: China's Voracious Appetite Spurs Farm Expansion'. Reuters, 20 April, available at http://www.reuters.com/article/2012/04/20/us-usa-china-food-factbox-idUSBRE83J05V20120420.
69. F. Zhong and J. Zhu (2005) 'Improving Security and Efficiency of the Government Grain Reserve System' in B. H. Sonntag, J. Huang, S. Rozelle and J H. Skerritt (eds) *China's Agricultural*

*and Rural development in the Early 21st Century.* ACIAR Monograph No. 116.

70. State Council, (1996) White Paper – Grains Issues in China.
71. J. Huang and R. Scott (1998) *China's Grain Economy toward the 21st Century.* China's Agricultural Press, Beijing; J. Huang, J. Yang and H. Qiu (2012) 'Reflections on the National Food Security Strategies and Policies in New Era', *Issues in Agricultural Economy*, 3, 4–8.
72. Royal Society (2009) 'Reaping the Benefits: Science and the Sustainable Intensification of Global Agriculture'; Foresight (2011) 'The Future of Food and Farming', Final Project Report (The Government Office for Science, London).
73. J. Huang, J. Yang and H. Qiu (2012) 'Reflections on the National Food Security Strategies and Policies in New Era', *Issues in Agricultural Economy*, 3, 4–8.
74. The Future of Food and Farming – Foresight Reports Implications for China (2012) (Government Office for Science, London).
75. As note 73.
76. H. Zhang and C. Zhao (2009) *The Basic Framework of Agricultural Policies in China* (Chinese Finance and Economic Press, Beijing).
77. X. Li, F. Qu, and W. Yun (2009) 'The Temporal and Spatial Distribution of China's Construction Land Increment', *China Rural Economy*, 4.
78. As note 45.
79. T. Liu, F. Qu, J. Jin, X. Shi (2008) 'Impact of Land Fragmentation and Land Transfer on Farmers' Land Use Efficiency', *Resource Science*, 10, 1511–1516.
80. L. Sheng, X. Guan and J. Jiang, (2009) 'Impact of Land Use Right Transfer on Food Security in China', *Modern Agricultural Science and Technology*, 9, 278–280.
81. Y. Huang, H. Zhang, W. Li and Q. Liu (2011) 'Investigation and Reflection on Rural Land Transfer', *Issues in Agricultural Economy*, 5, 4–9, 110.
82. R. F. Ash, 2011, Feeding Billions: Food Security in China, ISN Security Watch.
83. CCAP runs food projection based on its CAPSiM model and updates its projection every half year.
84. USDA (2012) *Agricultural Projections to 2021 Report No OCE-2012-1.* (USDA, Washington DC).
85. USDA (2012) as note 80.

86. E. Contini, and G. Martha (2011) 'Climate Change and Food security: Brazil', Presentation at International Conference on Climate Change and Food Security, 6–8 November 2011, CAAS/IFPRI, Beijing, China.
87. USDA (2012) as note 80.
88. As note 80.
89. FAO (2002) *World Agriculture: Towards 2015/30* (FAO, Rome).
90. Unpublished FAO supply utilisation accounts.
91. L. Mathews (2012) Global Sugar Market Review, Commodities: Agri Updates 18 January 2012, Commonwealth Bank of Australia.
92. OECD-FAO (2011) *Agricultural Outlook 2011–2020*, OECD Paris, June 2012.
93. FAO GAEZ Data Portal http://gaez.fao.org/Main.html accessed 28 August 2012.
94. G. Fischer and M. Shah (2010) Farmland Investments and Food Security. International Institute for Applied Systems Analysis, Laxenburg, Austria, for the World Bank.
95. L. Cotula, S. Vermeulen, R. Leonard and J. Keeley (2009) 'Land Grab or Development Opportunity?' *Agricultural Investment and Dand Deals in Africa*. (Rome and London: FAO, IFAD and IIED).
96. J. Huang, R. Hu, S. Rozelle and C. Pray (2005) 'Insect-Resistant GM Rice in Farmer Fields: Assessing Productivity and Health Effects in China', *Science*, 308, 688–90.
97. As note 68.
98. J.Wong and Y. Huang (2012) 'China's Food Security and Its Global Implication'. *China: An International Journal*, 10, 113–24.

# 8 Migration from China to the EU: The Challenge within Europe

*Bin Wu and Kevin Latham*

## Introduction

As a part of China's rise and 'going global' strategy since the late 1990s, more and more Chinese citizens have joined the flow of international migration (Wang and Liu, 2011). The unprecedented process of Chinese international migration has had a profound impact on major destinations in various ways.

With regard to Europe, the literature on Chinese immigration can be roughly divided into three areas: works dealing with the international movement and working conditions of low- or un-skilled Chinese immigrants (Pieke et al., 2004; Gao, 2010; Pai, 2008; Zanin and Wu, 2012; Wu and Liu, 2013); those looking at Chinese international student migration and circulation (Shen, 2009; GHK, 2011) and those considering the history and latest developments of Chinese diasporic communities (Benton and Pieke, 1998; Chan, 2005; Benton and Gomez, 2008). It is commonly recognised, furthermore, that overseas Chinese communities in Europe and beyond are diverse, segmented and fragmented, which prevent them integrating into the mainstream society (Liu and Hou, 2010; Wang and Liu, 2011; Wu and Sheehan 2011; Liu, Hong, 2013). With respect to the on-going transformation within local Chinese communities in Europe, it is important to ask: how has the new wave of Chinese immigration influenced Chinese communities in Europe and what are the new challenges for the community development and integration? The above questions will be addressed through an analysis of official information,[1] plus our own observations in Veneto and Prato, Italy (Zanin and Wu, 2012; Latham, 2011a, 2011b) and the East Midlands, UK (Wu et al., 2010). This chapter attempts to shed new light on the links between the latest developments in Chinese international immigration, changes in local Chinese communities in destination countries and their processes of integration.

## Chinese Immigration and Its Impact on the Growth of the Chinese Diaspora in the EU

China's economic reform and open door policies starting from the late 1970s have resulted in not only large scale capital and commodity flows across its borders but also increasing mobility of its citizens both internally and internationally (Benton and Pieke, 1998; Li and Roulleau-Berger 2012; Yeung, 2002). In relation to the new wave of Chinese international migration, furthermore, we have witnessed rapid growth in the overseas Chinese population world-wide. According to an estimate by Gui (2011: 54–5), the total overseas Chinese population worldwide has increased from 27 million in 1983 to 40 million in 2000 and 45 million in 2007. Despite a small share (less than 5 per cent) of the world total, Europe has experienced a rapid growth in the Chinese population from 0.60 million in 1980 to 1.45 million in 2000 and jumping to 2.15 million in 2007 (see Table 8.1). With a focus on the period from 2000 to 2007, in particular, the growth rate in Europe was about 48.3 per cent, considerably higher than the 12.5 per cent global growth rate over the same period. The impact of the new wave of Chinese immigrants varies greatly with region. Compared with other regions, Europe is more sensitive with regard to the new wave of Chinese immigrants due to the relatively small size of the Chinese population in the past and its low profile in public perception (Wang and Liu, 2011: 109–113, 166–171).

With a focus on the EU, the impact of the new wave of Chinese immigration in local Chinese communities varies greatly from country to country (see Table 8.1).[2] Some 87 per cent are concentrated in the top six countries by size of Chinese population: the UK, France, Italy, Spain, Germany, and the Netherlands. This is due partly to the colonial history of the UK and France and to the work, benefits and commercial opportunities available in those four states. Italy and Spain have implemented amnesties for illegal immigrants over the past couple of decades, and Italy has been a convenient place for Chinese to conduct business, particularly in the grey and black markets.

Table 8.1 also highlights (in italics) those countries which have experienced fast growth in the Chinese population over the last decade.[4] The majority of these countries are more peripheral countries of Europe (Italy, Spain, Portugal, Greece and Ireland), with their own histories of emigration in the past.

A number of observations can be drawn from Table 8.1. First, the new cohort of Chinese immigrants has, to varying degrees, made a significant contribution to an expansion of local Chinese communities in almost all EU member countries since the late 1990s. Second, we have witnessed accelerating growth of

**Table 8.1** Growth and distribution of the Chinese population in the EU, 1998–2008

| Rank | Country | 1998 | 2008 | 2008/1998 |
|---|---|---|---|---|
| 1 | *United Kingdom* | *250,000* | *600,000* | *2.40* |
| 2 | France | 225,000 | 500,000 | 2.22 |
| 3 | *Italy* | *70,000* | *300,000* | *4.29* |
| 4 | *Spain* | *35,000* | *168,000* | *4.80* |
| 5 | Germany | 100,000 | 160,000 | 1.60 |
| 6 | Netherlands | 127,500 | 150,000 | 1.18 |
| 7 | *Ireland* | *10,000* | *60,000* | *6.0* |
| 8 | Belgium | 23,000 | 40,000 | 1.74 |
| 9 | Austria | 20,000 | 40,000 | 2.0 |
| 10 | *Portugal* | *2,700* | *30,000* | *11.1* |
| 11 | *Sweden* | *12,800* | *30,000* | *2.34* |
| 12 | Denmark | 12,800 | 18,000 | 1.41 |
| 13 | *Greece* | *600* | *12,000* | *20.0* |
| 14 | Hungary | 10,000 | 16,000 | 1.60 |
| 15 | *Romania* | *3,000* | *10,000* | *3.33* |
| | Other | 16,320 | 19,970 | 0.54 |
| | EU Total | 939,720 | 2,153,970 | 2.29 |

*Source*: 2008 data are based upon an estimate by the European Chinese Association. The 1998 data are from Minghuan Li, 'Analysis of Chinese population in Contemporary Europe'. Both sets are quoted in Qu et al., 2011: 23, 57.[3]

Chinese populations not only in the new destination countries in southern Europe but also in those old destinations in western and northern Europe such as the UK, France and Germany.

## Factors Behind the New Wave of Chinese Immigration

Having identified the new wave of Chinese immigrants and its contribution to the growth of local Chinese communities in host countries in the last decade or so, this section attempts to identify some of the principal factors which have played a significant role in fostering this process. In particular, we concern ourselves with state-owned enterprise (SOE) reform, China-Europe trade, rising consumer power and inequalities in China, as well as the internationalisation of higher education.

*State-owned enterprise (SOE) reform.* In the late 1990s, SOE reform led to the closure or transfer of hundreds of thousands of small and medium-sized SOEs into private hands or joint venture administration with tens of millions of SOE employees being made redundant (CLIN, 1999). The effects of SOE reform varied greatly from region to region: Northeast China (or *Dongbei* in Chinese), the country's heavy industrial heartland and home to many SOE workers, was one of the most seriously affected regions. The vast majority of redundant workers were forced to migrate to other regions of China or to seek employment in the service sector, but a large number of former SOE employees also went abroad, mainly to Europe, in search of alternative business and job opportunities (Blanchard and Maffeo, 2011: 74–5). This has reshaped Chinese immigrant communities in Europe in terms of both local Chinese labour supply, and the geographical location of communities sending emigrants in mainland China. As a result, the proportion of Europe's Dongbei Chinese immigrant population has been growing rapidly, making people from that region a more prominent and influential group in some Chinese communities alongside those new immigrants from south China (mainly from Zheijiang and Fujian provinces).[5]

*China-Europe trade.* China's rise in the international community has seen an increasing interconnection and interdependence between China and Europe in all fields. This includes international trade and mutual investment, which has provided a sound base and strong demand for international migration. From 1999 to 2009 for instance, international trade between China and Europe increased from US$68.1 billion to US$427 billion, slightly faster than the average total growth rate of China's total international trade. Foreign direct investment (FDI) from Europe to China has remained fairly constant, increasing by only 15 per cent over this period even though the total scale of FDI has doubled. By contrast, there has been a rapid growth of outward direct investment (ODI) from China to Europe, from just US$500million in 2005 to over US$3 billion in 2009, an increase of 6.6 times in just four years. The rapid development of China-Europe economic collaboration in the past decade has had a profound impact on Chinese international migration to Europe in several ways. These include the diversification of Chinese business interests away from the traditional catering sector to other areas of commerce, manufacturing and personal services (Pastore and Castagnone, 2011: 9; Cologna, 2011) ranging from the sale of everyday items and hardware to traditional Chinese medicine and services, such as accommodation and catering, for the increasing number of Chinese tourists and business delegations coming to Europe (Arlt, 2006). It has also led to increasing demand for Chinese international migration in order to fill job vacancies in different sectors within local Chinese communities and beyond. For instance, many Europe-based small Chinese businesses, such as the tailoring and leather-goods manufacturers in Italy and France, employ almost entirely Chinese staff. Increasing business, which often means greater imports of materials from China, also means increasing staff levels and in turn greater demand for immigrants (Ma, 2011).

*Rising consumer power and inequalities in China.* The increasing importance of China in the world economy results from not only the rapid growth of its capital and commodity outflows, but also the purchasing power of Chinese citizens abroad, leading to the increasing demand for products and services in or from the EU. A good example reflecting this demand is the increasing popularity of outbound tourism (Arlt, 2006; CASS, 2011; CTA, 2011; Latham, 2011a) with more and more Chinese tourists visiting Europe in recent years. In 2010, trips to Europe, which numbered around 3.1 million, accounted for more than 20 per cent of all Chinese outbound tourism (excluding travel to Hong Kong and Macao) (ITB, 2011). Official statistics also foresee an annual growth in outbound tourism of between 15 and 20 per cent over the next few years (CTA, 2011). This tourism is strongly associated with the consumption of luxury goods (Moore, 2011) and also with investment migration and property purchasing in European cities such as London, Paris and Milan.

Although the vast majority of Chinese citizens have gained in some way from China's rise, the distribution of the benefits of its economic development have been quite uneven, with economic and social inequality increasing between different social groups. For instance, rural incomes continue to rise at a slower rate than urban incomes, leading to increasing income gaps between urban and rural residents in term of the ratio of annual net income per capita from 2.65 times in 1999 to 3.33 times in 2009 (see NBS, 2010). This uneven development has been closely associated with increasing rural-to-urban migration in China (Sun, 2007; Pieke and Mallee, 1999), and it has two important consequences for international migration. First, social inequality and discrimination, for instance against rural-to-urban migrant workers (Yan, 2003) is a major factor driving some Chinese people, including both rural and urban residents, to seek economic opportunities in Europe (Christiansen, 2003), even via illegal channels. Second, the authors' fieldwork in Europe has found that income inequalities, which reflect social stratification and labour market segregation in China, have also influenced economic and social structures in overseas Chinese communities in Europe, resulting in poor working conditions and forced labour in some European Chinese businesses (Wu et al., 2010; Zanin and Wu, 2012).

*The internationalisation of higher education.* The number of Chinese students coming to the EU has shown strong growth in the past decade. Chinese student numbers in the EU in 2010 were approximately six times those in 2000 (GHK, 2011: 18). It is difficult to give precise figures for student numbers but national statistics compiled by the European Commission and the Chinese Ministry of Education suggest that there were around 120,000 Chinese students in the EU in 2011 (GHK, 2011: 18). However, this figure should be taken as indicative rather than as a precise representation of student numbers, and more generous estimates would put it nearer 200,000.[6] These students come almost entirely from China's growing middle classes, who now find themselves with sufficient disposable income to send their children overseas to study. Many Chinese students return to China on completion of their studies but employment opportunities in the EU entice many to stay on. Consequently, the trend towards increasing numbers of Chinese students in the EU is also contributing to larger numbers of highly educated and white-collar immigrants.[7]

## New Features and Changes within Chinese Communities

Recent developments in Chinese international migration since the late 1990s have had a profound impact on local Chinese communities in the EU in a number of ways, bringing both new opportunities and new challenges relating to community development and integration. This section highlights some of the key changes that have occurred within Chinese communities in recent years and considers the implications for issues of integration. Further challenging issues will be dealt with in the next section.

### The transformation of the Chinese ethnic economy

The most salient impact of the new cohort of Chinese immigrants is perhaps an on-going or accelerating process of the transformation of Chinese ethnic economies in terms of industrial structure or ownership since the late 1990s. The former refers to the diversification of Chinese ethnic economic activities, leading to a significant growth of new business sectors such as retailers, tourism and student services in host countries. The latter is related to the emergence of new Chinese entrepreneurs as so many new immigrants have arrived in Europe who have different profiles from the old cohort of Chinese entrepreneurs in terms of the region of origin, educational level, professional background, and principles or visions of business operation.

Bearing in mind the great variation in Chinese businesses across EU member countries, it is impossible to generalise about the transformation of Chinese economies. Instead, drawing upon secondary data and our own observations in Italy and the UK, we would like to illustrate some recent developments in Chinese businesses in these countries.

Taking Milan, for example, until recently Chinese there were employed predominantly in shops selling Chinese goods, in catering, import-export companies and wholesale; some were also in fashion manufacturing and selling. Furthermore, in recent years some Chinese have even come to corner markets for some non-Chinese ethnic cuisines, running bars selling Latin American food to Latin American immigrants for instance (Cologna, 2011). Chinese now run wedding shops, newspaper stands, barber's shops, tailors, grocery shops and much more. Indeed, in 2012 the number of Chinese businesses offering personal services such as hairdressing, nail treatments or massage increased by 38.8 per cent compared with 2011 to more than 2,500 businesses (Europe China News, 2013). Many of these businesses are serving the general Milanese community, including Italians and immigrants of all kinds. In fact, there are indications that many Chinese, even first-generation immigrants, are changing their attitude to learning languages. Many are now learning basic conversational Italian, Arabic and Spanish because it is good for business (Cologna, 2011).

This kind of diversification is also happening elsewhere in Europe. In London, for instance, the past five years have seen a plethora of Chinese traditional medicine shops opening across the city. Many Chinese have opened nail parlours and it is becoming usual to find Chinese hairdressers and shops selling Chinese goods. This constitutes a significant diversification of Chinese business in the UK, which was for decades heavily concentrated on the catering industry.

The transformation of Chinese economies in the EU is not limited to the diversification of businesses alone but also relates to the changing Chinese entrepreneurial landscape in terms of place of origin. Taking the East Midlands in the UK as an example, our observations conducted in 2009, indicated that of a total of 61 Chinese businesses, including Chinese restaurants or take-aways, Chinese retailers and herbal medicine shops, over half (52.4 per cent) were controlled by established Chinese groups including Hong Kongers and other overseas Chinese from Malaysia and Vietnam, 30 per cent owned by Southern Chinese, mainly from Fujian and Guangdong, and the remaining one quarter were Dongbeinese or other Northern Chinese (e.g. Shandong, Inner Mongolia, Jilin). The Fujian, Guangdong and Dongbeinese groups between them owned or controlled nearly half of the Chinese businesses in the area, which, just a decade earlier were totally owned by Hong Kong and other established Chinese diasporic groups.

## Mobility and transnationality of Chinese entrepreneurs

Another distinctive characteristic related to the new wave of Chinese immigrants to the EU is their mobility and transnationality. Many Chinese stay in a place only for a few years before moving somewhere else, possibly within the same country but also often elsewhere in Europe. This mobility is especially visible within the Schengen treaty zone, where travelling between the countries with the largest Chinese populations, such as those in Italy, France, Spain and Germany, without a visa is possible.[8]

The transnationality of Chinese immigrants in Europe – the way that they live lives that are regularly informed or shaped by relationships, connections and social practices that cross or defy national boundaries[9] – can be partly understood in terms of this kind of mobility. The fact that many immigrants do not feel limited by national boundaries but extend their vision to other EU countries when making choices about their life and future in relation to work, education, business or family is an indication of how their lives are transnational. And many Chinese immigrants lead lives that are transnational in other senses. Especially noteworthy are their relationships with China, often conducted through media of one form or another (see below) and the way in which Europe is for many just one possible destination among several. Indeed, in recent years, with the downturn in the European economy, destinations such as Africa and South America have started to look more appealing to many immigrants or would-be immigrants with a keen eye for emerging business opportunities (Polyzou, 2011).

The diverse opportunities available to Chinese overseas are related at least in part to China's increasingly visible and active presence on the global stage. For example, Chinese government organisations and Chinese businesses investing in Africa, South America and Southeast Asia contribute to building up Chinese ethnic business networks in those countries. And Chinese outward direct investment, which, as we have seen, has been rising sharply in recent years, creates opportunities and markets for Chinese workers and entrepreneurs (Ma, 2011).

## The emergence and influence of new media

New media, predominantly the Internet and mobile phones and including new kinds of digital social media, has been increasingly popular amongst Chinese immigrants in the last decade.[10] With a great potential to influence the degree of integration of Chinese communities in Europe, they have been recognised as an important factor in diasporic identity construction and daily life among overseas Chinese (see, e.g., Sun, 2002; 2007). Chinese in Europe have for years been watching satellite and cable relays of China Central Television's (CCTV) overseas channels while reading a range of Chinese-language newspapers in Europe, where there are more than a hundred Chinese-language newspaper and magazine publishers (Zhou, 2011). Chinese-language newspapers have long played a central role in providing Chinese communities with news about Chinese community leaders in Europe and also important classified advertisements for those seeking work or to buy or sell businesses or other property.

However, an ever more important feature of overseas Chinese communities is their now extensive reliance upon new media. New media are accompanying a transformation of the way of life of overseas Chinese communities in Europe. They open up new links to China as well as to other Chinese in Europe or other parts of the world and also offer new opportunities for business, communication, entertainment and information-gathering. Although new media have been widely available for more than a decade, there has been a major expansion of new media use in recent years. In particular, online video and broadcasting have opened up new modes of mass media consumption, e.g. online television, radio and newspapers, while social media have created new possibilities for Chinese immigrants to link up with each other for social, business or leisure purposes.

In many parts of Europe, Chinese immigrants are now watching local television stations from China, e.g. Zhejiang Television or Wenzhou Television, over the Internet. They also often access Chinese newspapers and general Chinese web portals such as Sina.com, Sohu.com or QQ.com. The Internet is also used widely for instant messaging with other Chinese both in Europe and back in China, with QQ probably the most popular service. Some Chinese also read and write blogs and micro-blogs while many participate in online bulletin board system discussions. The Internet is also used widely for gathering news and information of all kinds and, perhaps most of all, as a medium for entertainment, such as online gaming, watching online television and film and downloading music.

In recent years, new media have played a big part in forming notions of identity among second-generation European Chinese. In the UK, websites such as www.dimsum.co.uk or www.britishchineseonline.com have created new spaces for reflection, dialogue and debate, information-sharing and expressions of emotional support (Song, 2011). Similar websites in other European countries have played a corresponding role. In countries such as the UK and the Netherlands, where the principal economic activity of overseas Chinese has been in the catering sector, a strong sense of community among Chinese was often lacking before the possibilities that new media offer. Chinese families, often running the one Chinese restaurant or take-away in a small town or village, had very little contact with other Chinese people. New media can thus be associated in some cases with the formation of a sense of second-generation Chinese diasporic identity (Parker and Song, 2006).

With the growing significance of new media in various aspects of identity-formation among Chinese immigrants in Europe, it is clear that new media have the potential both to link immigrants more strongly to their home communities and to detach them further from the immediate contexts of their host countries (Denison and Johanson, 2009; Johanson and Fladrich, 2011). However, Chinese immigrant media can also work to encourage better integration and affiliation with host communities (Zhou et al., 2006; Zhao, 2006).

## New Challenges Facing Chinese Communities

A range of complex factors including language and different cultural traditions have meant that the processes of integration of Chinese international migrants and overseas Chinese communities world-wide has been varied and uneven (Liu and Hou, 2010). Thinking of integration as a process of effective communication, interaction and cooperation of all Chinese groups with their counterparts in mainstream societies, this section aims to highlight a number of challenging issues facing Chinese communities: changes to immigration policies in many EU countries and social isolation and poor working conditions of Chinese migrant workers in some Chinese-owned workplaces.

### Impact of immigration policies

Given the increasing demand for Chinese migrant workers in host countries across the EU, it may be useful to consider a specific example. Table 8.2 illustrates the development of Chinese businesses registered in Veneto since the 1970s and strong demands for Chinese labour in Chinese-owned workplaces including Chinese catering, manufacturing, trade and retail shops up until the early 2000s. The rapid growth in the number of Chinese businesses led to a shortage in Chinese labour in many of them. Despite many amnesties in Italy and other countries (Denison and Johanson, 2009; Soothill, 2010), according to our observation (Zanin and Wu, 2012), irregular migrant workers accounted for up to 20 per cent of the total of Chinese workers in those factories sampled for that research.

A similar story can be told relating to the growth of Chinese catering outlets in the UK from 15,000 in 2001 to 17,500 in 2008. One recent estimate suggested that this new growth in labour demand led to a shortfall of more than 60,000 Chinese workers out of a potential 100,000 job opportunities (Lam, 2009). As a result, the shortage of Chinese migrant workers has become a serious issue facing Chinese businesses and the Chinese community in the UK. The gaps between the demand for and the supply of Chinese migrant workers via legal channels in the UK and other EU countries have inevitably led to

**Table 8.2** Chinese entrepreneurs registered in the trade chambers in Veneto, 1970–2005

| Sector | 1970–9 | 1980–9 | 1990–9 | 2000–5 |
|---|---|---|---|---|
| Bar/café/restaurant | 6 | 30 | 132 | 609 |
| Trade/retail | 0 | 3 | 61 | 934 |
| Factories | 0 | 1 | 104 | 1,299 |
| Other activities | 0 | 1 | 15 | 61 |
| Total | 6 | 35 | 312 | 2,903 |

*Source*: Elaboration by Valter Zanin based on data from InfoCamere, Unioncamere, Veneto, Italy (see Zanin, 2012).

the establishment and development of international networks for irregular migration from China to Europe (Chen, 2003).

The dependency upon irregular migrant workers in many Chinese businesses has serious consequences in terms of integration. First, it prevents Chinese businesses and Chinese communities from opening up to their host societies for fear of incurring penalties for the employment of irregular migrant workers. Second, it also deters Chinese migrant workers from communicating more fully with their local host communities through fear of the discovery of illegalities in their situation, about the potential loss of work opportunities and even deportation.

The constraints of migration policies have become even more salient in recent years. Owing to the global economic recession, many EU countries have adjusted immigration policies, leading to tougher border controls and efforts to clamp down on illegal immigration. As a case in point, the Italian town of Prato, for decades a fortress of the centre-left Italian parties, has been ruled since 2009 by a centre-right local government elected on the basis of a heavily anti-immigration, and particularly anti-Chinese-immigration, agenda. Since coming to power, the local government has sought to crack-down on illegal businesses, tax evasion, poor working conditions in Chinese workshops and other regulation violations such as rubbish disposal. This has led to tension not only between the two sections of the local population but also between the Chinese embassy and the authorities in Rome. It is too early to assess fully the impact of such hardening attitudes on immigration trends. However, initial indications are that they may deter some immigrants from coming to Prato and encourage others to consider moving, either as individuals or businesses, elsewhere in Italy or Europe.[11]

As immigration has become a more sensitive political issue in some major European countries, e.g. the UK and France (see Kofman et al., 2010), some countries have introduced stricter controls on immigration. After the UK general election in 2010, for instance, the coalition government followed through a Conservative Party election pledge to introduce a cap on the number of immigrants coming into the country from non-EU countries. The UK authorities have also introduced a range of measures aimed at reducing both regular and irregular non-EU immigration. Among them are tighter rules for Tier 4 visa applications (UKIN, 2011a), limitations on Tier 2 intra-company transfer visas (UKIN, 2011b), the introduction of biometric residence permits for immigrants (UKIN, 2011c) and tightening language test requirements for Tiers 1, 2 and 4 visa applicants (UKIN, 2011d).[12]

From the integration perspective, a friendly and mutually respective environment could be very helpful for those new Chinese migrant workers to develop their confident and effective communication channels with local counterparts including trade unions and civil society organisations for mutual understanding and support. In this regard, the changes of immigration policies in many countries may have a negative impact on those vulnerable immigrants who could benefit most from contact and communication with local host communities.

## Social isolation of Chinese migrant workers

The difficulty Chinese migrant workers encounter in integrating into local communities is not only caused by tougher immigration policies in host countries, but is also related to the structure of overseas Chinese communities which are characterised by closure, segmentation and fragmentation (Liu and Hou, 2010; Wu, 2010; Liu, 2013: 231–6). As a result, Chinese migrant workers are the most vulnerable group at the bottom of Chinese communities, whose voices, needs and sufferings can hardly be heard from the outside.

The nature of the social isolation experienced by Chinese migrant workers, according to our observation in Italy and the UK (Wu et al., 2010; Wu and Sheehan, 2011), can be measured by paying attention to the following features: whether or not their voices are to be heard by either the outside (local mainstream societies) or inside (Chinese community members); whether there exist channels for them to express their interests and communicate to other groups; whether or not there are external resources and social support available to them. Social isolation among Chinese migrant workers is therefore the most challenging issue facing Chinese communities in host countries.

There are many factors contributing to the social isolation of Chinese migrant workers today. Besides the Chinese community structure, according to our empirical studies, the following factors cannot be ignored.

- Poor language skills which prevent most of them from finding job opportunities with employers other than Chinese.
- Dependence upon Chinese employers or other Chinese community support groups in terms of not only employment opportunities but also other services such as translation, accommodation, dealing with bureaucracy and transport.
- Short-term vision or thinking focused upon making money to relieve poverty or service heavy loans for their international migration.
- Underdeveloped civil society organisations within Chinese communities capable of properly representing Chinese migrant workers.

Social isolation as a key indicator reflecting the poor status of Chinese integration in the new century has many negative consequences for Chinese migrant workers regarding both physical and mental health. The former can be seen in the difficulties that migrant workers face in accessing local medical services, for example, leading them to frequent popular underground Chinese clinics with a range of potential risks involved (Wu and Zanin, 2009). The latter are evident from many mental health issues amongst Chinese migrant workers (Wu et al., 2010).

## Poor working conditions and forced labour in some Chinese businesses

One of the consequences of the social isolation of Chinese migrant workers is the poor working conditions in some Chinese-owned workplaces in Europe where disenfranchised workers have no voice. The poor working conditions in Chinese-owned businesses can be seen from a detailed comparison between Chinese- and Italian-owned factories in the textile, garment and leather sectors (Wu and Sheehan, 2011). Research suggests that despite a higher income available from the former, many Chinese workers nonetheless preferred to work with Italian employers, where they were not compelled to work extremely long hours each day with no welfare and no insurance.

Another survey, conducted in the East Midlands in the UK by one of the co-authors and sponsored by the International Labour Organisation, suggests not only that irregular migrant workers are often abused and exploited in the workplace but also that some legal migrant workers with work permits such as Chinese chefs or doctors specialising in traditional Chinese medicine may also be subjected to conditions of bonded labour and abuse. In such cases, they had their personal identity documents confiscated by the labour agents who find them work or by their employers. They then have to pay either a large one-off payment or a large proportion of their monthly salary in the hope of eventually getting their documents back (Wu et al., 2010).

The issues of Chinese sweatshop labour that exist in some Chinese-owned businesses in Europe cannot be blamed merely on the bad behaviour of a few Chinese entrepreneurs. It is a more complex structural issue, related to many complicated factors, especially the characteristics of overseas Chinese communities (Wu, 2010). As a result, the voices, needs and sufferings of exploited Chinese migrant workers are rarely heard.

Just as in recent years there have been increasing protests and labour movements in China, so a new class consciousness has emerged among new Chinese migrant workers to Europe, even though they often have only limited influence (Wu and Liu, 2013). This trend is evidenced by several developments: violence against bosses in some workplaces and workers joining local trade unions and even creating Chinese trade unions, such as the Chinese migrant network in London.

## Conclusions

This chapter aims to reveal the latest developments, characteristics and new dynamics of Chinese immigration to the EU since the late 1990s, and their impact on local Chinese communities. A number of conclusions can be drawn as follows.

First, the new wave of Chinese immigrants to the EU, which started from the late 1970s, has experienced accelerating growth in the last decade, leading to an expansion of the Chinese population in almost all EU countries though to varying extents in different countries.

Second, recent Chinese immigration has been driven by a number of factors, which include but are not limited to: SOE reform in China, China-Europe trade growth, rising consumer power and inequality in China, as well as the internationalisation of higher education. These new dynamics, which, one could argue, are unique in the history of Chinese international migration, have had a profound impact on local Chinese communities in the EU in various ways, both *quantitatively* (increasing demand for migrant labour to support the growth of Chinese ethnic economies) and *qualitatively* (structural adjustment of Chinese businesses and communities).

Third, the impact on local Chinese communities across the EU can be analysed in relation to three features: (1) the transformation of Chinese ethnic economies in terms of business structure (diversification instead of single and traditional catering or manufacturing only) and profiles of entrepreneurship (pluralism in regions of origin, education and professionalism); (2) high mobility and transnationality across the boundaries of EU countries and between the EU and China; (3) mushrooming and increasing influences of new Chinese media.

Finally, a number of challenging issues facing Chinese communities have been identified, including: the constraints of immigration policies and changes in recent years; social isolation and in some cases poor working conditions in many Chinese-owned businesses. Further research is needed to identify the potential, space and new mechanism for local Chinese community development and integration.

## Notes

1. The following sources were used, where available: European Union and European Commission reports and statistical datasets publicly

available online or in published documents. The compilation of statistical data may be problematic, due to the following reasons: the variety of definitions and methodologies adopted by different sources of statistical data; inconsistencies across different data sources; comparability of different data sources.

2. In this table, 'Chinese' refers broadly to people of Chinese ethnic origin, including older generations of Chinese immigrants from Hong Kong and Indochina.
3. It is important to note that due to the variety of sources and methods of data collection, a certain caution is necessary when considering official statistics across the EU in terms of accuracy and consistency. For instance, irregular migrants are not included in official statistics, which leads to an underestimate of the true Chinese population.
4. That is growth of more than 2.3 times the mean growth rate of the Chinese population in the EU in the period from 1998 to 2008.
5. This is witnessed by some European Chinese newspapers which offer increasing numbers of news stories from the north-east of China. The Italian published Europe China News (欧洲侨报) for instance now regularly has a page for Dongbei and Fujian news in addition to its Wenzhou and Lishui section, the largest proportion of Overseas Chinese in much of Europe coming from the Wenzhou and Lishui areas of Zhejiang province.
6. There is much variation between definitions used to identify and count students across different EU countries, and in some cases there is a considerable lack of clarity as to how national statistics have been compiled. For a detailed discussion of the methodological difficulties associated with counting Chinese student numbers in the EU, see GHK, 2011: 19–22.
7. According to the Chinese Ministry of Education, of the 1,067,000 students who came to the EU to study between 1978 and 2006, only 275,000 returned to China (GHK, 2011: 40). However, the trend in recent years has been for a larger proportion of students to return home on completing their studies. The China Scholarship Council reported in 2009 that more than 50 per cent of Chinese students studying overseas did return to China (China Scholarship Council, 2009). But even though a higher proportion of students may be returning to China, the growing number of overseas students means that there are still large numbers who remain in the EU.

8. In the past, countries such as Spain and Italy have organised amnesties for illegal immigrants (see above), offering them the chance to legalise and make official their presence in the country. Such moves have led to surges of immigrants moving from elsewhere in Europe in order to take advantage of these opportunities. However, these surges do not account for the more mundane flow of Chinese immigrants between European countries.
9. This is broadly in line with Laurence Ma's approach (2005: 4–7) to transnationalism where following Schiller et al. (1992: 1–2) he takes transnationalism as 'the process by which migrants build social fields that link together their country of origin and their country of settlement.' Ma notes that this 'puts heavy emphasis on the process of creating transmigrants' 'social fields' and sees transnationalism as a dynamic social process' (Ma, 2011: 5).
10. By 'new media' we refer principally to the Internet and mobile telephony although other digital media, such as DVDs, satellite television, online video and broadcasting and digital photography, are important too.
11. No systematic statistical data is available yet to confirm this trend. It has only tentatively been identified by the authors of this report through interviews with Chinese immigrants and community representatives during fieldwork in Prato between May and September 2011 and Milan in 2013.
12. The UK immigration system is based upon the notion of five tiers with each tier having different conditions, entitlements, and entry requirements for potential immigrants to the country. Tier 1 is for entrepreneurs, investors and graduate students, Tier 2 is for skilled workers with a job offer, Tier 3 for low-skilled workers meeting temporary labour shortages, Tier 4 is for foreign students and Tier 5 is for youth mobility and temporary workers (UKBA, 2012: 5–6).

## References

Arlt, Wolfgang (2006), *China's Outbound Tourism*, London: Routledge.

Benton, Gregor and Gomez, Edmund T. (2008), *The Chinese in Britain, 1800–present: Economy, transnationalism, identity*, Basingstoke: Palgrave Macmillan.

Benton, Gregor and Pieke, Frank N. (eds) (1998), *The Chinese in Europe*, Basingstoke: Palgrave Macmillan.

Blanchard, Melissa and Maffeo, Carlotta (2011), 'L'immigrazionecinese in Italia e Torino', in Camera di CommercioIndustriaArtigianato e Agricoltura di Torino, *DiventareLaoban: Lavoroautonomo, percorsiimprenditoriali e progettimigratorideicinesi in Italia e Torino*, Turin, Italy: Camera di CommercioIndustriaArtigianato e Agricoltura di Torino.

Chan, Kwok-Bun (2005), *Chinese Identities, Ethnicity and Cosmopolitanism*, London and New York: Routledge.

Chen, James K. (2003), 'Reducing irregular migration from China', *International Migration,* 41(3), 49–72.

Chinese Academy of Social Sciences (CASS) (2011), *China's Tourism Development Analysis and Forecast (2011)*, Chinese Academy of Social Sciences Tourism Research Centre Green Book on Chinese Tourism. Beijing: Social Sciences Academic Press (in Chinese).

China Tourism Academy (CTA) (2011), *CTA Annual Report of China Outbound Tourism Development 2011*. Beijing: Tourism Education Press.

China Labour Information Network (CLIN) (1999), Research report on the re-employment training programme for former SOE workers who have been redundancy (in Chinese), available at: http://www.51labour.com/labour-law/show-4948.html (last accessed 1 October 2011).

Christiansen, Flemming (2003), *Chinatown Europe: an exploration of overseas Chinese identity in the 1990s*, London: RoutledgeCurzon.

Cologna, Daniele (2011), 'Getting closer: Shifting identities, socio-economic roles and perceptions of the other in the Chinese-Italian experience'. Paper presented to the China in the World Conference, 22–23 September, Monash University, Prato Centre, Prato, Italy.

Denison, Tom, Arunachalam, Dharmalingam, Johanson, Graeme and Smyth, Russell (2009), 'The Chinese Community in Prato', in Graeme Johanson, Russell Smyth and Rebecca French (eds), *Living Outside the Walls: The Chinese in Prato*, Newcastle-upon-Tyne: Cambridge Scholars Publishing, pp. 2–24.

Denison, Tom and Johanson, Graeme (2009), 'Community connections: The Chinese Community in Prato, Italy, and their use of technology', in Graeme Johanson, Russell Smyth and Rebecca French (eds), *Living Outside the Walls: The Chinese in*

*Prato*, Newcastle-upon-Tyne: Cambridge Scholars Publishing, pp. 161–73.

Europe China News (2013), 'The annual growth rate of Chinese business in the service sector has reached to 38.8% nation-wide' ('在意华人经营的个人服务企业年增 38.8%', 欧洲侨报), 27/08/13, page 4.

GHK (2011), *EU China Student and Academic Staff Mobility: present situation and future developments*, a joint study between the European Commission and the Ministry of Education in China, Brussels: GHK Consulting and Renmin University; available at: http://ec.europa.eu/education/external-relation-programmes/doc/china/mobility_en.pdf (last accessed 14 March 2012).

Gao, Yun (2010), *Concealed Chains: Labour exploitation of Chinese migrants in Europe*, Geneva : International Labour Organisation.

Gui, Shixu (2011), 'The contribution of overseas Chinese to China's development', in Qu, Zhang, Luo and Li (eds), *Annual Report on Overseas Chinese Studies (2011)*, Beijing: Social Sciences Academic Press (in Chinese), pp. 51–84.

ITB (2011), *ITB World Travel Trends Report 2010/2011*, Prepared by IPK International on behalf of ITB Berlin. Munich: IPK International.

Johanson, Graeme and Fladrich, Anja Michaela (2011), 'Ties that bind: information and communications technologies and the Chinese in Prato'. Paper presented at the fourth Chinese in Prato and second Wenzhounese Diaspora Symposia, Prato, Italy, 20 September 2011.

Kofman, Eleonore; Rogoz, Madalina and Lévy, Florence (2010), *Family Migration Policies in France*, International Centre for Migration Policy Development, available at: http://ec.europa.eu/ewsi/UDRW/images/items/docl_14977_276188113.pdf (last accessed 8 January 2014).

Lam, Jabez (2009), 'Labour shortage in Chinese catering', a presentation to the University of Nottingham-International Labour Organisation Workshop: *Employment of Chinese Migrant Workers in UK: Issues and Solutions*, 22–23 October 2009, Nottingham, available at: http://www.nottingham.ac.uk/cpi/documents/funded-projects/ilo-workshop-complete-report.pdf (last accessed 8 January 2014).

Latham, Kevin (2011a), *How the Rise of Chinese Tourism Will Change the Face of the European Travel Industry*, SOAS-Hilton Blue Paper, London: SOAS-Hilton Hotels.

Latham, Kevin (2011b), 'Media and discourses of identity in Prato, Italy'. Paper presented at the fourth Chinese in Prato and second Wenzhouese Diaspora Symposia, 20–21 September, Monash University, Prato Centre, Prato, Italy.

Li, Minghuan (2011a), 'Latest development and trends of overseas Chinese in Europe', in Wang and Liu (eds), *Overseas Chinese and Local Society in Europe: social integration, economic development and political participation*, Guangzhou: Zhongshan University Press (in Chinese), pp. 3–25.

Li Minghuan (2011b), 'The Chinese in Europe: population, economy and links with China in the early 21st century'. Paper presented at the China in the World Conference, 22–23 September 2011, Monash University, Prato Centre, Prato, Italy.

Li, Peilin and Roulleau-Berger, Laurence (eds) (2012), *China's Internal and International Migration*. London: Routledge.

Liu, Hong (2013), *The Conceptualization and Practice of Transnational Asia: China model, ethnic network and international relationship*, Nanjing: Nanjing University Press (in Chinese).

Liu, Hong and Hou, Jiaqi (2010), 'Chinese society and political participation in Contemporary Britain: A case study of the 2010 election', *South Asian Affairs*, 144(4): 49–61.

Ma, Mung Kuang (2011), 'Economic and social integration of migrants of Chinese origin in France'. Paper presented at the China in the World Conference, 22–23 September 2011, Monash University, Prato Centre, Prato, Italy.

Moore, Malcolm (2011), 'Chinese tourists bring £200m windfall for London retailers', *Daily Telegraph*, 24 May, available at: http://www.telegraph.co.uk/finance/china-business/8534189/Chinese-tourists-bring-200m-windfall-for-London-retailers.html (last accessed 8 September 2011).

National Bureau of Statistics of China (NBS) (2010), *China Statistics Yearbook 2010*, Beijing, China Statistical Press (in Chinese).

Parker, David and Song, Miri (2006), 'New ethnicities online: reflexive racialisation and the internet,' *The Sociological Review*, 54(3): 575–94.

Pai, Hsiao-Hung (2008), *Chinese Whispers: The true story behind Britain's hidden army of labour*, London: Penguin Books.

Pastore, Ferruccio and Castagnone, Eleonora (2011), 'Studiare l'imprenditoria cinese, oltre i luoghi comuni', in Camera di Commercio Industria Artigianato e Agricoltura di Torino, *Diventare Lao ban: Lavoro autonomo, percorsi imprenditoriali e progetti migratori dei cinesi in Italia e Torino*, Turin, Italy: Camera di CommercioIndustriaArtigianato e Agricoltura di Torino.

Pieke, Frank N. (1998), 'Introduction', in Benton and Pieke (eds), *The Chinese in Europe*, London and New York: Macmillan, pp. 1–17.

Pieke, Frank N. and Mallee, Hein (eds) (1999), *Internal and International Migration: Chinese perspectives*, Richmond: Curzon Press.

Pieke, Frank N., Nyir, Pal, Thuno, Mette, and Ceccagno, Antontlla (2004), *Transnational Chinese: Fujianese Migrants in Europe*, Stanford, CA: Stanford University Press.

Polyzou, Iris (2011), 'Chinese migration in Athens: Socio-spatial practices, new challenges and perspectives during the economic crisis'. Paper presented at the fourth Chinese in Prato and second Wenzhouese Diaspora Symposia, 20–21 September 2011, Monash University, Prato Centre, Prato, Italy.

Qu, Jin, Zhang, Yudong, Luo, Kereng and Li, Minghuan (eds) (2011), *Annual Report on Overseas Chinese Studies* (2011), Beijing: Social Sciences Academic Press (in Chinese).

Shen, Wei (2009), *Chinese Student Circular Migration and Global City Formation: A relational case study of Shanghai and Paris*, unpublished PhD thesis, Loughborough University.

Song, Miri (2011), 'Is the British Chinese case a typical trajectory of "integration"?' Paper presented to the China in the World Conference, 22–23 September 2011, Monash University, Prato Centre, Prato, Italy.

Soothill, Deborah (2010), *Eating bitterness: An ethnographic study of the Chinese migrant experience in Madrid*, unpublished PhD thesis, Department of Anthropology, University College London.

Sun, Wanning (2002), *Leaving China: Media, migration, and transnational imagination*, Lanham, MD: Rowman & Littlefield.

Sun, Wanning (2007), *Maid in China: Media, mobility and a new semiotic of power*, London: Routledge.

Sun, Wanning (ed.) (2006), *Media and the Chinese Diaspora: Community, communications and commerce*, London: Routledge.

UKBA (2012), 'Skilled shortage sensible: call for evidence: Review of the shortage occupation lists for the UK and Scotland and Creative Occupations', London: UKBA, available at: http://www.ukba.homeoffice.gov.uk/sitecontent/documents/aboutus/workingwithus/mac/uk-scotland-creative-occ.pdf (last accessed 25 February 2013).

UKIN (UK Immigration News) (2011a), 'UK universities war of negative effects of tighter tier 4 student visa rules' available

at: http://www.ukimmigration.com/news/2012-03-05/uk/uk-universities-warn-of-negative-effects-of-tighter-tier-4-student-visa-rules.htm (last accessed 14 March 2012).
UKIN (2011b), 'UK immigration could clamp down on tier 2 intra-company transfer visas', available at: http://www.ukimmigration.com/news/2012-03-02/uk/uk-immigration-could-clamp-down-on-tier-2-intra-company-transfer-visas.htm (last accessed 14 March 2012).
UKIN (2011c), 'UK immigration to expand biometric residence permits for immigrants', available at: http://www.ukimmigration.com/news/2012-03-02/uk/uk-immigration-to-expand-biometric-residence-permits-for-immigrants.htm (last accessed 14 March 2012).
UKIN (2011d), 'Changes to UK immigration English test for tier 1, 2 and 4 applicants', available at: http://www.ukimmigration.com/news/2012-02-02/uk/changes-to-uk-immigration-english-test-for-tier-1-2-and-4-applicants.htm (last accessed 14 March 2012).
Wang, Xiaoping and Liu, Hong (2011), *European Diaspora Chinese in Local Communities: social interaction, economic development and political participation*, Guangzhou: Zhongshan University Press (in Chinese).
Wu, Bin and Zanin, Valter (2009), 'Health needs of Chinese migrant workers in Italy: an survey report on Chinese-owned workshops in Veneto', *China Policy Institute Discussion Paper*, No. 48, Nottingham: CPI, available at: http://www.nottingham.ac.uk/cpi/publications/discussion-papers/2009/index.aspx (last accessed 8 January 2014).
Wu, Bin (2010), 'Overseas Chinese community building (CCB): Approach and practice', *China Policy Institute Policy Paper Series*, Issue 65, available at: http://www.nottingham.ac.uk/cpi/publications/policy-papers/2010/index.aspx (last accessed 8 January 2014).
Wu, Bin, Guo, L. and Sheehan, J. (2010), *Employment Conditions of Chinese Migrant Workers in the East Midlands: A pilot study in a context of economic recession*, a report submitted to the ILO, Beijing: International Labour Office for China and Mongolia.
Wu, Bin and Liu, Hong (2013), 'Bring class back in: Class consciousness and solidarity amongst Chinese migrant workers in Italy and the UK', *Ethnic and Racial Studies*, forthcoming, available at: http://www.tandfonline.com/doi/abs/10.1080/01419870.2012.715660 (last accessed 8 January 2014).
Wu, Bin and Sheen, Jackie (2011), 'Globalization and vulnerability of Chinese migrant workers in Italy: empirical evidence

on working conditions and their consequences', *Journal of Contemporary China*, 20(68), 135–52.

Yan, Hairong (2003), 'Spectralization of the rural: reinterpreting the labor mobility of rural young women in post-Mao China', *American Ethnologist*, 30(4), 578–96.

Yeung, Yue-man (2002), *Internal and International Migration in China under Openness and a Market Economy*. Hong Kong: Hong Kong Institute of Asia-Pacific Studies with Chinese University of Hong Kong Press.

Zanin, Valter (2012), *Immigrati cinesi operai e imprenditori nella terra di Marco Polo*, vol. I, *L'organizzazione del lavoro in Italia e nel Veneto alla luce delle migrazioni cinesi* [*Chinese migrants workers and entrepreneurs in the land of Marco Polo*, vol. I, *The organisation of work in Italy and Veneto in the light of the Chinese migrations*]. Padua: Cleup, ISBN: 978–88–6129–988–7.

Zanin, Valter and Wu, Bin (2012), *Immigrati cinesi operai e imprenditori nella terra di Marco Polo*, vol. II, *Condizioni di lavoro e salute degli operai cinesi tra Zhejiang e Italia (Veneto)* [*Chinese migrants workers and entrepreneurs in the land of Marco Polo*, vol. II, *working and health conditions of the Chinese workers between Zhejiang and Italy (Veneto)*]. Padua: Cleup, ISBN: 978–88–6129–990–0.

Zhao, Xiaojian (2006), 'Disconnecting transnational ties: The *Chinese Pacific Weekly* and the transformation of Chinese American community after the Second World War', in Sun Wanning (ed.), *Media and the Chinese Diaspora: Community, communications and commerce*, New York: Routledge, pp. 26–41.

Zhou, Yongming (2011), 'Social capital in print: Chinese newspaper publishing in Italy'. Paper presented at the China in the World Conference, 22–23 September 2011, Monash University, Prato Centre, Prato, Italy.

Zhou, Min, Chen, Wenhong and Cai, Guoxuan (2006), 'Chinese-language media and immigrant life in the United States and Canada', in Sun Wanning (ed.), *Media and the Chinese Diaspora: Community, communications and commerce*, New York: Routledge, pp. 44–74.

# Index

Printed and bound by CPI Group (UK) Ltd, Croydon, CR0 4YY